ALSO BY JAMES HARVEY

Romantic Comedy: In Hollywood, from Lubitsch to Sturges

MOVIE LOVE IN THE FIFTIES

MOVIE LOVE
IN THE FIFTIES

JAMES HARVEY

ALFRED A. KNOPF · NEW YORK 2001

Grateful acknowledgment is made to the following
for permission to reprint previously published material:

BMG Music and *Publishing Warner Bros. Publications Inc.:* Excerpt from
"Johnny Guitar" by Peggy Lee and Victor Young, copyright © 1954, copyright
renewed 1982 by Denslow Music, Inc. (ASCAP) and Chappell & Co. (ASCAP).
All rights on behalf of Denslow Music, Inc. (ASCAP) administered by
BMG Songs, Inc. (ASCAP). All rights on behalf of Chappell & Co. (ASCAP)
administered by Warner Bros. Publications Inc. All rights reserved. Reprinted by
permission of BMG Music Publishing and Warner Bros. Publications Inc.

Frank Music Corp.: Excerpts from "Spring Will Be a Little Late This Year"
by Frank Loesser, from the motion picture *Christmas Holiday,* copyright © 1943,
copyright renewed 1971 by Frank Music Corp. All rights reserved. Reprinted by
permission of Frank Music Corp., administered by Hal Leonard Corporation.

Henry Holt and Company, LLC: Excerpt from "The Oven Bird" from *The Poetry
of Robert Frost*, edited by Edward Connery Lathem, copyright © 1916, 1969
by Henry Holt and Co., copyright renewed 1944 by Robert Frost.
Reprinted by permission of Henry Holt and Company, LLC.

Library of Congress Cataloging-in-Publication Data
Harvey, James, [date]
Movie love in the fifties / James Harvey.
p.   cm.
Includes index.
ISBN 0-394-58591-7
1. Love in motion pictures.   I. Title: Movie love in the fifties.   II. Title.
PN1995.9.L6 H37 2001
791.43'6543—dc21   2001033821

INTERVIEWER: *How has your "relationship" with movies changed over time?*

PAULINE KAEL: *In front of the screen, I'm still a kid. Movie love is abiding throughout life . . . we're lovers who are let down all the time, and go on loving.*

INTERVIEWER: *When I'm at the movies, I feel like I'm swept up, lost.*

PAULINE KAEL: *I feel as if I'm found.*

—A 1998 INTERVIEW

CONTENTS

INTRODUCTION

I want to talk here not only about how some prototypical American movies of the postwar era look to us now but also about how they looked to us then. This is partly at least a book about—and a reflection on—the fifties through its movies, through its filmmakers and stars, through my own memories of the time.

In the fifties—and I use the term in this book to cover the whole postwar period from the late forties up to the early sixties—not just the big movie studios themselves were collapsing, but so along with them (according to some) were the movie genres that had sustained them. Postwar American audiences, the argument went, no longer so easy to please or entertain, had become too worldly-wise for the innocent old plots and conventions. Audiences were now demanding more adult, more "realistic" fare. And so, by degrees, they got it. At least sometimes. Mostly at first in movies about "hot topics" like racism, drugs, teenage rebellion. The "revolution" in the postwar Hollywood movie was in subject matter, not style—as the French critic André Bazin observed at the time.

But the old-fashioned genres persisted—the westerns and musicals, the mysteries and war films and family comedies and so on. And big-name directors like Hawks and Hitchcock and Ford, far from abandoning generic modes, seemed to be going deeper into them than ever before, with films like (respectively) *Rio Bravo* and *Vertigo* and *The Searchers*—odd and sometimes troubling movies, ambiguous even, that exaggerated their directors' styles and often left their earlier audiences puzzled, or cold, as in the case of *Vertigo.* It's hard to imagine *The Searchers,* for example, in the form in which it was released in 1956, at once dawdling and obsessive and a good two hours long (Hawks's *Rio Bravo* was nearly two and a half), getting past Darryl Zanuck, Ford's old boss at Twentieth Century–Fox, without a lot of cutting and tinkering to "improve" it (as happened to Ford's *My Darling Clementine* earlier on).

The Searchers is, of course, one of the monuments of the movie decade.

Other genres may have seemed to be running down then, but not the western, which was so clearly suited to the new wide-screen processes. A western in those days almost always made money, without costing that much to make to start with. It was the time, in fact, when the genre itself reached its richest and most expressive level—in the films of Ford and Anthony Mann, of Sam Fuller and Budd Boetticher, among many others. And if I've excluded the fifties western from this book—as I mostly have—it's only because the subject is so large and important: a book in itself.

This book will be concerned instead with a less easily defined topic—less with any particular genre or style or body of work than with a special kind of achievement that came out of the breakdown of the Hollywood system: namely, a conservative countertrend to the "revolutionary" new subject matter. Conservative as this counterreaction may have been, it nevertheless produced, I will argue, what was almost a new kind of Hollywood movie, establishing in the climate of general decline and dwindling box-office revenues a different relation with its audience, subverting at times just those securities in the audience—the reliance on narrative logic and linearity, on psychological realism, on the invisible camera and the self-effacing filmmaker—that the "classical cinema" of the big-studio heyday had so carefully built up. The *post*classical movie, instead of forgoing or disguising the genre, emphasized and aestheticized it, using the familiarity not to reassure but to astonish and even discomfit us—in films like Hitchcock's *Vertigo,* Welles's *Touch of Evil,* Ray's *Johnny Guitar,* and others.

Hitchcock and Welles and Ray are primarily lyric artists, it seems to me (as opposed to primarily narrative or dramatic ones). But they are also formalists—a trend that first begins to show itself in film noir as they and others practiced it, and that culminates near the end of the decade in the Technicolor-baroque movies of Douglas Sirk. And of them all, Sirk is the clearest example of "the termite artist," in Manny Farber's nice phrase—someone working steadily, quietly, almost unnoticeably against the predilections of his time and audience and employers, sometimes against those of his own movie. But in some way or degree these directors were all doing that.

And the movies of theirs that I pay the most attention to here are all marked for me by—among many other features—recurring little "epiphanies," as Stephen Dedalus called them: the sort of commonplace, often fleeting scene or detail that carries such a sudden pressure of meaning and beauty at once that you almost think it could implode the movie screen. Like, for example, the Arab watcher on the sand dune in *Bitter Victory;* the successive re-entrances of the heroine through *Out of the Past;* the rich boy's tilted walk and the rich girl's penitential black hat in *Written on the Wind;* the heroine bathed in the light of a neon-green sign in *Vertigo*—and so on. Though I'm not sure *when* I first fully registered the impact of these and other such moments—whether on the first viewing or later. Later, I should think, more often than not. Movie love may be abiding throughout life, as Pauline Kael says, but it can also be deepening.

Because that deepening is finally what this book is meant to be about—the *experience* of these movies. What I set out to do here is to help you to *see* them better—to experience them more deeply and sharply and richly, since that, it seems to me, is nearly the most valuable thing a critic can do for any of us. The method that I mostly use here is to follow the movie as it moves and changes and makes its points in front of us, *as* we experience it, not so much as we think and talk about it later—an approach that requires, as you will see, some considerable space and elaboration at times, especially when I come to the most crucial and powerful scenes or moments. And what I'm asking you to do is to collaborate in that process, to find (as I hope) that it justifies and rewards the attention it certainly asks you for.

"The critic's task," observed Pauline Kael in a recent interview (*Cineaste,* volume 25, number 2, 2000), with her characteristic forthrightness, "should be to help people to see more in the work than they might without him." This is not a thesis-driven book, though you'll find that it does get somewhere by the end, even to some conclusions. Its form is unconventional (perhaps) but organic, letting the various themes and connections emerge as it goes along—much as they did for me as I wrote it.

But I always seem to have known that it would *begin* where it does—with the stars of the time, and particularly with the great women of film noir: those villainous but glamorous successors, in fascination and complexity, to the radiant women stars of thirties romantic comedy; the noir women showing, of course, more sinister ways (appropriate to less humorous times) of being compelling. They got their start well before the fifties, as early as John Huston's *The Maltese Falcon* in 1941. They went through changes after that, of course. And it's just those changes that define them later in their postwar versions. So I'll begin even before the fifties: with the seminal figure of Mary Astor's Brigid O'Shaughnessy, with prewar film noir—with some women, and with Truffaut's wonderful (as it seems to me) epigraph . . .

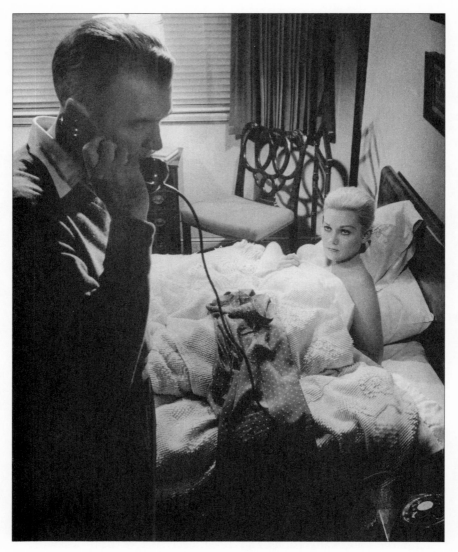

James Stewart and Kim Novak in Hitchcock's *Vertigo*

PART ONE

THE WOMEN

Cinema is an art of the woman . . . For me the great moments of cinema are when the director's gifts mesh with the gifts of an actress: Griffith and Lillian Gish, Sternberg and Marlene Dietrich, Fritz Lang and Joan Bennett . . .

— FRANÇOIS TRUFFAUT

One

NOIR HEROINES

There's a girl wants to see you," Sam Spade's secretary, Effie, tells him at the beginning of both the novel and the movie of *The Maltese Falcon.* "Her name's Wonderly." Sam replies by asking if she's a customer. Effie's not sure about that, but she thinks he'll want to see Miss Wonderly in any case: "She's a knockout."

But in John Huston's 1941 movie she's not exactly what you'd expect from Dashiell Hammett's description of her in the novel: "erect and high-breasted, her legs long . . . her full lips . . . brightly red," and so on—or even from Effie's introduction. She is Mary Astor, not Rita Hayworth, and she is no "girl." She is lovely, but more in a genteel, matronly than in a long-legged, high-breasted sort of way. Invincibly ladylike, she could pass for a delegate from the garden club come to ask for a donation. A jaunty little hat sits forward on her face and rises to a point above it; a fur stole is draped over arm and shoulder, her purse held firmly in front of her. But when she sits across from Sam and starts to talk—in close-up—you begin to feel that "knockout" is exactly the right word, after all.

Her real name, as it turns out (though "Wonderly" is certainly an inspired invention) is Brigid O'Shaughnessy. And she establishes early on one of the defining characteristics of the film noir heroine: she is a liar—and in Brigid's case, a virtuoso. Astor makes her falsity so multileveled that it feels almost witty. And so even after they've made love, Bogart's Sam never loses his irony about her—calling her "angel" and "precious" and "my own true love"—or his pleasure in her self-performance. He settles into their encounters, sitting back in his chair or leaning against the mantel, like someone watching a curtain go up. She is dazzling, all right—but tough to be in love with: a gambit that Spade finally and successfully refuses. "I haven't led a good life," she confesses to him earlier on. "I've been bad. Worse than you could know." Astor gives us the sense at such moments that Brigid has been worse than even *she* could know—just as she seems to be lying even when she says she is lying. But then again, as

Meeting "Miss Wonderly": Sam (Humphrey Bogart)
introduces her (Mary Astor) to his partner, Miles (Jerome Cowan),
in Huston's *The Maltese Falcon*

Sam observes, "If you were actually as innocent as you pretend to be, we'd never get anywhere." Looking on the bright side.

In their first scene together in his office, she tells him a phony story about her missing sister, chatting away with bright unseeing eyes, not looking at him, while Bogart measures her with his fierce, sorrowful stare—like a delinquent in love with the music teacher. Whenever she does look at him, he offers a polite business face—which falls, when she looks away again, into the same mournful attentiveness. One thing this generic heroine always demands, both from the hero and from us, is to be watched. From her first entrance—which is almost always memorable in some way.

Often in very obvious ways. Like Ava Gardner, first shown to us in a sexy black gown, singing by a piano in Robert Siodmak's *The Killers*. Or Joan Bennett, in a plastic raincoat, sitting in a Greenwich Village gutter in Fritz Lang's *Scarlet Street*. In his earlier film with her, *The Woman in the Window*, she makes an even more extraordinary first appearance: as the subject of an oil painting, on display in an art dealer's window, where it has for some time obsessed Edward G. Robinson, as a respected professor and happily married family man. He is alone one night gazing at it when the woman herself appears—her face reflected in the window glass next to the face in the portrait. And unlike the woman in the portrait, she is smiling at him.

The painting is sentimentally sensual, showing its subject in a sort of beseeching attitude, with undraped shoulders, luxuriant black hair, and melting canine eyes. But the woman beside him now seems more avian than canine, with her glittering dark eyes and raven hair encased in a cloche of black feathers. She has a crisp, genial manner and an infectious, side-of-the-mouth smile. She says she likes to look at people looking at her—that's how she happened to spot him—and she invites him for a drink. First to a lounge, then to her posh, mirrored apartment. Where he ends up killing the unnamed man who pays her rent. (She hands him the scissors.)

She is a much lower-class type in *Scarlet Street,* and the Robinson character is even more naive and unworldly. He first comes on her in the gutter where her sleazy "boyfriend" has knocked her down and left her. Robinson rescues her and takes her to a nearby restaurant. He wants to be sure she gets something to eat. But he is also troubled by her being on the street so late at night when it isn't at all safe. She was just coming from work, she says, as she leans across the table, lights her cigarette from the candle, and looks up at him provocatively. What does she do? he asks, wide-eyed. *"Guess!"* she says, falling back in her chair and smiling delightedly. He frowns and hesitates. Then it comes to him: "You're an actress!" She is amazed that he knew—the first guess, too.

Walter Neff, on the other hand—Fred MacMurray in Billy Wilder's *Double Indemnity* (1944)—is a man who does know women, just as he knows "all the angles" or "his way around," or the insurance game, the stuff he sells for a living. And he knows at first meeting what Phyllis Dietrichson (Barbara Stanwyck) is—available, among other things. That is, if you make the right moves, and if you're not afraid of the husband, or of trouble in general. She is standing at the top of the stairs (the housekeeper has let him in), so he has to call up to her to tell her that he is from the "Pacific All-Risk Insurance Company." But the name does catch her attention: "The Pacific All-What?" she asks, stepping forward to see him better. Since she is wearing only a towel, she explains that she's been sunbathing. "No pigeons around, I hope," he says roguishly—fatuously. She doesn't look amused by this, but she does look interested. She tells him she'll be right down.

When she comes downstairs she is in a rather incongruously girlish white frock, and white shoes with high heels and big white pom-poms on the toes—all of it highlighting her platinum-blond hair. She enters the parlor where Neff is waiting and goes past him to the mirror over the fireplace. He's a lot taller than she is, and he looms above her now with a faintly leering assurance. They look at each other in the mirror. "Neff is

Two versions of Fritz Lang's Joan Bennett: classy in
The Woman in the Window (above), trampy in *Scarlet Street* (below)—
and fatal to Edward G. Robinson in both

the name, isn't it?" she says briskly, as she unsheathes her lipstick and raises it to her mouth. "Yes," he says. "Two f's. Like in Philadelphia. You know the story?" "What story?" she says brightly, the words slightly muffled by the lipstick. *The Philadelphia Story,*" he replies. She looks at him blankly for a moment, then snaps the lipstick shut and turns from the mirror. "Suppose we sit down," she says, "and you tell me about the insurance." She smiles up at him, prettily. "My husband never tells me anything," she says, as she sits.

And in the tall wing-backed chair across from him, she looks very small and suddenly not formidable—until she crosses her long legs with those startling shoes and a chain around one of her ankles. He talks away while she examines a fingernail. He can't resist: "That's a honey of an anklet you're wearing, Mrs. Dietrichson," he says, and asks her what's inscribed on it. She looks down along her legs, slowly and wonderingly, almost as if she'd never quite noticed them before. There is a pause. "Just my name," she says at length, still gazing downward, almost as if she were answering her own question.

But mostly in this scene she offers him a kind of bright, strained encouragement. And Stanwyck makes you feel the enormous weariness behind the brightness, the deep, fatal impatience. She is "a native Californian," Phyllis tells him perkily. "Born right here in Los Angeles!" And the effect is almost as if she had announced that she was a Bruins fan, or a Girl Scouts supporter. You not only don't believe her; you understand something else as well: that she *hates* Los Angeles. You also understand why she does. Stanwyck's Phyllis is a woman who *knows* about emptiness, trying to pass for a woman who doesn't. This is a knowledge that none of the men in this movie (of mostly men) seem to have—at least not to the same degree. Not even her nemesis, the shrewd investigator played by Edward G. Robinson.

Phyllis's simmering, steady anger against ordinariness is nearly the most powerful thing in the film's early reels. When you see her playing Chinese checkers with her sweet young daughter-in-law, or performing the routines of wifeliness with her irritable and cloddish husband, you know why she wants to kill them both. You also know when you see her with Neff why she will eventually want to kill him too. Her monstrousness doesn't feel showy or exotic—it doesn't even feel "neurotic," but common and familiar and matter-of-fact, with the desperation just barely showing: "Born right here in Los Angeles!"

As the noir style goes on, into the late forties and beyond, the heroines tend to get more "realistic" and less glamorous. Compare Ava Gardner in

"That's a honey of an anklet . . .": Fred MacMurray and Barbara Stanwyck
in Billy Wilder's *Double Indemnity*

Siodmak's *The Killers* (1946) to Yvonne De Carlo in his *Criss Cross* (1948).
Kitty (Gardner) seems almost as clever as she is lissome and gorgeous,
whereas Anna (De Carlo) is something of a bumbler and, while certainly
sexy, looks a bit shorter and squatter than probably a femme fatale should,
especially in those baggy slacks she wears when she meets the hero at the
drugstore. She's also sort of a complainer. For sure, not one of life's winners.

But she can dance—as she does to a samba band at a local nightclub
while Burt Lancaster looks on at her. They were married once, and he still
hasn't gotten over her. He hadn't really expected to see her there, but he
spots her on the crowded dance floor as soon as the music starts. Noir
heroes do a lot of this hungry girl-watching, but probably no one else does
it with as much youthful nakedness and touching avidity as Lancaster does
here: he seems almost to *gleam* with longing in these close-ups, as he
watches Anna dance.

She starts with one of those it's-nothing-to-do-with-me expressions on
her face that good dancers often affect. And Siodmak's close-up framing of
her—over the shoulder of her barely visible partner (a bit player then
called Anthony Curtis)—shows almost nothing below her head and shoulders, implying more of her movement than it actually shows, so that what

Siodmak's *Criss Cross:*
Yvonne De Carlo and Burt Lancaster

we're looking at—as she dips, turns, passes, tosses her head, revolves her shoulder, and so forth—is less her dancing than her absorption in it, the concentration of someone who *really* dances, who becomes almost selfless. And as the musical fever mounts—a flute threnody, rising above the beat of maracas and drums, punctuated by piano fusillades—Siodmak's framing gets tighter and tighter, the cutting between De Carlo, Lancaster, the samba band, more rapid: from De Carlo shaking her shoulders and moving her hands on the air in front of her; to the hunched-over piano player pounding the keys; to De Carlo again, faster and closer; to the pianist's hands; to Lancaster, staring gravely, almost as if he were looking at a death; and so on. And it's hopeless. He's been *trying* to stay away from her. But at this moment, this otherwise rather frumpish, kvetching, dim-bulb young woman, in her strange combination of abandon and gravity, really seems wondrous. *Another* Miss Wonderly.

But does she *really* love him? That's always the question about these heroines—obsessive to the hero, central to the movie. De Carlo's Anna, for example, is willing enough to betray her racketeer husband for love of Lancaster, but *not* willing to stay with him once the husband catches up with them. Not when she can take the money and run. (She doesn't make it—

they are both gunned down by the husband.) It's one of the noir heroine's most invariable features that she is motivated by greed: she is poor and wants to be rich, or else she is rich and wants to be richer. She may inspire romantic dreams, but she doesn't have them herself. Not like *he* does, anyway. That's one of the advantages she has over him.

But no matter how venal or shallow she may be finally shown to be, it's still somehow the hero's earliest vision of her that defines her for us—the one that made her seem not only irresistible but *interesting,* endlessly, almost impossibly so. It's part of the underlying bleakness of these movies that that impression of her so often turns out to be an illusion. And yet not—not *quite . . .* There's no denying she can *dance.*

In Richard Quine's *Pushover* (1954), Kim Novak, a gangster's mistress, is the unknowing object of a twenty-four-hour police surveillance from the apartment across her courtyard. The guy behind the binoculars there is an aging, burnt-out cop (Fred MacMurray), for whom the job of looking at her day after day and night after night has become a kind of personal compulsion, no longer just an assignment. Even after they've met and made love, he's eager to get back to that courtyard window—where he can *really* see her. More or less the way we do, in fact: in a frame and at a distance, and larger than life.

But in other movies this heroine was getting smaller: by the mid-fifties Novak in *Pushover* seemed almost a throwback. She was too glamorous, too mysterious. And the movies themselves, which had always been pretty literal-minded, were getting even more so. And as the highly stylized sort of noir movie waned, so did the noir heroine, nearly disappearing. Where she did survive, she had become more reasonable, more comprehensible, altogether a more prosaic figure. In the fifties and even before, she became someone who could be either explained or excused, or both. Sometimes, like the hero, she was a victim herself, of some other man—as Lizabeth Scott is in André De Toth's *Pitfall* (1948). Sometimes—like Stanwyck in Siodmak's *The File on Thelma Jordon* (1950)—she reforms near the end. But mostly (it was the time of what was called the "psychological" thriller) she was insane: like Laraine Day in John Brahm's *The Locket* (1946)—or, best of all, Peggy Cummins in Joseph Lewis's *Gun Crazy* (1950), whose memorable first close-up is preceded by six-shooters (hers) going off in the air above her head, as the ferrety little eyes in the clown-white makeup appear at the bottom of the screen and rise into the frame. You know *she's* crazy, right away. With Faith Domergue in John Farrow's *Where Danger Lives* (1950), it takes longer to find out. Domergue is alluring and impenetrable in all the traditional ways for the first half of the movie. But by the second half (more action) she becomes such a coldly observed nutcase that the whole film collapses into unintentional farce. And even the Robert Mitchum hero's attraction to her gets clinically accounted for: by his getting hit on the head earlier on. There's nothing like having things explained.

But the heroine of Otto Preminger's *Angel Face* (1952) never really is. Jean Simmons's Diane is neither redeemable nor pathological. But she is deadly, implicating the hapless hero in murder and finally murdering him and herself. Frank Jessup (Mitchum again) is an ambulance driver who meets Diane when he is called to the Beverly Hills mansion of her stepmother—who has just barely survived, as we soon find out, her stepdaughter's first attempt to do her in. No one is suspicious, however; and Diane sets out to beguile Frank, trailing him to the hospital, inducing him to break a date with his nice, normal-type fiancée, Mary (Mona Freeman), even lunching with her later on to make more trouble for him. Finally she persuades him (it's not too hard) to move in with the "family" as their regular chauffeur. Mr. Tremayne, her father (Herbert Marshall), is a once-prominent British novelist whose talent for sponging—to his daughter's distress—seems to have displaced the one he recently had for writing. She blames this on Mrs. Tremayne (Barbara O'Neil), his rich and lordly American wife—who seems herself not entirely pleased with the marriage bargain she's made, nor with the father and daughter she is now supporting. She drinks, plays bridge, and manages the money they spend, condescending to them and others with a bored sort of graciousness that makes even Mitchum's Frank look a bit nervous.

But she is in fact a nice person—as Diane herself admits but only after she's finally succeeded in killing her. Diane had fixed the woman's car so it would lose control and go over the steep bluff outside the house, crashing into the canyon below. But she's killed her beloved father too, who was also in the car, causing both her and Frank (a mechanic as well as a driver) to be indicted for conspiracy to murder. Frank, of course, is clueless, but the shrewd and cynical lawyer who takes their case (Leon Ames) gets them acquitted—by tricks like having them get married in prison before the trial.

Simmons's Diane is the conventional noir heroine in almost every respect—except that the feeling Preminger's movie gives us about her is somewhat different. She is enigmatic without being impressive or glamorous. In spite of the black Cleopatra-style wig and the theme music she plays on the grand piano or the introductory slap that she exchanges with the hero—all the conventional theatrical details of her first appearance—

she turns out to be a sort of recessive, laid-back type, with a very hard-to-read face. Because of her, it seems to me, almost no one would be likely to mistake *Angel Face* for an earlier noir film: like its heroine, it's too impassive. The Preminger detachment: lots of long takes in evenly lit eye-level shots. And even though much of it takes place in the sort of labyrinthine Gothic house common to thrillers, there are few shadows, no odd or eccentric camera angles. It is all very matter-of-fact—regarding its heroine throughout with a kind of who-*is*-this-person? bemusement.

And you want to know—if only because the movie is so smart and clever, full of charged encounters between edgy, interesting people: between the novelist and his wife (Marshall and O'Neil are very good indeed), between her and Diane, even between Diane and the nice-girl fiancée. And yet while Diane's machinations are interesting, they seem passionless. It's even clear—for *once*—that she and the hero have *not* slept together. The most excitement they show to us is that early exchange of slaps. And so it comes as a sort of surprise when, toward the end, we hear Diane declaring to Frank that she has loved him totally and without conditions.

But then that is not the sort of thing that anyone else in this movie is going to understand—least of all the hero. When she demands earlier on that he admit that he loves her, he hesitates. He's not sure, he says—maybe he does. "How can you tell," he adds unhelpfully, "with a girl like you?" He is already thinking about going back to Mary, the normal one. But when he does (or tries to—she's taken up with his best friend), Diane returns to their lawyer and tells him that she murdered her father and stepmother and that Frank had nothing to do with it. The lawyer is not too impressed: he has to explain to her now about double jeopardy, about how she can't be tried again no matter what she confesses—though it's good, of course, that she has made this statement and gotten it off her conscience, he tells her, ending the interview. She looks at him in astonishment: "I will never have it off my conscience," she says. Of course, of course—as he shows her to the door.

It's a world in which nothing much is made of anything, either love or murder. And Diane's impassivity begins to seem almost defensive; her assertions of love and guilt are as out of place in it as they are in her busy lawyer's office. She tells Frank, when she goes back to the now empty mansion, that she cannot live without him. But that cuts no ice with him: he's leaving town, going to the railroad station, he's even called a cab to come for him. He's had enough. She gives up, offering him a lift to his train. He accepts, and even seems sort of pleased when she suggests that they have a last drink—of champagne. He brings the bottle and glasses as they go to

Robert Mitchum has one for the road, as Jean Simmons looks on,
in Preminger's *Angel Face.*

the car—Diane as unreadable as ever. As it turns out, the last words Frank
gets to utter are over that champagne and how it's getting spilled—
"Watch it!"—as she rams the gear shift into violent reverse and sends
them hurtling backwards into the canyon below, where the car explodes
and burns. The last thing we see then—in an extreme long shot of the
mansion driveway—is that cab Frank had called, pulling up to the door in
silence, waiting, then honking forlornly. The last shot of the film: an
image of shocking bleakness.

Earlier, Mary had told Frank, when he obligingly offered to come back
to her, that she was rejecting him because there were just too many Dianes
around. "I want a marriage, not a competition," she says. "I want a husband, not a trophy I'd have to defend over and over again." Sensible girl
(we saw Frank lying to her about Diane from one of the movie's earliest
scenes). And yet there is something so prudential about this speech, about
her tone as she makes it, that you are left with something like the dissatis-
faction Diane left the lawyer's office with. This prudential world is exactly
what Diane has been resisting all along. And by the end, surprisingly, you
are even a bit on her side. It's also the world that noir, in its growing realism, was moving into more and more. The fifties were dedicated to banish-
ing the shadows. The result was often, as in *Angel Face,* a clearer view of the
emptiness.

Two

OUT OF THE PAST

It wasn't much noticed at the time—a routine thriller, is what the reviews said about it—but Jacques Tourneur's *Out of the Past* (1947) has come into its own. Now it seems the richest and most lyrical of *all* the postwar noir movies.

With one of the most tangled and impenetrable plots. When it begins, the hero, Jeff Bailey (Robert Mitchum), is working as a garage mechanic in a small, scenic northern California town. He is hiding out, it seems. Until this tough guy from the city—in a black overcoat—comes to town and tries to look him up. But Jeff is off fishing in the nearby mountains with his girlfriend, Ann (Virginia Huston). His deaf-mute helper, known only as the Kid (Dickie Moore), comes to fetch him, letting him know that this stranger needs to see him—and in town. The tough guy's name is Joe (Paul Valentine) and he works for a big racketeer, who now wants Jeff to come to his Lake Tahoe mansion for an interview. Less an invitation, clearly, than a threat—and Joe drives to the meeting with the loyal Ann beside him, steadfast in spite of the fact that, as she points out, she knows nothing at all about his earlier life. And so, on the way to the ominous Lake Tahoe appointment, he tells her how he got into this jam, how he used to be a private detective. And the flashback begins . . .

. . . with a scene that shows the racketeer, Whit Sterling (Kirk Douglas), wrapped in bandages and confined to a chair, with Joe hovering nearby. It seems that Whit's girlfriend stole forty grand from him, plugged him when he caught her, and then disappeared. He wants her back, and he's hiring Jeff now (whose partner, Fisher [Steve Brodie], is also in the room) to find her. He won't hurt her, he doesn't even care about the forty grand, he insists to Jeff, who is understandably skeptical. "I just want her back," says Whit. "When you see her, you'll understand." Her name is . . . ? "Kathie Moffett," replies Whit—meditatively, as if he were pronouncing a koan instead of a name.

Jeff picks up her trail and follows it to Acapulco—where it stops. Until one day when he is sitting in a little adobe-walled café called the La Mar Azul, "half asleep with the beer and the darkness," as he says in his voice-over, "only the music from the movie next door kept jarring me awake" (we hear it too—a faint, jaunty Mexican dance tune). "And then I saw her. Coming outa the sun. And I *knew* why Whit didn't care about that forty grand . . ."

Jane Greer in Jacques Tourneur's *Out of the Past*

We hardly see her at first: a small figure, in medium long shot, strolling out of the distant street glare, passing under the shadowed arches of the café's long entranceway, in and out of the light—until she enters the main room and sits at a table. Kathie (Jane Greer) is (as noir women so often are) all in white, with a soft big-brimmed hat and a big white pocketbook under her arm. With her dark shoulder-length hair, her large lustrous eyes and rich contralto voice, she has a kind of brisk languor—beauty with a sardonic inflection.

She seems neither hostile nor friendly when Jeff first comes on to her—more like biding her time. He sits at her table. The awkwardness is considerably helped by the intrusion of Jose Rodriguez (Tony Roux) a street hustler who mistakes them for a couple and offers to guide them through Acapulco. Jeff is all for this—as he tells her, it's no good seeing the sights alone. "Maybe you ought to go home," she says coolly, smiling and exhaling her cigarette. And so it goes—not too well.

But her gaze never leaves his face: a detail that Tourneur heightens by cutting back to her (and away from Mitchum) at just those moments—emphasizing the dark and unrelenting eyes—when her lower face is hidden by her drink or her cupped hand with the cigarette. Her manner is

wary, vaguely wisecracking—in the general way of smart American heroines besieged, but not entirely discouraging. And behind the warning
intelligence of the eyes, there is not only ruefulness but a certain humor—
and that thin, provisional little smile, as if she were in fact waiting to
really smile, even to be amused, if someone would only give her a reason.

In any case, she seems to have successfully fended him off. She rises to
go. But then she's suddenly telling him about a local place called
Pablo's—a place, she says, where you can hear American music, sip
bourbon, and even imagine (they're both from New York) that you're at "a
little place on Fifty-sixth Street." "I sometimes go there," she adds—dropping her eyes for the first time, then turning and walking out, pocketbook under her arm, through the shadows, and out into the street glare
again.

And so he has to wait for her to enter again. Unlike the noir heroine
who makes her big entrance at the start (like Stanwyck in her bath towel
or Astor in her hat), Kathie goes *on* making it, again and again: into
Pablo's ("And then," says Mitchum in voice-over, "she walked in out of the
moonlight . . ."), onto the beach ("And then she'd come along like school
was out . . ."), and finally on the path to their hideaway in the woods
("And then I saw her walking up the road in the headlights . . .").

What does this remind you of? Dietrich, of course, also tends to reenter
her movies, especially the Sternberg ones; and Greer's Kathie is in the
same line of hieratic presentation, of remoteness and mystery. Greer would
later recall (in a British TV documentary) how elliptically Tourneur, with
his highly imperfect English, had instructed her to play the character. He
asked her if she knew the French word *impassive*. She said she did and he
told her that *that's* what she should play. Adding: "And no *big* eyes!"

No danger: Greer is, after all, like Stanwyck, a deeply American version
of the femme fatale—private and baffling, but direct in her way, and unexpectedly down to earth. Once Kathie and Jeff are lovers, her sardonic quality turns fond and playful, as if she were always just a little ahead of him in
seeing and enjoying the joke between them. "And then I held her and we
could laugh," says Jeff's voice-over at one point. In fact they seem to do a
lot of laughing together, and to be genuinely having fun—more like a
couple out of the great romantic comedies of the thirties than the doomed
noir lovers we know they are. Her baiting, half-mocking tenderness with
him, his humorous deadpan ardency with her, make them seem closer to
Powell and Loy, or Dunne and Grant, than to Stanwyck and MacMurray.

But we know it can't last. Just as we know that no matter how decent
Kathie seems now, she's going to turn out to be treacherous: a genre cer-

tainty. But for Jeff the point has always been not so much that she's honest as that she's irresistible. She tells him on that Acapulco beach that she shot Whit in self-defense and that she never touched his forty grand—she swears it. "Baby, I don't care," says Jeff huskily, as he leans forward into a clinch. But in a sense he is banking on the truth of her story when he decides to double-cross Whit, to spirit her away and then hide out with her. That's how they end up having that idyll in the woods, going to the city for the racetrack and movies during the days, returning by night to their secluded log cabin. Until someone tracks them down.

It's Fisher, Jeff's old partner, working now for Whit. And as soon as Fisher turns up, Kathie knows he has to get "taken care of." She also knows that Jeff would never do it himself—as she explains to him just after she's shot Fisher in the back, as she stands against the cabin's pine-log wall, gun in hand, looking fearful and cornered, while the light from the fireplace flames ripples like flowing water across her face. Jeff and Fisher had been brawling; as soon as the gunshot rings out and Fisher drops, Jeff turns—in a memorable close-up—to look at her, almost as if she'd just said something he hadn't quite heard, and can't quite believe, gaping at her, his hair falling across one eye. And as he turns to look after Fisher (too late—he's dead), he hears her car starting up and driving off. In her haste, she has left not only a corpse behind her, but a bankbook. It turns out she really did steal that forty grand.

And at this point, the flashback ends. Back to the present, in Jeff's car, as it pulls up to the gates of Whit's Tahoe retreat. Jeff gets out at the manorial entranceway, and Ann (as agreed between them) drives off, leaving him to his "appointment." Whit, who is now all no-hard-feelings bonhomie and joviality, tells Jeff he just wants him to do another job for him—after all, Jeff sort of owes him. The job is to get some incriminating tax papers back from a man named Eels (Ken Miles), who is Whit's former lawyer. To steal them, in fact—with the help of Eels's trusted female secretary (another sexy, double-crossing woman).

Jeff knows he is being set up, of course, but he doesn't yet know how. He has no choice in the meantime but to play along. And then there's a major surprise—both for him and for us. He and Whit are outside on the terrace with a view of the lake, exchanging verbal jabs. In a shot angled toward the room behind them, with Whit and Jeff in the foreground, a woman in a negligee enters in the far background. And just then, when you think you've seen Kathie again, or someone just like her (the movie encourages these uncertainties), Tourneur cuts away, reversing the angle: the two men against the lake. It isn't until she sits—silently, looking ner-

"I sometimes go there": Kathie (Jane Greer) giving encouragement
to her pursuer, Jeff Bailey (Robert Mitchum)

vous and abashed—in her place at the nearby breakfast table, that you're
even sure it's her: the first time Jeff has seen her since the night she ditched
him with Fisher's corpse. "Kathie is back in the fold now," says Whit, with
a huge and nasty grin.

She still hates the man, she tells Jeff once they're alone—she was afraid
of him, that's why she came back. But in fact, as we soon learn, she too is
involved in Whit's new plot against Jeff: a matter of sticking Jeff with yet
another corpse, once it's ready—it's Eels, the lawyer—and then framing
him for murder. But Jeff figures things out in time, and by getting to the
incriminating body first, he manages to hide it. When Kathie discovers
that he's defeated Whit's and her plot, she rallies by offering to recruit him
to another one—this time against Whit. And so on—and on. And yet
finally, with not just one plot proceeding against him, but multiple and
intersecting ones by several different people, Jeff outwits them all in the
end. Except that finally it doesn't matter—as we sort of knew it wouldn't.
While he is briefly away, retrieving the evidence that will save him from
both Whit and Kathie, Kathie kills Whit, overturning everything—as is
her way. (She is planning to frame Jeff *again*—for Whit's murder.)

"I don't want to die!" she pleads with him earlier on, when he threatens

Breakfast at Whit's place: "Kathie is back in the fold now."
Kirk Douglas is the ebullient host at right.

to expose one of her double-crosses. "Neither do I, baby," replies Jeff. "But if I have to, I'm gonna die last." And yet in the end he doesn't even manage *that* modest objective. She kills him too, as it turns out, just before her own death—shooting him in the crotch (no comment required) when they struggle over a gun.

But in this second half of the movie—the part that's in the present—Kathie is a different figure from the woman in Acapulco. Even her re-entrances (which go on) are different: less grand than furtive—less like *here*-she-is! ("And then I saw her . . .") than where-did-*she*-come-from? The way she appears on Whit's terrace, for example—or in Jeff's room just after that, to explain that she only returned to Whit because he'd threatened her if she didn't. "I couldn't help myself," she says: her inevitable fall-back line whenever she has to explain one of her betrayals. "You can't help anything," says Jeff. She even *looks* less attractive in this scene—uneasy and strained, as if her tireless ingenuities were beginning to cost her some sleep. Jeff regards her now with undisguised disgust: "Just get out now," he says, "I have to sleep in this room." Even the once besotted Whit now seems to have become more interested in humiliating her than in having her around for anything else.

Jeff has just discovered the new corpse—Whit's—when Kathie enters:
"You can't make deals with a dead man, Jeff."
She has dressed for traveling.

But soon she regains some of her old glamour and authority—though
to a different effect than she made in Acapulco days. More the bitch goddess now: with her hair pulled back in a bun, a fur over her bare shoulders,
wearing a regal low-cut black gown, stealing into another woman's apartment and impersonating her voice over the telephone, while Jeff in hiding
watches her, she looks more coldly beautiful than ever—like a sexy wicked
stepmother. And at the movie's end, dressed for the getaway, she looks like
a malignant nun—in a severe-looking suit, with her hair in a snood. This
is the scene where Jeff learns that she's just killed Whit. He finds the body
lying by the fireplace just as she comes up behind him and comments:
"You can't make deals with a dead man, Jeff."

Out of the Past shows the familiar noir mixture of depressive content and
exhilarated style. And if it's even grimmer than most such movies (noir
heroes are more likely than not to survive at the end, and especially so if
they are private eyes like Jeff), it's also *more* exhilarated. It's not just those
romantic scenes in the flashback: the whole movie has an oddly elated
rhythm and spirit. It offers the familiar noir ambience of the nighttime
city, with its clubs and apartments, its enclosing dark spaces and looming
shadows—but then it keeps leaving town, breaking into light and open

space and sweeping views, from Acapulco to Lake Tahoe to Telegraph Hill. And most of all the place where the movie begins and ends, and keeps returning betweentimes: the remote small California town where Jeff has his gas station, set in a vast landscape of field and sky, mountain ranges and canyon lakes and towering firs. It's the landscape that's under the opening titles as Whit's henchman Joe drives into town, and that's around Jeff when we first see him, from high above, striding along a stream with a fishing rod, while Ann waits on the bank. And Nicholas Musuraca's cinematography reminds you of all the ways black and white can seem more vivid and alive on the screen than even the best color can.

But it's also the visual rhythms, the fluidity of Tourneur's camerawork and editing, that make the film feel so high-spirited and expansive—as if it were riding some magical inner current, sweeping toward its ending almost as if it were going to be a happy one. For example: the way an elevator door closes on two men talking and then, on a trumpet blast and wail, dissolves into a close-up of a horn and its player, then pans across the band and the dance floor of a crowded Negro club, scene flowing into scene in what seems like one single broad, sweeping gesture of sound, imagery, and onwardness—just as this same nightclub scene will dissolve into a traveling aerial view of Mexico City, and so on. In Acapulco, there is a cloudburst and Jeff and Kathie run laughing through the rain to her seaside cottage. Inside she throws him a towel, and they wrestle on the couch, drying each other's hair, then kissing, as Jeff throws the towel across the room, with the camera following it as it lands on and overturns a lamp—the camera, with the soundtrack music swelling, moving majestically past the lamp, the table, through the open door and out into the pouring rain, past plants and trees and on and on, as if impelled only by the music, on to the dissolve into the next scene—the postcoital one—back inside the cottage. Kathie lifts the tone arm from her record player and the music stops.

This movie is unimaginable without that music—that particular music. It's variations on the melody of a song (uncredited here) written for an earlier RKO movie, where it was sung by Frances Farmer to Cary Grant.* Here it isn't sung, but played incessantly, in one guise or another—an outpouring of yearning with a mournful undertone and a soaring melodic line. And in Roy Webb's wonderful movie score it becomes something like the movie's "other" voice, its *emotive* voice, undercutting the deadpan mode. Played by the jazz band at the Negro club, by

---

*"The First Time I Saw You" by Nathaniel Shilkret and Allie Wrubel, from *The Toast of New York* (1937).

the string ensemble at Pablo's place, by the record on Kathie's phonograph, by the record on a jukebox, and so on, it's everywhere, it seems—most of all on the soundtrack itself. Seeming as inescapable as Jeff's fate, and a lot grander once it gets going: tending to swell into romantic exaltation in the early Acapulco scenes, then later—in full symphonic throttle—into powerful sounds of longing and nostalgia and Mahlerian melancholy. "American music," says Kathie, with a mocking little smile, when she and Jeff first hear it, in the thin tea-dance version of the string players at Pablo's.

But the *real* "American music" here is in the movie's conversations—cadenced, rhythmic, low-keyed, richly and intensely colloquial. In spite of what seems to have been Tourneur's uncertain relation to English, *Out of the Past* has nearly as distinctive a *talk* sound as a Hawks picture or a Sturges. It's a sound that you hear, along with the theme music, from the very beginning, when Whit's thug Joe comes to town looking for Jeff and stops at the local diner, telling the waitress behind the counter how he just happened to see his "old friend's" name on the sign at the local gas station. "It's a small world," says the waitress. "Yeah," says Joe, "—or a big sign." Playing roulette at an Acapulco casino, Kathie is losing badly when Jeff tells her that betting against the house is no way to win. "*Is* there a way to win?" she says. "There's a way to lose more slowly," he replies.

It's the tone and style of the comeback. "I lost her," says the cabdriver about the woman he was supposed to tail. "She's worth losing," says the private eye. "Your cousin is a very charming young lady," says the lawyer about the woman who's just left the room. "No, he's not," says the private eye. "His name is Norman and he's a bookmaker in Cleveland, Ohio."

If Mitchum's hero, as you'd expect, gives most of the best rejoinders, Douglas's gangster is nearly his match. Their verbal duets have extraordinary crackle and life but also an almost formal symmetry. Whit (on his terrace) expresses (or professes) surprise that Jeff has sunk to running a gas station. Jeff: "They call it earning a living. You may have heard of it." Whit: "I may have. But not from you." And so on. Douglas looks uncharacteristically small next to the towering Mitchum here. And his Whit is the insidious one of the pair—smiling, needling, and nasal-voiced. In Acapulco he compliments Jeff on his new shoes—but then can't resist a waspish afterthought: "Kinda sporty for you, aren't they?" Mitchum's Jeff is the seemingly imperturbable one, the tortoise to Douglas's hare, with his sleepy face (no one could look more awake than Douglas, even in this early role), his T-square physique, his drawling voice and comfortably centered baritone. Even though Whit has the power and the ruthlessness, Jeff has the personal authority. "Let's go down to the bar," he says in the hotel room to Whit, "so you can cool off while we try to impress each other." Doing to Whit, occasionally, the single thing that Whit can't ever do to him: make him look foolish.

As a clumsy imitator more than anyone else can and will do. Someone like Fisher, Jeff's detective partner ("a stupid, oily gent," says Jeff, introducing him in the voice-over) at the start of the early flashback. It's the two detectives' first meeting with Whit, at his office, where he is telling them about Kathie's disappearance, how she shot him and then cleared out. "Y'know," says Fisher from his corner of the room, "a dame with a rod is like a guy with a knitting needle—" "What's *he* doing here!" growls Whit at Jeff in a flash of anger.

Because Whit knows an inadvertent parody when he hears one (as he just has here). And the movie is smart enough, confident enough to make this distinction, this kind of joke, about its own style—to give us not only the sound of Whit and Jeff but that of Fisher the inept imitator too. It's a remarkable script altogether—arguably the best written, line for line, of all the noir movies—certainly the most *elegantly* written. And as scholar Jeff Schwager has conclusively shown,* it was predominantly the work of an obscure studio writer whose name never appears in the credits, Frank Fenton. It was Fenton (Schwager again) who gave the screenplay most of its wit and nearly all of its depth and subtlety.† And it was because of him presumably that the movie seems to find smart people nearly everywhere it looks. It's like an epidemic, spreading from the principals downward, through the minor characters to the walk-ons. Even the few slower types prompt some moments of colloquial splendor—like Joe, who "couldn't find a prayer in the Bible," according to Whit, or even "stupid, oily" Fisher ("Your picture don't do you justice, baby," he says to Kathie. "Why don't you break his head, Jeff?" she replies).

But as usual in noir movies, it's the women who stand out: one of the

---

*"The Past Rewritten," *Film Comment,* January–February, 1991.

†The credits say, "Screenplay by Geoffrey Home, Based on His Novel *Build My Gallows High.*" "Geoffrey Home" was the pseudonym that screenwriter Daniel Mainwaring used for his crime novels. But Mainwaring's early script for this movie was found largely unusable by Tourneur and producer Warren Duff. So were James M. Cain's two attempts to rewrite it. It was Fenton's screenplay that worked and that was finally filmed. He's a mysterious figure. Though many of his credited screenplays (almost half of the twenty scripts he worked on before *Out of the Past* were uncredited, Schwager says) show intelligence and taste—*The Sky's the Limit* (1943), and especially *The Man with a Cloak* (1951), with Barbara Stanwyck and Joseph Cotten—none of them approaches this one. Fenton died in 1971 and never did get credit for his script—a credit that Mainwaring, however, happily claimed and accepted.

excitements of late noir—of Rudolph Maté's *D.O.A.* (1950), of Robert
Aldrich's *Kiss Me Deadly* (1955), et al.—is the range and variety as well as
the individual fascination of the women. Eunice (Theresa Harris), Kathie's
onetime maid, for example. Jeff finds her in that Negro nightclub (the
only sequence she appears in). And she is a considerable personal presence,
sitting across the table from him, handsome and sharp-eyed, leaning back
against her rather doughy-faced boyfriend, playing with one of her gloves
as she looks speculatively at Jeff, who is trying to find out if she knows
where her ex-mistress may have gone to. She is not very helpful, until Jeff
assures her that it's a matter of Kathie's safety. She hesitates still—
"Florida," she suggests, after her boyfriend encourages her. Then she offers
Jeff a little "colored maid" turn: "That girl *sure* hated the cold!" she says,
almost chuckling. Jeff asks her if she is sure it was Florida. "Now I seem to
remember," she says, brightly, still playing with the glove, "and I'm sure."
She is still looking at him. And lying, of course—but unforgettably.

Then there's Marney (Mary Field), the waitress at the diner in Jeff's
small town, who appears in the film's opening sequence. She is one of the
first country rubes Joe inquires of in his search for Jeff. She is gawky and
gossipy, a younger, comelier Margaret Hamilton—no match for a city-
wise gunsel, you would think. That is, until she talks. "Tell me something," Joe begins. "You don't look like I could," she says amiably.

So it goes. But it's a characteristic moment. Even in passing, in this
film, people keep escaping their genre limits—in a film about no escape.
The nicest, most dazzling instance of this, perhaps, is someone who appears
(if that's the word) even more fleetingly than Marney or Eunice—someone
who's so inconspicuous and briefly present, we hardly see him at all. He
turns up when Jeff goes to the bus station to check the package (Whit's tax
papers) that his own survival more or less depends upon. He hands it to
the man behind the counter and takes his receipt, but before turning
away he offers an admonition. "You know," he says to the anonymous-
looking little man, "sometimes a bad memory is like what they call an ill
wind—it can blow somebody luck." "I always say everybody's right," mutters the attendant, as he turns away with the package and exits—as the
scene fades.

That flip, discouraged sound is the sound of the movie, as unmistakable
after a while as its musical theme: the dying fall into a bleak wisecrack.
And often *about* dying, like Jeff's announced intention to "die last," or his
reply to Kathie when she tells him that she's sorry Whit didn't die: "Give
him time," he says, crooningly, leaning back on his elbow and looking up
at the sky, and you know it's the kind of thing he *likes* to say. It's a style

that prides itself on being without sentiment or comforting illusion. Particularly without sentiment. Jeff tells Kathie when he's kissing her off (so he hopes) near the end why he will never go back to Acapulco: "because I'd keep thinking of *you,* Kathie—up there in the women's prison at Tehachapi." And he suggests in the same scene that Whit equip Joe's corpse (Jeff killed him in self-defense) with a suicide note: "He couldn't stand living with what he had done." Earlier on he tells Eels's duplicitous secretary that her boss is "an idiot." "You think so?" "Why not?" says Mitchum, giving the line all the force of his powerfully melancholy presence. "He's in love with you."

One of the movie's wittiest, most sardonic inventions is this latter character of the secretary, Meta (Rhonda Fleming). Another "knockout" (*"Nice!"* says Jeff's cabdriver buddy on first seeing her. "Awfully cold around the heart," replies Jeff. "Let's go") and *another* fatal woman, appearing midway through the film when Kathie has somewhat receded into the background. Whit has sent Jeff to Meta's Telegraph Hill apartment to meet her and get instructions on how to steal those tax papers from her boss. "I wasn't expecting you," she says, as she opens her door—wearing a revealing negligee. "I wasn't expecting *you,*" says Jeff. Neither, it should be said, were we: it's like finding that the western has *two* gambling-hall hostesses in the cast. "Should I take that as a compliment?" she says coyly, as she shows him to a nearby couch and takes his hat. In spite of the apparent come-on, and the ample figure in the negligee, she is like some little girl playing house—serving drinks ("You may have whiskey if you like") and making conversation ("Miserable weather we're having, isn't it?") just like a grown-up. And like the grown-ups too, she has her little affectations—what Jeff rudely refers to as her "Junior League patter" ("These old houses can be amusing when they're remodeled, can't they?") when he cuts it off impatiently. She is flirtatious, but in an utterly impersonal way—like a beauty contestant with one of her judges. And unlike Kathie when we first meet *her,* Meta is an utterly and amusingly familiar type—the American "girl" at her archest and most insufferable.

And normally, of course, she wouldn't make you think of Kathie—any more than Rhonda Fleming could remind you of Jane Greer. That is, if it weren't apparent from the moment Meta opens her apartment door and purrs her greeting at him that she is another version of Kathie (there's no escape!)—another seducer-betrayer. The two women even combine against him, or seem to, later on, even exchanging identities—as when Kathie appears without warning in Meta's apartment and impersonates her over the phone. There is even a fleeting but startling moment after that when

The *second* fatal woman: Meta (Rhonda Fleming) entertains Jeff.

we see the two of them together—from Jeff's point of view—as they go by in the backseat of a slowly moving car, sitting side by side (they are looking for *him*), at such a dimly lit distance that they look at the moment almost like twins.

But Meta is a *parody* version of Kathie. In Meta, Kathie's poise and natural elegance turn into gentility and ludicrous "refinement," her seductiveness becomes coquettishness, her mystery replaced by phoniness. But then, by this point in the movie—post-Acapulco—Kathie herself has moved from the realm of mystery to something more like irony. She has become, like Meta, less an object of romantic awe than of sardonic, despairing amusement.

After she has killed Whit, she tells Jeff—as they stand near the body in the central room of Whit's Tahoe lodge—that unless he wants to be fingered for Whit's murder, he has no choice but to come away with her again. She wants to go back to Acapulco and do the whole romance thing over again: to "walk into the sun and find you waiting . . . to sit in the same moonlight and tell you all the things I never told you," until he stops hating her, until he falls in love with her again. That's her plan anyway. She is all packed and ready to go ("Put some things in for me," he says. "I already did," she says) when she registers his hesitation. She tries to cheer him up a bit. "Jeff," she says gently, "we've been wrong a lot, and unlucky a long time. I think we deserve a break." And off she takes him.

"Unlucky," did she say? Deserve a *what,* did she say? But she really means it—never mind that corpse at her feet as she speaks. This remarkable reflection is so quickly gone in the flow of their talk ("We deserve each other," replies Jeff) that you almost don't hear it—and then almost don't believe that you *did.* And yet the revelation here that Kathie thinks of herself as being the victim of "bad breaks" is on the way to being the sardonic high point of the movie. And all the higher and the more sardonic for being so close to unnoticeable when you hear it, for being so casually and uninflectedly announced. It is, in its way, a wonderful moment.

Out of the Past is quite strikingly a film in two halves, not only in its narrative but in its tone. The lyricism and overt romanticism of the first part give way in the second—the part that takes place in the present—to an entertaining cynicism, a feeling of stoic, wised-up endurance: a fissure that gets reflected most importantly in the movie's changed perception of Kathie. Tourneur, like most studio directors, was not much given to discussions of character and motivation. Not at all, in fact—according to Jane Greer's recollection now. The only direction he gave her about the character was: "First half, good girl. Last half, bad girl." And that, more or less, is what we get.

Then why does the movie feel—as I think it does—so continuous, so close to seamless? Importantly, I think, because of that peculiarly heightened quality it had from the start—of almost-exhilaration. It never loses that feeling; it just transmutes it, so that what seems at first an elation about love and romantic experience can turn into what seems something like elation about seeing through that experience—about knowing the worst. And a movie that begins as a lyric-romantic experience turns, on the same arc of expansive feeling, into a lyric-sardonic one. Kathie, it turns out—a true descendant of "Miss Wonderly"—still inspires awe, but of a different kind than before: fulfilling our darkest forebodings—and then ("I think we deserve a break") surpassing them.

And because of this she becomes the ideal counterpart for the private-eye hero, whose own glamour comes importantly from his refusal of illusion, his wised-up outlook on things. What makes *him* compelling finally, even "heroic"—whatever his failings or his treasons—is his affinity for darkness, his final knowledge about what people are capable of, his propensity for facing the harshest facts and the bitterest truths. So that in the end "the quintessential film noir"—as *Out of the Past* has been rightly called—is a romance less about sex or love than about knowingness.

Three

VERTIGO

But one person in *Out of the Past* is exempt from that knowingness—
Jeff's small-town girlfriend, Ann (Virginia Huston)—and she is very
prominent. She's the one he wants to settle down with, who makes him
want to build a house in the cove by the lake and "never go anywhere else."
She is open and trusting and loving and fiercely committed to him, in
spite of her parents' opposition and the warnings of the sheriff (Richard
Webb), who is also in love with her. She is very certain about her own love
for Jeff. All he has to do, in her view, is make sure of what he feels for
Kathie *now,* if anything. She even offers to send him back to her one last
time, so that he can "be very sure that there isn't even a little bit of love left
for her." But he knows there isn't, and that's enough for her. The past is
past, she tells him: "I told you whatever happened, it's done." She is dead
wrong, of course. The whole burden of the movie, including its title, is
against her.

Which may be less important in the end than the way she sounds. Her
voice is so different from the others, from the ironic, humorously self-
deprecating voice that movies like this one teach us to value and love.
Even when she talks about death, as everyone does in this movie, the
chord she strikes is more like wistful transcendence ("They say the day
you die your name is written in a cloud") than grim acquiescence. She is
no sap and she is genuinely nice. But while the movie never exactly undercuts her, it does give us room to feel uneasy about her—even about her
virtues. It shows her, for example (in a medium close-up), dropping Jeff
off at the gates of Whit's Tahoe lodge, looking at him through the window of the car before she drives away. Her face shines with reassurance and
tenderness, but with something like complacency too. At moments like
this one her loyalty seems a little too conscious, her faith in him a little
too close to a faith in her own power to be wonderful. And the more Jeff
declares his growing love for her, the more we hear the dissonance
between them. As in their last urgent conversation, just before Jeff goes

back to meet Kathie and his doom. They are talking about Kathie. Says magnanimous Ann: "She can't be all bad. No one is." "Well, she comes the closest," says Jeff.

Of course one way of describing the gulf between them is the way her childhood sweetheart the sheriff does: she is simply too nice for a guy like Jeff. But the final truth is that she is too nice for us as well: too reasonable, too mild, too upbeat and life-affirming for anyone who is genuinely in collusion with the film itself. And the fact that she has to be lied to at the end of it (the Kid tells her that Jeff meant to go off with Kathie, so that Ann will feel "free" to go off with the sheriff) only confirms our sense that the movie we've been watching is really beyond her. And her actually being *in* it only underscores the point.

In fact, she is nearly always in these films—whether she is called Ann or something else. She is the available (and distinctly advisable) alternative to the noir heroine, to the woman we and the hero are really interested in. She is the innocent stepdaughter in *Double Indemnity,* the rejected girlfriend in *The Killers,* the loyal secretary in *D.O.A.* and *Kiss Me Deadly.* In *The Big Heat* (1953) she is the wife who gets killed, in *Pitfall* (1948) and *The File on Thelma Jordon* (1950) she is the wife who gets left. She is played by Maureen O'Sullivan as a loving nurse in *Where Danger Lives* (1951), by Mona Freeman as a neglected fiancée in *Angel Face* (1953), and by Dorothy Malone, again a nurse, in *Pushover* (1954). In one form or other, she is the domestic angel the hero turns his back on.

And as the noir film goes on, she gets more prominent—and less insipid. The earlier noir pattern that kept her, like Ann in *Out of the Past,* in almost a separate compartment of the movie—in the country or safely at home, quite apart from that woman in the city or the nightclub or the *other* guy's home—begins to erode in later noir films, where she may even encounter the bad woman and look good doing it—as Mona Freeman does in *Angel Face:* that nice girl is not only on to the other woman's tricks, but even has the scene's best lines.

But the problem is and remains that no matter how much the movie idealizes and celebrates her, she is just not very interesting. Not like the *other,* anyway. Some noir films seem uneasy about this—like *The Strange Love of Martha Ivers* (1946), whose good girl (Lizabeth Scott) seems to get even more screen time than the bad one (Barbara Stanwyck) does. And in general, especially toward the fifties, the nice girl seems to get nicer, even sexier—to get closer to having "everything": looks, brains, warmth, understanding, and so on. She even—as established noir heroines like Stanwyck age—gets younger and prettier. As if it were becoming some-

Jean Heather (left) is the nice girl in *Double Indemnity*—here playing
checkers with her stepmother (Barbara Stanwyck), who is not at all nice,
and who loathes her.

how more urgent to make a case for her. But then her "case" was always her
strongest suit—even, in a way, her liability.

It's Hitchcock who gives, toward the end of the fifties, both the
shrewdest and most moving account of her, with Barbara Bel Geddes's
Midge in *Vertigo* (1958). In her cardigans and horn-rimmed glasses, with
her wholesome, round-faced prettiness, she is meant to be a very appealing
figure, humorous and sensible and straightforward. And though she is
unhappily in love with the James Stewart hero—who seems fond of her
but no more—she is without self-pity: gallant and, except for an over-
cheerful smile and a tendency to give the ends of her sentences a plaintive
upward inflection, making no show of her pain. Scotty (Stewart) is an ex-
cop, retired because of an accident, a fall caused by his acrophobia, and still
recovering, lying on her couch in an early scene while she works at her
drafting board—a nice image for the deliberate way she sustains the sepa-
rateness from him. Midge will never press him or lean on him. Scotty
refers banteringly to the fact that they were once engaged, and we learn
that she was the one who broke it off. And when he accuses her, in the
same conversation, of sounding like a mother, she looks up (a high-angle

close shot) from her work and gives him a glance over her glasses. All the important recognitions in the scenes between them belong to her.

But when he *needs* her to be a mother, she obliges. In this same early scene, he offers to defy his vertigo by climbing a stepladder for her and then doing some no-hands boasting: "I look up, I look down . . ." Until he looks down and out the window—and falls down and onto her shoulder, drooping there like a vine while she comforts him.

Much later on, after a second vertigo attack has kept him (as he supposes) from saving the life of the woman he loves, Midge visits him in the sanatorium he's been confined to with a breakdown. "Acute melancholia," says the doctor—as rat-faced and ersatz-looking as Hitchcock's "experts" usually are. Midge, crouching on the floor by Scotty's chair, attempts to break through his catatonia. "Oh, Johnny, Johnny," she pleads (she is, significantly, the only one who calls him by this diminutive of his first name). And Stewart's expression of devastated vacancy is genuinely unnerving. "You're not lost," she says. "Mother's here." No response. Mozart plays on the phonograph, and she chats about that, and about the doctors—and circles the room, looking at him. "Oh, Johnny, you don't even know I'm here, do you?" she says at length. "But I'm here," she adds. It's a moving afterthought: it's what she's resigned herself to being, after all—almost purely generous.

She is very much *there,* in lots of ways. One of the qualities she is characterized by in her first scene is a healthy forthrightness about sex and its anatomy. The first subject she and Scotty talk about in that lightly comic exchange is corsets: he is wearing one, due to his accident. And she is at her drawing board, as they talk, sketching a brassiere—which is designed on the principle, as she explains to him, of the cantilevered bridge, and so on. He asks about her "love life." "Normal," she says—and why not? Later on, when she feels threatened by the out-of-the-normal spell cast on him by the Kim Novak heroine—involving as it does a museum portrait of the beautiful "mad Carlotta" of San Francisco legend—Midge tries to restore his perspective by playing a joke on him. She has painted a "mad Carlotta" of her own—a copy of the museum one but with her own sensible face, horn-rims and all, replacing the tragic beauty's. And when Scotty comes to visit again, she unveils it for him—and for us.

An audience may laugh, but *he* doesn't. He is, in fact, appalled. He makes a strangled protest: "It's not funny, Midge," he says. Then says it again, and leaves. And Midge is left behind, tearful and berating herself for being so "stupid," for not having known better. And indeed, she should have known. This, after all, is a movie where the heroine talks to redwood trees—and we are *not* meant to laugh. We don't, in fact. It's not a place for jokes and common sense—and Midge's Carlotta joke only confirms her own out-of-placeness here. She sees it herself, of course—with her usual clarity. "But I'm here," she says later—and then she is gone. There is that long, sad shot of her walking away down the hospital corridor—and leaving the movie for good, as it turns out. It's at its halfway point.

Like *Out of the Past*, *Vertigo* falls into distinct halves: the enchantment and its aftermath. And like the earlier film, it takes us powerfully *inside* the enchantment, the hero's experience of the woman, making us see and feel her the way that he does. But Scotty, in Stewart's transfixing perfor- mance, has almost none of the movie-hero self-possession of Mitchum's Jeff Bailey; what he has instead is Jimmy Stewart's hesitation and plain- tiveness and middle-aged irritability. Plus a surprising store of credulity, which Gavin Elster's story doesn't at all seem to exhaust. Elster (Tom Hel- more) wants him to follow and watch his wife, Madeleine, who, he believes, is being "taken over" by her suicidal ancestor Carlotta. Scotty sits glumly in the corner of a long shot of Elster's office as he listens to the Car- lotta story—as if he wanted to get as far away from it as he could and still be in the room. Looking more threatened than skeptical, he reacts almost peevishly to Elster's job offer, which is also a request from an old friend. "I'm suppos'ta be retired," he says querulously. "I don't wanna get mixed up in this darn thing." But he relents. Still, though, how will he even *know* Madeleine, whom he's never met? Elster will arrange to take her to Ernie's, the posh landmark restaurant (a real place), so that Scotty can see her there. "Ernie's," repeats Scotty—on a lap dissolve from his close-up to a medium shot of the restaurant exterior, with the camera tracking silently forward toward the entrance door, adjoining a gold nameplate.

Then, just as we seem about to enter through the door, there is a cut to a close shot of Scotty, already inside, sitting at the crowded bar. The interior is in a Gilded Age style, with red plush walls and hanging brass lamps, all the tables filled, the conversation buzzing. At the bar, Scotty leans uneasily back on his stool, craning his neck, looking furtive, like a guilty eavesdropper. And as he moves, the camera takes off on its own, tracking and panning, in a slow, stately survey of the crowded dining room—until it spots her, near the back wall with Elster, and stops, before tracking stealthily, discreetly forward, through the people and tables, toward her. And Bernard Herrmann's melancholy theme music—a slow, ascending four-note plaint, rising in pitch as it repeats—begins. A solemn, almost ominous moment: our first sight of Madeleine . . .

She (Kim Novak) is turned away from us, facing Elster across the table, her head, with its blond back-knot, moving in conversation. She is posed like a foreground character in a Renaissance painting: her bare back inclined toward her companion, her wrap fallen in folds onto the floor around her chair. Cut back to Scotty again, in close shot—looking disturbed.

Next we see her from farther away, framed through a doorway—rising from the table and gathering her wrap around a low-cut black gown, turning and coming toward the doorway and us (Elster lingering to talk to a waiter) alone. With her slow, sidling walk, her enigmatic, crooked little smile, she seems almost apologetically ravishing, even a bit uneasy. Until she walks into the close-up Hitchcock has waiting for her, strolling into apotheosis—where she stops: her face in profile flooded with traveling and rising light, first side-lit, then shadowed, then backlit, as Herrmann's strings soar exultantly, almost hysterically, and the red plush wall behind her glows and burns, her beauty made not only unearthly but uncanny. And Scotty now, in his separate close-up, looking anguished.

But he can't be seeing what we're seeing, can he? He's still at the bar— and she's in the restaurant foyer now. But as she turns her face around to the left, seeming to greet someone behind her (Elster, presumably, rejoining her), Scotty—in his close-up—turns his face in the same direction, less as if seeing her than thinking her, as if registering her on some level beyond sight. And in the following shot she is turned away once again, gliding off into the background, next to Elster, past a mirror, and out the door. Leaving Scotty (in his final close-up here)—and us—behind.

This exit through a door in the background of a shot will be as characteristic of Madeleine as the multiple entrance was of Kathie Moffett. And the profile close-up becomes a signature for her too. Except that the *next* time, we're in no confusion about Scotty's spatial relation to the vision she offers: he's right on top of her, peering into a florist's shop from behind an alley door, and after that skulking among the headstones in a graveyard— both times unseen and thrillingly close to her. Just as we are. Much of the odd, creepy excitement of such scenes comes from how close he gets to her *without* being seen (later, as we learn, he even undresses her—in one of the movie's most famous ellipses—without being noticed: getting her out of her wet clothes while she's unconscious). Being near her at these moments—both for Scotty and for us—is like an encounter with a natural wonder, an experience more impersonal than not. Which, in a curious way, seems to be how Madeleine experiences herself, as we watch her—seeming most present to herself in moments of intensest isolation—standing before the red wall at Ernie's, gazing at the flowers in the florist's shop, walking

Vertigo: After fishing her out of San Francisco Bay, taking her home,
and undressing her, Scotty (James Stewart) serves Madeleine
(Kim Novak) some hot tea—and looks at her.

among the graves at the Mission Dolores, and so on. Her lack of any imperiousness seems as striking as her looks. It's as if the stake she had in her
own beauty were as uncertain and finally impersonal as the onlooker's—
something visited on her rather than fully possessed.

The San Francisco the movie takes place in looks singularly unpopu-
lated. Instead of the range and variety of people and types that a noir
movie like *Out of the Past* offers, here there are mostly places, all of them
beautiful and almost all of them empty: a museum, a church, a graveyard,
an ancient forest—*Madeleine's* sort of place, carrying, as she does, not only
associations of spirits and romantic legends, but of lines to eternity as well.
As in the redwoods scene—among the movie's most dangerously hyper-
bolic—where, falling into a kind of trance, she traces the times of her life
and "death" ("Here I was born—and there I died") between the dated rings
of a giant cross-sectioned tree. "It was only a moment for you," she says to
the tree, with a gloved finger on its trunk, "you took no notice." Then she
strolls away, into the eerie half-light between the trees, and for one startling moment, to Scotty's dismay, seems to have disappeared into them . . .

It is all, of course, a fake, an elaborate fraud—just as Madeleine herself

is. She is really, as we later learn, just this girl who works at Magnin's—
who wears too much makeup, big earrings, and tight knit dresses. Her
hair is brown, not blond, and she wears it long, in a kind of ponytail, and
in spitcurls around her forehead (the Carmencita look). She has a big
frame, a lounging walk, a tendency to talk out of the side of her mouth,
and poor diction. She left her native Kansas for "sunny California" (as she
calls it) mainly because she didn't like her mother's new husband, and she's
living now at a hotel in downtown San Francisco—where Scotty, after
Madeleine's "death," first sees her, walking with some girlfriends. Her
name is Judy.

But in fact she is Scotty's Madeleine, all there is of her or ever was, the
rest being Gavin Elster's invention. And whatever she may have learned
from the suave Elster's coaching seems not to have survived his departure:
Judy is not a "classy" type. For her, all that belongs to "the other," in her
own phrase for Madeleine. She stays with Scotty now, in spite of the exposure she risks, in hope that he will come to love her for herself. Elster had
hired her, as we learn, to impersonate his wife as part of a scheme to pass
off her murder as a suicide with Scotty as the crucial witness.

This revelation, however—the "solution" to the Madeleine mystery—is
much less surprising than the fact that we get it not at the end of the
movie but in the middle: with Judy, just after re-encountering Scotty,
back in her hotel room writing him a letter she never sends, explaining the
whole plot (with voice-over and flashbacks). The extreme awkwardness of
this device clearly mattered less to Hitchcock than the radical effect it
makes on our relation to the rest of the movie. We are now no longer
exclusively inside Scotty's view of things, trapped in his obsession, but
outside it too, inside "Madeleine's" view of it as well, through our sympathetic connection with Judy. First half, he was her victim; last half, she is
his—reversing the noir paradigm.

They have their first "date," and he takes her (no surprise) to Ernie's,
where she looks rather out of place. It's not a successful evening. Nonetheless, when he brings her back to the hotel and they are saying goodnight in
the hallway, he asks her to quit her job, to let him "take care of" her. She
treats this disdainfully, as a conventional, if extreme, make-out move—
though she knows better, of course. Like Midge, she knows very well—
just as much as he does not—what's going on between them. She walks
away from him into the darkened room and sits on the arm of a chair near
the window. From outside it, the big "Hotel Empire" electric sign gives
off an eerie aqueous blue-green glow that floods her corner of the room.
But she is in darkness, as she removes her glove—her face turned in pro-

ABOVE: Madeleine in the graveyard
BELOW: Judy (Novak again) in her hotel room

file, a black outline, like a silhouette cutout, against the green unearthly
light. Scotty stands in the doorway, talking to her across the room, uncomfortably. His intentions are honorable, he tells her—he only wants to see
more of her. "Why?" comes her voice from the darkness. "Because I remind
you of her?" (pronouncing it "remind-juv"). At this, Scotty looks pained,
the music rises, and the camera sweeps suddenly forward, right up to the
black, unreadable profile, where it stops—the movement an almost visceral register of Scotty's longing and frustration. The next shot, however, is
Judy's—inside the darkness: a frontal close-up, her face half in shadow,
half in the sea-green light. She is gazing out the window into the light:
one of those moments when Novak's unmeditated, cornered-animal quality seems most vivid and moving. The unearthly light makes the misery in
her opaque dark eyes look almost luminous. She shifts her gaze from the
window: maybe, she says, she could get the day off from work.

But it's hopeless. The more she gives in to him, the more she loses herself. She just wants to be ordinary, to be "just a girl," as she describes herself to him defensively, in love in the ordinary way: like the necking young
couples in the park she looks at with envy as she walks beside him—in
silence. This, apparently, is what he calls "seeing more of" her. But it's precisely that he *doesn't* see her, under any condition or circumstance. The
more avidly he looks at her, the more he seems to be seeing something
beyond her. She knows what the something is, of course—and she knows it
isn't her.

Now he wants to dress her like Madeleine, and he takes her to a coutu-
rier. "The gentleman seems to know what he wants," says the saleswoman,
trying to deal with his demands, and with her own aversion to him, audible in her voice. By this time, Scotty is not only behaving like a creep but
sounding like one too. "Judy, I just want you to look nice," he says when
she rebels, barely controlling his anger at her. "I know the kind of suit that
would look well on you"—like a pedophile reassuring his prey. The suit
that he's urging upon her is an elegant gray pinstripe, chic and understated—not Judy's sort of thing at all. But it is the suit Madeline was
wearing the last time he saw her, when she ascended the bell tower to die.

But his unctuous, patriarchal manner at the dress shop disappears when
they get back to her hotel room, and she refuses to wear the things he's
bought her. Now he's just someone in pain, pleading with her. She's given
him the first relief from his unhappiness that he's known in a year, he tells
her. "Because I remind you of her," she says. "And not even *that* very
much!" she adds bitterly, as he draws away from an embrace: "You don't
even want to touch me . . ." Not, it seems, until she puts on those clothes.

And if that's his last hope, soon it's hers too. "All right," she says finally, "I'll wear the darn clothes."

But he doesn't even seem to be listening now. He is looking at her dark brown hair—and Hitchcock's camera begins, ominously, to circle them. "The color of your hair!" he says. "Oh no!" she cries despairingly, and turns away from him. But he persists. "Please, Judy—it can't matter to *you*," he says—incredibly. Again she gives in to him—"I don't care about myself anymore," she says—and he takes her to the beauty salon. At such moments, *Vertigo* offers the kind of ironic fulfillment you expect from the noir mode. But it comes here not from the duplicitous heroine but from the obsessed hero. Instead of Kathie Moffett's "We deserve a break," we get Scotty's "It can't matter to *you*."

Scotty's madness of desire is more Buñuelian than Brontëan: it doesn't do a lot for the higher romantic vision when the hero makes her dye her hair and shops for her shoes. And if Scotty reminds us at such moments—however uneasily—of the artist's passion for perfection, he even more forcibly suggests the fetishist's: the necessity less of getting it right than of getting it up. When Hitchcock starts his camera circling the two of them here—with Judy protesting about the clothes and Scotty staring at her hair—there can be no doubt that Hitchcock is showing us (and enjoying showing us) something creepy. But he's also, by this time, implicated us, the audience, in the creepiness—as he is famously adept at doing. We can, of course, put Scotty's obsessiveness at a distance, but not too *great* a distance. The satisfaction we feel in this scene, from being in touch with the ironic intention behind it, carries also a feeling of danger. Hitchcock is inviting us to see through something we've already bought into, and are *still* buying into. *We* want Madeleine back too—who wouldn't? And we've been wondering, in fact, when he'd bring up the hair.

But it's *still* not right when she comes back from having it dyed, walking slowly and stiffly down the long empty hotel corridor while he waits for her, standing at the open door to her room. She is wearing the compulsory gray suit, purse and gloves in one hand, the other hanging clawlike at her side, the hair blond at last—but still long: it's her final resistance, and the effort makes her look sheepish and uncomfortable, as she approaches him and walks in front of him into the room, neither of them speaking. So there's going to be another struggle. And now more than ever, in their grim pursuit of tenderness, installed together in this empty hotel (we never see any other "guests"), they seem locked in a compact of madness. And yet we know how they got there. It's one of the features of *Vertigo*'s power over us that it gets madder and larger at the same time—the more outrageous it becomes, the more familiar it feels.

He can't control his exasperation—just that one last thing of the hair would make it perfect: "It should be back from your face. And pinned at the neck . . ." And at the mirror *she* can't control a sudden revulsion when he touches her pleadingly: she whips defiantly around and faces him, leaning back against the dresser with her hands, staring up at him. "Please, Judy," he says. Pause; her face softens. She drops her eyes, leaves the dresser, and walks past him to screen right, as he turns away from her to the left. Turned from each other, as if in shame—as she goes in silence to rearrange the hair, crossing the room and disappearing behind the bathroom door. While he waits . . . by the window, looking at the door, which is flooded now by that same blue-green haze we saw her in the night he found her, when *she* sat by the window. No electric sign to account for it now, however; only Scotty's perfervid attention.

He doesn't see her come out again—nor do we. There's just the sound of the door unlatching. And he rises—with the face of someone in torment—and turns to look.

In that intense blue-green haze, she's barely visible at first. As she moves out and toward us, Hitchcock—as he did at Ernie's—cuts between her and Scotty's reaction, to the sound of Herrmann's "Vertigo Theme." Edging forward, at first she looks abashed and even hostile, while Scotty simply looks staggered. Getting nearer, she looks more self-possessed, but unreadable, her eyes opaque. She is Madeleine now. And yet not exactly—there's a difference somehow from the Madeleine of earlier, of the church graveyard or the redwood forest. There's now an odd, dramatic sort of plainness about her, something clearer and purer, something almost ascetic. Or is that just her discomfort? Her beauty now, in any case, has none of the lushness of the Madeleine at Ernie's. And it is even more moving to contemplate. At least, now that she's got the hair right. At last.

She is smiling (it's going well) by the time she gets to her close-up—and Scotty's arms. And as they hold each other—in relief and exaltation—and kiss, the music hymns away and the camera circles slowly and deliriously around them—as the dingy backdrop of the hotel room gives way to Scotty's hallucinatory memory of the carriage museum (a similar kiss, a similar camera movement, before she "left" him)—a discordance reflected in the music—then dissolves into a background of rich empyrean blue, as the scene fades out and the music climaxes with a series of serene, triumphant resolving chords.

She ruins it all in the next scene when she wears Carlotta's necklace, having Scotty fasten it for her in front of the mirror. And once he sees it there, he understands everything. Instead of going out to Ernie's, where she thought they were going (she now calls it "our place"), he drives back

The hair is "right" at last—Judy has become Madeleine—
and they embrace, as Hitchcock's camera begins to circle them.

to the Mission and to the bell tower. He drags her to the top again, triumphing over his vertigo, and frightens her into admitting her own deception and Elster's entire scam. She begs him to take her back: "You love me!" she cries. But he tells her it's too late: "There's no bringing her back!" But in the next moment they are kissing—when she is frightened by a suddenly looming shadow, and in panic bolts away and falls from the tower to her death. The elderly nun who cast the shadow crosses herself and tolls the bell, while Scotty steps to the edge of the belfry and looks down, spreading his empty hands. It's this image of loss that the film ends on.

Most of all, *Vertigo* is about impossible love. Just how impossible is made clear in the final belfry scene. "Carlotta's necklace," says Scotty. "There's where you made your mistake, Judy. You shouldn't keep souvenirs of a killing," he says—and the anguish in Stewart's face and voice is nearly as terrifying to us as it is to her. Then he adds, "You shouldn't've been—" and stops, choking up at the bitterness of what he's saying. He starts over: "You shouldn't've been—that sentimental"—both swallowing that last crucial word and coming down on it at the same time. The moment is powerful if only for the way it breaks our sympathetic connection with Judy (Hitchcock has put us so much inside her victimization by Scotty), reminding us that she is someone who has just connived at a killing for money, that the Judy who values the ordinary world, who is "just a girl" who wants to be loved for herself, is capable of appropriating even a murder to her "ordinary" landscape. She certainly seemed pleased with her new necklace. Not a "high-class" character, even when the hair and clothes and speech are right. It's the pain of this recognition that Stewart—remarkably—gets into the word "sentimental" when he says it, with all his bitterness and grief. And his next words, different as they are, are even more searing. "I loved you so, Madeleine," he says, in tears, raising his head. No longer looking *through* the insufficient Judy, but upward and away.

But, of course, there never was a Madeleine. She existed only in Gavin Elster's contrivance (one of Scotty's bitterest recognitions) and in Judy's imposture—and then only when *everything* was exactly right. Madeleine is a phenomenon both impossibly specific and finally transcendent, so that Scotty's cry of love for her in the bell tower feels not only moving but oddly heartless—like this movie itself. There is never a point in its unfolding when you expect—or indeed even want—Scotty to give in to Judy's dream of normalcy, to stop hectoring and controlling her and to love her "for herself." We all know what kind of movie ending *that* might call for: seeing her off to Tehachapi, say, with a promise to "wait." Hitchcock hardly cares about Judy. But then he hardly cares about Scotty. Neither of them has an imaginable existence beyond the situation they are in—none, anyway, that Hitchcock cares to imagine. What he cares about—as we do—is "Madeleine"; and the movie shows what that caring involves. Judy thinks that together the two of them can bring her back—and Scotty in the bell tower seems at least tempted to try (that final kiss). And we know they can't. Just as we know—or so it seems once it happens—that she will go off the tower after that kiss, and that he will be left standing on the edge looking down: a final image that seems as inevitable as it is memorable. Because *this* is the vertigo—this madness of longing, this almost infinitude of painful desire, of longing *beyond* longing—that Hitchcock has been drawing us into all along, and with all the equanimity of someone who knows *exactly* how the hair should look.

The now fashionable view of *Vertigo,* in academic circles anyway, is as an *exposure* of romantic passion, as a "deconstruction" of the romantic vision. And indeed the support for such a reading is all there in the film itself, even offered by Hitchcock (as I've suggested above) with a certain glee. Irony at the expense of Scotty's obsession is one of the principal pleasures the movie offers. And the meanings are quite amazingly up-to-date, even "politically correct": the tyranny of the male gaze, the commodification of the object of desire, and so on.

But to reduce *Vertigo* to such meanings, even to such ironies, is to bypass the fact (who could miss it?) that the film itself is a romantic experience of the intensest kind. A *knowing* sort of romantic experience. And it seems, for us at least, no impediment to the experience that it's all a kind of swindle, really. Our difference from Scotty—our advantage over him, so to speak—is that we guessed it would be. We know the genre. We're not surprised when the magic turns out to be sleight-of-hand. Never mind: we still register it as "magic," as fully and powerfully as if it had been on the level, and *not* a trick or deception. Could anyone, *re*seeing this film (as most of us have by now), watch the first half of it, with its all-out romanticism, for signs of the fakery behind it, for clues to Judy's counterfeit or to Gavin Elster's coaching and control, *instead* of entering into the enchantment, giving yourself up to it fully and without significant reserve?

It may be, in some sense, the most romantic film of all. It's the *defiance* of its romanticism that makes it finally so powerful and lingering—and maybe even unique. In prototypical romantic "texts" like *Wuthering Heights* and *Peter Ibbetson,* both book and movie versions, the romantic passion survives death. In *Vertigo* it survives disbelief.

Four

BETTY GRABLE TO DORIS DAY

We wanted Madeleine—and the movies gave us Judy. Or worse yet, Midge. It was a trend that began to take over in the forties, during the war years. There was a comfort to be found in the girl-next-door star that was decidedly missing in the woman-of-experience type. And every studio, it seemed, was producing its hometown sweethearts—from Joan Leslie at Warners to Jeanne Crain at Fox to Joan Caulfield at Paramount to Kathryn Grayson at Metro. It was like an epidemic—at a time of national crisis when the celebration of ordinariness had come to seem like a patriotic duty. And the biggest and brightest female star of them all was Betty Grable.

Myrna Loy, a star in the older tradition—the womanly woman, glamorous, self-possessed, definitively grown up—tells in her memoir (cowritten by James Kotsilibas-Davis) *Myrna Loy: Being and Becoming* how she met Grable early in the war. Loy, ten years older, had temporarily retired from movies to do war work and was then stationed in New York. She had prevailed on Grable—whom she discovered she liked quite a lot ("a game gal, direct and unaffected")—to do an impromptu show for the wounded at a Staten Island military hospital. But when Loy came to pick her up that morning, Grable had a bad hangover: "Harry James and I were out on the town last night." Never mind: Loy tells their driver to stop at "a little roadhouse" on the way, where she proceeds to make Grable "take some beer to appease the gremlins," and they go on again. It's almost like a scene from one of Loy's early movies with Harlow—like *Libeled Lady* (1936), with the Loy character dealing generously and even warmly (as she always did) with this other, very different sort of woman. Anyway, they arrive at the hospital, and Grable, Loy reports, was "a sensation":

. . . Can you imagine? This was the pin-up girl of the Navy, the Army, and the Marine Corps. They were so thrilled, so excited—some of them shy, some of them forward—and she was absolutely

43

terrific, which wasn't easy in her condition, particularly since she hadn't been prepared for all that horror. Overcome at one point in the burn ward, she sat down on the edge of an empty bed, looking up at me like a little girl ashamed of being naughty. "That's all right," I said. "You can sit and rest." . . . So she stayed quite a while . . . giving kisses and autographs, putting her lip-prints on plaster casts as the men moved joyfully around her, some on crutches, some legless in wheelchairs . . .

The horror . . . But in a way that horror was what Grable was all about: turning away from it saucily, as in Frank Powolny's famous pinup photo—*who needs it anyway?*—smiling back at us over a provocatively upraised shoulder, with her high heels and her upswept hairdo, showing us the trim little behind in the gleaming white bathing suit. This famous image, as inelegant as almost any of Loy's would have been the opposite, became the most popular pinup in history (five million copies distributed free to U.S. servicemen during the war), and had a force that went far beyond its obvious erotic message. It was an image of American tackiness: consoling, sustaining, inescapable—about to take over the world, in fact. Sexy—but evoking the candy counter in the lobby as much as the beach or the bedroom.

On the screen she was flip and friendly, just like the carhop or the cute waitress she reminded you of. She sang and danced jauntily, she had great legs, an infectious energy, and small, watchful eyes. Her mechanical-doll quality was in fact part of her appeal: whatever her problems, you knew that she would never (unlike her successor Marilyn Monroe) lay them on *you*. She was so spectacularly self-armored that it gave her a kind of charm—even at times (though rarely, and mostly when she sang) a kind of pathos. It's sort of staggering to think of her, as in Loy's anecdote, doing one of those perky little numbers of hers in the burn ward—but it also seems deeply right somehow: you don't stagger *her* very easily.

She was the tough type, really; but in the forties she wasn't allowed to *be* that, the way leading women in the thirties had been, from Jean Harlow to Joan Blondell, so that she gave an impression of aspiring to vulgarity without quite achieving it. But the plots of her films told a different story. If she started *out* seeming common and low-class (in 1943's *Coney Island,* her best film, the hero has to handcuff her to the scenery to keep her from butt-twitching her way through a love song), she was claimed for gentility well before the end—though so discreetly, and with so little effect on her looks and manner, that we hardly notice it's been done. Her movies were nervous about this issue of class, because finally we were being asked to believe that she was just like the Girl Next Door—and *not* just the one in Hollywood or Vegas. But then, as often happens with the movies, the girl next door, wherever she lived, was getting to look more and more like *her.* And so Grable's vulgarity—which might have linked her to the best and strongest traditions of Hollywood comedy—became instead a sort of touchy matter, even a potential embarrassment. And her toughness on the screen, instead of giving her comic life, became a constraint, suggesting less freedom and boldness than complacency and thickness. Where Harlow at her crassest had been interesting and enlivening, Grable seemed merely lively.

But the growing genteel-ism, as James Agee called it, of forties movies affected Myrna Loy too. Like all the great romantic heroines of thirties comedy—Carole Lombard and Claudette Colbert, Irene Dunne and Jean Arthur—she depended upon a certain brashness in the fantasy world she inhabited, a kind of challenging vulgarity. These heroines were not only equal to the raffishness, they were in touch with it too; in some mysterious way it was part of what they *were*—a point that's made memorably explicit when Irene Dunne imitates a stripper in *The Awful Truth,* or when "Nora Charles" (Loy) entertains her husband's "friends" in *The Thin Man,* all the mugs and crooks from his days as a private eye. We were always interested in how the elegant Loy (it came naturally to her) would react to tough guy Gable or tough girl Harlow—and always heartened somehow when she made it clear that the gap between her and them was less important than the shared vitality or the shared joke. Her glamour, like Dunne's and Lombard's and Arthur's, was a reflection of the openness and possibility of American life. Even her remarkable beauty didn't "place" her in any way that seemed limiting, or cut her off from the risk. It was just one of those qualities she had (her humorousness and her adventurousness among the others) that saved her from refinement.

But these rather complicated, definitively grown-up types (it was hard to imagine someone like Loy *ever* being a teenager) were on the decline in the forties—and then even scarcer in the fifties. Their last redoubt had been the noir films, and they too were declining by mid-decade. The fifties woman star was nicer, simpler, younger (at least in spirit), more girlish than womanly, whether the style was baby doll (Marilyn Monroe) or butch (Doris Day), sophisticate (Grace Kelly) or gamine (Audrey Hepburn). The trend was apparent not only in the abundance of starlet-stars—Debbie Reynolds, Shirley MacLaine, Janet Leigh, Mitzi Gaynor, Shirley Jones, et al.—and in the popularity of recent child stars like Elizabeth Taylor and Natalie Wood, but in the changes that came over some of the older stars who were still around.

Like Lucille Ball, who made probably the most astonishing transformation of anyone. She had had a two-decade-long movie career, going from Goldwyn Girl (*Roman Scandals*) to familiar supporting player (*Stage Door*) and B-picture lead (appearing in eleven films in 1934 alone) in the thirties to an above-the-title star at MGM in the forties (*DuBarry Was a Lady, Best Foot Forward*). Almost from the beginning, and certainly by the time at Metro, her persona was fixed and familiar: an extension and elaboration of the wisecracking tough cookies in *Stage Door*. You knew, for example, if she was in a movie called *Two Smart People* (as she was in 1946), that she'd be one of them. She was comic, but in a dryly commanding way, specializing in the knowing glance and the stinging remark. With her statuesque figure and showgirl walk, the eloquently arched eyebrows over the unblinking stare, she had a sort of instinctive hauteur, sardonic but good-natured.

In Douglas Sirk's melodrama *Lured* (1947), she is an American chorus girl in London, helping Scotland Yard in their hunt for a serial killer. Her cop protector (George Zucco) is a fatherly plainclothesman, who has just intervened to save her from a madman (Boris Karloff), and after emerging from the melee that ensued, she and the cop are sitting together in the backseat of the police car. She is badly shaken and the cop, kindly but stern, is admonishing her to be more careful in the future. "Here's your toy," he says—by way of driving the point home—handing her back her gun. "Thanks," she says blankly, taking it—but you know from the way she hesitates that there is Something Wrong. She stares straight ahead, rises slightly in her seat, and reaches wearily into her coat: "Here's yours," she says, producing a second gun, not looking at him as he takes it. "Thanks," he echoes—as they both look front. "'S all right," she mutters, out of the side of her mouth, turning tactfully to the window, while Zucco continues to stare at the camera, a startled and discomfited fixed gaze.

It's not that the Zucco character was meant to be maladroit. It's that Lucille Ball—the pre–*I Love Lucy* one—was almost *helplessly* smart and competent, even when frightened nearly out of her wits. It was almost embarrassing it was so inevitable.

That was, at any rate, the Lucille Ball audiences knew. Until she reached the age of forty—in 1951, the year the *Lucy* show began—and turned into an innocent. The Lucille Ball of the fifties was a lovable ditz, impractical and fanciful, brought down to earth usually and eventually by her (marginally) more worldly husband. And she achieved in this role a popularity she'd never even come in sight of in movies. *I Love Lucy* ran for six years ('51 to '57) at the top of the ratings, making her the most popular star of the television decade.

In the movies it was Doris Day who was the most popular woman—some say the most popular movie actress ever (she was the *only* woman to appear in *Variety*'s 1980 list of the top ten all-time box-office champions, with John Wayne being Number One). An infectious and engaging performer, with a boundless energy, a great singing voice (she had been a big-band singer), and a klieg-light smile, her appeal was direct and open. Never coy or affected, more tomboy than tease, she seemed like good feeling incarnate when she first appeared (in 1948's *Romance on the High Seas,* replacing Betty Hutton)—the Girl Next Door in excelsis.

Or on amphetamines (though she never touched them). Even at rest she was a strenuous presence. And for all her cheeriness, real gaiety seemed beyond her. Determination, however, was not. You can see that in her early Warner Bros. musicals in her perky shoulder-switching little walk, holding her back in and her chest out while the rest of her tootles along below. She moderates that perkiness later on, but she never entirely loses it. There is always something faintly pedagogic about her energy: the quality that would make her both amusing and utterly convincing as a Columbia journalism professor in *Teacher's Pet* (1958)—in front of her night-school class, with her combination of enthusiasm, goodwill, and carefully suppressed irritability. It's a controlled and intelligent, even subtle comic performance. And she is good too with her co-star, Clark Gable—who is also funny, though in a much broader comic style, as a tough but aging newspaperman. They seem to galvanize each other.

But that wasn't the sort of performance—a serious, self-aware woman—that Day was widely identified with, or often asked to give. She was better known for all those brisk, bouncy, low-rent musicals that first made her popular: *Calamity Jane* (1953), for example, one of her most frenetic and charmless performances. She loved making that film, she later claimed, playing, in the words of *Doris Day: Her Own Story* (told to A. E. Hotchner), "a rambunctious, pistol-packing prairie girl" in buckskins, who doesn't wear a dress until the last reel. But her androgyny was never really interesting; it was too frantic and overassertive—another way of flattening her persona, of keeping herself and us on its surface. Like all those beedle-dee-ump songs they wrote for her films—with their irritating, imbecile refrains ("Que se-*ra,* se-*ra!*")—she could seem very relentless.

She was so popular that even Hitchcock got around to working with her—arguably the only really major director she ever had. But it was more than her box-office clout that interested him, as is clear from the performance that resulted. And although the film, *The Man Who Knew Too Much* (1956), wasn't one of his best, it became one of his—and Day's—biggest

Lucille Ball is the decoy and George Zucco is the Scotland Yard man
looking after her—in Douglas Sirk's *Lured.*

hits. It's an inflated remake of a movie he'd done in England twenty-two
years before (1934) under the same title—with Leslie Banks and Edna
Best as an impeccably upper-class English couple traveling abroad when
their child is kidnapped, drawing them into an international assassination
plot. In the new version, they are suburban Americans, James Stewart as a
midwestern doctor, Day as the wife and mother, a retired musical-comedy
star, traveling with their little boy in French Morocco. Now, instead of the
British couple's Pooh-like resilience, their pull-yourself-together-old-girl-
or-old-boy reserve, you get a lot of just falling apart, of overt emotionalism. Through most of the movie Day is distraught, and Stewart (as he
often was in his fifties films) alternately seething and exploding.

Hitchcock was the first director to discover and mine Day's hysteria—
or rather (it may be) to ask to see it. It was never, after all, very far below
her performing surface. She stunned the people on the set, she later
boasted, by doing the whole harrowing scene where she discovers her son
has been kidnapped on the first try and in a single take. Her recent co-star
James Cagney had also been impressed with her—comparing her to Lau-
rette Taylor in her combination of power and simplicity.

But she had a hard time. More than any other star of the era, she embodied our national will-to-happiness. Not surprisingly, she was given to

Doris Day in *Teacher's Pet*—teaching her Columbia journalism class

breakdowns. The first one, she later admitted, came right after all the happy hijinks of *Calamity Jane;* the second, after the thriller hysterics of *Midnight Lace* (1960), one of her worst later movies. She had always been someone who survived setbacks—like the girlhood auto accident that nearly crippled her and dashed her hope of being a dancer; so she became a singer. Her religion—again no surprise—was Christian Science. Her sunniness in "real" life was distinctly shadowed (she was distant and even unfriendly on her sets, reportedly), and even on the screen it's more precarious than she seems to know. When she's not smiling, her mouth falls into a disconsolate set; her eyes look desolate. She never made happiness look *easy* exactly—though she was mostly confined to movies and songs that asked her to do precisely that.

But not *Love Me or Leave Me* at MGM (1955)—probably her best movie, and she is extraordinary in it, with the extraordinary Cagney as her co-star. She plays singer Ruth Etting, and he is Marty Snyder, Etting's manager and first husband. The movie seemed a kind of breakthrough at the time, when Hollywood was looking to produce more "adult" sorts of pictures: a biographical musical in which the leading characters were more unsavory than not. The real Etting had been a mildly scandalous figure in the 1920s, married to a small-time gangster who used his muscle to promote her early rise, and who ended up going to prison for shooting the musician she had fallen in love with. She later married the musician.

Day's Etting is just sort of nervously calculating. Not really a tramp, just a sort of hard number from the chorus—manipulating Cagney's lovestruck hoodlum while not quite admitting what she's doing, least of all to herself. First he calls her "Ettling," like a gargling sound—that's early on, when he just wants to lay her, a kid in the chorus who says she

Day as Ruth Etting, James Cagney as Marty Snyder—making his
early discovery of her "talent"—in *Love Me or Leave Me*

wants to sing. And she is going to hold out until she does sing—that's
clear. Soon he's calling her "Ruthie," showing us how you look both fierce-
eyed and calf-eyed at the same time. And she's *still* holding out. But she's
singing—better than he ever imagined she could. Nevertheless, he's still
in charge—except that he's vulnerable and she's not: the sort of bind that
makes you nasty, as Marty is. Finally, after mutual hysterics and recriminations, he throws her on the bed and *makes* her come across. Some of the
strongest parts of this scene, Day would later complain, were cut because
of censorship; but it is still very powerful, with an authentic hell-is-other-
people terror and pain.

Before that turning point, the backstage scenes between Marty and
Ruth—confronting each other with their opposing hopes and stratagems,
their interacting self-deceptions, their inventive little nastinesses—have a
rich comic-ironic life. It's an often witty and accurate screenplay, with the
confidence of something telling painful human truths plainly, by novelist
Daniel Fuchs (who also wrote Siodmak's *Criss Cross*) and Isabel Lennart,
directed by Charles Vidor (who directed *Gilda*). And Cagney is wonderful.
He's shorter than she is. And with his high-speed moves and manner and
his game leg (Snyder had a limp), he rocks and bobs through the movie's
action like some demented dwarf, ever hopeful, ever wary. It was one of his

favorite films, he said later in his autobiography ("I rate [it] among the top five of the sixty-two pictures that I made"). But it's less interesting as it goes on. It's over two hours long, and the last third—as Marty declines into frustration and failure and Ruth rises into the love story with her piano accompanist (a thankless role but attractively played by Cameron Mitchell)—is draggy and conventional. It makes you feel they're trying to take back what they've already done: by turning her into a romantic heroine. Even the wonderful songs disappear—the ones that Etting actually sang. Now we get the new ones. And though they are somewhat better than Day usually got to sing in her films, they are still a letdown—Tin Pan Alley giving way to Mantovani.

But she is some kind of great singer. That had been fitfully apparent in movies before this one, but here it seems such a constant and exciting fact that it feels like a discovery. Beginning with "It All Depends on You"— which she sings for the pianist in a darkened empty rehearsal hall. His piano is at the edge of the bandstand and she is standing on the floor below, her face at keyboard level, her hands resting on the wood, almost prayerfully. She sings the song, to piano alone, in a single take that's like a held breath, moving slowly in on her as she begins and holding her in a semi-profile close shot till she ends. And you realize that the point about this hard, manipulative, small-minded, narrowly ambitious, and frankly irritable heroine is that she's transfigured—almost literally—when she sings (at least when the song is as good as this one, by DeSylva, Brown, and Henderson).

Day's way with it can be contrasted with Barbra Streisand's treatment of the same song in her 1995 concert on HBO: she rattled off the first lines, offering them as an instance of the kind of thing she wouldn't sing anymore—what she called "victim songs." As most of Etting's songs were: it was a time when both men and women were more likely to sing about being blue and bereft than feeling good about themselves. And you can understand how the central conceit of the song, in verses like the bridge—

> I can save money—or spend it.
> Go right on living—or end it.
> You're to blame, honey,
> For what I do-oo-oo . . .

—might be off-putting to a successful analysand. But when Day sings it, she really *gives* herself to the song, making its moony exaggerations, its witty dislocations and juxtapositions (like the "spend it" / "end it" rhyme) sound like pleasurable little victories. Just as she finds meanings in the tensions or incongruencies between words and music: the way, for example—in the verse above—she transforms the ordinary burden of a word like "blame," making it sound like the lightest sort of endearment, coming after the mild agitation of the two lines that lead up to it, and then into the release and relief of "For what I do," with its bluesily drawn out final vowel, lifting and dipping, and then rising and sailing into blissful irrelevance at the end.

Her absorption, her meditative intensity as she sings, makes you hang on the notes and words as if you were following a plotline—even when you know what's coming: her repetitions of the title line, "It all depends on you," for example, each time suggesting a more complicated tenderness than before. Her feeling for the dramatic shape of a song is extraordinary, as in the controlled power she brings later on to the singing of Ahlert and Turk's "Mean to Me"—stepping onto the CinemaScope screen as the camera pans slightly to show her in close-up at the side, where she takes her stance in front of the band and begins to sing. You know right away *this* person is no pushover or whiner ("You treat me *coldly*") but someone with the confidence of both an unanswerable case and a great song, as she moves surely through its wittily ambiguous transitions and exciting little rhythmic shifts. Till she comes to the usually merely wistful final line—where the refrain of "mean to me" turns into "what you mean to me"—giving it a kind of sexy serenity, both inviting and self-contained.

"Ten Cents a Dance" is a more over-the-top sort of performance—in front of a curtain, in a sexy black gown with fringes. She sings with feet apart and hands on hips, swaying in place to the drumbeats: "Come on, big boy! Ten cents a dance!" The stylization is firmly this side of camp, if only for the reason that the feeling she gives is as much *about* the song as inside it—the sort of thing she also signals when she comes out onto the nightclub floor to sing "You Made Me Love You," with a distinct gleam in her eye and an undertone that feels almost antic (it's Ruth's first big chance), as if she is really letting us in on something terrific. As it turns out she is. The song is nearly the most standard of pop standards, now as in 1955; but by the time she gets to the release ("Give me give me give me / What I cry for . . ."), still gleaming, you feel as if you've never heard it before.

She does this for nearly all the Etting songs—except for the very clumsily staged "Shaking the Blues Away," the movie's single approximation of a big production number (these were cost-cutting days even at Metro). With her warmth and intelligence, her musicality and uncanny phrasing—the sudden dry inflection in the middle of emotion, the artfully bro-

Marty made her and now he can break her—or so he says. But she's
not very breakable—as she shows here, while Robert Leonard,
as her manager, looks on.

ken note in the middle of a sustained intensity, and so on—Day in this
movie seems a pop singer on the level of her greatest contemporaries:
Dinah Washington, Mildred Bailey, Jo Stafford.

But this is Cagney's movie too. And he, too, is a kind of singer—as we
hear very clearly in the last spoken line of the movie, which he delivers
under the strains of Day's final song ("Love Me or Leave Me"—at last).
Marty is standing at the back of his posh, crowded new nightclub, at the
bar, overlooking the dance floor and the band. He has just gotten out of
prison, where he went for shooting Ruth's pianist, and Ruth has arranged
this surprise for him: the club, the crowd, and everything. And she is
singing in front of the band, a last favor to Marty before she's off forever
(we presume) with the pianist (he survived the shooting). Marty, of course,
has mixed feelings about this "favor," and in fact about this whole occasion, as he looks back on his ruined marriage and failed life. But as she
sings, he leans back against the bar and listens, shushing his companion
when he tries to say something. Then, after a moment: "You've gotta hand
it to her," he says slowly, under the music, "the girl can sing." Then adds,

as an afterthought (pronouncing "was" New York–style, to rhyme with "Oz"): "About *that*—I never *was* wrong . . . ," as the song and the movie end with a crane shot of the club's interior. And you're reminded that Cagney has *his* sound too, and the elegiac zest he gives to these climactic words is as thrilling as her song. This ending—her voice and his, followed by the swelling music and that final camera lift-off—gives you that feeling of lingering splendor that you can sometimes get from great old-fashioned movie endings, fitting in this case not so much the size of the story we've witnessed (small, inconclusive, rather depressingly "true to life") as the finally very moving outsizeness of its two stars.

It wasn't the first movie she and Cagney had done together (they had been in *The West Point Story* five years before, something neither of them could have wanted much to remember: it was a musical, and a very odd one, with Virginia Mayo too). Nor was *Love Me or Leave Me* the first time she'd had an impressive leading man, someone more considerable than her usual Warners co-stars, Gordon MacRae and Jack Carson. Her seventeenth and last film on her exclusive Warners contract—she'd been doing two or three a year since 1948—was *Young at Heart* (1954) with Frank Sinatra. And it wasn't, she later said, a particularly agreeable experience—in contrast to working with Cagney. Sinatra was aloof and difficult, and made problems about the script. Day, who never made problems, it seems, didn't get on with him. And the resulting movie, while in no sense a good one (or even particularly a moneymaker), is interesting for its stars, and for what happens on the screen because of them.

It was a remake, with songs added, of one of the studio's biggest and most fondly remembered hits of the thirties, Michael Curtiz's *Four Daughters* (1938)—the one that introduced John Garfield and made him an instant star. Day's heroine (Priscilla Lane in the original) is the happy center of a happy family: her widowed music-teacher father, two unmarried sisters, and a grouchy, lovable old aunt (Ethel Barrymore's next-to-last movie role). They all live on a Candy Cane Lane sort of suburban street in a picture-window house with pink rooms full of chintz and tchotchkes. A dashing young songwriter, Gig Young, visits and falls in love with her. Then Sinatra—in the Garfield role—arrives: he's the songwriter's arranger, from New York, and very sullen, making dour jokes about his own invincible bad luck and life in general. Day can't resist, of course: she sets out to cheer him up. She doesn't. But he does fall in love with her, even though she is now in love with the songwriter. However, when she discovers that her favorite sister loves him too, she gives him up and marries Sinatra, the loser. But then her sister marries another man, leaving the songwriter both lovelorn and still available—as well as having a big new hit on Broadway—while Day is stuck with this very difficult, and jobless, new husband.

At this point in the original, the Garfield character, convinced (quite rightly) that Priscilla Lane has never really loved him and that she still loves the songwriter, kills himself—running his car off the road and making it look like an accident, freeing her for the other guy. And it all would have happened like this again, except that Sinatra—sensibly enough—refused: either he survived his suicide attempt *and* got the girl in the end, or he walked. Unsurprisingly, he got his way. The movie's final scene (after the one in the hospital) has Sinatra and Day singing together (for the first time in the film) at the piano by the picture window, Gig Young forgotten.

It was—at least before Sinatra's intervention—the sort of soap-opera scenario, *very* familiar to movie audiences, where a character seemed to get killed mainly for being more interesting and alive than the others, and therefore unsuitable for the obligatory happy ending. Analogous to those punishing films (*The Yearling, The Biscuit Eater,* et al.) about kids and their animals where the boy at the end is compelled to shoot the fawn or the dog or whatever because it isn't sufficiently socialized (eating the crops, killing the hens, etc.), the way *he* will become by shooting it: learning to grow up. It's the same point about the Garfield character—he is also not socialized, the undependable sort. And in a domestic tearjerker, that's an often fatal failing: it's the suit who gets the girl in the end, not the rebel. That's how *she* learns to grow up.

So Sinatra was probably right—whether he meant to be or not. One of the few ways that *Young at Heart* improves on its source is by forgoing the sort of heart-wringing resolution that the movie itself is neither serious nor smart enough to support. We *want* Sinatra and Day to end up together: they are the most appealing people on the screen (by some distance). So why not give us what we want—instead of trying to affect us deeply, or at least emotionally—at a movie like this? Hollywood's penchant for happy endings often had an aesthetic soundness it rarely gets credit for.

Unlike *Four Daughters,* this film maintains a degree of suspense around the heroine's final romantic choice—a suspense you get to share with the Sinatra character for part of the time. He is still not sure she really loves him after they are married and living meagerly in their New York flat. For one thing, she still wears that charm bracelet Gig Young gave her—and now Sinatra, in a fit of unreasoning and unprovoked jealousy, tells her to get rid of it, right away, and storms out of the apartment. He pauses worriedly on the stairs a moment, but then goes on out. The sequence fades out on a close-up of Day, looking distressed. In the next scene, he's at his job, sitting at the saloon piano on a platform above crowded tables, singing and playing "One for My Baby." Day enters, coming in off the street, and sits alone at a table in the middle of the well-lit room. She catches his eye as he sings. Her elbow on the table, she raises her forearm and pulls her glove down to show him her wrist—*without* the bracelet—as he finishes the song. End of scene.

Day makes the moment so simple and so serious—yet with a little smile of pride, a how-about-*that?* glint in her eyes—that it becomes moving. It's what Cagney called her "simple line of performance, directly to you"—without sentimentality or falsifying self-consciousness, plain and powerful. She gives you a person you can take seriously in the midst of otherwise indifferent filmmaking. And you really believe at this moment in the depth of the commitment she is making to him. Partly it's a matter of what actress Helen Mirren—in a 1995 *New York Times* interview—called Day's "wonderfully expressive and subtle face." ("Unfortunately, she had horrible material and those dreadful clothes and horrible hair, always.") But it's also that, in spite of the plasticene look and deadness of the film itself (the original at least has a lot of life, and a convincing family feeling), there really seems to be something at stake between these two. His disillusionment is the sort of thing that you might want to see Doris Day—or at least the "Doris Day" we know from family musicals like this—come to terms with. And when, earlier on, she sets out to give him a more cheerful view of things, taking up the challenge of his alienation and melancholy, the situation has real interest and promise. And though the movie never really delivers on that promise, the contrast between the two stars is oddly touching: it gives her sunniness a poignance it doesn't often have.

But there is another kind of poignance in the movie's division of musical labors. In that respect, the two of them seem to be in different movies altogether. (And guess who's in the bad one.) Day sings her usual brace of awful new songs (her four-flusher husband—shades of Marty Snyder—was now managing her career and commissioning songs he could take a cut on). One of them, an appalling hop-and-chirrup number, she does capering on a beach at a picnic; for most of the others, she's sitting at the family grand piano in the living room. Sinatra, on the other hand, at his saloon upright, with a cigarette usually, sings Porter ("Just One of Those Things") and Gershwin ("Someone to Watch Over Me") and, most wonderfully of all, Harold Arlen's "One for My Baby," in the scene described

The joy of cooking—or baking. In *Young at Heart,* Doris Day shows
Frank Sinatra his gingerbread man.

above. But except when he's singing, his performance seems mostly perfunctory, without any of the feeling of danger in the character that
Garfield so famously brought to it. With his sour jokes and falling speech
rhythms, Sinatra evokes someone more like Oscar Levant (who actually
was in a lot of movies of this sort), more depressed than dangerous—
though when he is with Day, *she* is precarious enough to make him *seem*
dangerous.

Because it's partly through Sinatra's presence—and even in an Oscar
Levant mode, it's a considerable one—that you register how hard, and
almost gallantly at times, she works. It's easy enough to lounge around
cracking wise, looking downcast and disdainful, as he does for most of the
movie. But she is the one (as she usually is) who has to carry and sponsor
the movie's *official* meanings: getting him to accept the complacent
domesticity he's set himself against. But the happiness in this family house
is about as real-seeming as the Astroturf lawn in front of it. And *she* has to
sell it—like an infomercial for suburban fulfillment—as she did in so
many of her movies.

You saw a lot of actresses at the time (and since) doing this sort of thing
in the movies—without your feeling specially bad about it, or feeling any-

thing except wishing that it was over: Debbie Reynolds or June Allyson or Sandra Dee, all the perky blondes. But with Day—in spite of her relentlessness—you felt the injury went deeper somehow. That they really shouldn't be doing this to her—even *with* her cooperation. And they would do much worse, as her career went into the sixties—in all those coy sex comedies about her not coming across for Rock Hudson or Cary Grant, the ones that inspired the famous Oscar Levant quip that he'd known Doris Day before she was a virgin. But she deserved better—much better, as she would sometimes demonstrate.

If Marilyn Monroe died for our sins, as a saying of the time had it, then Doris Day smiled for them.

Five

MARILYN MONROE

If not the most popular woman star of her time, Marilyn Monroe was certainly the most vivid, and has turned out to be the most haunting and lasting—along with Brando and Dean, a fifties icon. Her career spanned the decade: she made her first impact on audiences in small roles (*The Asphalt Jungle, All About Eve*) in 1950 and made her last completed film (*The Misfits*) in 1961, going in the course of eleven starring movies from comic dumb blonde to a very uncomic sort of earth mother. And she was a significant figure both in the dumbing down of the American heroine and in the redefinition of the female movie star. Unlike Kim Novak, said to be the "studio-manufactured star," Monroe was manufactured by no one but herself, it seems—self-created from the start. She became one of those rare cases in movie-studio history of someone who made such a powerful early impression that they all but *had* to make her a star. She was—as Billy Wilder said of her after her death—an original. And she was—not to put too fine a point on it—adorable. There was almost no one in her audience who didn't come to feel *that* about her.

Though that's not necessarily what they first felt when they saw her in her earliest roles. By the standards of the time she was an almost astonishingly libidinous presence. The wet lips and the wiggling fanny and the way she always seemed to be bursting out of her clothes both fore and aft: she seemed more overt than anyone had been before, and it was startling. It made audiences laugh, too—as if one of your most ambitious carnal fantasies had suddenly come to life, in public, in front of everyone. Not that she cared—she was so much inside the fantasy herself, so alive with it, that she made everyone else around seem almost like an abstraction of sexiness.

But she was also a little grotesque. Like a walking dirty joke—too outrageous for the politer company of the leading players, and so most of the time she was cast in the generic role of the sexpot, as in the two films that first made her famous: as Louis Calhern's sad, spooky, gold-digging mistress in *The Asphalt Jungle,* and in *All About Eve,* as George Sanders's dimwit date at the party, worrying about how to call for the butler without getting someone *named* Butler instead. Even in these nearly minuscule roles, the Monroe persona was already fully formed, and made such a sensation that Twentieth Century–Fox (which had dropped her two years before) was now scrambling to sign her up. After the rough Hollywood years this turnabout must have been very satisfying to her—and there is a wonderful apocryphal story (repeated by Norman Mailer, among others) about her signing the contract: "That's the last cock I eat," she is supposed to have said as she threw down the pen.*

But as Sharon Stone once observed: "You can only sleep your way to the middle." Those were bad days for the movies, and the studio needed new and authentic stars—but if they could have chosen, they wouldn't have wanted this one. She was too peculiar—too hard to cast in leading roles. It was a one-joke talent at best, in their view. But then, as Charles Coburn says of her in *Monkey Business* (1952), when explaining why he's hired her as his secretary: "*Anybody* can type." And her name on that movie—in which she appears very briefly—meant more at the box office than his or Ginger Rogers's did—probably even more than Cary Grant's, the top-billed star's. This was about the time when the nude calendar story got out (she admitted it was her). That year, the studio put her into four films. Why not? Anybody can act.

One solution they came up with that year to the problem of her limitations (as they perceived them) was to "star" her in the multistar, multistory film then in vogue—as a beauty contestant in *We're Not Married,* and then as a streetwalker in *O. Henry's Full House*—where *all* the roles were brief. It wasn't just her inexperience with acting that made a problem. In any case, she was working hard on that (with a coach, Natasha Lytess), and in her one loan-out that year—Fritz Lang's *Clash by Night* at RKO—she is very good. In the supporting role of a small-town cannery girl who is briefly beguiled by Barbara Stanwyck's big-city ways, Monroe is appealing and persuasive, with just the right underbred prettiness and controlled poignancy. But what is more surprising is that she is perfectly unmannered, seeming for all the world like an ordinary girl. Maybe Lang scared her into going straight. It was almost the last time anyone would.

Because ordinarily she was extraordinary. There was even, for many people, something unsettling about her—an extraterrestrial quality that

---

*Apparently it wasn't—even if she really did say this. Screenwriter Henry Ephron (Nora's father), in his memoir, remembers Monroe on the set of *Bus Stop*—a time when she was at the peak of her fame and power—being suddenly summoned to the office of a studio executive. "Don't go away," she said to Ephron as she left the soundstage, "he only takes five minutes."

might have put audiences off more if she hadn't also seemed rather innocent and nice, like all our favorite extraterrestrials. The problem with casting her was that she had already created this persona, this Marilyn Monroe person—and it was undeniably sort of odd. The glow she gave off in full throttle—with her lips parted, her eyes narrowed, her breasts angled forward, and her head thrown back—was both real and remarkable. But was all that wattage, all that insistent radiance, just about *sex?* . . . Probably it was. So you hoped, anyway. But she was unsettling enough at first to suggest that she belonged in noir film, doing bad and sexy things, if she belonged anywhere. Her first big leading role was in a low-budget thriller with Richard Widmark, *Don't Bother to Knock* (1952). Anne Bancroft was in it too, as a nightclub singer, but Monroe was the top-billed attraction—and the Dangerous Woman. Not a conniver, however, but a psycho—a loony baby-sitter trying on another woman's negligees and menacing a child in a hotel room, until she's led gently away at the end by the hero and his "normal" girlfriend (Widmark and Bancroft). Monroe's role called for her to be both scary and pathetic. But these were not the possibilities in her that her fans wanted to dwell on very much, and the movie wasn't a great success. But her next one—*Niagara* (1953) was.

Niagara was even more in the noir vein—and this time it's the Joseph Cotten hero who's demented, and Monroe, his wife, who is planning with her stud lover to murder him. And Monroe is spectacular—in the movie's chromium-bright Technicolor (the ads compared her to the Falls themselves, another "natural wonder")—wearing a red dress or walking away from the camera in a tight skirt or lying nude and squirming under a sheet in her motel room. But the role itself, both as written and as performed, was a neon-sign version of a hard, nasty bitch. That, conjoined to the eye-bugging sexiness, made her seem almost monstrous. If *Niagara* was a turn-on for audiences, it marked another dead end for her—and a continuing dilemma for the studio.

Which *Gentlemen Prefer Blondes,* her next film, seemed to solve. They'd tried her scary and they'd tried her vicious: now she went back to "dumb blonde," triumphantly. The strange demonic energy of self-display seems for the first time entirely in her control—as shaped and aimed as her comic line readings are, even when (as often) the jokes aren't so great (asking the steward if this boat goes to "Europe, France," for example). But there is so much good feeling between her and co-star Jane Russell (both on and off the screen, as it turned out) that it makes the film at its best feel, as Norman Mailer said, like "a magic work." In a way Monroe's Lorelei is really the supporting role—the comic sidekick to Russell's Dorothy. Russell

Monroe vamping the shipboard jeweler in *Gentlemen Prefer Blondes*

becomes that inevitable and by now familiar figure in a Monroe film: the "normal" sexy woman (Bancroft in *Don't Bother to Knock,* Jean Peters in *Niagara,* Lauren Bacall in *How to Marry a Millionaire*), presumably meant, in the face of the other's oddity, to reassure us. Monroe plays her love scenes in this movie with another grotesque, the comic Tommy Noonan, while Russell gets the serious romance and the handsome leading man (Elliott Reid). But Monroe gets the movie.

She is supposed to be very dumb indeed: trying to put a tiara around her neck, or indignantly telling an Olympic athlete who boasts that he's the only four-letter man on the team that she should think he'd be ashamed to admit it. She is obsessed with rich men and with diamonds. "A mercenary nitwit" is how the romantic leading man describes her, and nothing in the script belies him. Except that Lorelei's dumbness, as Monroe conveys it, seems more like an ecstatic sort of slyness, a wonderful liberation that makes her responses to other people—the widened eyes, the sudden little panics, the serene risings above sense and caution—the most compelling events on the screen. Her outrageous ribald mugging (she uses her face, keeping it in constant motion, much the way Mae West used her hips) has a coherence it's never had before—especially the transitions from round-eyed wonder to slant-eyed lasciviousness, then back to wonder again, even rounder-eyed than before. When her rich fiancé's father (Taylor Holmes)

Dorothy (Jane Russell) and Lorelei (Monroe) perform "When Love
Goes Wrong" for a Paris café crowd in *Gentlemen Prefer Blondes*.
(The little Arab boy is next to the accordion in the right background.)

asks her if she isn't marrying his son for his money, "No," she replies, "I'm
marrying him for *your* money"—sending the line through inflections of
hurt, then defiance, and out into triumph at the end: the kind of virtuoso
comic effect that makes you want to both laugh *and* applaud.

But it's in the song-and-dance numbers (the movie was based on a hit
Broadway musical) that she really seems wonderful. "Diamonds Are a
Girl's Best Friend" is a justly famous turn, though so overproduced that it
almost swamps her at times—but never quite. And it's perhaps finally not
so memorable as the soft, crooning way she sings in her cabin a very slow-
tempo "Bye Bye Baby" into Tommy Noonan's ear—clinging to him, leaning her chin on his shoulder, cupping his face in her hand and turning it.
All because she's sailing to Paris and leaving him behind: "I'll be lonely,"
she sings, in her creamiest voice—and though the line is meant to be a
joke, implying its opposite, her exaggerated mimicry of dejection (a sudden downcast face) is so generously offered and so sweetly funny that it
almost seems better than a real emotion.

If the movie's script more or less confines her to shtick, the musical
numbers liberate her into that complexity of effect you associate with the
authentic star. In "When Love Goes Wrong (Nothin' Goes Right)," she
and Russell sing and dance at a Paris sidewalk café. The number starts as a

soft, bluesy lament, the two of them singing forlornly at their table—
where they are joined by two little Arab street boys. Whereupon each of
them takes a turn singing to each of the boys. But where Russell (who is
very charming here) ever so slightly condescends to her underage fan, taking him by the shoulders and singing at him with big eyes, Monroe gives
hers the full steamy treatment: sloping her eyelids at him, leaning forward
and shaking her torso, making him a partner in the mischief. "A man ain't
fit"—emphasis of drums—"to live with," she sings, in her most guttural
register. "Dîtes-moi, mademoiselle!" cries the boy—as she contemplates
him through smiling, half-closed eyes. Just then the bluesy, moaning
music shifts to a driving, propulsive rhythm mode, with lots of slow drags
and jazzy riffs—as the two women rise abruptly, to perform for the crowd
that's materialized around them. The dance (by the ingenious Jack Cole, a
specialist with nondancers) is a sort of strut-and-slide display, which the
two women begin (a kind of fanfare) by spreading their arms and shaking
their chests, burlesque style, then stilling the agitation with modestly
placed hands before continuing (this "step" recurs throughout the film).
But it's Monroe who gets center stage at the climax of the number (Russell
withdraws discreetly)—shaking her little Arab friend's hand and taking
off in front of the crowd, with her sultry, heavy-lidded smile of satisfaction, on her break-out promenade. And at this moment you see something
you hadn't seen in her before: a kind of imperiousness rising up through all
the baby-dollishness, so unexpected it's moving. It is, of course, a conventional Big Moment for a musical-comedy lady—taking over the stage, or
screen, to do her stuff. But Monroe is as far here as she could be from the
kind of razzmatazz performer—a Liza Minnelli or a Shirley MacLaine—
who overbears you with her big talent, her larger-than-lifeness. Rather
than *willing* herself into the largeness, Monroe seems to get carried into it,
and then beyond it, by the attention around her: her radiance grows in
front of your eyes like something in stop-motion photography. And the
deepest connection she makes with any other player in the movie, it seems,
is the one she makes with that briefly seen Arab boy, whose dazzled attention spurs her performance. The sequence fades out, just as you feel it
should, on a shot of him and his friend, waving goodbye to her.

She is enchanting in her next film too, *How to Marry a Millionaire*
(1953). But it is much the same role, though a toned-down version of it,
without music: another blond gold-digger, with nearsightedness replacing
nitwittedness as the comic shtick. Pola (Monroe), one of a female trio
hunting rich husbands in New York, is nearly blind without the glasses
she refuses, out of vanity, to wear—so she walks into doors, reads books

upside down, and so on. Given the limits of such a joke, it's not surprising that she ends up with less screen time than her two co-stars, Betty Grable and Lauren Bacall—even though Monroe is top-billed and was clearly, next to the CinemaScope (it was only the second film released in that process), the movie's biggest draw.

She was at last cast as a more or less "straight" leading woman in her next two films, a western (*River of No Return,* 1954) and a backstage musical (*There's No Business Like Show Business,* 1954), but she is poor in both of them, and the films themselves (the musical especially) are even worse, though they are in CinemaScope and they made money. Her next movie, *The Seven Year Itch,* however, was a huge hit, and by the year of its release, 1955, Monroe had become the studio's hottest star.

But it's another dumb-blonde role. And The Girl—as she is listed in the credits—is even dumber in some ways than her predecessors, most of whom (certainly Lorelei and Pola) at least knew how to get what they wanted, even if that turned out to be the comic nerd playing opposite them. In *How to Marry a Millionaire,* it's David Wayne, who is *also* nearly blind without his glasses. But the nerd in *The Seven Year Itch* (Tom Ewell), though radically unappealing, is also unavailable, being happily and securely married. And although he is tempted by The Girl (he is a "summer bachelor" and she has sublet the apartment above him), it never goes much farther. She remains a fantasy object, both in his head and in the movie, which itself is more or less confined to his head (comic enactments of his romantic daydreams) and to his apartment (it was based on a hit play). And The Girl herself—as her namelessness implies—has practically no identity, neither a history, it seems, nor a personal life (no friends, lovers, etc.). What she has instead, apart from her almost unbelievable delectableness, is an obsession about getting cool in the summer heat (the gimmick that keeps bringing her downstairs to his air conditioner), as well as her innocent (entirely) provocativeness. In a way, it is Monroe's most insulting role yet. And it was her biggest hit.

She is eager to show him her nude photograph because it's so artistic. She comes out of the movie house feeling sorry for the Creature from the Black Lagoon—then squeals with delight to find a subway grating that will blow her skirt up over her head (the coolness). At home, she tells him, she always keeps her panties in the icebox. She is a sweet kid, without even a hint of anything problematic—except, if you like, for the childishness; but you're not invited to see that as alarming. As The Girl, Monroe comes the closest to fitting Mailer's designation of her as "the sweet angel of sex." She appears like a vision to the hero in his distress, even at a climactic point coming down to him through the ceiling (a trapdoor). And she brings him solace too: when he confides to her at the end that he knows no "pretty girl" could ever really want him (in his fantasies, he's always irresistible), she contradicts him passionately, in her longest and most emotional speech. He is just, she tells him, what a pretty girl always wants: someone unattractive, it seems. "But then you kind of sense he's gentle and kind and worried—and that he'll be tender with you, nice and sweet. *That's* what's really exciting!"

This was the summit of her popularity, and you can understand why. Her "Marilyn" is sex without shadows—the antithesis of the noir heroine, with all her connections to danger and mortality, her irremediable (for good and ill) grown-upness. Monroe is a Disney version of the sex goddess: soft and sweet and user-friendly. "My name is Lolita!" she sings in a later film (*Let's Make Love*)—only to remind you that Nabokov's Lolita, however much younger, is also a lot tougher and smarter, not to mention more dangerous, than the iconic "little girl" Monroe comes to embody, and especially in *The Seven Year Itch*. She's an angel—and that full-hearted speech she makes to the beady-eyed Tom Ewell about his desirability ("If I were your wife, I'd be very jealous of you") makes her mission on earth clear. She has come to us—to the Creatures in the Black Lagoon of the movie auditorium—not only to turn us on but to shore us up, provoking our lusts, but then redeeming them by her innocence.

No more slyness from now on, no more wet lips or narrowed eyes. Except that there is something slightly awry. It's there even in *Bus Stop* (1956), which was in most ways a considerable personal triumph. It was the movie she made after her hysterically publicized flight from Hollywood to New York and the Actors Studio and the ministrations of the Strasbergs. The movie, coming after all this, was meant to establish her as a serious actress, and it more or less did—to general surprise. Yet though her Cherie (played on Broadway by Kim Stanley) is coherent and touching, it's not a performance that wears well. It's too heavy, too *distressed,* for the fragile pathos and sitcom epiphanies of the play (by William Inge)—until you almost feel the pain beginning to displace the character. Nevertheless, it was impressive, and promised well for her announced ambitions, outsize as they were (Grushenka in *The Brothers Karamazov,* Lady Macbeth—one suspects she drank during her interviews as well as her films).

But each of her films that followed *Bus Stop*—slowly and painfully and with a maximum of media attention to all the problems she had in making them or even making it to the set (there were only four of them)—seemed to renege on that promise, in different ways. In *The Prince and the Showgirl*

(1957)—directed by and co-starring Sir Laurence Olivier—as an American chorus girl who helps a stuffed-shirt nobleman to find his inner child, she is almost alarmingly girlish (a giddy mouse-squeal laugh, a finger poked quizzically into her cheek or the corner of her mouth, and so on) and seems ill at ease in general. The picture, in spite of the firestorm of publicity surrounding it, was something of a dud, and she was off the screen for well over a year. But her next film, Billy Wilder's *Some Like It Hot* (1959), was (and is) enormously popular, and the reviews spoke of it as a comeback for her. But her role was a throwback—another dumb-blonde turn, though a heavier and woozier version of it (as if to account for this, the writers give the character a drinking problem). And once again she is distinctly secondary to the two leading men. She fulfilled a contractual obligation to Fox by doing *Let's Make Love* (1960), another leaden musical, in which she seemed less like herself than like a smudged and indistinct copy. And so John Huston's *The Misfits* (1961) was to be, at long last, something worthy of her talent—conceived and written for her by her husband, Arthur Miller, a serious film and her first unequivocally serious role. And yet it was *still* about the men. It was her last and saddest film.

A gift from her husband (who already sort of hated her—and with good reason, apparently) and she is trapped in it, along with the other things like pills and booze and sleeplessness that were also trapping her. She knew the role was wrong, and you can *see* her knowing it, and *that* becomes, as it turns out, the most compelling thing about her performance. "Childishness isn't all fun, is it?" she says to Olivier in *The Prince and the Showgirl.* And *The Misfits* shows that it can even be bitter.

Roslyn is a kind of eternal child who enters the lives of a trio of aging and discouraged men, and if she doesn't quite transform their lives, she at least lights them up a little. The men—Clark Gable, Montgomery Clift, and Eli Wallach—are cowboys, the last (as we are told) "real men," radically displaced by modern American life, but clinging futilely to their independence ("Anything's better than wages"). Roslyn comes among them, fresh from her Reno divorce, not as an "angel of sex" exactly (she beds down with the Gable character but not with the others), but as an unsettling sort of moral sensibility: a Holden Caulfield type, even sounding like him at times—she is an *anti*-phony. She tried to be a *real* dancer, she tells Gable, while the other girls at the club would just fake it. "I really tried. You know? Whereas people don't know the difference."

But even if "people" don't know the real thing when they see it, the three cowboys do, and she is it. They are dazzled by her spontaneity and eagerness. "You really go all out," says Gay (Gable), as he watches her eat her breakfast. Her smile is "like the sun comin' up," he says. "How tiny the seeds are," she exclaims as she plants vegetables in Gay's garden, "and yet they know they're supposed to be lettuces." Gay looks at her dotingly: "You say the darndest things," he says. And all three of them stand and look at her with silent awe as she dances drunkenly on the grass and then hugs a tree. Perce (Clift) asks her: "How come you got such trust in your eyes, like you were just born?" And Guido (Wallach) tells her she has "the gift for life." "The rest of us," he says, "we just lookin' for a place to hide and watch it all go by."

You really have to wonder if they were trying to do her in (*she* certainly thought so) with this movie—and these lines. Because it's Roslyn, not anyone else in the movie, who looks like she wants to "hide." Where Perce sees trust (*trust!*) and newbornness in her eyes, the audience sees alarm and anxiety. And where Roslyn is meant to look uncomplicatedly happy, Monroe looks dazed, with almost a Stan Laurel–like complacency and out-of-touchness. She was in bad shape at the time. But in most conditions she was probably (on the evidence) just too natively shrewd a person for this sort of crap. (This was the woman who remarked about Norman Mailer, after she'd read some of *The Deer Park,* that "he's too impressed by power, in my opinion.") Too shrewd to be comfortable with it, at any rate—and discomfort is what she conveys. Especially when the men talk to her about her "gift for life."

Clearly the Marilyn of *The Misfits* no longer believes, if she ever did, in the innocence she's asked to perform for us. What she does believe in—and so do we watching her—is Roslyn's pain. But instead of enlarging or inspiriting the character in the ways the script suggests, she is like someone whose sad experience has hollowed her out, left her depleted. She moves heavily and gracelessly, the breasts seeming almost to weigh her down—especially when she has to frolic, little-girl-style, for the besotted daddies around her ("I can go in and I can come out," she sings over and over, jumping on and off the front porch while Gable grins at her). But she has none of the free, expansive movement such moments would seem to call for. Her most characteristic gestures are of clutching things *to* her, as when she feeds some scraps to Gay's hound dog, crouching beside his muzzle and holding the food so close to her own face as he takes it that she seems to be competing with his hunger as much as feeding it. Roslyn loves animals (as Monroe did). And her reverence for life of all kinds is her principal claim to the kind of moral stature the movie finally wants to give her. She can't stand to see anything killed, she tells Gay when he wants to shoot some rabbits eating his garden. And the movie's climactic episode has her

Monroe in *The Misfits,* her last completed film,
with Thelma Ritter at right

turning hysterically on all three men for their mistreatment of some wild
mustangs (who seem really to be mistreated—but never mind).

"You *care,*" Guido tells her when she complains to him about missing an
education—and caring, he claims, is better than knowing. Because "whatever happens to anybody happens to you," he says. "You're really hooked in
to the whole thing, Roslyn—it's a blessing." And when Perce is gored by a
rodeo bull, the movie's emphasis is so much on Roslyn's suffering, her
sympathetic prostration, her choked and wracking sobs, that for a moment
you think the ambulance has come for *her.* But the effect of all this is quite
different from the one (presumably) intended. Roslyn by this time seems
less someone "really hooked in" to life than someone who appropriates,
with her pain and her sensitivity, all the life around her. What's proposed
to us as a universal sympathy comes across on the screen as a radical self-
absorption. The daddies may not mind this, but the audience finally does.

She never completed another film. She was fired from *Something's Got to
Give* at Fox and died shortly thereafter. The public grief was extraordinary.
And it was only then in a sense that the *real* Marilyn Monroe movie
began—the one we thought of as her life, and that was so much more
interesting and surprising and moving than any of the Hollywood productions had been.

It was television that first brought us this "movie"—beginning with
the news reports of her death, through all the memorials and tributes to

her life that followed, showing her in clips from her movies, but mostly in newsreels: entertaining the troops in Korea, waving at the crowds as she stands over that subway grating in New York, holding a press conference, having a wedding, emerging from a clinic, and so on. She had been perhaps the most photographed woman in the world (Olivier thought that her real talent was for being an inspired "model")—even more compelling in the informal footage than in the stuff that was posed. Or so it seemed at the time. The public appetite for her image—if not necessarily for her movies—began to be insatiable. As it still is.

It seemed a simpler story then than it ever would again. And its *meaning* seemed unmistakable: Marilyn Monroe was a victim. And swelling the grief over her was a sudden clear sense of collective anger at her victimizers—a buried but now uncovered public rage at the pop-culture machine that had exploited her (and "pop" as in "patriarchal" as well—though that latter word was not so predictably pejorative as it's become today), that exploited us all; at the *men,* both powerful and weak, who had abused her; at all the daddies who had betrayed her, both privately and publicly. Her movies looked different now, after her death—more like a record of that betrayal. And when her studio, a year later, released *Marilyn!,* a feature compiled (by the daddies) of high points from her movies, almost no one would go to see it. It was quickly withdrawn, but not before the studio bosses had been accused of continuing beyond the grave the exploitation they had inflicted on her life. The idea that they should make even more money from her death struck many people, in the mood of the time, as obscene.

But we had exploited her too: that's one reason her death hit us so hard. "I'll be whatever you want me to be," she promised Richard Widmark in *Don't Bother to Knock.* And as a sex symbol she deliberately made herself outlandish, hating herself for it, she said, but feeling she kept a kind of control by doing it. The reactions she got told her that. Her model in this line, she said, was Mae West, improbably enough. But Mae West, who clearly knew all about *control,* would seem to have been a stranger to the dominant emotion we were seeing in Monroe now that she was dead—namely, humiliation. In her films she had always threatened to be heartbreaking; now, at last, she really was.

It's extraordinary to realize that the emotion she finally evoked, and still stirs in us, should be so much like what we feel for a victim of child abuse—this middle-aged woman (thirty-six when she died) who was not aging very well. But even the baby-dollishness she more and more affected was somehow sympathetic: probably because there was a real and compelling "baby" somewhere behind it—in her eyes, in her uncanny radiance, in the claim her distress seemed to make on us, in her final helplessness.

But in the end America is rough on babies (as we now know better than ever), whether they are real or imagined ones. That's one of the truths she inadvertently made us look at. We're hard on innocence and then we want it back. Monroe embodied both these impulses for us, as well as the torturing contradiction between them. It's no wonder we wept over her.

Six

HITCHCOCK'S BLONDES

In spite of the exceptions, movies in general in the fifties seemed to get blander and safer—like American life in general. You could feel the decline of things in the movie houses—those great, glorious palaces, nearly empty most of the time, sometimes neglected and moldering. (The studios no longer owned them, after the 1948 Supreme Court decree ending the studio monopoly over exhibition.) They belonged to a past that promised imaginative experiences that were grander, more outsize and outrageous, than the diminished thing we were now mostly seeing on the even bigger screens. And *especially* on the bigger screen: CinemaScope, the most popular wide-screen form, seemed always to be out of focus, and to effectively do away with the spatial depth and complexity we had gotten used to from forties black and white. It was back home on your television set, often enough, that you could really see what had been lost—in stars and films of the past, with their uniqueness, their mysterious inspirations and energies. The Marx Brothers and W. C. Fields, Garbo, Astaire and Rogers, the young versions of Cagney and Bogart and Davis, *The Awful Truth* and *The Thin Man* and *The Lady Eve*—and so on. If you had any doubts that the movies had "lost something," as people used to say, the Late Show could settle them.

The wry and intelligent sort of comedy so happily rampant in the thirties had disappeared, surviving only—in a mostly ironic form—in the noir thrillers. But *they* weren't surviving so well, either. Toughness and irreverence, those onetime Hollywood specialties, seemed to be losing out to a kind of national sanctimony—and surviving in individual movies only when combined with that sanctimony, a trick the talented Billy Wilder had more or less perfected by then. But even in 1948 an unidentified studio boss told Lillian Ross, the *New Yorker* writer, that Hollywood had "a new kind of self-censorship." Now, when he read a script he had to pass on, he no longer did it through the eyes of *his* boss, but through those of "the D.A.R."—while "beating my breast and proclaiming my patriotism and

The Smith family at church in *The Next Voice You Hear:* (left to right)
James Whitmore, Nancy Davis (Nancy Reagan-to-be), Gary Gray,
and Lillian Bronson (as Aunt Ethel)

exclaiming that I love my wife and kids." It was the time of the investigating committees, when family values and anticommunism became synonymous. When Andy Hardy returns to Carvel as a grown-up, in *Andy Hardy Comes Home* (1958), it's not only to raise his own family there but as an engineer to build a missile plant.

In MGM's *The Next Voice You Hear* (1951)—personally produced by studio head Dore Schary—an aircraft-plant worker named (according to the cast list) "Joe Smith, American" (James Whitmore) is listening to his radio one night when his favorite show is interrupted by the voice of God. Or so we're told (we never hear the voice ourselves). "Maybe it was one of those Orson Welles things," suggests his wife, Mary (Nancy Davis), when he tells her about it. But it's not—it really is God. And He is being heard on radios all over the world, not just in the California suburb where Joe and Mary and Bobby, their little boy, live, with its bungalows and driveways and flat-surfaced lawns repeated in mirrorlike succession down the block.

But then God makes a radio appearance the next night, too—and the next. It's beginning to make people nervous. Especially when He alludes cryptically to one of His nastier precedents: those forty days and forty nights of rain. This thinly veiled threat so disturbs Mary that she gets hysterics at the next thunderclap. At this point, Joe, too, begins to feel sort of put upon—and puzzled as well: why would God want to upset *Mary,* of all people? (Though since we know her now as Nancy Reagan, we may feel we have an idea.) Just what, he wonders, is God's problem? Aunt Ethel (Lillian Bronson), a religious type, starts to carry on about "sin" and "punishment"—but she, of course, is nuts. It's true that the Smith family has its bad days now and then, some anger and frustration at times—mostly Joe's (what reason could Mary have?), like when he drives poorly, or snaps at the kid, or quarrels with Aunt Ethel. At his lowest, he goes to a bar and gets drunk. But he is sorry when he sees how he's upset Bobby and Mary. Especially since Mary is now pregnant.

Soon, however, they begin to see what God is getting at. "Just teachin' us to take it easy," is how one of Joe's buddies at the plant puts it. And that seems to be about it. For six of His nightly appearances (He rests on the seventh) God offers a brief inspirational instruction (the rain idea seems forgotten): be thankful, love each other, appreciate nature, enjoy life, and so on. These messages appear to do the trick: by the end of the movie the Smith family and everyone else in town are in Sunday church lifting transfigured faces toward the pulpit and the camera. "Taking it easy" at last: Aunt Ethel has stopped talking about sin, Joe has made up with her, Mary has had her baby (it's a girl), and little Bobby has learned to trust and love his parents even more than he did before. They are even nicer than before, of course—and if not *greatly* nicer than they were at the movie's start, they have learned by its end to thank God for their niceness.

It wasn't a very popular movie, but Schary was proud of it and even wrote a book about it (*Case History of a Movie*). But it was symptomatic: Hollywood was championing American family values almost as strenuously as it had recently championed the war effort—the idealism of the war movies giving way to something more like simple self-congratulation. The movies, like their audience, were moving to the suburbs. So were movie stars—especially the women. The idea of feminine stardom was no longer much associated with any kind of exceptionalism, let alone mystery or remoteness. It was more like the star next door—where she belonged. And women faced even more limited opportunities *in* the movies than outside them. Now, if you went to a movie called *Woman's World* (1954), it would *not* be—as it would have been in the thirties—either a soap opera about being victimized by a man or a comedy about triumphing over him, but instead a "comedy-drama" about advancing his career. The "next voice you hear" in this film—more worldly than Schary's—belongs to an all-wise corporate boss, Clifton Webb, who is not only interviewing three potential magnates but sizing up their wives as well. In spite of the cosmopolitan veneer, it's the kind of movie where Arlene Dahl, looking out her hotel window at New York, says, "This is where I belong," and you know right away she is unredeemable; where June Allyson, given money by her husband to buy an evening gown, buys an outdoor barbecue instead, complete with chef's hats for the whole family; and Lauren Bacall, looking misty-eyed at her, says, "What an idiotic, *won*derful thing to do!" Though Bacall, you're sure, wouldn't be found dead in a chef's hat, she has certainly learned how to deliver this sort of line: with an appropriately wistful inflection.

To embody scenarios like these, however, you didn't really need or even want women who were *too* interesting—women like Jane Greer, or Eva Marie Saint, or Gloria Grahame, all of whose starring careers in the fifties began to decline almost as soon as they'd begun. The era of the great women stars seemed over by then. And the newer, blander woman star—without a strongly defined persona, with a certain comforting vacancy in her screen presence—was changing our experience of the movies themselves, which could no longer so plausibly seem (in Truffaut's phrase) "an art of the woman." Frank Capra, for example, who collaborated with Barbara Stanwyck and Jean Arthur in the thirties and forties, worked in the fifties with Coleen Gray, Jane Wyman, Eleanor Parker, and Hope Lange.* Howard Hawks, who had worked so notably with such unforgettable women as Ann Dvorak, Frances Farmer, and Lauren Bacall (all three of whom gave their most vivid early performances in his films), was well known for a recurring feisty heroine who was independent as well as sexy, even before cineastes started talking about "the Hawksian woman." But the versions of her he offered in the fifties and sixties—declining from personable near-stars like Joanne Dru, Margaret Sheridan (in *The Thing*), and Angie Dickinson to multiple interchangeable starlets (Laura Devon, Michelle Carey, Gail Hire, Elizabeth Threatt, et al.), suggested a growing desperation, until his pictures began to be *crowded* with spunky, outspoken girls (*El Dorado, Hatari, Red Line 7000;* each had three or four)—as if quantity might help.

The burden of allure and mystery in the movies had shifted now to the men. And as the women got less interesting, it seemed, the men got more so. They also—like the women, like the movie audience—were getting

---

*In *Riding High* (1950), *Here Comes the Groom* (1951), *A Hole in the Head* (1959), and *Pocketful of Miracles* (1961), respectively.

younger: in looks and manner, more like boys than ever before. And yet these "boys" were trouble, and made trouble—just as women stars had so recently been and done, in their roles as noir heroines and as screwball-comedy heroines before that: the ones who stirred things up, the social and cultural subverters. No longer. From *Theodora Goes Wild* in 1936 to *Rebel Without a Cause* in 1955, that role had devolved to stars like Brando and Dean, who embodied an even more open sort of dissidence: against "the system," against conformity and material ambition and suburban domesticity. They were brooding and sensual and disruptive, like Brando's biker with small-town girl Mary Murphy in *The Wild One,* while the women had now become cheery, conventional, and conciliating, like Day with Sinatra. On the whole, it was women stars who now emblemized what was most complacent and repressive in American life.

And not just the girl-next-door stars: the "sophisticates," too. Like Grace Kelly in *Rear Window* (1954)—as Lisa Fremont, a *Vogue* editor and girl about town, visiting her fiancé, James Stewart, in his apartment, where he is laid up with his leg in a cast—the latest result of his exciting career as a photojournalist. She wants him on Wall Street: "I could see you looking very handsome and successful in a dark blue flannel suit." She is breathless over the cocktails she's just shared, she tells him, with Leland and Slim Hayward (real celebrity names in this movie). Tell me, says Stewart mockingly, what *was* Mrs. Hayward wearing? "She had on the most *divine* Italian hand-printed—" Then she breaks off, as his mockery registers on her. "Oh, *you*!" she cries. Then, pouting: "To think I planted three nice items about you in the columns today." And so it goes.

It must have seemed a bit amazing to audiences who still remembered the Loys and Dunnes and Lombards. In a thirties romantic comedy (never Hitchcock's forte, even at the time) this sort of talk would have been more than enough to nail Lisa as a hopeless airhead, and *not* a harmless one—someone not only silly but also poisonous. But times had changed—and so had the view of rich feminine airheads. Hollywood, like the advertisers, was beginning to promote a more upscale version of American life, even embracing the sort of petty snobberies that would have been automatic targets of scorn in movies past—and that are abundantly illustrated in this one by the Grace Kelly heroine: in the character's name-dropping and pettish manner, the giddy talk about the posh life, the aggressive gentility and "refinement." As when she reproves Stella, the maid (Thelma Ritter), for her outspokenness about a murder they've been discussing: "Oh, Stella, your choice of *words*!" she exclaims, knitting her brow at the impact of Stella's vocabulary (who has just referred to blood "spattering").

But Hitchcock liked this refinement. He found it stimulating; his favorite publicly shared fantasy was of "the real ladies, who become whores once they're in the bedroom." ("Poor Marilyn Monroe," he said in 1966, "she had sex written all over her face.") He described to Truffaut how he first showed Grace Kelly to us in *To Catch a Thief* (1955): "I deliberately photographed Grace Kelly ice-cold and I kept cutting to her profile, looking classical, beautiful, and very distant. And then, when Cary Grant accompanies her to the door of her hotel room, what does she do? She thrusts her lips right up to his mouth." It's a justly famous scene by now, and it really does work the way he meant it to: the first shot of Kelly over Grant's shoulder as she turns in the doorway and looks up at him challengingly, almost makes you catch your breath. It's partly the consciousness in her eyes (which have been opaque up to now) as she moves in on him, both smoldering-sexy and little-girl-mischievous—and radiant. She puts her arm around his shoulders (in the same shot), an elegantly splayed hand on the back of his neck, and kisses him (you suppose) deeply, as a saxophone growls on the soundtrack—then draws slowly back with a lingering knowing gaze as she closes her door on him.

But, it seems to me, her beauty is too self-aware, too complacent. Even when she is struggling with inexperience, as in *High Noon* (1952), or with a big-time acting challenge, as in *The Country Girl* (1954), she conveys, in the fashion of the time, something like placidity, and it keeps her from ever seeming truly exciting. The closest she comes to being so is in a few moments with Grant in *To Catch a Thief.* In *Rear Window,* her opportunities are restricted by the hero's temporary invalidism (as well as by the film's ingenious single set) to her bringing him gossip and company, as well as meals from "21," and some interludes of sexual teasing, as when she models a new nightgown for him (she calls it "previews of coming attractions"). But in spite of these efforts, the relation between her and Stewart comes across as stubbornly noncarnal. And not just because of his irritableness and enforced celibacy. Kelly's Lisa gives the impression that even if she *should* undress for him, as she hints at doing, there'd be an even more stunning outfit underneath.

Nevertheless, she was hugely popular, though her career before she retired was short (1951–56) and comprised only eleven films. They gave her the 1954 Academy Award for only her third starring movie (*The Country Girl*). Like Audrey Hepburn, she embodied "class," but hers was of a distinctively American kind. And for that reason she was seen to be in the tradition of that other Hepburn, Katharine, for whom Philip Barry over a decade earlier had written *The Philadelphia Story* and the leading role of

Kim Novak—with Pyewacket—in
Bell, Book and Candle (her next film
after *Vertigo* and again with Stewart)

Tracy Lord, all about the Main Line
society world that Kelly herself had
come from. When MGM remade
their 1940 movie of the play as *High
Society* in 1956, with songs by Cole
Porter, they cast Kelly as Tracy (her
last picture) and Crosby and Sinatra
opposite her (in the Grant and Stewart roles, respectively). But Kelly's
performance never begins to suggest
the virtues that made Hepburn's so
memorable: the nervy, high-strung
quality, the feeling of wit and danger. Kelly was a star partly because
she *didn't* make us nervous.

But if Kelly often reminded you
of a triumphant hostess, Kim Novak
seemed more like the unwanted
guest. Joshua Logan said of her that
she bore her extraordinary looks like
a physical disability. "Her dumb suffering beauty," said Pauline Kael
(about *The Man with the Golden Arm*),
is "very touching." Novak, unlike
Kelly, was never taken very seriously by Hollywood—and apparently not
by Hitchcock. He had planned *Vertigo* around his new protégée, Vera
Miles, as Madeleine/Judy. When Miles got pregnant instead, the much-
relieved studio heads pressed Novak on him, someone who had clout at the
box office. But then they made the mistake of showing him her most
recent film, *Jeanne Eagels*. "That girl is going to ruin my movie!" he is
reported to have said when the lights went up. And he seems never to have
quite got over either his resentment of Miles for getting pregnant or his
feeling that Novak had been forced upon him—never conceding much
more to her than that she did not ruin his movie, after all.

Even at the peak of her stardom most of Novak's publicity seemed to be
about what a miracle had been worked *on* her, by Harry Cohn and his studio. *Time* magazine did a 1956 cover story about her, offering her the
ambiguous accolade of being (as they claimed) the first "truly manufactured" star. And it's true she was inexperienced, even for a starlet—emerging mainly through beauty contests, touring refrigerator demos (she was

"Miss Deepfreeze"), and some unbilled movie bits. But "this former tough Polish broad from Chicago," as dance director Jack Cole described her, would be transformed by experts. She made her Columbia debut in a starring role (when another actress didn't work out) opposite Fred MacMurray in Richard Quine's *Pushover* (1954), a low-budget noir, one of those quiet triumphs of straightforward genre filmmaking that always made "the movies" seem worthwhile again when they came along, in spite of all the junk. It was sort of *Double Indemnity* over again, except MacMurray was older and wearier, and a cop instead of an insurance salesman—and quite wonderful. Novak was the woman who gets him to do murder for her: you're meant to believe she's irresistible, and you do. She's in an old-style glamour mode, marked by languor and angst. All she does is smoke and stare at the wall, says one of the cops who's staked out her apartment (Dorothy Malone, the nice girl next door to her, does her exercises and gives parties). He's wrong: she also drives to the beach and stares at the ocean. And, in a surprising forecast of *Vertigo,* the hero follows her around in his car. She's a gangster's girl who wants to get rid of the gangster. She talks about money, as she does about everything, with a kind of sadness. She seems at home in the noir shadows, moving in and out of them with diffident ease. And when she looks in a mirror, it seems less to check her hair or makeup than to confirm her gravity. In spite of the artifice and constraint of her Hollywood makeover, and the anxious care of her presentation (there were many retakes and some apparent postdubbing of her lines), she is appealing and convincing, giving a real performance of a real person, with a powerful erotic effect on the screen.

They decided they had the "new" Marilyn Monroe—only classier and less eccentric than the original: the big healthy girl they'd get it *right* with this time. But then they began to get it wrong. In her next Columbia picture, *Phffft!* (1954), a lame Judy Holliday–Jack Lemmon comedy, she had the supporting comic role of the cute ditzy blond mantrap. But she wasn't funny—unlike Monroe, she had no comic talent. She wasn't "cute," either: that wasn't her line any more than antic comedy was. You can see the sort of problem the studio had with her when you look at some of her early publicity stills. In spite of her physical qualifications, she can't really carry them off. Crouching on top of a bed in a negligee, with her head thrown back in a provocative gaze along her shoulder at the camera, she seems so unconvinced you think she might be joking. Except that she never is. She has a solemnity that always defeats the sex-kitten stuff. If she is feline, it's less because she seems sensual and playful than because she seems finally inaccessible. And the poignancy of that makes her sexier.

Novak with Sinatra in Preminger's *The Man with the Golden Arm*

But she was beautifully at home in her fourth released film, Otto Preminger's *The Man with the Golden Arm* (1955), as the saloon girl in low-life Chicago with a crush on Frank Sinatra's heroin addict, who helps him to go cold turkey ("You mustn't touch that dirty stuff no more!"). The movie was a hit. So—even more so—were her next two: *Picnic* (1956), her first movie in color and her biggest hit of all, and *The Eddy Duchin Story* (1956), where she plays the bandleader's socialite first wife, and is made to look (again in color) and sound so much like a heavenly visitation that her death in the middle of the movie ("The wind frightens me! Oh, I hate the wind!") feels like a romantic fulfillment. At the end of 1956, she was named the most popular star in America, number one on the exhibitors' list of top ten box-office draws.

It didn't last long. Her next pictures for Columbia, *Jeanne Eagels* and *Pal Joey,* both in 1957, were big letdowns, the latter being widely resented for the way it mangled and bowdlerized the Rodgers and Hart original. And *Eagels* seemed terrible enough to be almost inexplicable. Perhaps they thought, with the impact she made on the screen (the *Hollywood Reporter* had compared her to Garbo and Valentino)—and since she couldn't sing or dance or do comedy—it was time for her to *act,* in a big way. And what better way to persuade us that she could than by having her play a Great Actress—who was also a scandalous one? And in case we missed the latter point (or had never known about it), the writers gave Eagels an invented early career as a carny cooch dancer—a chance for the star to appear semi-nude in the movie's early part, and in *all* of the ads, if necessary. It pretty much was.

Her performance is hectic and grotesque; her straining is apparent in every scene she's in. And she seems to be in nearly all of them—almost as if she were being disciplined. The movie runs nearly two hours and requires her over its length to impersonate not only the genius-type artist's stormy rise to fame, but also her long decline into dissipation, disgrace, and death, so that Novak's discomfort and inadequacy seem not only exposed to the audience, but imposed on it too—the sort of experience that turns audiences against you. She did better in *Pal Joey,* in the ingenue role, but the movie was so flat it didn't help much. By the time she came to do *Vertigo,* she was still a big star, but a more problematic one. And *Vertigo* too was a box-office disappointment, and mostly poorly reviewed.

Hitchcock, she later said, would never talk to her about the characters she played. And he would later say that she had had too many ideas about "acting." He got rid of those soon enough. "You see, she's a bit confused," he told an interviewer, explaining how he got the *Vertigo* performance out of her. "On the one hand people are telling her that she's America's top woman star, on the other, that she's a dumb ox. I convinced her the truth lay somewhere between the two." She submitted to Hitchcock—as she did two pictures later to pioneer TV director Delbert Mann in his film of Paddy Chayefsky's *Middle of the Night* (1959), a no-frills New York location shoot, with a cast of theatrical pros and Actors Studio types. It was a whole new world to her, and a new way of working, opposite to Hitchcock's: "getting inside yourself" instead of taking orders. And she has a kind of triumph in it (though the film itself wasn't popular), as the dishy but neurotic working girl with whom older man Fredric March falls in love.

She was reportedly shaken by Monroe's death in 1961; it confirmed her own fears of Hollywood. But the fact seems to be that she was tougher than Monroe—and with fewer self-destructive habits. She was widely known to be "difficult" and was unpopular with directors and fellow actors. But that kind of stubbornness may be part of what saved her from Hollywood in the end. Just as it seems to have played a big part in what she salvaged from the disastrous production of *Of Human Bondage* (1964), the third movie version (and the most widely maligned one) of Maugham's novel, filmed in Ireland and London to constant publicity about its problems.

Mildred (Novak) is glad to get away from Laurence Harvey's Philip even
if it's with his best friend, Griff (Jack Hedley), in *Of Human Bondage.*

She is, of course, less powerful than Bette Davis was in her legendary
1934 performance; but Novak is more nuanced, and—to my sense anyway—finally more interesting. Her Mildred, unlike Davis's frightening
virago, isn't so much cruel and vindictive as she is coarse-grained and
rather ordinarily calloused: the sort of person who, you know, feels really
sort of *bad* about the things she says and does, but who says and does them
anyway, and so what if she did. This was not a conception of the role,
apparently, that was favored by *either* of the movie's directors—Ken
Hughes, the credited one, or Henry Hathaway, the first one (who said,
when he quit, that he'd always wanted Monroe for the part anyway). But
Novak stuck to it, in spite of all, and there it is finally, on the screen, clear
and coherent. But the movie was her biggest flop yet. And her radically
un-Davis-like performance—except for a few strong dissents (Siobhan
McKenna, also in the cast, admired it vastly—so did the *Newsweek*
reviewer)—was widely judged to be another example of her inadequacy,
when it seems now, at least, to show just the opposite.

By then, however, she was no longer somehow the Kim Novak of the
fifties. She was still beautiful, of course (as she is now, in her sixties). But
that incredible bloom of the *Picnic* and *Vertigo* years wouldn't come again.

Nor would her surefire power at the box office. She worked less after *Of Human Bondage,* but still managed to make two more remarkable movies—Billy Wilder's wonderfully lubricious *Kiss Me, Stupid* in 1964 and Robert Aldrich's *The Legend of Lylah Clare* in 1968. She's affecting in both of them—a hooker in the first, a movie star in the second—and victimized in both. And both movies were reflections—Aldrich's explicitly so—of the passing of old Hollywood, Wilder's tireless smuttiness being as alien to that world as Aldrich's self-reflexive games with genre were. But the retro aspect of the two films seemed appropriate to Novak, young as she still was. She was, after all, the last great star to come out of the old studio system.

The kind of star James Baldwin is talking about when he writes (in *The Devil Finds Work*) of people like Bogart and Davis and Wayne: "One does not go to see them act: one goes to watch them *be.*" "Films can be made," says the great filmmaker Robert Bresson, "only by bypassing the will of those who appear in them, using not what they do but who they are." And when the studio remade Novak into "this ethereal 'who-am-I-what-are-you-saying-to-me?' girl" (Jack Cole again), giving her the relatively blank persona of the glamour star, they were effecting (however different their intentions) something at least analogous to Bresson's recommended bypassing of the film actor's will. So was Hitchcock—as when he told Novak (according to the story anyway) that he would not ask her how to direct as long as she didn't ask him how to act.

She is as moving as she is in *Picnic* partly because of all the acting going on *around* her. It's a seriously misbegotten (if entertaining) movie—beginning with the casting of a middle-aged, worn-looking William Holden as the hero, the kind of homoerotic fantasy stud ("I like to keep in shape") so common to fifties drama, but normally played by younger, more knowing performers. Holden, often stripped to the waist and shorn of body hair, mainly seems embarrassed, which only makes him work harder than usual—especially when he has to play a scene with Rosalind Russell, as the repressed but ravening spinster schoolteacher (her big moment comes when she tears his shirt off at the picnic). Only Betty Field, among a cast of theatrical pros (Arthur O'Connell, Susan Strasberg, et al.), playing Novak's mother, seems as if she could really live in the actual midwestern town director Josh Logan insisted on filming in, crowding the backgrounds of his wide-screen shots with uneasy-looking townspeople. But in the midst of all the shrillness and falsity, in the midst of all that *acting,* there's Novak—with her simplicity of just *being* there, as it seems, inhabiting a character she clearly felt close to: a girl who feels patronized and dis-

Novak, a publicity still from *Of Human Bondage*

counted by the way people react to her beauty. Whether it's acting or not, she seems the only *serious* human presence in the film.

That's the sort of thing Preminger seems to have understood about her in *The Man with the Golden Arm* (released before *Picnic* but filmed just afterwards): a "sexpot" with *gravitas*. "She gives you a feeling of compassion," he told an interviewer, trying to account for her power on the screen. And you can see what he's talking about in her very first moment in the movie. She enters in the background (of course) of a shot of Sinatra, just sprung from jail, talking animatedly on the tenement's hallway phone. She is going out the door with a guy she has a date with, who is in a hurry and hustling her along, when she stops and looks at Sinatra—who doesn't at first notice. Then he looks at her—and looks quizzically at the impatient party at her side. "A guy I met while you was away," she says softly, in her diffident, thrillingly husky voice. With a single line she evokes that mixture of intense longing and an even deeper resignation that would come to seem characteristic of her.

What Preminger called "compassion" in her, Hitchcock turns into Madeleine's generosity and graciousness (almost the opposite of Grace Kelly's kind of classiness), as they show in her openness of feeling and response to Scotty in their early encounters. There are other versions of the same qualities in the way she looks at flowers in a shop, the way she studies the stones in a graveyard: a fullness of concentration, of stillness in the moment. Then there's the way she reverses most of those qualities in Judy—who is all yearning *without* resignation, who is gauche and querulous and defensively closed off. And Novak makes her moving, too.

We can never know what a Vera Miles *Vertigo* would have been like. Except that it would have been different—and perhaps less moving. Hardly anybody at the time wasn't a little puzzled by Hitchcock's enthusiasm for her (he had her under personal contract)—especially after *The Wrong Man* (1957), in which he gave her a big and showy role opposite Henry Fonda (as a wife going mad) without her making much impression at all. It's true that Miles had by then some experience as an actor (supporting movie roles as well as TV work). But then people were even more puzzled by Tippi Hedren, his next "discovery" (also under personal contract), who had none at all (he had seen her in a television commercial). It was clear that she at least was meant to be a replacement for Grace Kelly (who had fled to Monaco and princesshood). But for audiences Hedren's narrow-eyed, carefully coiffed prettiness seemed a long way away from Kelly's "classical" beauty and cool sexiness—as indeed it was.

What they did have in common—Kelly, Miles, and Hedren, these three Hitchcock blondes—was a kind ordinariness, a blandness no one could ever have attributed to heroines of his like Ingrid Bergman or Eva Marie Saint or Novak. The "discoveries" were closer to the heroine of one of his earlier masterpieces, Teresa Wright in *Shadow of a Doubt,* in the way they evoked, in spite of differences, the "nice" American girl of their time, the kind of daughters that nice American mothers had learned to wish for (Grace Kelly, especially).

Hitchcock was interested in this feminine version of commonplace, innocent Americanness. Partly because it was deceiving—like the lady with the whore inside her. There was the violence inside the girl next door (Wright in *Shadow of a Doubt*), the criminality inside the respectable working girl (Hedren in *Marnie*), the hysteria and fear inside the suburban mom (Doris Day in *The Man Who Knew Too Much*). Hitchcock was both drawn to the generic American girl and not quite convinced by her. But his deepest response of all to her, it seems to me, is Janet Leigh in *Psycho*.

Seven

JANET LEIGH AND *PSYCHO*

The heroine of Orson Welles's great film noir, *Touch of Evil* (1958), is on her honeymoon in a sleazy Mexican border town called Los Robles. She and her Mexican husband, Mike Vargas (Charlton Heston), are walking to the American side so that he can buy her a chocolate soda (you can't get them in Mexico) when suddenly a car bomb explodes at the border crossing, killing two people and plunging Mike back into his work as a cop. He sends her back to the hotel ("We'll have to postpone that soda, I'm afraid"). But then she is waylaid on the street by "Uncle Joe" Grandi (Akim Tamiroff) and his "nephews," who have a score to settle with her husband. They hustle her into a shabby hotel lobby and start to threaten her. She admits to being pretty scared, but if she doesn't show it, that's because *bullying* makes her so angry. She calls Uncle Joe "a silly little pig," and her cold fury is impressive. She accuses him—with apparent accuracy—of seeing too many gangster movies. And when he bears down on her with a cigar in his mouth, she swats it away.

They let her go. They're not daunted, but they have other plans for her: a series of traps and violations so baroque and improbable that we experience them almost more as being contrived by Welles the filmmaker than by the bad guys in the film. Nonetheless, she walks into them all—eyes blazing and breasts jutting (she mostly wears sweaters)—intrepidly. That chocolate soda was misleading. So are her looks. This is no spoiled American bimbette, no campus-queen sweater girl, but a courageous, self-possessed young woman. On her honeymoon.

It's true that she shows some of the complacency that goes with white American privilege—especially when it is visiting a poor country full of dark-skinned people. She tells her husband the Mexican that she thinks that she might be safer, after all, in an American motel (she is disastrously mistaken), and when he takes offense, she amends "safer" to "more comfortable" (wrong again). Her automatic response when she is spoken to on the street by a native is to say that she doesn't want any more postcards.

Janet Leigh in *Touch of Evil,* shadowed by "Pancho" (Valentin De Vargas)

She tries some fractured Spanish but instantly gives it up—enough of *that* nonsense, her manner seems to say. When a young Mexican stranger approaches her with what he says is a message from her husband, and since she is nervous about following him as he tells her to, she adopts her hearty wisecracking mode: "Lead on, Pancho," she says, as she goes off behind him—a moment that makes you cringe for her.

But then it turns out that his name really *is* Pancho. He and his uncle, Grandi, are puzzled about how she knew it. It's one of the times (and there are many) when this movie undercuts *our* complacency. Even her nervousness about strange Mexicans—what a contemporary critic calls her "unconscious racism"—is, as it turns out, more than justified by events several times over. She is, in fact, almost the best type of American-in-a-strange-place. She is high-spirited, uncomplaining, and (up to a point) adventurous, open and free. She is never officious or demanding, even when you think she's entitled to be: in a hotel room without window shades, for example, or in the accommodations she later endures "on the American side." She is inexperienced, of course, and quite unprepared for the depravity she encounters in Los Robles (who wouldn't be?). And she is played by one of the most engaging new people in fifties movies, Janet Leigh.

Leigh was a lesser sort of star, but an adaptable and dependable one, and she made a lot of movies, most of them negligible or worse. But partly because she had intelligence and spirit, as well as looks and charm, she lasted longer as a star than most of her counterparts did: it's hard to imagine many of *them* (Jeanne Crain, say, or Pier Angeli) slapping Akim Tamiroff's cigar away—or coping so womanfully with the ordeals that *Touch of Evil* imposes on her. Indeed, Leigh's main function through the film, it seems, is to be threatened and violated, at length and in some detail. At that American motel, the Mirador, where she asks her husband to leave her off—for a start. It's ominously isolated, in the middle of the desert, with an obviously crazy night man and no other guests. But soon it's invaded by a motorcycle gang, a dozen or so leather-jacketed thugs with a radio, slavering and jittering to a rock-and-roll beat as they take over the place. She is alone in her room trying to sleep. Then comes the extraordinary scene where she is crouched at the head of her bed, in a virginal short nightie, her eyes like saucers and her ear pressed against her own shadow as she listens through the wall to a woman's Spanish-accented voice on the other side. It's one of the gang members warning her about the others. "You know what the mainliner is?" says the voice. "I think so," says the wide-eyed Susie, "but what's that got to do with me?" "You take it in the arm," replies the voice. Susie struggles with this idea: "You're trying to tell me those boys are drugged?" she says ("those boys" is nice). But soon the boys resume their music, and Susie is careening around her motel room in a panic as they surround it and her. Silently (the radio music drowns out every other sound) and implacably they file into the room and gather around her bed, as she crouches on top of it, clutching a sheet to herself, as their shadows fall across her face one by one, and someone shuts the door, and fade-out.

But after all this, it turns out in the end that "nothing" has happened to her. "The kids were all faking," a detective later tells her husband. All there was in the hypo they gave her was some sodium pentothal: "no harm in it at all." And she was not raped. *That* thought seems to have occurred only to us: not, in any case, to the boys who encircled her on her bed, who lifted her off it and spread her legs before they closed the door on us; not even to the lesbian in leather (Mercedes McCambridge, one of the movie's unbilled "guest stars," and also the voice behind the wall) who was heard to say huskily, as the door closed: "Lemme stay—I wanta watch." What she got to watch, apparently, was the gang scattering reefer stubs around the room, lighting some and then blowing the smoke (the devils) into Susie's clothes. The idea is to frame her on a drug charge. "You kids didn't use none of that stuff yourself, huh?" says Uncle Joe Grandi later. "We're not doing this for *fun,* Uncle Joe," replies one of them. It turns out they were doing it for money. What a relief.

All this improbable revisionism, which comes toward the end of the movie, was Welles's way not only of complying with the Production Code of the time but of making a joke about it. But there's another joke involved—about Susie: because the fact that nothing has happened to her only confirms the suspicion the film has already given us that in a way nothing *could,* at least not very deeply. Welles has many ways of making this point about her, it seems, including the remarkable sequence where Mike phones her at the Mirador before all hell breaks out. She is half-reclining on her bed, in a sexy negligee (*not* the chaste nightie she wears for "the boys"), looking like the ultimate calendar girl, and whispering horny endearments into the phone: "my own darling Miguel" and "I was just listening to you breathe, it's a lovely sound." But Mike is phoning from a dingy general store that looks almost as collapsed as its blind lady proprietor. The film cross-cuts between Mike and Susie as they talk. But the way Welles has arranged the shot in the store, it's the blind woman, not Mike, who is foregrounded—and whose image is contrasted in the intercutting with that luscious vision of Susie. Mike is in the left background of the shot, talking on the wall phone, while the woman is in the right foreground, in dramatic close-up: with stubby features and stringy hair and her mouth clenched downward, she is turned away from him and toward us, one eye squinted nearly shut and the other wide and staring sightlessly at us. And challengingly, it seems—a feeling that's confirmed by the hand-lettered wall sign that hangs just above her: IF YOU ARE MEAN ENOUGH TO STEAL FROM THE BLIND, HELP YOURSELF.

The kind of challenge, you feel, that would be lost on Susie. Probably Welles's harshest comment on her is the one implied by this juxtaposition of shots: the blind woman being as clearly the real thing—in several senses—as Susie, in several senses, is not. Mostly she is too oblivious, too safely secured from the sort of reality, both grubby and tragic, that this "real-life" blind woman evokes for us. Of course, *all* the Susies—and the Midges and Anns and so on—are out of place and out of their depth in their own noir movies: that's just the point about them usually. But Welles makes that point imply a more radical judgment of her than either Tourneur or Hitchcock does, or would want to do. Otherwise, he offers his nice-girl a kind of arm's-length admiration. He is amused by her, even a bit impressed, but not much interested in her, so that in spite of her centrality to the plot—to its melodrama and Grand Guignol theatrics—to the movie itself, finally, she is peripheral.

Alfred Hitchcock, on the *Psycho* set

But for Hitchcock the Janet Leigh heroine in *Psycho* (1960) is central, and to deep and upsetting effect. She is also—only two years after the Welles film—once again being menaced in an empty motel by a nutty night man. And it's the same familiar "Janet Leigh" in both films: the pretty, self-confident young woman who inevitably reminds you of that *very* popular girl in high school you could never get a date with. But there's a difference that's apparent from the first moments of each film. Where Susie enters Welles's movie, striding purposefully forward arm-in-arm with her glamorous hero-husband (on the way to that chocolate soda), Marion Crane, the *Psycho* heroine, is first seen lying down, in a situation and image that imply her subjection, even her humiliation.

And so she seems vulnerable from the moment the movie begins—first of all to Hitchcock's camera, panning across the skyline of Phoenix, Arizona, and then swooping down to a window and passing through closed venetian blinds into the dingy hotel room where she has just had sex with her boyfriend, and is lying on her back on the bed, in a white bra and half-slip, gazing up at the shirtless male figure standing beside her: she is silent and he is talking. Though we don't see his face at first (the framing cuts him off), we see her eyes looking up at him. Even her breasts in the low-angle shot seem to be pointing up at him, in that almost luminous white bra. She never touched her lunch, he says—and Hitchcock gives us a close-up of the lunch tray. The boyfriend, Sam (John Gavin), wants Marion to stay with him a bit longer, but she has to go back to work, she says. She makes it clear, as they talk and dress, that she doesn't like these lunch-hour quickies, or the hotel they have them in. It's equally clear that he likes it all, just this way. This is the last time, she tells him—from now on he has to come to her sister's house (less action there, for sure)—as she moves to the mirror, where she buttons her blouse. He agrees: "All right," he says, as he lounges in a chair by the window. And at that moment she turns from the mirror to look at him.

It's the first time we see Leigh up close in this film, and it's rather star-tling. The style is still girlish—the Junior Miss look, with floppy shirt collar, streaked and tousled hair, and so on—but the effect this time is an unexpected sort of dignity: her face seems older, hair darker, eyes wider and sadder than they did in the Welles movie. In some way it's a maternal face: not passing judgment on this guy, but not really expecting much, either (although hoping for something) as she looks at him and listens to him talk. He is talking about money now—that's the reason they can't get married, he says, because of all the alimony he has to pay to his ex-wife. She's heard it before, you know—and she turns back to the mirror. "I haven't been married once," she says softly, almost to herself. Sam responds to this: he rises and saunters toward her, displaying a wide grin. "Yeah, but when you do, you'll swing," he says—all of a sudden making like this hip sexy guy coming on to her.

It's one of those moments when Hitchcock's nastiness toward the Sam character (he was nasty to the actor too, by some accounts) seems *almost* out of control. Except that it isn't—just the opposite, in fact. Sam's radiant smugness at this moment (for him, you can see, that's what the sex is about too) places his character for us exactly and powerfully—especially when he is being watched by Marion's sad, alert eyes. So that when she suddenly responds to this the next moment by embracing him and crying, "Oh, Sam, let's get married," the effect is more than a little disturbing.

But about Marion, there is something disturbing altogether. Partly it's that music—a soft, slow pulsing of strings—whenever she is alone on the screen. And from the start—in these hotel-room scenes and after that at her office—the film gives us the uneasy feeling of some urgency about her that we are not quite understanding yet: the way the shots and the fram-ings make her smallest choices (like that uneaten lunch on the tray) seem somehow momentous. And the camera, which had felt invasive at first, now begins to seem attentive, almost solicitous in the way it tracks forward to reframe her (to get *next* to her, as it seems) once Sam walks out of their shot.

And the attention feels obsessive. We are immersed in all the inflections and details of her behavior in these opening and even later scenes. Of course, you recognize a genre characteristic in all this: in a conventional thriller any detail or minor circumstance may be either a clue to the puzzle or a signal of the danger. But in *Psycho* there is no puzzle and the danger is everywhere at once. The details feel ominous but we don't know why. Like that title just before the action starts, giving the exact location, date, and time of what we're going to see, the hotel tryst—detailed information that turns out to have no importance at all. Except, perhaps, to introduce a pattern of seemingly pointless emphasis that runs throughout the movie. Like all those striking close-ups of insignificant objects: Marion's unwanted lunch, the license plates on her car, the envelope she scribbles some figures on at the motel, and then tears to pieces, the toilet bowl she flushes the pieces down, and so on. Here it's no longer a matter, it seems, as it was in more conventional Hitchcock movies, of such things as the identity of Mr. X, or the poison in the milk, or the Maguffin in the wine cellar. In this movie, it's a general and persisting unease in the nature of things, a matter of what William James called the "pit of insecurity beneath the surface of life."

And one of the things the movie observes closely is how much at home on that surface Marion seems to be. Why shouldn't she be? She has all the natural authority and ease of someone who is physically attractive, who is used to being smiled upon. You see that self-possession operating at her dismal job. She is—not surprisingly—a secretary, one of two (the other is Hitchcock's daughter, Pat) sitting at their desks in a storefront realty office, when a blowhard Texas millionaire named Cassidy (Jack Albertson), who's had too much to drink, comes in with Mr. Lowery, the boss (Vaughn Taylor). The millionaire is buying a house for his eighteen-year-old daughter as a wedding present; but before Lowery can get him into his private office, Cassidy is sitting on Marion's desk and coming on to her—waving a wad of big bills under her nose (the forty thousand dollars cash that he is closing the deal with) and talking about his beloved "baby" and the wedding he's giving her and all the things that his money will do for her, as he perches on the edge of Marion's desk, looking down on her roguishly. Marion listens to all this (all she is really being asked to do), balancing her chin on the tips of her fingers, smiling, even making little faces of sympathy and agreement, but gazing at him unforgivingly all the while—though he does unsettle her a little at one point. "You know what I'd do about unhappiness?" he asks her rhetorically, then answers: "I'd buy it off." Then, looking at her searchingly: "Are you unhappy?" She hesitates: "Not inordinately," she replies after a moment, with a complex little smile.

The irony of this is that at this point in her life Marion seems "not inordinately" anything *except* unhappy. Though it would seem she "has it all," or ought to have—at least from the points of view of the people around her, the lecherous millionaire who seems willing to buy her cash down, or the plain-looking secretary at the other desk who is distressed (an emphatic close-up) because Marion is getting all the millionaire's attention. "I guess," she says to Marion after he's gone, "he must have noticed my wedding ring"—*another* person who's married.

When of course it's Marion, of all people, who should be—who should be having a better time in every way than she is. What cries out, to her and to us, is the simple *wrongness* of what's happening to her and what's *not* happening to her. She is so clearly like the all-American girls you saw on the magazine covers, in the cigarette ads, even the movies—like Janet Leigh, to put it plainly—the ideal daughter, the ideal wife. But not only is Marion no one's wife (not even once), but not even, in a sense, anyone's daughter, as the encounter with Cassidy suggests painfully. "My sweet little girl!" he exclaims when he enters the realty office. And for a moment Marion (you can see from the way she starts) thinks he's talking to her. He's not: he's thinking about his "baby" back home, who will have everything an adoring rich daddy (a real one) can buy her. Thanks to him, he tells Marion as he sits on her desk, his "little girl" has "never had an unhappy day in any one of her eighteen years." And he shows Marion the forty thousand dollars once again. "I never carry more than I can afford to lose," he says, flapping it at her.

And so she steals it. Not right away, of course. Her boss, nervous about having so much money on the premises, asks her to deposit it in the bank. But in the next scene, she is in her bedroom, again in bra and half-slip, packing a suitcase and circling the money, which reposes in an envelope placed in the center of the bed—where it exerts (as Hitchcock objects often do) a kind of magnetic field: an example of what Catholic moral philosophy calls the occasion of sin. Marion yields to it in any case (the bra and half-slip are black this time). She dresses, stuffs the envelope in her handbag, and steps out the door—into a dissolve that puts her (to the throbbing Bernard Herrmann score) in a series of tight frontal close-ups at the wheel of her car, on her way to Sam (who manages a hardware store in another town), and hearing inside her head the voices of the people she left behind, all of them—the boss, the other secretary, Cassidy himself—reacting to her disappearance and their discovery of the theft. Still she drives on. In her daydream, she hears Sam's voice too—his astonishment when she turns up at the hardware store: "Marion, what in the world . . . ? What are you doing here?"

But then, after all, what *is* Sam supposed to say, when she comes to him with money everyone will know she's stolen? It's Cassidy's reaction she imagines most vividly: "I'll replace it with her fine soft flesh!" says the Cassidy voice—as she smiles and drives on. The voice can't get over it: "She just *sat* there," it says, "while I dumped it out. Hardly even *looked* at it, plannin', and even flirtin' with me!" Much as she likes savoring the Texan's distress, she seems not to be thinking about the distress she's bringing to Sam. But of course if she did think of it, she might not be able to bring it to him. Nor, for the same reason, can she afford to recognize the daddy identity Sam shares with the odious Cassidy—or with Lowery, her boss. "A girl works for you ten years," exclaims the Lowery voice in her head, "you *trust* her!" So she's fucked him too. *Good.* (Ten years!)

She's in Hitchcock's world now—no longer in that "normal," on-the-surface world she's used to commanding without question or qualm. She has a guilty secret, and a lot of deep bad feeling, dimly registered but powerful and controlling. Neither Miss America nor the girl-next-door any longer, she's stolen something—she's entered into lawlessness, and momentousness, and escaped banality. Like Tippi Hedren's thieving heroine in *Marnie* (1964)—a real Miss Priss, busy at her desk, sitting posture-perfect at her office typewriter, where she can eye the company safe and plan her big score, while Hitchcock's camera circles her adoringly. Like Marnie, Marion has become a subverter of the same conventions she appears to embody so well, a covert challenger to the daddies who run things—and improbably "glamorous" as a result.

She's also, at first, very much out of her depth. She's lost the assured manner we've been observing—the mixture of obeisance and condescension she normally offers to the men around her. She's awkward and furtive, arousing the suspicions of a highway patrolman, and then so unnerving a used-car salesman that he almost declines to sell her the car. Marion is so accustomed to making the right effect, it seems, that she hardly knows how far she's missing it. "Am I acting as if there's something wrong?" she challenges the cop. "Frankly, yes," he says. And she really is. What she is doing is clearly crazy—"a temporary madness," she later calls it. But then we know exactly why she needs to do it: the *emotional* logic is clear and inarguable.

So she drives on: the passing headlights blind her. The rain does too. The windshield wipers falter. And the upsetting soundtrack music pounds

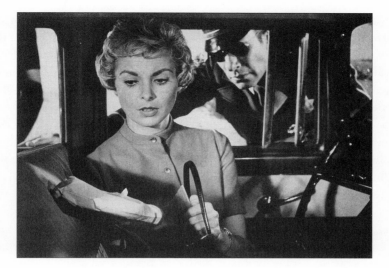

"Am I acting as if there's something wrong?": Janet Leigh in *Psycho*
(Mort Mills is the cop.)

and swells, rising to a commotion that turns out to be the prelude to a sudden silence, only the sound of the rain and the windshield wipers, as she eases the car onto a side road and toward a distant light, barely visible between the swipings of the wiper blades, and a neon sign that says BATES MOTEL. The car rolls to a stop. *This* place is quiet. And empty too. Ever since they moved the highway, says the desk clerk and manager, Norman Bates (Anthony Perkins). "I thought I'd gotten off the main road," says Marion, as she signs in. And that's exactly what she's done—even what she meant to do.

When she admits she's sort of hungry after her drive, Norman invites her up to the house to have something. He'll come back and get her when it's ready—"with my trusty umbrella," he adds, his voice breaking with pleasure and excitement. Who could blame him? She is so lovely and so nice. And he is all boyish eagerness. Except that this is a boy (a young man, really) who can't say the word "bathroom" in her presence when he's showing her her room. It's in the background of the shot, the door open and the light on, glowing like a spaceship in its whiteness: "And that's the, uh—" he says. "The bathroom," says Marion, helpfully. He concedes it is.

So it is clear to Marion that there's Something Wrong with him—to say the least. She smiles at him: certainly nothing she can't handle. For the first time since she's left Phoenix, we can see she's regained her aplomb. More than that: Norman is the first person we've seen her with who hasn't impinged on her in some threatening personal way, who isn't somehow involved in her dilemma. He is someone she can be *disinterestedly* nice to—and she is. Their unexpected encounter frees her to be generous and friendly, impulses that seem natural to her but that we haven't seen much of up to now. It's like a revelation of her final attractiveness—a fulfillment of something that's been held back since that first tense scene in the hotel room. And it's a relief—in spite of all the ominous portents of the Bates Motel itself, and not excluding the fact that Norman is distinctly odder than he ought to be, in spite of his charm. But in a movie with a Sam in it, that kind of charm—a function of shyness and uncertainty—is bound to register strongly.

He goes to the towering, haunted-looking house on the hill behind the motel and leaves Marion to unpack in her room. But through her open window (the rain has stopped at last) comes the obscene voice of Norman's mother berating him—for his wanting to bring a woman "home" with him, for his "cheap erotic fancies," and so on. Marion listens reluctantly (too loud *not* to listen), embarrassed and half turned away. And when Norman comes back down from the house with a tray of food, she is standing in her doorway. "I'm afraid I caused you some trouble," she says, emphasizing the "you," defusing the situation as best she can. Norman responds gratefully, and with characteristic verbal delicacy declares that his mother "isn't quite herself today"—a remark that reveals its full mischief (by now it's famous) only to those who've seen the movie before. "I wish you could apologize for other people," he says, holding the tray and visibly suffering. Marion comes to his rescue: since he's brought the food they may as well eat it, she says. But he hesitates at the moment he's about to step into her motel room. She is still in the doorway, arms crossed, and smiling at him. "Well?" she says, as he stands with the tray. And for the first time, we notice her condescension, and a certain amusement she shows in her control of him, her control of the situation. Instead, he suggests they eat in another room, the one behind his office—and he turns away to go there. Marion shrugs, smiles to herself, and follows him along the porch to the office door.

But when she gets there, and pauses at the doorway (in the foreground of a close shot) to look back over her shoulder and up at the sky and to remark that the rain has stopped, while Norman (in the background of the same shot) stands with his tray in front of the darkness of the *second* doorway inside, we get the sense of *another* kind of control: in the sudden power of Norman's unmasked presence, in the force of his longing as he looks at her at the precise moment she's not looking at *him*. The moment passes;

she turns and follows him into the
inner room—and into what turns
out to be the richest, most extraordinary sequence in the movie: a
sustained conversation in which
these two already compelling figures become almost mysteriously
large and interesting and moving.
Leigh, in a memoir, has called it
"their strange kind of love scene."
But it's also a scene where Hitchcock plumbs his own complicated
feelings about the kind of nice
American heroine Janet Leigh
represented.

"You eat like a bird," says Norman, as she slowly tears a piece of
bread. But then he adds, "Birds
really eat a tremendous lot." That
remark gets a grisly sort of
emphasis from the presence all
around the shadowed room of
mounted stuffed birds, many near

"Their strange sort of love scene"—as
Leigh later called it—is about to begin
here. With Anthony Perkins

the ceiling in full attitudes of predatory flight. Marion, sitting near a window in the midst of all this as she eats, has her give-nothing-away look:
wide-eyed, studiedly impassive, slightly dazed by the lamp she's sitting
near, whose light she must look through to see Norman, buttering her
bread, then turning to him when he speaks. She is at the left of an unbalanced, slightly low-angled medium shot (the lamp is at the right) with
lots of space above and around her. Norman is in a closer, more tightly
framed shot—also at the left, leaning forward, arms on knees, looking
steadily at her. The contrast in their seeing—her blinded look juxtaposed
to his intent gaze—turns out to be important. Hitchcock isolates them,
cutting between their respective shots: only at the beginning and the end
of the sequence do we see them in the frame together.

He doesn't really know about birds, he says—he only likes to stuff
them. Marion holds her bread in front of her, chewing thoughtfully. "A
man *should* have a hobby," she says, sagaciously, as it were. Norman sits
back, turning his face away. "It's more than a hobby," he says, stretching a
long arm out until his hand rests on a stuffed bird. "A hobby's s'posed to

pass the time—not fill it." "Is your time so empty?" she asks sympathetically, still holding her toast in front of her. Not really, he says: there's the
motel to take care of and the errands he does for his mother—"the ones she
allows I might be capable of doing," he amends with a grin. She asks him
about his friends. He looks disturbed, then blank; then, putting his hands
between his knees: "Well, a—" he says with mock solemnity, "a boy's best
friend is his mother." Marion does not reply to this, merely looking down
at the bread in her hand—a difficult case, after all.

What she's been offering him is a tactful sympathy. But the threat that
she inevitably poses to him lies in the limits of that sympathy, in the limits of Marion herself—which are sometimes in this scene almost cruelly
evoked. When she says something like "A man should have a hobby," as if
it were unbeatable wisdom (a woman, presumably, being too busy with
her house), she is really only speaking for the complacencies and fatuities
of that "normal" world Norman has so little part in. Marion may be generous and nice, but she carries the threat—for him—of conventional standards and judgments. Even if a man should have a hobby, Norman is not a
man; he is a boy—as he himself ("a boy's best friend . . .") has just
reminded her.

On the other hand, *she* is a boy's dream: not just because she is so sexy,
and in an unthreatening way, but because she is so close to the agreed-
upon ideal of the American girl—by conventional standards, a winner.
Norman's next remark reflects just such a judgment of her: "You've never
had an empty moment in your entire life, have you?" he says, grinning
broadly. She looks down at her toast. "Only my share," she replies softly,
with the dignity she usually musters for such questions. She is less ready
for his next one, when he asks her where she is going and what she is running away from. "Why do you ask *that?*" He shrugs, not pressing her, but
launching into an extended, excited, and very disturbing speech about
how we are all in our "private traps," how we think we can run from them
or get out of them, but we can't. Marion is struck. "Sometimes," she says
with a sigh, "we deliberately step into those traps." For her—a positive
thinker, as you knew she would be—"private traps" are something you
choose to get into, and so can choose to leave as well. But of course the
whole force of the movie is behind Norman's meaning, not hers.

But then something remarkable happens. Norman says that he was
born in his trap, and that he really doesn't mind it anymore. "Oh, but you
should," says Marion with sudden feeling, "—you *should* mind it!" Almost
the first response in the movie she hasn't hesitated before making, it just
comes out—so spontaneously, so directly and genuinely concerned for *him,*

that it's touching. And just when we had been noticing in their exchanges how often she misses the point—how much more Norman "sees" than she does—we are surprised by a larger point, and it's just the one she makes here: far different from Norman's glib and rather complacent pessimism, and "truer" as well. One *should* mind, of course—one should always mind what causes suffering. And her openness of feeling is very winning—as opposed to his caginess. But then, just as we have been surprised by her, so we are by him now—by his answer to her. "Oh, I do [mind]," he says— then, with a wide but sheepish grin: "But I say I don't." The little boy again—open, artless, engaging. It's the closest they will come to coming together. And it *doesn't* feel negligible—only hopeless.

And it encourages Marion to try for something more. She is in profile, looking toward the same sort of window she'd earlier heard Norman's "mother" through, so upsettingly. "You know," she begins, slowly and carefully, still looking toward the window, "if anyone ever spoke to *me* the way I heard—the way she spoke to you . . ." She doesn't finish: on these last words Hitchcock cuts back to Norman, who is suddenly *not* smiling. And who is reframed very dramatically: an extreme low angle, placing him in profile under one of his fierce mounted birds of prey in full wingspread above him. But the anger he gives words to in this shot—to your relief—is for his mother, not Marion. As he talks, and Hitchcock cuts back to Marion, she is reframed in a closer shot—and looking startled but *very* still. He would like to go away and leave his mother, he says, but he can't because she is ill. "She *sounded* strong," says Marion dryly in a small voice—still in her close-up, wide-eyed and watchful, chewing thoughtfully, the bread held at an angle in front of her. "No," says Norman, "I mean *ill* . . ." And he tells the story of the onset of his mother's madness. When first his father, and then the man who succeeded him in her bed, both died, she had nothing left, he says. "Except you," says intrepid Marion, persisting. "A son is a poor substitute for a lover," he replies, with a grown-up bitterness that seems almost to come from another person. But it's a reply that says as much about his present relation to Marion as any past one with his mother.

What *really* sets him off, however, is Marion's rather nervous suggestion after this that it might be better if his mother were, as she says it, "put . . . someplace." He just looks at her, in close-up—then leans forward ominously: he wants to know if she means "an institution," a subject he seems to know a suspicious lot about, as he goes on, angrily. Marion, in an even tighter close-up now, looks glassy-eyed with apprehension: sitting folded in on herself, her arms crossed, one hand moving absently on her upper arm as he talks. She apologizes carefully: "I didn't mean it to sound uncaring," she says. But this prissy platitudinousness only inflames him the more. She was only concerned for him, she persists—she meant well. It doesn't help: people *always* mean well, he says. But then he subsides—threateningly. He leans forward again. After all, he says, with exaggerated reasonableness, his mother is not a *maniac*. "She just goes a little mad sometimes. We all go a little mad sometimes." Then, sitting back again, genial and expansive, smiling at her: "Haven't you?" he says—inviting her.

He knows the answer, of course. It's some sort of madness that's given this delegate from the outside world her passport into his. Now she thinks she can revoke it—being Marion, being someone who "minds." But Norman knows better. So does Hitchcock—so do we. "Yes," she answers, her eyes dropping, looking into herself, as it were, "sometimes just one time can be enough." She looks up at him. "Thank you," she says, by way of concluding their chat. He corrects her: "Thank you, *Norman,*" he says, the familiar boyish grin reappearing. Except that the smile now—like the correction it comes with—is a social one. And *very* nasty.

And it's a terrible moment—it feels like a violence, as real as the ones ahead, this sudden condescension of him to her. He's taken her measure—and she won't do. So that when she then rises to leave and he asks her if she can't stay and talk some more, it's not (as before) the pressure of his loneliness that we feel behind his words, but something close to playfulness. Because even though he'd still like her to stay and talk with him, he's discovered he doesn't *need* her to—and Hitchcock makes that recognition seem quite awful. She'll be leaving early in the morning, she tells him: she has stepped into a trap of her own and she wants to get out, she adds cryptically. She is standing over him as she says all this and he looks up at her: "Really?" he says, with the same nasty smile. And so they part.

But he still desires her: he can't get past that. He watches her through a peephole in the wall (an upsettingly "beautiful" extreme close-up of his eyeball and lashes in profile) as she undresses for a shower. And when she is in the shower—the thing that no audience quite "expects" even when they know it's coming (as nearly everyone does by now)—"Mother" rushes in and slashes her to death, in that famously artful, now legendary montage that culminates in the extraordinary close-up image of Marion's dead staring eye on the floor of the shower and the camera's slow track into its sightlessness.

In a way, it's all there beforehand—in that moment I've just described. He's "killed" her before, when he gave her that boyish smile. His impotence is a torment; it means there could never be anything more between them, of course, than what they've achieved here. He can't have her, so he feels superior to her—transforming a sexual emotion into a reflex of contempt. That's not exactly, of course, an unknown human strategy. But Hitchcock here makes us feel its special awfulness. The wit and sudden power of the moment (like the "Battle Hymn of the Republic"'s "terrible swift sword") make you register the moral discrimination, both radical and delicate at once, at an almost visceral level. It's like the moment in *Vertigo* when Scotty says, "Your hair"—and like that moment too (where we share Scotty's obsessiveness), Norman's little smile of dismissal makes us complicitous: we do, after all, understand the contempt, not just as a displaced longing, but as a reasonable response. By this point, we are closer, however uneasily, to Norman than to her.

The second half of the movie is devoted to finding him out, to unmasking him and his "mother" and stopping them. So the surviving people in the film have to solve the puzzle of Marion's disappearance. This is undertaken first by an amiable private detective named Arbogast (Martin Balsam)—and then taken up, when *he* disappears too ("Mother" strikes again), by Sam and Marion's sister, Lila (Vera Miles). Eventually these two trap and expose Norman—surprising him in his Mother costume, with knife upraised and preparing to kill again.

It's in this second half that *Psycho* becomes a somewhat more routine sort of thriller. But hardly a routine experience: Hitchcock's orchestration of anxiety and surprise and shock effects (like "Mother"'s ambush of Arbogast on the stairs) never lets up. And the movie was an unparalleled sensation on its first release in 1960. No one could be admitted once it had begun, an unprecedented policy for theatres and strictly enforced. Reviewers and publicists were enjoined not to give away anything at all about the story and its events (Hitchcock in the movie's trailer tells more than anyone else did, in fact), so that the entire audience in those days was on the same roller-coaster ride together, on the same stomach-plunging turns and drops, unsure where it was going from moment to moment. *Psycho* was the intensest sort of *audience* experience at a movie that most people had ever had—just at a time, ironically, when the larger American movie audience was breaking up and breaking down, irrevocably.

But then *Psycho* itself is an experience of breakup, a terrifying vision of emptiness and anomie. That is something that is implicit in even its biggest and most daring surprise, the main reason (as everyone understood) for keeping its secrets ahead of time: the "premature" death of Janet Leigh, the heroine and top-billed star. Now *that* had never been done before—as Hitchcock loved to point out. If you want to shake an audience up, that would do it. Though not without consequence, to say the least, to the rest of the movie. Whatever the final impact of that "strange kind of love scene" between her and Norman, we have become intensely, almost uncannily, caught up with Marion, in her feelings and experience, so lovingly and minutely observed, up to her death. Hitchcock has been fascinated with her: so have we.

Her disappearance from the film even changes our experience of Norman. Once she is gone, he loses his odd sort of authority—becoming furtive and cornered and hunted down, once the movie becomes committed to "catching" and finally "explaining" him. Instead of the genuinely mysterious figure he had been, he becomes a generic one: the Dangerous Madman. And the conventional pair who then step into the hero-and-heroine roles—Sam, the empty-suit hunk, and Lila, a harder-edged version of Marion herself—are not only unappealing but relatively characterless, becoming more so, it seems, the more we see of them. Until at the end they sit stony-faced and all but ignored on the sidelines, listening with the rest of us to the smug, fat-faced police psychologist (Simon Oakland) who gives a self-important and ludicrously pat "explanation" of why Norman turned into his mother and became a murderer.

Although Martin Balsam's Arbogast, the dumpy and unglamorous private eye who first traces Marion to the Bates Motel, has some of the distinctiveness and vitality we miss in the other surviving characters, he too is quickly—and sickeningly—killed: like Marion, and again by "Mrs. Bates." It's as though Hitchcock intended to depopulate the movie, so that for almost half its length there would be no leading or sympathetic or genuinely interesting character. It's a radical program. If we don't quite register it as that—at least not right away—it's because the thriller mechanism has revved up. The excitement grows and grows. But so do the feelings underneath of desolation and sadness. The effect is of a kind of agitated emptiness. "Life goes on," as we say. The resolution of the crime of Marion's death (and Arbogast's) diverts us from the fact of it. But the movie never really does recover from it. As the imagery of its final frames reminds us: not the usual and formulaic scenes of comforting conclusion—i.e., Sam and Lila getting together romantically, the police psychiatrist wearily but triumphantly closing his file, familiar stuff like that—but instead, Norman alone in his cell, with his dead mother's voice inhabiting him wholly at last, as his face in close-up turns into a death's head, which dissolves in turn into Marion rising from the grave, as it were, in the trunk of a car (her own) being hoisted from the swamp. *Psycho* is the only film I know of that could be described as both—and at the same time—exciting and inconsolable.

Hitchcock was once asked (as famous men used conventionally to be) what words he wanted on his gravestone. His answer was: THIS IS WHAT WE DO TO BAD LITTLE BOYS. A serious joke. He was *not* a positive thinker. He

Hitchcock, with his "Marian," on the set

was as apart from the America of his time as his movies, at their best, invite us to be. But he felt that apartness, like many of us, partly as a superiority, partly as a disqualification—or an impotence. It's this complication of attitude and self-judgment that helps to account, I think, for the odd and special power of *Psycho:* the *second* Hitchcock movie where the heroine "dies" prematurely—that is, in the middle of the film. In *Vertigo,* however, there is no possible distraction from the loss, only an intensified obsession with it. And a hopeless one: not only because of Judy's criminality and commonness, but because even at her most Madeleine-like, she will always be—with her needs, and her longing to be loved "for herself"—a sentimentalized version of Madeleine, just as Madeleine can be seen as a transcendent, almost religious version of *her.* But the spirit of *Psycho* is very different: slyer, more malicious, more "secular."

Obviously, Marion is no noir woman, in spite of her crime (this movie will show her what a *real* crime is). "A man should have a hobby": she is really in the line of Midge and Ann and even Susie (she is, after all, "Janet Leigh"), in her simplicity and at-homeness in the world, in her refusal of glamour and obliqueness, in her essential niceness, in her optimism and essential conformity—the secular virtues of the American girl. But hers is a spirit and a temperament that Hitchcock is debarred from. Quite unlike Welles, Hitchcock feels the removal painfully. *Psycho* is partly and importantly a meditation on that removal—on the human insufficiency behind it.

Eight

THE BIG HEAT

Noir movies, with their shadows and angles, tended to stylize reality. But the new trend in postwar Hollywood was toward greater realism, especially in thrillers—toward location filming, and seemingly new forms like the "semi-documentary." That name was coined in 1945 to describe 20th Century–Fox's *House on 92nd Street,* an espionage "true story" set in New York, produced by Louis de Rochemont (of the *March of Time* news shorts) without stars, and a surprise hit. More followed, in the same hyperrealistic mode—the movie that looked like a newsreel: Elia Kazan's *Boomerang* (1947), Henry Hathaway's *13 Rue Madeleine* (1947) and his *Call Northside 777* (1948), among others. It was director Jules Dassin—then on contract to Universal—who made the most sudden and radical adjustment to the new trend, going in the same few months (in 1947) from the extreme noir mannerism of *Brute Force,* a prison picture, to the unmediated head-on views of real New York places and streets in *The Naked City,* a *policier,* again with no stars—and a *very* big hit. And so the set-bound thrillers still being made—like Michael Curtiz's *The Unsuspected* (1947), Edmund Goulding's *Nightmare Alley* (1947), Douglas Sirk's *Sleep My Love* (1948)—were getting to seem like something from another era.

But there were hybrids, too: semi-documentary noirs—combining the real and the unreal, as it were. Like Anthony Mann's *T-Men* (1948), about a couple of treasury agents (Dennis O'Keefe and Alfred Ryder) going under-cover in a counterfeiting ring. The movie stakes its claim to authenticity by opening (as these films often did) with a real government bureaucrat sitting behind his desk and droning into the camera about "the film you are about to see." The case is a "composite," he tells us, drawn from several such in the Treasury files, and so forth. Until the talking-head shot gives way to a postcard view of the Treasury building (the same shot also ends the film), and the voice of the narrator (just like in the newsreels) takes over, recurring regularly then through the movie. All the signs in place, then: this is no trivial fiction, but a real and worthwhile account from the "files."

But then what we see is more like a dream (even those reassuring bulletins from the narrator can't change that). Everything, it seems, goes on at night, and Robert Alton's gleaming black-and-white photography, with its tilted spaces and skewed perspectives, its vertiginous diagonals veering off into deep-focus backgrounds, gives you the feeling of an epidemic corruption. The government agents, of course, are incorruptible, if not invincible. But since they are disguised as crooks, the "normal world" they are presumably defending—their homes, families, etc.—has no real presence in the film. Unless we count those glimpses of the Treasury building. The action mostly takes place in long dark alleys, shabby rooms lit by overhead bulbs, a steambath, a harbor and its dock, the passageways of the labyrinthine cargo ship where the Big Boss, the ring's mastermind and chief, waits to settle with them all at the end. That this nemesis figure should turn out to be when we see her—even in this nearly all-male film—a young and glamorous woman (Jane Randolph), seductive and executive at once, made for a familiar sort of surprise at the time. But was *she* in the Treasury files? Probably not. The noir impulse in these movies had many ways of co-opting the documentary one.

But in the fifties, the documentary style won out. Thrillers—like the country itself—were moving to the suburbs. Where the favorite locale of the crime story had almost always been New York, or its unnamed rough equivalent in urban atmosphere, now it was Los Angeles—as in Robert Aldrich's *Kiss Me Deadly* (1955) or Stanley Kubrick's *The Killing* (1956). And where New York had been created in the studios, Los Angeles was the real thing. And the look of fifties noir—with its shootouts on freeways, its heists of parking-lot banks—was daylight and sunlit. It was the look of new cities that didn't—unlike the towering and crumbling older ones—aspire to anything beyond comfort and convenience and bright light. But in the best sort of thrillers—movies like Aldrich's and Kubrick's and Phil Karlson's *The Brothers Rico* (1957)—this brightness felt more ominous than ever. The threat *now* seemed to be everywhere. And the private eye, when he appeared (less and less frequently)—as with Ralph Meeker's Mike Hammer in *Kiss Me Deadly*—was a balls-up character, utterly out of his depth. We needed the FBI, or the DA, or the police at least—institutional heroes, to fight institutional enemies, like organized crime, or corrupt local government, or international crime rings, or the Reds at home. These institutional-style thrillers often *tried* to be reassuring—just as those talking-head prologues were meant to be ("We have this under control")—and rarely were. "Never get the people stirred up," says the mob boss in *The Big Heat*. "They start doing things." But in fact—as this and other movies seem to show—the people don't do anything. Depend on *them* and you're really done for. And even when they *can* be roused, the evil is only partially stanched at the end—a cancer in remission only—as in Phil Karlson's *The Phenix City Story* (1955), about mob control and municipal corruption, and one of the decade's most harrowing thrillers.

In any case, it's no place for a woman. These are movies about men, and about power struggles between men, with women relegated to the background roles of wives, girlfriends, mothers. And the noir heroine, as we knew her, is on the wane. Fifties noir is less about men being seduced than about their being bullied—by other men.

The greatest of these films—the one with the keenest insights into the ways power feels and works—is Fritz Lang's *The Big Heat* (1953), with a script by Sydney Boehm. Glenn Ford is the cop who comes up against the mob and its boss, the immensely powerful Lagana (Alexander Scourby) and his henchman Vince Stone (Lee Marvin)—the people who really run the (unnamed) city. Including (as it turns out) the police department that Dave Bannion (Ford) works for.

A high-ranking police official named Duncan has shot himself in his living room—but without, apparently, leaving a note of any kind. His widow, Bertha Duncan (Jeanette Nolan, Orson Welles's Lady Macbeth) is grieving rather showily in her room when Bannion, the cop on the case, comes to question her. She says her husband was secretly but terminally ill. Bannion clearly doesn't like this woman, but he has no reason to disbelieve her until he gets a call at the station from a B-girl named Lucy Chapman (Dorothy Green), who wants to talk to him about Duncan. Bannion meets her at the nightclub she works at, and she tells him that she was Duncan's mistress. He wasn't ill and he wasn't depressed, she says, but he *was* planning to leave his wife for her. Lucy can't believe that it was really a suicide, but Bannion, of course, knows that it was. Anyway, he is fairly suspicious, even a bit contemptuous, of his barfly informant, suspecting her of setting up a shakedown. But when he goes back for another talk with Mrs. Duncan, she reacts by ordering him out of her house. We know by now what Bannion doesn't: that Duncan had been on Lagana's payroll, that Bertha has the suicide note confessing to this (she finds it by the body in the movie's opening scene) and is now using it to force Lagana both to pay and to protect her.

Back at the station, Bannion is in big trouble. His boss, a lieutenant (he's a sergeant), has orders to relay from the police commissioner himself: Bannion is to stay away from Mrs. Duncan. But then some cops find Lucy Chapman's body, thrown from a car on the highway. She was killed, appar-

ently, right after talking to Bannion—so brutally that the police patholo-
gist calls it a sex crime: "You saw the cigarette burns?" "Yeah, I saw them,"
replies Bannion. Then, under his voice: "Every single one of them."

And they don't want him snooping around the Lucy Chapman murder
case, either. But he does anyway. Until soon, his wife, Katie (Jocelyn
Brando), with their little girl clinging to her mother's skirt, gets a threatening phone call. That does it for Bannion—Lagana's strong-arm stuff
reaching into his home! In a rage, he drives off to the big man's suburban
estate. Do you like this job? he asks the uniformed cop on duty outside. "I
do what I'm told" is the reply. The one Bannion expected: "That's what
we're all supposed to do, isn't it?" he says. And barges inside.

Lagana can't believe it. "You came *here?*" he says, "To my house—about
a *murder?*" And some house: they meet in the high-ceilinged, Tudor style,
wood-paneled library, below a portrait over the fireplace of Lagana's
deceased mother ("A great old lady . . . She never got over being surprised
at my success"), with a formal dance party for his teenage daughter taking
place in the room across the vast front hall. And this lowly cop is accusing
and "warning" the boss of the city; he even slugs Vince, when he comes in
to do his job. But Bannion doesn't care: he is so angry that even Lagana
seems a touch impressed with him. Anger is power in this movie, and Bannion almost always has more of it than anyone.

Foolhardy as he can be, it's the sort of thing she loves him for, his wife,
Katie, tells him—his refusal to compromise, even when everyone else
does. She is afraid, of course, but she can't tell him to stop. She tells him all
this just before she goes out to their car in the driveway to pick up their
baby-sitter, while Bannion is in the little girl's bedroom telling her about
the Three Little Kittens. But Lagana's goons have had the car wired, and
when Katie starts it, it blows up. Bannion pulls her body from the burning
wreck. Fade-out.

And the most shocking thing in the movie so far is the little smile we
see on his face, in close-up, in the next scene (no time for mourning in this
film). He's in the office of the police commissioner (Howard Wendell), a
walrus-faced little man with a salesman's élan—whom we realize we've
seen before this: playing cards with Lagana's "boys" in Vince Stone's apartment. The commissioner offers his heartfelt sympathies, instructing Bannion's boss, Lieutenant Wilkes (Willis Bouchey), who is also present, to
work his police force night and day until they find the person or persons
who killed Mrs. Bannion—probably someone, he supposes, that Sergeant
Bannion sent up once, getting revenge now. "Is that what you think too?"
inquires Bannion, with his little smile, turning to Wilkes. Wilkes is

embarrassed and evasive. Once again, that's just the answer Bannion expected; just as the commissioner has made the suggestion Bannion expected (someone he sent up did it). Hence his little smile. And pretty soon, he is denouncing both the commissioner and Wilkes, and storming out, leaving his badge and his job behind. In the next scene, as he is closing up the house he shared with Katie, a cop friend accuses him of being "on a hate binge" and advises him (your heart sinks) to "see Father Masterson."

But he doesn't. Not in *this* movie. Bannion's anger is too enlivening— for all of us. Says the same cop friend to Dave: "You can't set yourself against the world and get away with it." No, but you can try—if you're transfigured by rage the way Dave Bannion is, both sick with it and glowing from it. Like this movie—even when it's quiet. The wit and knowingness of an earlier noir movie like *Out of the Past* have devolved in this one to that sick little smile on Bannion's face. As well as (in another key) to that image (one of the movie's most powerful) of Bannion in the flames, locked in a Sisyphean contortion—pushing with one arm and pulling with the other—against the immovable car door his wife is trapped behind.

But the rage in this movie is always threatening to be out of control (Bannion looks disturbingly at home in those flames). You get onto the high of the movie's anger, but then you sort of dread the payback: the violence you *can't* get high on, that you almost even don't want to know about—almost as if it's directed at you, in a way. And that happens often here: all the movie's significant violence involves squirm-inducing episodes of burning people's flesh—as in Katie's death, or Lucy Chapman's cigarette burns. Then soon to come is a scene in the nightclub where Vince puts his cigar out on the hand of the girl running the twenty-one table (he doesn't like the way she handles the dice)—all of them rising to the truly horrific moment when Vince throws a pot of scalding hot coffee in his girlfriend's face. (Probably the most upsetting single shot in the movie for most audiences is the one just before this: a close-up of the coffee in a rolling boil.)

Vince is a malignant scum. But Mike Lagana—the movie makes clear—is even worse, remaining comfortably remote and detached from the horror he directs ("You came *here*? To my house—about a *murder*?"). Vince, at least, must bear the day-to-day burden of his own malignancy— that can't be easy, after all, even for him. But the Laganas of the criminal world—like the Henry Kissingers of our governmental one—inspire a special kind of rage: the ones who never have to see or smell the burning flesh, or even look at the scars. It has nothing to do with *them;* they hardly even take it in, after a while. It's Dave Bannion's particular heroism then

Bannion in the flames: Glenn Ford in Lang's *The Big Heat*

that he *looks,* directly and steadily: "Yeah, I saw them . . . Every single one of them."

And it makes him a little crazy. Certainly Lagana thinks he is. What else do you think about someone who invades the well-guarded home of the most dangerous and powerful man in the city in order to threaten him to his face and to beat up his bodyguard? And yet—for us—if Bannion seems enlarged by his anger, he never seems really endangered by it. The script offers an explanation for this (Lagana claims early on that it would "stir up too many headlines" to do Bannion in), but it's not a very convincing one.

Curiously, it's only *women* in this movie (including Bannion's little girl) that you feel directed to worry about, to feel a kind of continuing apprehension for. In fact (until Vince's girlfriend takes her revenge at the climax), it's only women who get hurt or killed—who pay for helping or talking to Bannion (it's always women who do help him). The only one who seems to escape retribution for it is an elderly secretary in a junkyard office, Selma Parker (Edith Evanson), who gives Bannion a name after her boss (a man, of course) has refused to do so out of fear. But then she is *already* crippled—walking with a leg brace and cane.

This pattern of female vulnerability has a notable exception: Bertha

The women's world of *The Big Heat:* the spinster (above),
the widow (below), the bar girl (opposite page)—among others.
They are Selma Parker (Edith Evanson), Bertha Duncan
(Jeanette Nolan), and Lucy Chapman (Dorothy Green), respectively.

Duncan, who is invulnerable because Mike Lagana protects her (if any-thing "happens" to her, her late husband's suicide note will go to the papers) but also because she is one tough lady. After reading the suicide note while standing over Duncan's body (glancing at it with distaste, as if to say, "You *would* write something like this"), she instantly calls Lagana and orders his boys to wake the boss up. And they do. The next time we see her is when the cops come to investigate. She is in her bedroom, touch-ing up her face in front of the three-paneled mirror on her dressing table—just before Bannion comes in to question her for the first time. She is wearing a tatty bathrobe, her hair gathered into a shapeless, reproachful clump on top of her head. She directs Bannion to the cheery, chintz-curtained window seat, while she sits sufferingly in a chair against the wall (good enough for *her*) and talks about her husband-that-was ("many friends," "clean and wholesome," etc.) like a proper grieving widow, with Lang's camera moving discreetly but exploringly around her. Bannion's close-ups, however, show that he is repelled by her—just as we are, of course.

But then he seems repelled by Lucy Chapman too—as we are not. Where Bertha Duncan—with her imperious eyes and tight thin mouth—has the look of someone who simply refuses misfortune of any kind, Lucy Chapman is clearly someone who attracts it. Like Bertha, she is dark and fortyish and small. But her widely spaced eyes, big and moist and full of hurt, are crossed with an ominous shadow in the close-ups of her scene with Bannion. And in that lighting, the skull-like shape of her face is as disturbing as the spaniel eyes. A loser but not a liar. That's not how Bannion reads her, however. A barfly and a B-girl, after all—why should he believe her?

That's his righteousness—which is a problem through the whole movie, even when he *is* right. Even his early confrontation with Lagana makes you pull back from him a bit, satisfying as it is. But even in the nature of these narrative satisfactions, this one feels too soon, too much. After all, shouldn't it occur to Bannion that he's endangering his own family by threatening Lagana and his? And there is a disturbing element of personal resentment in the tirade—a note that comes easily to Glenn Ford with his permanent air of curdled boyishness—when he taunts Lagana about "your immaculate home" being "no place for a stinkin' cop" like himself. Early on you get the sense that Bannion may be brave and incorruptible but is probably not as smart as the movie he's in.

Perhaps not even as smart as Debby (Gloria Grahame), Vince Stone's live-in girlfriend. Vince keeps her in his penthouse apartment, where he holds his poker games with his buddies (the commissioner included) and plays host to Lagana's imperial visits. None of this has much to do with Debby. She drinks and goes shopping and makes jokes that no one else in the room seems to appreciate. Since her jokes are all more or less about the way Vince sucks up to his boss, it's safest to ignore them. She's bored, and not at all thrilled with the company she keeps. But as she "explains" to Bannion later on: "I been rich and I been poor—*believe* me, rich is better." She's a realist: "You'll never get anywhere in this town without liking Vince," she also tells him. ("I'm not trying to get anywhere." "*That's* obvious.")

As those Vince-and-Lagana jokes of hers show, Debby in the end probably knows more about how power works than Bannion does. It's not just a matter of being afraid of someone but of being really *impressed* by him: the way Vince is impressed by Lagana, and the way the boys are impressed by Vince, and so on. It's a religion of bully worshipers, and she is the only unbeliever on the premises. Even Lagana gets put on by her when he visits—though he is only dimly, if uneasily, aware of it. She invites him to talk about his teenage daughter, whom he dotes on. He tells her about how the girl's "going out formal" on a date with a football player—how grownup she suddenly is, and so forth. "Oh, sometimes the father means more than the football players—they come and go, but Dad's around for keeps," says Debby, in her "cutest," chirpiest voice and manner, looking at Vince for approval when she finishes. Lagana says stiffly that he certainly hopes his daughter feels like that. But when Debby leaves the room (an order from Vince), he blames Vince for her unsettling behavior. He lets her drink too much: "She's a young girl, Vince," he reminds him. Always the father.

What seems to sustain Debby in this bind—apart from the clothes and money and booze—is the sight of herself in the mirror. She never passes one, it seems, without stopping to have a long look. That's when the guys in the apartment seem to come on to her, coming up beside her: joining her in the glass so they can *both* look. "That's a real pretty kisser," says Vince at one such time. "Isn't it?" she says complacently, without looking away. She doesn't look at herself the way Bertha Duncan does, or Vince's sidekick Larry does (arranging his hair and his tie before greeting Lagana)—to prepare a face for those others. Debby's face is who she is—it's her essential value in a world of power arrangements, where "Dad's around for keeps."

The first time in the movie she really looks *at* someone else is at the club by the bar—after Vince has put his cigar out on the girl's hand, causing a commotion in which Bannion intervenes. At the sound of his voice—he is challenging one of Vince's thugs ("Where yuh goin', thief?" says Bannion, planting his hand on the gorilla's shoulder, while Vince, Debby sitting next to him on a stool, slumps over his drink at the bar, now hoping not to be noticed)—she turns (in close-up), with one eloquent eyebrow lifted, and looks, over Vince's back, at Bannion. Who now turns to Vince: "You like workin' girls over, doncha?" he says to Vince's back. But in the image of the two men's standoff—Vince's hunched and resisting back at frame left, Bannion's angry profile at right—it's Debby's reaction that Lang centers the shot on, placing her in the light between them, with that raised eyebrow, looking at Bannion.

She seems never to have thought anyone could actually stand up to the Vinces of the world—not the world she knew. It's an eyebrow raiser, so to speak. She walks out on Vince and trails after Bannion, trying to pick him up. She succeeds, but only because he wants to question her. He doesn't succeed—she didn't come to his hotel room to do *that,* she tells him—and goes home to Vince. But someone has squealed on *her* (Larry, the guy she's been turning down) and Vince is waiting for her with that boiling coffee. After that, she is back in Bannion's room—a concealing bandage over the left side of her face—ready to help him get the goods on Vince and Lagana and the whole bunch.

But Bannion doesn't know how to do that, *even* with her help. It's Mrs. Duncan, and she alone, who holds the evidence (her husband's posthumous confession). And as long as she's safe, so is Lagana. It's this frustration that

Debby (Gloria Grahame) baiting the boss, Lagana (Alexander Scourby)—
who worries that she drinks too much—while Vince (Lee Marvin, at right),
her nervous boyfriend, looks on (Adam Williams as Larry at left)

prompts Bannion to visit Bertha and even threaten her—starting to choke
her at one point. Until Lagana's man arrives: "Mr. Lagana is an excellent
insurance policy," crows Bertha, as Bannion beats an ignominious retreat.
Later he tells Debby (whom he's installed in his hotel) that he almost
killed the woman. But Debby tells him he'd have been just like Vince if he
had killed her. "I don't believe you could," she says. (*We* are not so sure.)

But Debby could—and does, turning up at Bertha's front door, with
her prized mink coat on, the bandage over her face, and a revolver concealed in the coat pocket. Bertha is also in *her* mink, about to go out, but
she invites Debby in for a moment. "Were you in an accident?" Bertha
inquires sympathetically, noting the bandage. "Yes," says Debby pleasantly, and tells her what a nice house she has. Bertha knows that, of course,
but not why this woman has come to it. "I've been thinking about you and
me," says Debby, one hand holding her coat together at the throat, the
other in her pocket, "—how much alike we are." She looks Bertha up and
down and adds: "The mink-coated girls." And when Bertha, getting a little testy now, calls her "Miss Marsh," Debby insists on first names—since
"we're sisters under the mink." Bertha thinks maybe her visitor is not well,
and goes—as is her custom—to the phone to call "Mr. Lagana." Debby
tells her she never felt better, and shoots her dead.

Slapping down the bully (Vince): Debby thought it couldn't be done—
and so Bannion gets her attention when he does it.

She goes back to the penthouse and ambushes Vince, when he returns, with a face full of boiling coffee. And when he's lying on the floor moaning, she unbandages her face to show him what *he'll* look like in a while. Bannion arrives with the cops and there is a shootout in which Vince dies and Debby is mortally wounded. With Bannion leaning over her, she lies on her mink and asks him to tell her about his wife, Katie. "I like her," she says—and dies.

It's not unusual at all, of course, for a secondary character to steal a film. But it's another thing when she takes over the plot, and the case—and brings everyone to justice in the end. Especially when the hero has failed to. That is, anyway, a fair enough description (and it even leaves out her big death scene) of what Debby does in this movie. What follows her exit from it is both hasty and perfunctory. A headline: Lagana is indicted! Then a scene in the station house, Bannion back at his old desk, going cheerily out on a new case. Even the tone of all this seems to belong to another movie. And so this one ends—in this flurry of numb banalities.

And yet it feels oddly right that it should—once all the women are gone from it. After all, it's a movie about conflicts between men, between cops and mobsters, where it's *women* who settle things, who determine all the big outcomes. And not just Debby, but the even more conspicuous unfortunates, like Lucy Chapman and Selma Parker—a loser whore and a crippled spinster. Without them, Bannion wouldn't have gotten even as far as he does. And finally it's a woman who stands in his way, and another woman who defeats her. What we took for Bannion battling Lagana turns into Debby defeating Bertha.

The famously closed worlds of Lang's best films have the power they do partly because of the hidden worlds behind them—the *real* ones—that they imply: like the literal nightmare under the apparent reality of *The Woman in the Window,* unrevealed until the end, or the organized-criminal underworld of *M* (1931), which both mimics and surpasses (by bringing the child killer to trial in its own "court" when the police fail) the official world of the police. In *The Big Heat,* there's a kind of reality associated with women and their arrangements that both mocks and subverts the world of men, the power of the fathers and husbands. It's not unlike the point the romantic comedy movies once conventionally made—with the woman outsmarting the conventionally "dominant" man. But here—as in much of fifties noir—the analogous point is a much grimmer one. In the pervasive corruption, the almost holocaustal menace of the world of this movie, women are seen as primary victims. And yet, it seems, it's only the ones we make victims of who can—finally, and just possibly—save us. The power of *The Big Heat*—particularly its power to move us—comes importantly from that developing meaning.

Julie Harris and James Dean in Kazan's *East of Eden*

PART TWO

THE MEN

*You come into this world alone and you go out of it alone,
and you're going to be alone a lot of time when you're on
this earth—and what tells it all, it's the music. You tell it
to the music and the music tells it to you. And then you
know about it. You know what it was happened to you.*

— SIDNEY BECHET

*I've always felt the most important thing in acting is hon-
esty. And if you can fake that, you've got it made.*

— GEORGE BURNS

Nine

CLIFT, BRANDO, DEAN

Like the women stars, the men too got younger. But they were more surprising. For one thing, stars like Dean and Clift and Brando were sexy in ways, provocative and seductive, that had been more or less reserved for women up to then. And though their masculinity was pronounced (even overpronounced), it was inflected with an air of danger and sexual challenge and had a homoerotic charge. To be sure, there had been plenty of boyish male stars before them—like James Stewart and Henry Fonda in the thirties, Van Johnson and Robert Walker in the forties, and so on. But this new boy-hero was something different, almost like a mutation in the idea of masculinity itself—with his deep, aching vulnerability, his sensitivity and alienation, and, above all, his hunger for love.

The first time we really noticed him was in Montgomery Clift's "aggressively sexual" performance—as Pauline Kael calls it—in Hawks's *Red River* (1948). It was the first important leading-man performance to make an audience feel that a hero could have almost the same *sort* of fascination—and androgynous mystery—as a heroine: an impression that Brando and Dean would soon confirm.

Of course, the older, established men were still around, staying through the fifties and even beyond that—Cooper and Grant and Stewart (no longer a male ingenue) and Gable and Crosby et al.—and they were still major stars (John Wayne was the decade's top box-office draw). But they showed the strain—especially when asked to go through the moves of their youth again. As in MGM's hard-boiled action romance, *To Please a Lady* (1950), where the now avuncular Gable has to tell the equally mature-looking Barbara Stanwyck that "you're just another dame to me." Later on, these two dignified people must slap and bite each other as prelude to a hot close-up kiss—a scene that plays so awkwardly that it feels more like something from a Samuel Beckett scenario than a major studio movie.

There was a remedy for the men stars, however, that wasn't available to the women who were aging—i.e., vastly younger co-stars. Usually the same three, in fact: Audrey Hepburn, Grace Kelly, and Sophia Loren. Kelly held the record, appearing in her brief career (1951–56) opposite Gable, Cooper, Stewart, Grant, and Crosby—all but Wayne. This strategy led to awkwardnesses, like the portable shadow following Cooper around in *Love in the Afternoon* (1957) as he pursues Audrey Hepburn's young (and brightly lit) Parisienne. Only Grant seemed really ageless, requiring no shadows even in the sixties—until that phenomenon came to seem the point of his appearing at all, in increasingly lifeless performances. Even if he didn't *look* uncomfortable, he seems to have felt that way, and retired in 1966.

But they stayed popular and they stayed long. It's always *men* who've been the biggest movie stars. None of the women we think of as the great stars of the past—not Garbo certainly, not Davis or Bergman, not Stanwyck or Lombard, not even Marilyn Monroe—were securely popular with audiences in their own time. Women, it seems, inspired too much ambivalence; the quality that makes them "starry" can also make the audience nervous about them in the end. For one thing, they were often seen to *act*—something the enduring males rarely seemed guilty of, and when they *were,* it could be a sign of their box-office decline: hero to character actor, like Crosby in *The Country Girl* (1954) or Wayne in *True Grit* (1969). Although some, like Spencer Tracy, went on "nonacting" to the end.

Above everything else, they were *dependable,* these iconic patriarchal males—representing all that was strong and reliable and solid. They offered the kind of reassurance (it's all in control, nothing we can't handle, etc.) that was one of the feelings we went to the movies for in those days. "As certain as the sunrise," said the *New York Times* obituary of Clark Gable, "he was consistently and stubbornly all man."

He wasn't a type the movies ever tried to do without. But the newer and younger versions of him that came along in the fifties tended to be less monumental than their predecessors, less like the dream fathers we'd been used to. Sinatra, for example, was not so soothing and untroubling as Bing—nor was Dean Martin, with his blissed-out-boozer shtick. William Holden was less stoic and unflappable than Gable; Gregory Peck and Rock Hudson were less authoritative than Spencer Tracy or Gary Cooper; and so on. Robert Mitchum, of course, was in the same impassive male tradition, but he offered such an extreme of it ("Paint the eyes on my eyelids, man, and I'll walk through it") that it almost felt like something else—something slyer and wittier than a sunrise, and not at all so reliable.

Marlon Brando in the film version of
A Streetcar Named Desire

This patriarchal star embodied an antinarcissist idea of maleness. And while he never disappeared (the younger versions of him were almost as popular as the originals), his hegemony was challenged when the new teenage audience of the fifties arrived. Where only recently, it seemed, you had to be grown-up in the movies to be interesting or glamorous (even the kid movies, like the Andy Hardy series, had been about the humiliations of being one), movies *now,* instead of inviting us to grow up, were commiserating with us about failing to. And the exciting new Clift-Brando hero, far from being "consistently and stubbornly all man," was partly a boy—*that* was the stubborn part of him. Instead of being the ur-father we went to movies to see, *he* was looking for him too, as it turned out—generally without much success.

Like Paul Newman, who was hyped as "the second Brando," starting out in all the requisite Brando-type roles: the sensitive jock (*Somebody Up There Likes Me,* 1956), the sexy interloper (*The Long Hot Summer,* 1958), the rebel "delinquent" (*The Left-Handed Gun,* 1958), and so on. In his second film, *The Rack* (1956) he was an ex-POW in the Korean War, on trial for collaborating with the enemy (Communist "brainwashing" was a big public concern at the time). His own testimony, before his military judges, climaxes with the revelation that his father, a four-star general played by Walter Pidgeon—one of the most reserved and monumental of the older stars (Mr. Miniver, Pierre Curie)—had never kissed him, even when he was a boy. His lawyer, Edmond O'Brien, offers this as ultimate explanation for the defendant's failure of character in the POW camp: *we* are guilty, he says; we have failed our young men by leaving them "uninspired and uninformed," "virtually ignorant of communism," and depriving

The Rack: Anne Francis is the fiancée, Paul Newman the troubled
Korean War vet, and Walter Pidgeon his father the general.

them of "the warmth" they needed "along the way" (to Korea, apparently). It's no wonder they can't stand up to the Commies. The hero
finally does get that kiss—a scene in the back seat of the general's limo
(Pidgeon is visibly embarrassed, but he is a pro)—but he also gets court-
martialed and convicted: an outcome that's assured once he breaks down
on the witness stand and accuses himself, demanding to be punished, in
the final scene.

As movies like this one showed, we had a lot of uneasiness and ambivalence about this new, not-so-reliable boy-man—not *blaming* him exactly
(we were too "understanding" for that), but still hoping he'd be "man
enough" to blame himself at least. He was a worry, for all his charm, even a
social problem—in movies like *The Wild One* (1954) and *The Blackboard
Jungle* (1955)—someone we should *do* something about, and sooner rather
than later. This was the patriarchal view (the enlightened version). But it
was also the sort of "mature" and "responsible" take on things that Brando
and Dean seemed to demolish just by appearing on the movie screen—
making everybody around them (especially if they were older) seem radically less authentic. Whereas Newman—like the "second Brandos" who
came after him, not really having that same sort of power—soon became a
more conventional (and dependable) sort of star.

East of Eden: Cal (Dean) in his bean field
with one of the workers (Nick Dennis)

It's importantly the way James Dean *moves* through Kazan's *East of Eden* (1955) that makes him so compelling. His slight and rangy body is as speaking and eloquent as his face. That face, under tousled hair, is often pained, sometimes impassive—it's the body that conveys freedom and exultancy and rebelliousness. And Kazan shows him in nearly constant motion: dancing and darting through a crowd at a carnival or through a parade of marching war recruits on Main Street, walking with a girl and darting off the path to pivot with his arm around a tree, leaping onto a passing freight train, scrambling monkeylike up an icehouse chute—and most thrilling of all, probably, when he dances and leaps shamanlike over his bean field in the valley, as rubber-jointed and spacily intent as Ray Bolger's Scarecrow. Dean's Cal (his name in the film) makes grown-upness (they are everywhere!) look like solitary confinement.

Clift's Matt Garth in *Red River,* on the other hand, makes his impact mostly by standing still, contemplating the turmoil around him—a dangerously restive cattle drive—with his unnervingly intent but dazzled-looking gaze. He's like someone who looks into a blinding light and sees all the more clearly. A sexy seraph in buckskin—his gaunt form balanced on his hips, or else seeming to hang from his upraised shoulder like a coat on a tilted rack—he is this steady shining consciousness among the closed-

John Wayne and Montgomery Clift in Howard Hawks's *Red River*

off faces of the older men around him. Especially next to Dunson—John Wayne, who brings his own kind of gruff sidelong wistfulness to the role of the overreaching cattle baron, Matt's surrogate father and climactic antagonist.

And that turns out to be, I think, one of the most inspired pairings in movie history, and one of the most inspiriting: pitting Clift's subtlety and sensitivity against Wayne's macho force and bluntness—the new idea of manliness against the old, and yet suggesting a continuity between them, too. Hawks's movie really does persuade you (no other movies of the time even tried to) that Clift's Matt *could* actually "come from," and even belong to, the world of this familiar "father" and still belong—like all shining "sons"—to another order of being, more adventurous, more hopeful.

Terry Malloy's (Brando in Kazan's *On the Waterfront*), on the other hand, is a much grimmer case. He's already been compromised by *his* "fathers." A washed-up ex-boxer, now a dockworker, with puffy eyelids and a scar across one eyebrow, he seems not so much at home in his powerful, big-muscled body as resigned to it, slumped in it almost hopelessly, with his rolling walk and his hands plunged deep into the pockets of his plaid windbreaker. Standing with some buddies, all older than he, outside the local poolroom, he holds his head on an angle, chews gum, looks speculatively into nowhere. Some guy named Joey Doyle, suspected of ratting to the feds, has just been killed—pushed off the tenement rooftop that Terry himself (following orders from the waterfront boss) has just come from calling the guy out onto. It was a setup, of course, for a murder. But what did Terry know? Until *now*—as he takes it in, if slowly, while the buddies beside him crack wise and laugh (can stool pigeons fly? and so forth). Terry leans back against the poolroom window, pushing his hands ever deeper into his windbreaker pockets, and looking off toward the fatal rooftop. "Wow . . ." he says, in his slow, wandering way. Again: "Wow . . ." Then adds: "He wasn't a bad kid, that Joey"—looking puzzled.

Terry is a kid himself—though pushing thirty, as his older brother (Rod Steiger) keeps reminding him. And the waterfront boss (Lee J. Cobb) treats him as if he were about ten—throwing playful punches at him, calling him "Slugger," bear-hugging him off his feet, making fun of his inarticulateness and delayed (apparently) comprehension. They all treat him as if he's not too bright: he's the only one around who could get away with saying "Wow" like that—like a kid—and then repeating it.

But for Terry—as *we* see him—it's not so much the recognition of things that takes the time as the feelings that come *after* it, the backwash of awareness. The way it hits him later, for example, that the very pretty stranger he's been teasing and flirting with is Edie Doyle (Eva Marie Saint), Eddie's bereaved sister: his face simply collapses, looking suddenly, stupidly heartsick—beyond even a "Wow." Kazan later on took no credit for such moments, or for the performance as a whole. Brando, he said, was the only *actor* genius he'd ever known—it was "like directing some genius animal." And indeed Brando's face does have an animal sort of inadvertence—the undefended expressiveness that goes with not being able to *make* a face, the way people (and actors) do.

In a later scene Terry takes the grieving Edie to a neighborhood saloon for a beer. They sit down at an out-of-the-way table. He really just wants to get to know her, to have a nice talk. But *she* is a woman with a mission, and distraught with it, suddenly imploring him, "for God's sake," to help her find the men who killed her brother. She doesn't, of course, have any idea that Terry unwittingly aided the killing, or that the men who did it, as well as the boss who ordered it, are all Terry's buddies—and Terry doesn't want her to know any such thing. He tries to finesse the situation with his streetwise bravado, even trying to cheer her up. But that isn't easy to do when he finds himself feeling so helplessly sorry for her—especially when she starts to weep, right there at the table. As she cries, he slumps forward, dropping his head onto the tabletop, his chin resting on his

Terry (Brando) and Edie (Eva Marie Saint) at a local saloon,
talking about her murdered brother, in Kazan's *On the Waterfront*

folded hand, and looks up at her from below, his eyes wide and pained, gazing at her miserably, his thumb working his lower lip. But what can he do? And she keeps *on* crying. After a moment: "Here," he says softly, shyly pushing the glass toward her," have a little beer . . ."

She refuses, and he looks stupidly at the glass—as if *that* were the problem. She thinks she'll leave, she says, and tells him—kindly—to stay and finish his drink. "I got my whole life to drink," he says, his chin still on the table. He wants to know if maybe she is "sore at" him. For what? she wonders. "For not—for not bein' no help to you," he says, looking searchingly up at her, thumb still resting on his underlip but no longer moving.

What happens next is genuinely shocking. In reply, Edie says nothing at first, but puts her hand tenderly on his face, in its suppliant position below her. And at that moment it's as if you can actually *see*—in Brando's face— Terry lapsing away behind his eyes, that sickening drop into the gut, the moral nausea. And as Edie then moves her hand caressingly up the side of his face, his eyes fall downward and close—and they've become so awful by now you're glad they're suddenly hidden. "You would if you could," she says in gentle reply—twisting the knife almost unbearably. Prompting his eyes to open, swimming with pain, then look blearily sideways.

Terry's a boy—as all these early Brando heroes are—and that's part of what makes his guilt so poignant. Like Clift and Dean, Brando reminded us that whenever we imagined innocence as a *force* rather than as a passive or incomplete state (or a dirty joke), we rarely imagined a girl. Even as Stanley Kowalski, Brando is irreducibly boyish—as well as brutish and cruel. He seems to have been a revelation even to Williams, the playwright, who later claimed that he had never imagined the character could be cast so young (Brando was twenty-three when he appeared in the 1947 stage production). He "humanizes" the character, Williams wrote to his agent, Audrey Wood, after Brando had first read the part for him—and as a result Stanley's cruelty "becomes the brutality or callousness of youth rather than a vicious older man," and became therefore closer to the sort of moral complexity both Kazan and Williams wanted in the play.

Brando gives Stanley a note of adolescent puzzlement and vulnerability—like a terrifying big kid. Tearing angrily through Blanche's big steamer trunk (he's convinced she's only pretending to be poverty-stricken) in front of the protesting Stella (Kim Hunter), doing a running commentary on Blanche's belongings, the jewelry and dressy clothes, he inflects his words with the faint hesitations of someone who feels precariously out of his depth, or beyond his age. As he pulls out a rope of "pearls" and holds it up, incredulous—not slugging the next line across but trying it out, his eyes sliding off to one side as he says it: "What *is* y'r sister—a deep sea diver?" The sound of a smart kid hazarding a joke for the grown-ups.

He is all the more destructive in his war on Blanche for being a kind of innocent. Since she is a kind of phony—just his meat in a way, with her pathetic pretensions and strenuously self-deceived gentility. Critics like Harold Clurman thought that Brando unbalanced the play, putting the audience too much on Stanley's side, and taking necessary sympathy away from Blanche. (Kazan gave his old Group Theatre colleague the chance to redress the balance when he assigned him—but uncredited—to direct the Chicago company, with Uta Hagen and Anthony Quinn.)

But for audiences this "unbalancing" was often a relief—freeing us sometimes from our sympathy with Blanche, from the oppression of her insistent claim on our pity, and on our "higher" feelings (something it's harder to imagine Anthony Quinn doing). Brando's Stanley—not necessarily Williams's (and not at all Alec Baldwin's in the recent American revival, with Jessica Lange)—felt at times like the kind of explosive truth-teller the culture will occasionally produce just when the cant and banality seem most unchallengeable, someone who cuts through all the bullshit and to hell with it.

But of course he only *felt* like that to us: even in Brando's person he was

Blanche (Vivien Leigh) is being kittenish here, giving Stanley (Brando)
a little spritz of her cologne. It doesn't work.

too mean and stupid, and still too much Williams's rough-trade nightmare, to really *be* that figure. The one who *was* for most of us was in a book,
not a play or movie: it was Salinger's Holden Caulfield in *The Catcher in the
Rye* (1951). It's almost impossible to say, it seems to me now, how much
this single book meant at the time (the original paperback cover—with
Holden in a deerstalker's cap in Times Square—was one of the most familiar sights of the decade), or to exaggerate how much it determined so many
young people's view of themselves and America. Holden's obsession with
"phonies," wonderfully comic and entirely serious, both echoed and gave a
rich, special voice to the very American concern with personal authenticity, with the sort of plainness and directness and honesty of character that
we wanted to think of as ours—or at least as potentially ours. And it was
such an enlivening voice—in spite of the fundamentally depressed view it
took of us, of our contemporary lives, and of American culture in general.
"Nothing is more exhilarating than philistine vulgarity," says Nabokov
(also a Salinger fan) in his afterword to *Lolita,* another seminal text of the
time. And *The Catcher in the Rye* seemed to capture both the vulgarity
and the exhilaration as no one had before—or perhaps has since (except
for *Lolita*).

"Phony" was a comically comprehensive term, as Holden employed it,

Terry, after testifying against his buddies, has
just found the pigeons he was raising on his
roof slaughtered—in *On the Waterfront*.

and yet over and over he makes it seem the *exactly* right word. And not
only for the obvious and aggressive cases—poseurs and big shots and
secret snobs—but for the ones who are *sad* too, the ones who settle for the
familiar *thinness* of American life that the book evokes so brilliantly, for its
rewards and goals and enthusiasms: people who are always washing their
cars, or standing in line for some dumb movie (Holden among them).
From the kind of "hot-shot lawyers . . . who make a lot of dough and play
golf and play bridge and buy cars and drink Martinis," to the kind of old
man who comes back to his prep school and looks for his initials carved in
a bathroom stall, to "the kind of a phony" at intermission in the theatre
who has to give himself "*room* to answer somebody's question" about his
opinion of the show, and stepping on the feet of the lady behind him, and
so on, and on. "The phonies," as Holden later recalls, were "coming in the
goddam windows."

Partly because "phony" is also a crucial *aesthetic* category. He applies it,
for example, to Ernie, the saloon piano player who puts in "dumb, show-
offy ripples" on the high notes; to the hero of *A Farewell to Arms* (Holden
wonders how his draftee older brother "could hate the army and war and

all that and still like a phony [book] like that"); to the sort of movie "that was supposed to be a comedy, with Cary Grant in it, and all that crap."

But when Holden is pressed to think about his future, he draws a blank—or a movie-derived fantasy, like being (since he has to be *something*) one of those "lawyers who go around saving innocent guys' lives all the time." But even so, as he says to his sister Phoebe,

> . . . How would you know if you did it because you really *wanted* to save guys' lives, or you did it because what you *really* wanted to do was be a terrific lawyer, with everybody slapping you on the back and congratulating you in court when the goddam trial was over, the reporters and everybody, the way it is in the dirty movies? How would you know you weren't being a phony? The trouble is, you *wouldn't*.

That's partly why he likes children and animals so much: because they don't have, in his view, this falsifying self-consciousness. Where the rest of us are always in danger from it—of being more concerned about the impression we're making than what we're actually doing, even if we're only making that impression on ourselves. And even if we resist phoniness, we may only be falling into a more insidious—and characteristically American—form of it: the pose of not posing. Like the Beats—or the Hemingway hero. Holden trusts such stances of dissent and rebellion even less than he does middle-class conventionality—which is at least likely to be less ego-driven. When he imagines for himself what would come to be called an "alternative life-style," it's more like a monk's—a cabin in the woods. With a *very* few visitors, and one house rule: "If anybody tried to do anything phony, they couldn't stay." You're never entirely safe—even in the woods.

A similar concern with anti-phoniness, the same radicalism about personal authenticity, animated the Actors Studio movement, the most exciting new theatre of the time. *Not* the sort of theatre that Holden goes to and complains about: Olivier in his 1948 *Hamlet* movie ("too much like a goddam general"), and the Lunts in their 1949 Broadway hit, *I Know My Love*—who didn't act like people or actors but "more like they knew they were celebrities and all . . . I mean they were good but they were *too* good."

But the Method actor was as alert to the phony as Holden was—and a sworn enemy to the external, image-conscious acting styles of the "theatrical" stars, whether self-delighted show-offs like the Lunts or British school technicians like Olivier. The Method was as much a moral revolution in the theatre (and the movies) as a technical or stylistic one.

Kim Stanley in *The Goddess*—Paddy Chayefsky's roman à clef
about Marilyn Monroe

Still, it was generally the Method *men,* not the women, who went to
Hollywood and became movie stars—a pattern that has held good more or
less up to this day (De Niro, Nicholson, Pacino, et al.)—whereas the most
celebrated Actors Studio women (Julie Harris, Geraldine Page, Maureen
Stapleton, Kim Stanley) were mostly stage stars. Kim Stanley, for example,
made only two starring movies, *The Goddess* and *Seance on a Wet Afternoon*—
both failures—and of all the studio women she was the most remarkable:
"the most gifted acting artist" he'd ever known, said Studio co-founder
Robert Lewis in his autobiography. Stanley had the ability to transform
otherwise negligible plays (like Anita Loos's *Chéri* in 1959, or William
Inge's *Natural Affection* in 1963) into major experiences, and theatre people wanted to see anything she was in. They usually had to hurry: she was
rarely in hits (*Chéri* lasted fifty-six performances; *Affection,* thirty-six).
General audiences were somewhat less taken with her—and understandably. She had a Brando-like power and glamour, but more neurotically
inflected and lacking his charm and sexiness. She generally played vulnerable, screwed-up heroines (she originated Monroe's *Bus Stop* role on the
stage, in 1955), but she made them more upsetting than most audiences
wanted them to be. She was the uncompromising, even harrowing sort of

A Place in the Sun: Elizabeth Taylor and Montgomery Clift on the terrace in the famous "Tell Mama" scene

artist who gives no quarter. In 1958, when she was starring in New York in O'Neill's *A Touch of the Poet,* a story circulated about an offstage exchange between her and her co-star Helen Hayes, who was famous for her practiced charm. Hayes wanted to know why Stanley hadn't looked at her in the scene they'd just played. "I can't stand to see you *act,*" Stanley supposedly replied. Whether it happened or not, the story certainly *sounded* true. Watching Stanley with the redoubtable Hayes was a little like watching Brando with Blanche DuBois: the truth teller and the phony.

Because the Method—with its commitment to interior truth—could not only make it hard to act with Helen Hayes, in the long run and for some it could make it hard to act at all. Brando has often described facing the same quandaries as Holden does: how do you know you're not being a phony? The trouble is, you *don't.* And the impossibility of resolving the issue can contribute—as it does for Holden—to a kind of breakdown. Stanley made her embittered retirement from the theatre in the mid-sixties. Brando, Clift, and Dean had all self-destructed—in their different ways—before that.

In the early days of his stardom, Clift would often go to Central Park and read Salinger out loud with a friend. He had Holden-like dreams for his movie career then—to play "rebel hero" types, truth-telling young saviors. But what he played instead (and wonderfully), after the sensation of *Red River,* was eager fakes: the fortune-hunting charmer of William Wyler's *The Heiress* (1949), the desperate social climber of George Stevens's *A Place in the Sun* (1951). In the Stevens film, he has the same funny bent posture as in the Hawks western, but this time it was as if something was crumpling him from inside. And he never looked more beautiful—more martyrlike. With Elizabeth Taylor in their famous love scene on the ballroom terrace—a succession of ravishing alternating close-ups, where he looks at her almost as if he needed her even more improbable beauty to support the weight of his own—"Tell Mama," she says, "tell Mama all": one of the most surprising (she looks barely fifteen) and moving utterances in the history of romantic filmmaking.

In Hitchcock's *I Confess* (1953), he is a young priest falsely accused of murder, bound by the secrecy of the confessional from revealing the real murderer. He became obsessed with this character, his close, longtime friend Jeanne Greene later said (to biographer Patricia Bosworth), talking to her endlessly about the priestly ideal, the priest's transcendence and martyrdom: "Good priests," he said, "assume the guilt of the world." On his movie set, however, he had to assume the daily burden of facing Hitchcock—who had his own ideas about guilt, and whose method of directing Clift was often to tell him what look he wanted on his face in the next shot. Clift was appalled. The fact is, he was starting to look more and more absent on the screen, the dazzled look more like a dazed one. His co-star Anne Baxter sometimes found him, she said (again to Bosworth), so "blank and distant" in their scenes together that she had to *imagine* an affect to play to to get through them. Off the set, he was drinking more. The movie that resulted was a high point neither for him nor for Hitchcock.

But his Private Prewitt in *From Here to Eternity* (1953) was a return to form. It was also arguably his last great performance: another martyr hero, but an even more ingrown one, more hapless and outcast. And even at his best now, Clift seemed to be retreating from us on the screen. Then, in the middle of filming MGM's *Raintree County,* a megabudget Civil War spectacular—a movie he had never wanted to do in the first place—he had his drunken, disfiguring car accident, and the clarifying radiance was gone for good. That was the same year—1956—that James Dean died in *his* car accident.

While Brando, it seemed, was making his own kind of retreat. After his widely publicized but disappointing Marc Antony (in Joseph Mankiewicz's *Julius Caesar,* 1953), he seemed bent on proving himself in diverse lightweight roles like Sky Masterson in *Guys and Dolls* (1955) and Sakini in *The Teahouse of the August Moon* (1956)—not the sort of things most of us wanted to see him in. And it was almost worse to see him in something like the more ambitious *Sayonara* (1957)—an enterprise (a Joshua Logan production) whose corruption and vulgarity he seems to

"Good priests assume the guilt of the world": Montgomery Clift
in Hitchcock's *I Confess*

have taken the full measure of, while turning in a creditable and complex performance nonetheless. Still, it's a performance with a clear undertone of complacency—and contempt. This undertone grew stronger as his movies got worse. And soon you almost didn't want to see him at all. In any case, he had stopped being a serious actor. It was not, in this would-be serious man's view, a serious activity. So that it makes a kind of sense that his one great mid-career performance (excepting 1971's *The Godfather*), after the early films, should be in John Huston's *Reflections in a Golden Eye* (1967), as a repressed homosexual army officer, someone in a tormented relation to his own public image. (Someone like the homosexual Clift, in fact.)

Unhappily, the movie was a terrible flop. Both its stars—Brando and Elizabeth Taylor—were well past their surefire box-office days; and the film's coldly engrossed view of its peculiar-to-grotesque characters was too unsentimental, too obliquely comic for most audiences. It's a richly funny movie at times (especially in Brian Keith's performance as the amiable, bearish officer having an adulterous affair with Taylor—who is also very funny, as Brando's hearty army wife), but the audience never laughs: the movie's feeling is too detached and astringent. But it's exactly that feeling, the bemused Guignolish point of view, that characterizes Huston's best (though not necessarily his most popular) movies—from *The Maltese Fal-*

Marlon Brando as Major Pemberton and Elizabeth Taylor as his coarse-grained
wife, in John Huston's *Reflections in a Golden Eye*

con (his first) to this one, to *Fat City* (1972), *Wise Blood* (1979), and *Prizzi's
Honor* (1985). Huston is probably the only director who could have filmed
Flannery O'Connor's great comic novel and gotten the voice and vision—
the sense of humor—so close to right. ("He's an auditory [director],"
Brando later said to Lawrence Grobel, "and he can tell by the tone of your
voice whether you're cracking or not.")

At the beginning of *Reflections in a Golden Eye,* Major Penderton
(Brando) is at home lifting weights in a T-shirt, sweating and puffing in
close-up—then flexing his fat arms in the mirror. Later, we see him in
uniform, leaving his study to go upstairs to bed. There is another mirror
at the foot of the stairway and he stops to study himself in it, gravely at
first, then jauntily: he gives the mirror image (*Hi there!*) a tentative little
smile—but the eyes above the smile look unfriendly, almost hostile. Then
he starts trying a few more public faces. He is giving an order to someone:
the lips move silently. Then he is angry, barking a command: the eyes
blaze—almost. Then a sharp, snappy salute—a silent *Dismissed!* He
brings his hand down—the eyes melt, the shoulders sag. Now, lounging
on his hips, becoming "just one of the boys," candid and manly, then
breaking into a roguish smile-verging-on-a-grin—a little manly charm,
why not? Until the eyes, with their disapproval, recall him to "himself"—

which he now contemplates: he stares, blinks, lifts his chin and squares it solemnly. Then turns and goes up the stairway, giving a hopeless little bound at the top.

It's a thrilling scene: so daring and witty, so "private," it might be titillating if weren't so genuinely embarrassing—and it still feels new and daring, even now, long after De Niro's great mirror scene ("Are you talking to *me?*") in *Taxi Driver*. That one—sooner or later as it goes on—makes you laugh; this one strikes you dumb. The consciousness in the major's eyes makes it impossible to put him at an entirely comfortable distance: It's the sort of private moment when the self betrays the surface *under* the surface, the inner you even shallower than the outer one. And Brando's version of this is unsparing, but with such sympathy and fierce imaginative life that it feels not just reductive and malicious—the major "exposed"—but moving and large: that bound at the top of the stairway, for example.

The major lives in a fearful isolation. An aristocratic sort of southerner, he is meant to be a natural leader (he even teaches a class in the subject to the junior officers), stoic and sure and self-sufficient. He is, in fact, utterly unsure, self-pitying and self-despising. And ravished with loneliness—humiliated by his braying, tough-as-nails wife, tormented by his sexuality, and secretly obsessed with the dark, brooding enlisted man (Robert Forster) who tends the yard and stable and takes care of the horses and rides them naked through the nearby woods ("Bare-*back* and bare-*ass,*" as the major's wife puts it, crowingly). The major becomes more and more—as his fixation with the soldier grows—out of touch, but still going through the motions of his professional and social life, not always successfully. Teaching his class one day, he breaks down, unable to go on. And one evening, in an after-dinner tête-à-tête in the parlor with his wife and her neighbor-lover, the major launches into a speech of sentimental tribute to the manly closeness and beautiful camaraderie of enlisted men in their ranks and barracks—leaving his two coarse-grained auditors (Taylor and Keith), not too swift on their *best* days, merely baffled. When he's alone, he prowls around the post after the soldier, who remains at a distance, opaque and unacknowledging.

That's what the major is more or less doing one day when another officer runs up to him excitedly to tell him that a mutual friend, a woman named Allison (Julie Harris—as Brian Keith's fragile, neurasthenic wife) has suddenly, unexpectedly died. Brando doesn't seem to quite take this in at first—he hardly seems even to be listening. Then the actor does something extraordinary. He turns away from the other man while saying the name "Allison" as if he were suddenly, instinctively looking to see her—but then you realize that, no, he's looking for the soldier, who has gone off while the major was being distracted by this news. "Allison!" he says softly again, stepping off toward the nearby bench where the soldier has just been lounging—now empty. He's gone. And she's gone. And Brando evokes the sort of loss that feels so pervasive and absolute that almost any name for it (the soldier seems to have none) will do. Like the "Ou-boum!" in Forster's Marabar caves (*A Passage to India*), the echo comes back the same.

For the patriarchal stars, the Gables and Coopers, the problem with being a movie actor was that it seemed unmanly—narcissistic, something only women were supposed to be. For Brando it's simply that acting is unimportant—it's "childish" and "neurotic" and seduces those who do it into lives of self-indulgence, he told Joe Hyams in 1958. "It all adds up to nothing." His later views, in his autobiography, are no different, only calmer and loftier. He explains that he doesn't "condemn" other actors, nor does he condemn what they do: it's just that he prefers not "to be counted among them." "Quitting acting—that's the mark of maturity," he told Hyams. But of course he doesn't quit. He needs the money, as he keeps telling us—putting "maturity" on hold. And yet if acting is "nothing" on the one hand, on the other hand it's really too much. Praising a Jack Nicholson performance (in *The Crossing Guard*, 1996), he reports: "I told Jack that one of the reasons I don't want to really act anymore is that I don't want to have to reach that far down into myself to get that kind of result." He doesn't want to learn lines, either; he has long preferred to have them posted around the set where he can read them—even, on occasion, on another actor's face. All this, he says, not only saves time (his, of course) but preserves spontaneity; after all, we don't memorize what we say to each other in real life, do we? And so on.

"I coulda had class," he says to Rod Steiger in *Waterfront* (the famous I-coulda-been-a-contender scene), in his thin, highish voice with its faint lisp and odd, gargling undertones. And as he pronounces "class" with its nasal vowel, his face seeming to lift on its own agony, he conjures up not only the respect Terry wanted and never got, but some almost unimaginable dignity beyond it. Brando's most mythic-size moments on the movie screen, the ones he's permanently imprinted on the rest of us, are most often—it seems to me—scenes like this one: like Stanley howling for Stella at the bottom of a stairway, or Major Penderton saying an absent person's name and stepping toward an empty bench—scenes of pure, painful, powerful *loss*. And so it almost seems appropriate, in an unhappy, ironic way, that he gave us a botched career in the end—or at least an unfulfilled one.

Ten

METHOD MOVIES

Hollywood didn't just change the shape of the movie screen in its efforts to stem the loss of audience. It knew it had to change "the movies" themselves: the endlessly repeated genre plots (the familiarity meant it hardly ever mattered if you came in at the middle or even after that), the shtick of old character actors and overfamiliar stars, the outdated restrictions of the Production Code, and much more. All the unreality—more clearly that now after the war than ever—was losing its point, if it ever had one, for everybody. And when postwar Italian "neorealists" began showing us what some approximation of real life might look like on a movie screen, the shock of it felt almost sexy, like your first movie nudity.

But television was offering the same sort of shock, and closer to home, in all those weekly live dramas (*Studio One, Philco Television Playhouse, Goodyear Playhouse, Kraft Theatre*), all from New York at first, later on from L.A. too (*Playhouse 90*). And amid the prevailing inanity of television (even worse than the movies), these shows seemed even more remarkable—not least for showing us the new Method actors, as well as the kinds of plays (by new writers Paddy Chayefsky, Reginald Rose, Horton Foote, Rod Serling, et al.) they did their best in: intensely and minutely colloquial, dense with the sound and texture and quality of everyday American life. These plays, and most especially their actors (Kim Stanley was prominent in them, for example, and James Dean began in them), were as much a revelation to people as the new European cinema had been. And they made "the movies" as we knew them look even thinner and emptier.

But then some of these shows (the critically applauded ones) were made *into* movies. Movies that (for the most part) looked and sounded just like TV plays, and that gave rise in turn to movie "originals" that *also* looked and sounded like TV plays—"Method movies," as they were sometimes called: small-scaled, urgent-toned comedy-dramas centering on domestic events and mundane crises and issues, the action set in New York, as a rule, or somewhere in the small-town South. And they were usually directed by

Kim Stanley with Steven Hill (DA Adam Schiff for ten seasons on TV's *Law and Order*) as her soldier boyfriend in *The Goddess*

the newcomers from TV, people like Sidney Lumet, John Frankenheimer, Martin Ritt, Delbert Mann. After the surprising success of *Marty* in 1955 (and its Academy Award for best picture), the number of these movies—and of jobs for these directors—seemed to increase.

They were "psychological" stories, but more therapeutic than analytic, generally climaxing in a leading character's successful "adjustment" to reality and its limitations: sending the potentially wayward young husband back to his pregnant wife and cheerless city apartment (*The Bachelor Party,* 1957); freeing the troubled baseball player from the control of his baseball-zealot father (*Fear Strikes Out,* 1957); reconciling the domineering Irish mother to her daughter's desire for a small, quiet wedding (*The Catered Affair,* 1956); enlightening the idealistic businessman about the boss whose hard-nosed realism he mistakenly took for capitalist greed (*Patterns,* 1956); and so on. They were movies that *meant* to be anti-generic, as much committed to truth above convention, to character above plot, as their actors and directors were.

But all too soon they began to seem like a genre of their own. Most predictable of all, perhaps, in the inevitability of a telling-the-ugly-truth scene, where a weeping character confesses some embarrassing personal

Helping Mama with the supper dishes:
Ernest Borgnine and Esther Minciotti in *Marty*

fact: like the dirty-mouthed aunt in *The Dark at the Top of the Stairs* (1960) owning up to her frigidity, or Marty to his ugliness (Ernest Borgnine in the movie, Rod Steiger on TV): "I'm a fat little man! I'm a fat ugly man!" he cries, and even his loving mother, sitting across from him at the dinner table, cannot bring herself to deny it.

These movies meant to be about *us*—really. About what we worried about and the everyday problems we faced and the ordinary discontents we felt, about our families and marriages and boring jobs. And not at a fictionalized remove, but up close and personal. Instead of unfolding before us in dreamlike self-assurance the way the movies used to do, they were trying to get next to us, to console us, to snuggle up even. Even (were we imagining this?) to *help* . . . They weren't just about finding love, for example, but about getting a date—or failing to (you're not alone). It was the decline of what Italo Calvino has called "the cinema of distance"—his inspired phrase for the genre movies of the thirties and forties. Those, for the most part, were movies that *kept* their distance—if only through their conventionality, their artifice and equivocation, even their dishonesty.

We were told that all this was progress, and it certainly appeared to be: not only all these extraordinary new actors, but the shocks of recognition movies sometimes gave us now—scenes we recognized not just from other movies, as in the past, but from our own lives, like the family arguments in *Middle of the Night* or the guy talk in *Marty* (both by Paddy Chayefsky). Suddenly (as it often seemed) there were movies that we could verify from our own experience, even from the conversations in the movie-house lobby.

Except that we could—and we couldn't. That was the catch. Because the final and lingering effect of most of these movies, both singly and in aggregate, was of an essential sort of falsity. They seemed wrong even when they seemed true. It was the falsity of a diminished reality. And at its worst, it offered characters who might have been "real," but who were caught and fixed in a vision of self-regarding pathos.

The drive to make the movies more true to life also affected the retold versions of older movies—like the musical remake of *A Star Is Born* (1954) as a comeback vehicle for Judy Garland (she had been off the screen four years after being dropped by MGM). Garland had become, without benefit of the Actors Studio, her own kind of Method performer, mainly through her stage shows—what Margo Jefferson has called "Method vaudeville." It was in these shows that she began to draw noticeably and creatively on the upheavals of her by then highly public "private life." And the narrative of the old movie, starring Janet Gaynor and Fredric March and released in 1937—about the love of a rising Hollywood star for the falling one she is married to and attempting to save from the self-destruction that finally claims him—suited Garland's penchant for tremulous emotionalism. It had been a big hit in the thirties, though even then the material had seemed a little out-of-date. The more "realistic" sensibility it had to be given in 1955, however, produced a rather strange hybrid. While the fifties version has the same fan-magazine breathlessness about Hollywood as the original (and even more so: the studio boss, for example, is even kindlier, and—since he's played by Charles Bickford—even more emphatically WASP than Adolphe Menjou was), it also has a heightened and more brutal emotional tone, particularly in its central performance. But the total result is less convincing than before, and mostly because of that performance. While Janet Gaynor, with her tiny voice and big baby-doll eyes and genteel performing style, was no one's idea of a truth teller exactly, Garland's heroine seems even more complicatedly false.

One trouble is that while it's James Mason, as Norman Maine, the alcoholic has-been husband, who is supposed to be out of control, it's Garland's Esther who mostly seems to be. (Except in the movie's big song numbers, most of them composed by Harold Arlen and Ira Gershwin, where she is almost more thrilling than ever.) So that by the three-hour-long film's climax, Mason's skilled and sensitive performance has come to seem inappro-

priately, not to say tastelessly, self-possessed. In the early scenes, Garland
offers a resolute version of a woman so compliant that she inflects even her
most casual "Hello"s beseechingly. But that's before she gives herself up
later on—gasping and crying and staggering and clutching—to the hysteria of the "tragic" scenes: sobbing and falling apart on the chest of the
grandfatherly studio boss as she recounts the horrors of living with a
drunk; weeping on her patio as she tells the boss she must give up her
career to go away with Norman and try to save him (the boss: "But you're
at the very height of your career, Esther—the very peak of your success!");
having hysterics in a darkened room at home after Norman's suicide; and
so on. We have to believe, of course, if such heavily emotional scenes are
going to work the way they're supposed to, that Esther's upset and grief
are principally about Norman's pain and suffering—more than about her
own, that is. Indeed, if the whole heartbreaking narrative is to work at all,
we have to believe in Esther's nobility, even her essential selflessness,
when the kind of overwrought feeling and hysterical self-pity that Garland seems to be drawing on at these moments persists in suggesting the
opposite.

And that sort of problem was one of the drawbacks of the Method itself
as some actors practiced it: the obsessive self-reference of its "inner truth."
Kazan, among others, was alert to this trap. He had been one of the three
co-founders of the Actors Studio in 1947 (Robert Lewis and Cheryl Crawford were the others), but he had become critical of much of the Studio
training as it went on under Lee Strasberg. Mostly Kazan disapproved—as
did Lewis, and Brando's great teacher, Stella Adler—of Strasberg's exaggerated emphasis on the Stanislavsky technique of "affective memory"
(supplying the character's emotion by reliving on stage some past one of
your own). He thought Strasberg's teaching encouraged trancelike, self-
adoring performances—and self-pity and self-indulgence; that it produced
actors who communed with themselves on stage instead of with their fellow actors. Like *not* looking at Helen Hayes: almost alone among theatre
people, Kazan did not much admire Kim Stanley.

But for audiences the problem was larger than Strasberg or his training.
An acting movement that had begun as a protest against the phony was
developing its own distinctive kind of phoniness: the actor who didn't
seem to know that something strongly felt can also be something worked
up and misplaced, something factitious—that the "deeply felt" can also be
all the more deeply fake. The danger of that kind of fakery is probably
more familiar to us now than it was in the fifties—in this time of public
"privacy," with its eager and widespread soul-baring. But it's always a

threat—and it begins with the audience inside your head. That's why it can feel almost inescapable, whether in Holden Caulfield's cabin in the woods or on Brando's Tahitian island.

Brando's torn-from-the-gut acting in Bertolucci's *Last Tango in Paris* (1972) is an example, I think, of how such performing, even on the highest level, can go subtly wrong. Brando's performance is an extraordinary tour de force. And unlike his Terry Malloy or his Major Penderton, it is unapologetically a performance of *himself.* The script was all but nonexistent, and the star was encouraged by his director to wing it, to invent and improvise throughout. That was the sort of thing, of course, that

Brando with director Elia Kazan on the set of *Streetcar,* having a party with the crew

Brando loved to do. But on Bertolucci's scale of doing it, he was a little uneasy. Six years later he would say that he still didn't "know what that film was about."

But could he really *not* have known? That it was about *him*? So that when the character is being confessional—as he often is—we have the feeling the actor is too. And his long speech to the Girl (Maria Schneider) about growing up on a midwestern farm with two drunks for parents, is of course a speech about Brando's own family history. And when he describes going on his first big prom date with cow shit on his shoes, because his boozing old man made him milk the cows just before he left, his tone, far from being at all whining or poignant (he even suggests when it's over that he'd been making the whole story up), is insolent and defiant (as it is through the movie), challengingly unsentimental. But there is so much satisfaction in the challenge, so much final complacency in the remembered pain, that what you feel more than the "truth" of the moment is its

Brando in Bertolucci's *Last Tango in Paris*
(Maria Schneider is turned away at left.)

ultimate self-pity and narcissism—its truly *deep* phoniness. The trap of confessional performance, whether on or off the screen.

Writing in 1932, the distinguished critic Stark Young disputed the widely held notion that acting is just a matter of "being the character," of "being natural." That's what the audience thinks they want from their actors but it really isn't. "What people want in acting is acting," he argues. He was writing about Garbo in *As You Desire Me* (1931). She's as compelling to audiences as she is, he says, partly because of her "removal" from them: she is not affected or unnatural, but she is somehow different. Her acting is not a reproduction but a "creation"—a "new birth with a nameless difference" from "real" life, giving us what we *really* want from acting: "illumination, unreality and remoteness." Garbo maintains in every way—what was so important to this critic—"the distance that style in art assures."

Of course, hardly anyone talks about acting in this way any longer. And that's importantly because of the Actors Studio and its enormous impact on all kinds of theatre. And by the fifties it would have been virtually impossible to argue that "distance" and "a certain removal" were what American movie audiences wanted in their stars, even unknowingly. We wanted our stars to be like us—having become more than ever before the stars of our own lives. It's true the Method actor offered a certain residual mystery, but most of all he suited the tone of his time by his obsessive turning inward. Nineteen-fifties America, with its strangely hollow cheerfulness and then unparalleled general prosperity, its unprecedented world dominance, was also—with its paranoia and blacklisting and incessant self-celebration—a time and place of increasing insularity and provincialism. The expansion we were feeling—after the rigors of the depression and the war—was also a kind of closing down. A lot like the experience the new actors were giving us. After all.

Eleven

IN A LONELY PLACE

I t's the sort of set piece in the middle of a movie that director Nicholas Ray almost came to specialize in: his two stars, Humphrey Bogart and Gloria Grahame, in the kind of glamorous, grown-up romantic scene that you may never get out of your head once you've watched it—unfolding, with its movements, with its framing and cutting rhythms, in sync and in counterpoint to a haunting standard song. The scene (as with a similar scene in Ray's *Johnny Guitar* later) even has the formal shape (verse, chorus, finale) of a popular song, as it proceeds from an introductory mime to a dialogue and a crescendo sort of wind-up. The movie is *In a Lonely Place* (1950).

The setting is in the sort of minimalist form that the economy-minded studio Columbia often favored: a piano bar that looks more like a cheap movie set than the real thing—a few booths and some concealing drapes between plaster pillars, with the piano itself in the center of the straight-on, evenly lit long shot that opens the sequence. Dix and Laurel (Bogart and Grahame), seated among the couples on high stools around the big white piano, are directly across from the singer-pianist, Hadda Brooks—who gets the scene's first close-up, as she leans forward into the first words of her song (it's Ray Noble's "I Hadn't Anyone Till You," from 1938). Brooks is a regally beautiful black woman, in a shoulderless gown and a glittering necklace and earrings, with a manner at once benign and remote, and large, lambent eyes. Her voice is a sort of teary contralto, exactly suited to the song's melancholy and heavily climbing exultancy. What Ray shows us here is not only how intimately and tenderly easy these two people, Dix and Laurel, are with each other, but how easy they are in this saloon setting—not only the personal relation but the impersonal one: to this song, and to the luminous and kindly singer. Her yearning and open emotiveness (the sequence now alternates close-ups of her and them) qualifies their playfulness with each other, giving another, richer level of feeling and effect to what we see.

In a Lonely Place: the piano bar scene.
Gloria Grahame and Humphrey Bogart

Dix sits forward, leaning on his elbows over his drink. Laurel is beside him in the same close-up, sitting straight and slightly turned away from him. He lights a cigarette and puts it between her lips, then says something we don't hear (we only hear the song). She likes it, whatever it is, and laughs, with a sort of I-should-have-known-better look on her face. And as he turns away, pleased with her response, looking back toward the singer, Laurel directs a glance of rueful affection at the back of his head—something only we see. He turns and whispers again; they laugh, then together look offscreen at the singer again—who is now retarding the tempo and raising the emotional charge as she launches into the song's bridge (*"Now* I see . . .*"*) and release (*"I was the only* one—*till you . . .*"*). And the camera pulls slowly and majestically back over the two leads, the piano, the singer, the room . . . then returns to the singer's close-up as, lifting one elegant bare shoulder, she begins the final refrain.

After that she launches into an instrumental reprise, very uptempo and jaunty. "Anything you want to make you happy?" Dix (audible now) says to Laurel, in a husky voice. Laurel smiles and puts her mouth to his ear. He lowers his head in the close-up—obscuring all but her forehead and eyes, as she whispers slowly, soundlessly, insinuatingly. As the piano riffs in the background, her eyes drift sightlessly above his head—until she sees something offscreen, her eyebrow arching in alarm. "What's *he* doing here?" she says gutturally. Dix turns suddenly toward the camera, his angry face rising into the frame and filling it, obscuring Laurel's—his rage blotting her out from us. The effect is memorably unnerving—and as jarring as a scream. (And it will be repeated later on, more insinuatingly, when he seals their engagement with a kiss.)

What's occasioned it is the entrance of a cop they both know. Dix is now a murder suspect, and he instantly assumes (mistakenly) that he's being tailed. He rises abruptly, jamming his cigarette out on the piano ashtray so violently (the sound is amplified) that the singer starts at the piano and hits a discord. The sudden rage makes Laurel look dazed, as he grabs her by her elbow and hustles her to the exit, cracking wise to the puzzled cop as they go out the door. "I can see why that guy gets into a lot of trouble," says the cop to his girlfriend as they take Dix and Laurel's stools, and as the singer repeats the song's refrain, and the sequence returns to its opening long shot of the club interior.

Nicholas Ray was a Method sort of director, an "actor's director" and a onetime actor himself, and an early associate of Elia Kazan's (whom he later credited with introducing him to the techniques of Stanislavsky). But Ray also had an affinity for genre moviemaking that Kazan neither had nor seems to have wanted. Ray knew how to make movies that were *about* their stars, in the tradition of old Hollywood.

His *In a Lonely Place* was the last of the great Bogart movies—the last one both in the noir line and about the Bogart hero. Ray's movies generally are more about men than women. And in this one, it's not the noir heroine but the hero that the movie obsesses and speculates about—it's the Bogart character who is dangerous, mysterious, unalterably ambiguous. And like other noir heroes, he is a doomed man. He is also his own nemesis, at once the victim and the mysterious "other" who does him in.

And of course the director identifies with him. *In a Lonely Place* is Ray's most personal movie—even to its circumstances. Gloria Grahame was married to him at the time, though acrimoniously: they were on the edge of divorce, and she was made to sign a preshooting agreement binding her to play the role the way he told her to. By some accounts he might have preferred Lauren Bacall in the part (almost certainly Bogart would have) if Warners hadn't refused to lend her. As it was, he had been threatened with Ginger Rogers (Harry Cohn's preference). Grahame would have to be borrowed from Howard Hughes's RKO, but in the end Ray insisted on her; she was simply *right* for the part. If not, it seems, for going home to: Ray took to sleeping on the movie's principal set—which was an exact replica, built to his specifications in the studio, of the apartment complex he'd lived in when he first came to Hollywood (it's where the hero and heroine live). And he filmed the exteriors of the place (as when Dix comes or goes) outside the real Los Angeles building.

Dix is a Hollywood screenwriter, whose reputation for being troublesome has made his jobs scarcer and scarcer. He openly hates most of the stuff he's asked to work on, and his drinking and temper (he socked the producer on his last job) don't help his career, either. Ray saw himself in the character's self-destructiveness, his tormented relation with Hollywood, and his frustrated artistic ambition. But he also identified with his star, his (by then) buddy Bogart—who seemed to have somehow beaten the Hollywood game, and to have done it on his own stubborn terms. Never mind that he'd made a lot of crap—who hadn't in the movies? Bogart had emerged from it all a figure of beleaguered integrity—a role that Ray, a relative newcomer to the game, himself aspired to. "He was much more than an actor," Ray would later say of his friend and star, with characteristic grandiosity, "he was an image of our condition. His face was a living reproach."

But to whom or to what? Bogart's face had become by 1950 not only "an image of our condition" but of our final best hopes for it: the face of someone not only battered by experience but deepened by it too—a face of dreadful beauty. Ray seemed to believe (again, characteristically) that something or someone should be *blamed* for this face. But when it came to filming it, he clearly knew better. Bogart in this movie looks and seems both fiercer and sweeter than he's ever seemed before—and more tormented. His gift for a kind of judicious doting—over women, some kids, lovable character actors—is more pronounced than ever, and especially in the scenes with Laurel, the out-of-work starlet he's fallen for. He's older, after all, and his *need* for this heroine makes the romantic longings of all those other Bogart heroes—of Rick for Ilsa, even Sam for Brigid—seem soft and generalized, almost painless by comparison. But it's a little unnerving for Laurel. His first kiss (after the suspense of waiting for her word of encouragement) is vampirelike: she is sitting near the floor on an ottoman and he stands and rises out of the frame, then bends down into it again, taking her face in his hands, fingers on her throat, lifting her mouth to his. Laurel needs him too, of course (her life is at least as screwed up as his is); but confronted with *his* need at such moments, she looks almost frightened. And as the movie goes on, that will make him very angry . . . once he's become a murder suspect.

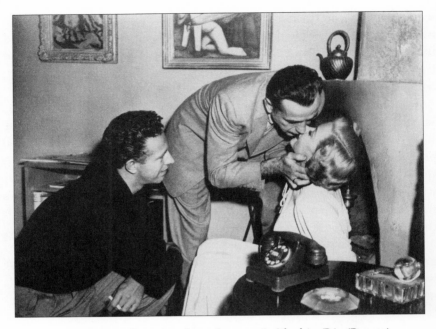

Nicholas Ray directing the early, vampirelike kiss Dix (Bogart)
gives to Laurel (Grahame)

He's a more vulnerable sort of Bogart—in the style of the time—not only in his neediness but in his submission to it. It's the latter that makes him so especially moving here. This Bogart hero can no longer *afford* to send the heroine away at the end, as he did with Brigid and Ilsa—as he knows. His puzzling over that grapefruit knife in Laurel's kitchen, just before he straightens it, is more than the standard little joke about the incompetent helpless male; it's also a kind of realism—humbling and late in coming, perhaps, but in Bogart's case it's touching. Embracing the domestic, Dix is making breakfast for himself and her (she is just getting up). He's really feeling great—that is, he *should* be feeling great. They're getting married, and Laurel has to set a date. But on some level of himself that he doesn't want to be in touch with, he knows something is wrong (*we* know she's wanting to back out by now, but is too afraid to tell him). As she comes into the kitchen in her fur-collared floor-length negligee (the one he first saw her in from across their courtyard)—gliding rather ominously across the floor, as if she were on casters—laughing and coming to save the grapefruit knife, you see him both understanding and refusing to. He goes on with the breakfast: "A good love scene," he says, in one of the movie's best speeches, "should be about something else besides love"—

should be like this one. He knows, of course; he writes them. And he's trying to write this one now—to make it be something it isn't—while Laurel sits across the room from him, on a high stool near the doorway, literally with her back against the wall, looking uneasy. But he's not looking at her—he's too busy at the sink, preparing the breakfast tray. Done at last, he carries it to the living room. He sits and looks up as she comes in after him. We don't see the look on her face *now*—but we see *him* seeing it, and the way the sickened alarm rises in his eyes. Momentarily. He goes on—chatting and joking, pressing her about the wedding date. Ray builds the entire scene on Bogart's close-ups (Grahame's are secondary), on his ability to register conflicting levels of feeling and recognition. And though the scene is inconclusive in the end (Laurel goes along with him, he kisses her and rushes out to buy a ring), it leaves you feeling numb afterwards. It's the Bogart hero, after all—not the psychos the star sometimes and uncharacteristically played, in forgotten vehicles like *Conflict* and *The Two Mrs. Carrolls* (as a nonstar in the thirties, of course, he specialized in psychos)—and we'd never before seen him so *hopeful,* and so close to breakdown.

Another thing that was new to us at the time was the way the Dix role seemed to play off allusions to Bogart's "private" life. That is, the one we'd read about in the papers: the drinking, the expressed contempt for Hollywood, the nightclub fights (the most notorious was the one at El Morocco, where he got himself banned for shoving a woman who laid hands on his stuffed panda; he was also permanently banned from the Stork Club), as well as the violence against his pre-Bacall wife, Mayo Methot. And yet the point of all this suggestion for an audience at the time was neither titillation nor revelation exactly: not so much that they were getting the "real" Bogart as that they were getting a more realistic, more "psychological" version of the fictional one. And in any case, we never supposed that that public version of the private Bogart could be anything much more than a feeble extrapolation from the "real" Bogart—the one we knew from the screen.

He's introduced in this movie by a close-up of his tormented eyes in the rearview mirror of an open convertible he is driving through nighttime L.A.—under the movie's opening titles and the ominous George Antheil music. And at the first stoplight he nearly gets into a fight, with a mouthy guy in the next car (who drives away when Dix starts to get out of his car). He *looks* like he's going to a murder, but he's only on his way to a Hollywood business-meeting-cum-social-occasion, at his favorite hangout, a place called Paul's (a replica of Romanoff's—who appears as himself), where he meets Mel, his agent (Art Smith), a fussy, white-haired little man who worries out loud a lot, and Charly (Robert Warwick), an alcoholic old ham whom Dix affectionately calls "Thespian." With both these figures, Dix is strikingly protective, even paternal. When a hack producer at the bar—another bigmouth—insults the old actor, Dix knocks the guy to the floor. "There goes Dix again!" says a woman in a nearby booth—who turns out to be his ex-girlfriend, someone (it's implied) who may have gotten knocked around by him too. By now you have the impression he doesn't just take offense; he seizes it.

But he has good reason to be angry. He's surrounded by phonies and bullies. And his writing career isn't going a lot better than his love life. "You haven't written a hit since before the war," says the director he's just described as "a popcorn salesman" while drinking beside him at the bar. "I won't work on something I don't like," Dix replies. But you know that he has, and that he will again—and so does he. What else is he doing in Hollywood? Or at Paul's now, with his anxiety-ridden little agent pleading with him to accept the writing assignment on the crappy best-selling novel the hatcheck girl is reading eagerly even as they speak? (She's borrowed Dix's copy.) "Remember," Mel says to him, "*she's* your audience." If Dix says yes to the job tonight, he can go on salary tomorrow, Mel promises him. After all, it's not as if it should be *difficult* to do: "All you have to do is follow the book," says Mel.

But Dix doesn't even want to read it. At least not tonight—at home by himself. It's in this mood that he asks the hatcheck girl, the soon-to-be-murdered Mildred (Martha Stewart), to come back with him to his place, where she can tell him the story of the thing. Why not? She seems eager to talk about it, and to oblige him, once he assures her that his intentions are honorable, as they seem to be—mostly, anyway.

She is chattering away at his side when the two of them walk into the next shot, entering the enclosed courtyard of the apartment complex he lives in. It's familiar California-baroque, with palm trees and spikey plants around a central fountain, amid tiles and fancy grillwork. "Sort of hacienda-like, huh?" says Mildred, as she stops to look around. You can see he is already depressed by her. He leaves her alone in her full-length shot as she stands and gawks—then he re-enters it from the right to bring her along impatiently, taking her by the arm. That's the moment when Laurel (her first appearance) walks in from the left, her hands in the pockets of her light-colored, high-collared coat, coming silently up behind them on the narrow pathway, exchanging a glance with Dix as she passes between them. "Excuse me," she says softly—and she's gone. All in the same medium shot. Then a much closer shot of Dix and Mildred, in side-by-side profiles, looking after her—with Dix moving ever so slightly forward, as if drawn in her wake. And the soundtrack music (which up to now has been noodling away idly, in the spirit of Mildred's chatter) introduces the movie's desolate, deep-sighing romantic theme, in full orchestral flourish. A neighbor of yours? asks Mildred. No. He's never seen her before.

They go into the apartment and he gives Mildred a drink (ginger ale) as she launches on her task of telling him the story of the book, called *Althea Bruce* (she keeps calling the title character "A-lay-thee-a," in spite of his irritated and repeated corrections). It's the story ("It's what I call an epic," she says) of a beautiful young woman who really didn't mean, in spite of the way it looks, to drown her rich, elderly husband, and who falls in love with a lifeguard who is "really" a student at Columbia, and so on and on, with Mildred, drink in hand, prowling excitedly around the room (the camera following) as she relives all the high points for her now very unhappy host. At one point, she even bears down on the camera, looking directly into it (i.e., at Dix), nattering away as she approaches: she looks wild-eyed, even menacing. As indeed she is, from Dix's point of view: "Remember, *she's* your audience."

He flees to his bedroom, assuring her through the doorway that he can still hear her in there. Unhappily, he can. " 'All you have to do is follow the book,' " he says to himself with a grim laugh, registering the full hopelessness of Mel's words. That's the moment when he sees Laurel a second time (she's a neighbor, after all), out his open window and across the courtyard, standing on her balcony in a negligee, dim but distinct. He stares longingly, while the childish voice in the other room prattles away. He goes back to the living room: he's heard enough, he tells Mildred, kindly but firmly. But instead of offering to drive her home, he gives her the cab fare, almost propelling her out the door in his eagerness to be rid of her now. Later during the night she is brutally murdered—strangled and left by a roadside.

Laurel, in the gray light of the police station the next morning (she's been called there to be questioned about her sightings of Dix the night before), is no longer the enigmatic figure of the courtyard, but a very down-to-earth girl, in slacks and a checkered jacket, who has been gotten up too early but is still remarkably clear and cogent in response to questions about Dix's movements. "You've paid quite a bit of attention to Mr. Steele," says her avuncular but stern interrogator, Captain Lochner (Carl Benton Reid). "I have at that," says Laurel dryly, with an amused smile, as Dix, sitting behind her, watches the back of her head steadily and gravely. But she's never met him, Lochner persists. "I noticed him because he looked interesting," she says. Then adds: "I liked his face."

This remark gets echoed soon afterwards when Dix goes back to his

The cross-currents at the police station: (left to right) Frank Lovejoy
as Brub, the cop; Carl Benton Reid as Captain Lochner;
Grahame; and Bogart

apartment and looks Laurel up in his casting directory. "*Won*-derful face!"
he exclaims over her photo, talking more or less to Mel, who has turned up
full of excitement and worry over Mildred's murder. But Dix is not much
interested in that subject. Nor is the movie. What's interesting from now
on is the emotional current between him and Laurel. In the face of that
phenomenon, even Lochner seems to lose his thread—at least momentarily. Do young women often react to his face so favorably? he asks Dix at
that first interview. If they do, says Dix, "they're not usually as outspoken
as Miss Gray." And he tells Laurel later on what *he* felt when he first met
her at the police station—in the form of what he said to himself: "There
she is: the one that's different. She's not coy or cute or corny—she's a good
guy, I'm glad she's on my side. She speaks her mind and she knows what
she wants." But, as she tells him in reply to this speech, she also knows she
doesn't want to be "rushed."

Because "not-coyness" has its own formalities and indirections. Laurel is
no Mildred, and certainly no one's easy mark. She can be as direct as she
first was because Lochner made it possible—he even made it witty—to
respond that way. Both she and Dix have a taste for elegant parrying—as
when he stands in front of a hallway mirror after this exchange and asks

her how she could possibly *like* a face like that. Then he promptly puts his first move on her, which she eludes deftly by turning his face away with her hand and slipping out from under his arm. "I said I liked it, I didn't say I wanted to *kiss* it," she replies. And he seems almost as gratified by the wisecrack as he is disappointed by the rebuff.

Next to *his* ravaged face, Grahame's heart-shaped mask looks almost unbelievably burnished and smooth, with its hooded eyes and long, immobile upper lip. Her prettiness is sulky, humorous, sardonic, with one or the other eyebrow rising on an elegant diagonal, a faint smile lurking permanently at the corners of the mouth and the back of the eyes: the face of someone who might seem insolent *if* she could be bothered to. And her simple *appreciation* of the Bogart hero in this film—even when she's blocking his pass—is wonderfully appealing. Laurel is a person, Grahame convinces you, who really would "know" faces.

After she and Dix have become lovers (very discreetly indicated, but unmistakably, as usual), Dix's apartment seems to turn into a kind of familial nest, with Dix at its center, working steadily at last on the new script (it seems to be *Althea Bruce* after all), without letup, and with Laurel acting as house mother, taking care and giving orders, and Mel and Charly supplying their different kinds of childishness and dependence—the whole group surrounding Dix as he writes and giving off a powerful feeling of well-being and achieved serenity. Something that reaches a strange and moving climax in the domestic ceremony of putting Dix—written out at last—to bed in the middle of the day: leading him, numbed and half-staggering, solemnly across the room, a procession in which Charly—with little Mel beside him, the acolyte at his elbow, and Laurel ahead of him, becoming the guardian at the bedroom door—recites these lines from a Shakespeare sonnet (**XXIX**: "When, in disgrace with Fortune and men's eyes . . ."):

> *For thy sweet love remember'd such wealth brings*
> *That then I scorn to change my state with kings.*

Thus blessed, and ushered to his bed, Dix goes to sleep. His romance with Laurel has not only transformed his writer's block, it's given him a new rich life as the center of a "family." And it's a typical Bogart fulfillment—the tough guy as reluctant patriarch (*To Have and Have Not, Casablanca, High Sierra,* et al.)—as well as a typical Nicholas Ray situation and event: the improvised family.

"If it were all in the script, why make the movie?" Ray once said—a remark frequently quoted in defense of the "auteur theory." And his favorite procedure was to rewrite his scripts (when the studios would let him get away with it, and they were in such disarray themselves that they often did) *while* he was filming them—usually with and in response to his actors. As with this film: his biographer Bernard Eisenschitz says that only four of the original pages of the screenplay (solely credited to Andrew Solt) were filmed as they were written. Most of these changes seemed to have taken place on the set (from which Bogart had insisted, for whatever reasons, that Solt be barred), coming out of discussion and improvisation. The movie's original ending had Dix, driven over the edge by Laurel's attempt to run out on him, strangling her in a rage, then sitting down, with her body in the bedroom, to type the concluding lines of his uncompleted screenplay—the words that he had recited to her earlier: "I was born when she kissed me, I died when she left me, I lived a few weeks while she loved me." Just then, a cop friend arrives to tell him that he's been cleared of Mildred's murder, that they got the man who did it (a jealous boyfriend). Cleared of one murder just as he's caught at another: It's what they call an irony, as Mildred might have said.

Ray and his stars actually did shoot this ending, at midpoint in their production schedule—which only confirmed their sense that it wouldn't work. Instead, they improvised the ending as it now is. Dix attacks Laurel but is brought suddenly down from his rage by the phone ringing. He answers it: it's the news about the boyfriend confessing to the murder and clearing him. He hands the phone to Laurel. "Man wants to apologize to you," he says to her in a dead voice. It's Captain Lochner on the other end, giving her the good news. "Yesterday," says Laurel into the phone, "this would have meant so much to us. Now it doesn't matter, it doesn't matter at all . . . ," as Dix walks out of the apartment and across the courtyard. Laurel, hanging up, watches him go: " 'I lived a few weeks while you loved me . . .' " she says aloud, leaning against the doorway—as Dix, in a long shot from her point of view, walks off into the end title.

Not only the final film but the presence and performance of both Grahame and Bogart make that earlier rejected ending, with its trashy, dumb irony, seem all but unimaginable. The grown-upness of Dix and Laurel is so central to our sense of them—their ability to recognize too-lateness, to accept what cannot be unsaid or undone. Whatever their problems or flaws (sizable in both), they are not the sort of characters who need to be arrested or killed to understand finality.

His violence, of course, is no surprise. The Bogart hero was associated with that. There were clear suggestions of sadism in his Sam Spade and

Captain Lochner's too-late phone call: "Now it doesn't matter.
It doesn't matter at all."

Philip Marlowe, and in Harry Morgan, the hero of *To Have and Have Not.*
But that element was never foregrounded: it complicated his heroism
without changing its nature. Here, however, the besetting question is
about that nature, and it concerns everyone else in the movie: is Dix really
normal? Not a question that could have been posed about those earlier
Bogart heroes—except for a joke or a wisecrack. But this is the fifties
already, and here it's crucial, and not just for Laurel. It becomes the focus of
Captain Lochner's interest: he is much struck by the undisturbed way Dix
seems to look at the grisly photos of the murdered Mildred—is *that* normal? But none of us could tell what he felt about anything, says Brub
Nicolai (Frank Lovejoy), Lochner's assistant, who knows Dix from the
recent war, having served with him in combat. His men trusted and liked
him, Brub says, but no one could ever "figure him out."

But there is a self-announced "psychology major" in this movie too—
something Bogart's never had to face before. It's Brub's wife, Sylvia (Jeff
Donnell), a perky little wife-and-homemaker. And if Brub is content to
rest with and accept his old army buddy's impenetrableness, Sylvia is not.
She serves supper to the two of them (a scene right after Dix's first encounters with Lochner and Laurel) one evening. They are seated in her compact

little dining area, among the knickknack shelves, the organdy curtains, and the plaid-covered "rustic"-style furniture. Sylvia does not like her husband's friend—that's apparent from her first close-up. She smiles as Dix talks, but weakly—weaker still when they all adjourn to the living-room area and Dix begins to give, at Brub's request, his own imagining of how Mildred was killed, and what her killer was like. As he talks, a sinister close-up (a shaft of light across his avid, gleaming eyes) underscores the creepy enthusiasm the subject of murder brings out in him. We know by now that Dix has an affinity for violence (the guy in the next car, the big-mouth at the bar). But his expression of it here seems as much and as reasonably a response to Sylvia and her living room as to any inner prompting. When he next stages a demonstration, with Brub as the killer and Sylvia as Mildred, of the method of Mildred's strangling, he gets Brub so momentarily carried away enacting the killer's emotions that Sylvia almost gets choked. The Sylvia smile that follows *that* episode—once she gets loose—is very weak indeed.

"I'm glad *you're* not a genius," she says to her husband once Dix has gone. "He's a sick man, Brub." But Brub won't buy that. Sylvia persists: "Well, there's *something* wrong with him." What it is, says Brub, is that Dix is just so out of the ordinary—"a superior person" and "an exciting guy." "He's exciting because he isn't quite *normal*," she retorts—adding that she prefers the way Brub himself is, "attractive and average" (and reminding him again about her major).

Laurel is a bit out of the ordinary herself. She is an ex-starlet, down on her luck, who has just run out on her situation as a Beverly Hills real-estate man's mistress. Her only apparent friend—"all that's left of my movie career"—is a burly and sinister masseuse named Martha, who tries to frighten her off Dix (she wants her to go back to the rich guy) by telling her the gossip about how he treated his last girlfriend (the one we saw briefly at Paul's). Lochner, too, is trying to scare her about Dix—showing her his photo gallery of *other* likable faces, all of them belonging to convicted murderers. She tells Lochner that she loves Dix and is going to marry him, and walks out. But she doesn't tell Dix about this interview—she knows how it would upset him, with his paranoia.

But Sylvia *does* tell him—while the two couples are picnicking on a beach. "I don't know why I said that," she announces, after Dix has stormed off in a rage. "Brub especially asked me not to." Laurel goes after him, and they drive away, not speaking. And then he gets into another fight on the road—with a college kid he cut off. And Laurel sits helplessly in the car, looking on in horror, screaming when Dix (who is winning) picks up a rock to brain the guy with. He drops it and gets back in the car. He calms down as they drive on. She accuses him of having really wanted to brain *her.* No, he says—it was the kid, and his smart mouth . . . showing the same lack of self-awareness Sylvia has just displayed.

And Laurel turns to Sylvia, visiting her alone one day. "This is just what I want someday," she tells her, "a small, cozy house near the ocean." It isn't just Lochner who's upset her, she confides to Sylvia, but her own suspicions of Dix. She's ashamed, of course, for even having them—but at her most desperate, she's no longer so sure that he *couldn't* have killed Mildred. She appeals to Sylvia: "But there *is* something strange about Dix, isn't there?" Sylvia doesn't exactly answer, but she doesn't deny it either.

It's *his* fault in a way. As she exclaims to the ever-faithful Mel later on: "Why can't he be like *other* people?!" "Would you have liked him if he was?" Mel responds. She wouldn't, of course—any more than we would. And as the movie goes on, the issue becomes less and less "what's wrong" with Dix—we never learn and we never really expect to—and more and more what Laurel will do about him. The question for us has never been whether he killed Mildred (we're never invited to suppose he did) but whether Laurel can really put up with the uncertainty (for her) of whether he did: another way of asking whether she can put up with the ultimate uncertainty of Dix himself, with all his trouble and complication and even danger.

She can't, of course. How could she? We understand that, and we are closer to her than we are to him. She starts, mid-movie, to have bad dreams about him—which we see (we never, of course, see *his* dreams)—only to wake up and find him sitting beside the bed and watching her curiously, wanting to know when she started to take sleeping pills (he's found the bottle). This is how the Dix-making-breakfast scene begins—and it ends with her agreeing at his urging to get married right away. They kiss; and once again his head rises into the frame and blots her out. She's lying—and playing for time—as she tells Mel when he comes in, just after Dix has left to buy the ring. It's all going too fast for her, and she has become too afraid of his violence to confront him and tell him she wants out. She tells Mel she's written a letter "explaining" everything—for Dix to read once she's gotten away on the plane flight she's reserved for that night.

In the meantime, though, there's the engagement party at Paul's to get through—she and Dix and Mel and Charly, the whole family, together in a booth. Dix, increasingly edgy because of the feelings he's picking up from Laurel, explodes at Mel and slugs him, smashing the little man's glasses, then follows him to the washroom to apologize, while Laurel, more terrified than ever, slips out and goes home. She is trying to pack and get out when Dix comes in, flying into the sort of towering rage she's been afraid of, and starting to choke her ("I'll never let you go!"), when the exonerating phone call comes, followed by the bleak-spirited ending I described above.

But if Dix didn't kill Mildred (who was nothing to him), it certainly looks—to her and to us—as if he could have killed Laurel. Never mind that her mistrust and deception, on top of Lochner's investigation, have driven him to it. As she says, just before he starts to throttle her: "I can't live with a maniac!" Of course she can't—and of course you can't blame her.

But you do, nonetheless. It's the paradoxical final effect of this movie to make you feel that Laurel's rejection of Dix is not only justified, even inevitable—after all, *she's* not crazy—but also somehow "wrong." At the same time as the movie has been building the case against him (not as a murderer, but as a hopeless, even dangerous, prospect for a husband), it's been making us feel that Laurel's inability to trust him amounts somehow to some kind of moral and human *failure* on her part. Not quite comparable to his, of course, but still a failure.

How so? Early on, we're told she has a record of running out on people—a "get-out-before-you-get-hurt type," as Dix puts it. And then there's the constant presence of the indomitably loyal Mel. ("You make me feel ashamed," she says to him.) But equally important—perhaps even more so—is that Laurel begins to sound like Sylvia ("Why can't he be like *other* people?").

It's the sound of commonplace judgment—just the sound that people like Dix and Laurel, you presume, might have left their hometown or old neighborhood to get away from. But try getting away from it now—in the fifties, even in L.A. In so many ways, Sylvia's was the sound of the broader culture, complacent, understanding, "psychological," and final: "He's a sick man, Brub"—the voice of doom. "Well, there's *something* wrong with him": Try appealing *that* judgment. Sylvia is inescapable.

Worst of all, in this case, she's right. As she often is. There is quite a lot wrong with Dix. And Ray's movie makes you feel all the oppression of her rightness—even, if on some level, it has to side with a "maniac" to do that. The maniac is Bogart, after all—the most interesting, compelling, and appealing figure in the movie. And he gives this hero's need for this movie's heroine a power and primacy that overwhelms everything in it. And yet, finally, it's all as hopeless as Dix's way with a grapefruit knife. The movie makes you want Dix and Laurel to get together probably most of all when it's let you know they won't.

In his most celebrated roles after *In a Lonely Place*—in *The African Queen* (1951), for example, or in *The Caine Mutiny* (as Captain Queeg) or *Sabrina* (both 1954)—Bogart appears (wisely) as someone else besides the familiar Bogart hero. There were a couple of halfhearted stabs at re-embodying him—*The Enforcer* and *Sirocco* in 1951—but Ray's movie was this hero's final effective appearance. It seems very right indeed that it should be in such a painful and poignant movie—and one where the hero retains to the end, walking into the final fadeout, all his privacy, ambiguity, and essential mystery.

Twelve

JAMES DEAN

N ick and I were much alike," says Elia Kazan in his autobiography (*A Life*, 1988). He and Ray both started out in the workers' theatre movement of the 1930s (the Theatre of Action, a New York collective drama group presided over by Kazan). They bummed around the country together during the Depression, hitchhiking all through East Texas. And later, when Kazan got his first film-directing job, on *A Tree Grows in Brooklyn* (1945), he brought Nick to Hollywood to be his assistant director. Ray would always claim that he learned almost all he knew about moviemaking from watching Kazan—and that Kazan was the greatest actors' director of their generation (Kazan, born in 1909, was two years older). Their active movie careers ran roughly parallel in time—from the postwar forties to the early sixties—but not in prestige or prominence. When Kazan was making his *Streetcar* movie, for example, Ray was at Howard Hughes's RKO shooting something called *Flying Leathernecks* (1951). While Kazan was making *On the Waterfront* with Brando and all those hot new actors (Saint, Malden, Steiger), Ray was at Republic directing an over-the-hill but still unmanageable woman star in a so-called "Freudian western" (*Johnny Guitar*, 1954)—and congratulating himself that he was at least getting his own producer's credit, his first. (He never got it—the shoot was too troubled.) While Kazan, it seemed, was going from success to success in both theatre and film, and to history-making effect in both, Ray remained a marginal figure at best, experiencing more frustration and failure than not, struggling with doomed projects in often ludicrous circumstances. And it didn't help at all that his self-defeating appetites—for drink, dope, gambling—were legendary even by the prevailing Hollywood standards.

"Nick"—as he almost universally (and mostly affectionately) came to be called—was, it soon became apparent, the sort of person who is less deepened by his experience than used up by it (and he used up most of his friends too). That sense of things, and of his own situation, usually found

Nick Ray, circa 1978 in New York

its way into his most remarkable work. Into *In a Lonely Place,* of course, and, just as notably, *Bitter Victory* (1957), his last great film—among others in between. He was credited with directing twenty movies altogether (there were others uncredited) in his Hollywood career—which ended in 1963 after a couple of disastrous (and expensive) European co-productions (*King of Kings* and *55 Days at Peking*). Some of these films were just assignments, which he performed efficiently (like *Flying Leathernecks,* with John Wayne); some (especially later on) were calamities, both personal and professional (like *Wind Across the Everglades,* 1958). But close to half of them were extraordinary in some way.

He was "a dear and sad man who had a hard life" said Kazan in 1971 (to Michel Ciment), when Nick's life was at its hardest. In 1988, a decade after Ray's death, Kazan alludes to him as someone who trashed his own talents in the Hollywood mills: "I saw him give himself over and be lost among the moguls of the film world"—in contrast to Kazan's sense of his own history, as someone who had early taken possession of his own career (as, for example, when he refused Darryl Zanuck's offer of a studio contract in the late forties, returning instead to New York and the theatre) and who consolidated that possession at each crucial juncture, going from being a collaborative artist in theatre and films to being a film auteur and finally a best-selling author of autobiographical novels like *The Arrangement.* And his account in his autobiography of this development—like the one he gives there of his HUAC cooperation—is mostly triumphalist. In any case, it's a very different career story from Ray's "sad . . . hard life," with its early sellout (as Kazan sees it) to the moguls and final decline into illness and unemployability. Kazan never offers an assessment of Ray's work, beyond remarking in passing on his "unique talent" for directing actors, or expressing distaste for *Rebel Without a Cause* for "the way Nick Ray showed the parents."

But on the other hand, he finds himself wondering, toward the end of his old friend's life, and at a time when his own films "began to not quite come off," whether Nick hadn't, after all, been "more of an artist" than he had. "Was my life too even-keeled," he asks (again in the autobiography), "while he'd been living as an artist should?" It's true that Ray had led the sort of life that might make even the most reckless observer feel "even-keeled"—and true as well that Kazan's own excesses (as a proudly tireless and coldhearted sexual operator) ran more to control than the loss of it. But still that last speculation is a startling one—especially in view of what Kazan has said and implied earlier about Ray's life and its destructive effect on his career. But then he says this too: "We'd both started as actors and become directors. But he went 'all the way,' and I did not. I was more disciplined, more in control, more cautious, more bourgeois. Perhaps, I thought, he's been more of an artist, more of a gambler." As an observation about the two men's *movies* (though it's not entirely clear) this seems to me both true and honest—even if it's rather ambiguous praise for Ray. Kazan's movies *are,* on the whole, "more cautious, more bourgeois," less really daring. Whereas Ray, with his odd intensities, his naive enthusiasms and overwrought pretensions, his lack of a certain sense of the ridiculous, took chances in his work (without, perhaps, always knowing they were chances) that Kazan would never have been tempted by.

One result of all this is that while Kazan's high reputation as a filmmaker has been open to reservation and some discounting, Ray's—once the French began to assert it, at any rate—has been liable to disbelief and ridicule. Nicholas Ray *is* the cinema, Godard famously wrote in 1958—at a time when you could have fooled *us.* For the *Cahiers* reviewers generally—with their enthusiasm (the French have no word or phrase for "common sense," as Margery Sabin points out in her brilliant essay comparing French and English literary traditions*), with their bias toward form over

*Margery Sabin, "The Life of English Idiom, the Laws of French Cliché," *Raritan Quarterly,* Fall 1981.

content, for mise-en-scène over plot or (not surprisingly given the language gap) over dialogue—Ray was the cynosure of American filmmakers struggling gallantly inside the commercial system. Whereas to most American audiences and reviewers at the time, the work just looked like the usual junk, or worse. Gore Vidal has told about Orson Welles's highly distressed reaction to a French cineaste's pronouncement in his presence that the three greatest directors of all time had been Griffith, Orson Welles—and Nicholas Ray: it's always that last name that lets you down, Welles appended. And Vidal himself refers elsewhere (and dismissively, of course) to the kind of critic who calls *Johnny Guitar* a great movie. Depending on us to know the type—as indeed we do, by now (there's a lot of us).

Elia Kazan with friend John Steinbeck

Kazan didn't have a very high opinion of his friend Steinbeck's 1952 novel, *East of Eden* ("certainly not one of John's best"). He wasn't alone. What had attracted him to this long, turgid (and badly reviewed) "modern-day" biblical allegory was the last third of it, about a pair of Cain-and-Abel brothers contending for the love of their stern, virtuous, Abraham-like father. Kazan right away thought of Brando, his favorite actor, for the role of Cal, the Cain figure (they had just finished *Waterfront*). But when playwright Paul Osborn, who was then working on the screenplay of the Steinbeck novel, saw the then unknown James Dean on Broadway, playing a seductive Arab houseboy in *The Immoralist* (from the Gide novel), he told Kazan about him. Kazan went to see the show, and even let the kid take him on a motorcycle ride through Manhattan traffic afterward ("he was showing off"). And he seems to have disliked the young actor (as he told it later) from that first meeting. But—"I called Paul and told him this kid actually *was* Cal." He sent Dean to visit Steinbeck, who also disliked him ("a snotty kid") but who agreed that he was indeed Cal to the life.

But then—by his own account at least—so was Kazan himself. This movie, he tells us, was meant to be "part of an autobiography," an early installment. Like Cal in the novel, Kazan also had had a father he could never really please and who favored his brother. He writes of his satisfaction upon discovering that Dean too had such a father. "I saw the story of the movie was his story," just as it was, he adds, "my own." Kazan was a Method artist, after all. He admits that he could never successfully direct anything (forget "the classics") that he couldn't intimately connect to his own life in some way.

Like everyone else, Kazan called his new star "Jimmy," but his other name for him (reportedly) was "Creep"—presumably referring to Dean's propensity for activities like taking endless and indistinguishable snapshots of himself in his dressing-room mirror. And unlike Brando, Kazan reports, "the kid" had no training or technique to get him through scenes where he had a problem. But mostly Dean just never had a problem, he was so close to the character. When he did, however, no direction could solve it, and Kazan had to try other things. For a rooftop conversation scene with Julie Harris that just wasn't working at all, he got Dean drunk on Chianti (and the scene *still* doesn't work, though Kazan appears to think it does). When the director discovered that Raymond Massey—playing Cal's father Adam—disliked Dean even more than he and Steinbeck had ("couldn't stand the sight of [him], dreaded every day he worked with him"), he relayed this news to Dean—and then told Massey what Dean had said in reply, and so forth, until "the screen was alive with precisely what I wanted": their visible mutual loathing. And when his young star seemed distracted, Kazan moved him onto the set to live, and then moved in next door to him—thus discovering that the problem was Pier Angeli (he could hear them "boffing" through his wall). Until she married Vic Damone (Kazan takes no credit for that), and then "I had Jimmy as I wanted him, alone and miserable."

But all this surveillance and control turned out to be worth it, for Dean as well as Kazan. Even before the movie opened in 1955, Dean became known as a hot property, and began work on his next starring picture, Ray's *Rebel Without a Cause*. Kazan felt well rid of him. For sure he'd gotten what he wanted from him, but he was still astounded at the sensation "this twisted, fidgety kid" could make. Beginning with his movie's first pre-

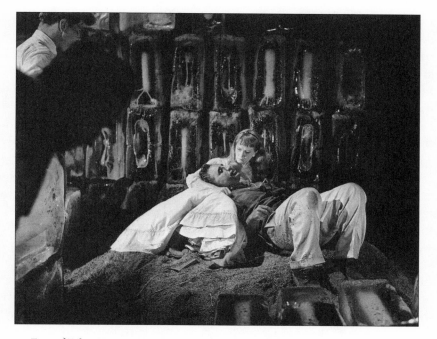

East of Eden: Kazan is showing Dean (just visible at left) how to play—
and be—Cal, in the icehouse scene with Julie Harris (as Abra).

view—where "hundreds" of girls began to scream at the first sight they
had of him. It was, Kazan says, as if they'd been waiting for him, "how
come or why, I don't know." In any case, "the goddamn kid became a legend overnight." Kazan still disapproves of that legend, and steadfastly
refuses to contribute to it, declining all inquiries or interview requests
relating to it. Dean, says Kazan, was "self-pitying, self-dramatizing, and
good-for-nothing," just like the teenage heroes he played in his film and
then in Ray's, both of them promoting the mistaken idea that parents are
the enemy and that kids are all sensitive and misunderstood. And if Kazan
had disliked the actor the first time he met him, by the end of *Eden's* filming—when Dean started abusing the underlings and generally behaving
like the star-from-hell—he positively despised him. He warned Nick, he
says.

He doesn't report the response. But whatever it was, he had the wrong
man: if anyone *could* like the offscreen Dean, it would be Nick. Here was
someone over thirty who really *did* believe that parents were the enemy.
Especially if they belonged to his and Kazan's generation, the ones who
had come of age during the Great Depression. It was Nick's conviction,
often reiterated, that they had betrayed the generation that followed them

in some specially egregious way. It was a vague notion at best—no one seemed to know quite what he meant by it (apart from his guilt about his own kids)—but it grew on him in the fifties, and made him feel very much at home later on in the cultural currents of the sixties. The sentimental populism of the thirties left-wing theatre movement he and Kazan started out in was congenial to Ray's temperament in a way that it never could have been to the shrewder, more cynical Kazan's (who says now, quite credibly, that he was faking it much of the time). But come the rigorously "nonpolitical" fifties, when class struggle in America was supposed to have been made unnecessary (Ray had been a Communist in the thirties but somehow later on never got interrogated or blacklisted—he was said to have been protected, improbably enough, by his friend Howard Hughes), for Nick it was as if, in a more up-to-date set of emotional allegiances, the workers and their bosses had been replaced by kids and their parents.

But in many ways he was himself an example of what Erwin Knoll called "that peculiarly American phenomenon, the lifelong kid." Ray had not just a sympathy with the contemporary young but almost an anxiety to ally himself with them, both in his life and in his work—being surrounded much of the time, in his late years especially, by adoring circles of them, and leaving behind (as such adored figures often do) many bitter feelings and memories.

His first movie, *They Live by Night* (1948)—produced by his friend John Houseman, at RKO when it was still under Dore Schary's management—was a feverishly romanticized version of the Bonnie and Clyde legend, hapless young lovers on the lam. Like the pair in Fritz Lang's *You Only Live Once* (1937), only younger and more innocent, and with a concern that never touched Lang's lovers (Henry Fonda and Sylvia Sidney) about "fitting in" and seeming like "normal" people. Where Lang's couple are victimized by society in *spite* of being "just like the rest of us," Ray's pair are victimized *because* they're *not* like the rest of us. The main thing that Bowie (Farley Granger) has got to learn now that he's out of prison, his older jailbreak partner tells him, is to "look and act like other people." Not easy. On their "honeymoon," Bowie and Keechie (Cathy O'Donnell) watch normal people at their normal diversions—playing golf, riding horseback, dancing in a nightclub—without quite understanding what they're seeing. "People sure do act funny," observes Bowie. But they hope to get the hang of it themselves and learn to live "like real people," as Bowie puts it. "This boy and this girl," says the fancy script appearing on the screen even before the movie's title does, over a ravishing close-up of the lovers entwined before a fireplace, "were never properly introduced to the world we live in."

If this seems a bit overexplicit, it turns out we can use the help it gives us. They are such a bland couple—being "different" mainly by being prettier, though in a nonglamorous way (Cathy O'Donnell's stirring plainness is specially effective). They have none of the awkwardness and oddity, the truly marginal quality, of the Bowie and Keechie in Robert Altman's movie version of the same novel (by Edward Anderson), *Thieves Like Us* (1974), with Keith Carradine and Shelley Duvall in the roles. Ray's couple are too idealized for that: they carry the burden of standing—even in an otherwise rather brutally realistic movie—for his general sentimental idea of victimized kids.

Given this bias of his, it's not hard to imagine how galling the job (for a quickie outfit at Paramount called Pine-Thomas) of directing a movie like *Run for Cover* (1955) must have been for him. A low-budget western starring James Cagney as an aging gunfighter, it was (like a lot of westerns at that time) a thinly disguised juvenile-delinquent movie. But it dealt with that issue in a way that made Ray very unhappy—in spite of the unalloyed pleasure of working with Cagney ("a good man," Cagney says of Nick in his autobiography). The Cagney hero comes to the town and befriends a troubled gunslinging boy (John Derek) who has become the town scourge. The townspeople have given up on the kid, but not Cagney, whose own dead son would have been the same age. He sets out to make a man of Derek—and fails: the town was right, this kid is hopeless. And in the ritual climactic gunfight, Cagney shoots him dead.

Luckily for Nick, it only took thirty days to film—and left him more eager than ever for his next assignment, the *Rebel* picture. After talking Warners into it, he began his preparation: making copious research notes, hiring and firing successive writers (before settling on Stewart Stern, author of *The Rack*), interviewing experts at Los Angeles Juvenile Hall, even hanging out with the youth gangs in the Valley (until they decided to invade and wreck his house). All this went on so long that the studio almost pulled the plug on him. But his sense of the importance of this picture was, if anything, growing—so much so that two weeks before he commenced shooting, he undertook to write a book about the whole project, calling it *Rebel: Life Story of a Film.* Though he only finished two chapters (later revising them for publication), one of them records his early encounter with Dean.

> Late one evening he arrived at my house . . . On entering the room he turned a back somersault, then from the floor looked keenly at me.

The fatal climactic gunfight in *Run for Cover:*
Cagney exchanges shots with the irredeemable John Derek (at far right).
(Ernest Borgnine is the stiff on the ground.)

"Are you middle-aged?"
I admitted it.

You wonder if Nick ever told his friend Kazan about this meeting. And if he included the star's dramatic entrance by somersault, or his *faux-naïf* questioning. It isn't hard to imagine what Kazan's reaction would have been ("then from the floor looked keenly at me," indeed). But Nick not only bought the whole show, he joined it—as best he could in his prose. "First there was the revolver" is how he opens the reminiscence, his breathless way of telling us that Dean kept a Colt .45 in his dressing room ("where he also slept"). He says Jimmy "threw himself on the world like a starved animal," approaching each person he met "with the same urgent probing curiosity: *'Here I am. Here are you.'* " On the other hand, he also reports—without apparent irony—the young star's announcement that he has decided to stop being "nice," so that he can be respected for his work alone.

Ray had only thirty pages of written screenplay when he first approached Dean about playing the lead. And Dean was cagey at first. Ray describes the decisive exchange, after dinner at a New York restaurant:

. . . He looked up at me. Something in his expression suggested he was about to impart a special confidence. He was restless, more so than usual.

"I got crabs," he said. "What do I do?"

I took him to a drugstore and introduced him to Cuprex. Outside in the street, we parted. He thanked me for the help, smiled, then said:

"I want to do your film but don't tell those bastards at Warners."

I said I was glad, and that I wouldn't tell Warners anything except that I wanted him. We shook hands on it.

This bonding over Cuprex and crabs—like a Hemingway parody—was a crucial one, Ray implies. The kid reminded him of himself: they were both "cat-like" ("a wound to the pride of a cat is serious. Ask any of us cats"); both thought of themselves as rebels; they both hated phonies and studio bosses and the Hollywood game; and both had had bad fathers. And so it developed that Dean now had for his director—on his second movie—not a masterful and doting dad like Kazan, but an easygoing big brother, who seemed less concerned with controlling him than with making him a collaborator, involving him at every stage of production, from planning to filming to writing.

In fact, all the kids in Ray's cast would contribute dialogue to the final version, it seemed. And yet if it was sometimes hard to tell who was writing, it could be even harder at other times to tell who was directing; Dennis Hopper, who played one of the gang members, claims to have thought it was Dean. "He did certainly control all the scenes he was in, and he's in almost every scene," he told Bernard Eisenschitz. Hopper remembers Dean chewing out Ray in front of everyone because the director had called "Cut" during the knife fight scene when the actor felt he was still on a high ("Don't you ever say fucking Cut, man, I'm the only one who says Cut here").

Ray's laid-back directing style, along with his apparent eagerness to bond with his cast, may have left his star feeling the contrast with Kazan in some uneasy ways. "This man," he told a friend at one point, "does not know what he's doing." On the other hand, everyone knew what he was doing with the underage Natalie Wood (she was fifteen, Nick was forty-four) once they were caught in the shower together by Dennis Hopper, who was also sleeping with her. It was Hopper, however, who got caught by her parents—thanks to Nick, who told on him. That's how Hopper tells it now, in any case.

But Nick and Jimmy became, and stayed, friends. The actor then went on to *Giant,* and George Stevens—whom he *really* never got along with. *Rebel*—opening after his death—was a huge hit, bigger even than *East of Eden.* It was Ray's biggest commercial success, and his last one. And it was the biggest moneymaker in Warner Bros. history.

"Focus always on the kids," Ray wrote in his preliminary notes for the movie. "Adults should always be seen through eyes of kids. Same for places." And that's the way he did it, however disconcertingly. The movie has the same lack of curiosity about its grown-ups as an adolescent like Jim Stark (Dean) might have. His parents, as well as his live-in grandmother, are in a lot of the movie, but we never learn too much about them—not what the father does, for example, nor what any of them do besides say good-bye to Jim when he goes out and then wait up for him to come home. We know that the family has had to move a lot—but that too was always about Jim, the successive schools he got in trouble in.

And what isn't dreamlike about this family is cartoonish (even literally so: the voice of Mr. Magoo, Jim Backus, plays the father). We recognize them from comic strips: the mother-in-law (Virginia Brissac) heckles the wife, and the wife (Ann Doran) nags the Milquetoast husband, who goes about the house in an apron, taking the wife (her nerves have given out) her meals on a tray. And when his son comes to him with a real life-and-death sort of decision to make (about the "chickie run" challenge), Dad suggests they sit down and make a list ("I'll get a pencil!").

The reviewers who had been impressed by Dean's first movie were more or less appalled by this one. What was specially off-putting was the way it seemed to flatter its teenage audience. Not so much by portraying the kids in general as in any way admirable or even particularly attractive (the gang are a collection of bullies and their toadies), but by taking them so seriously, showing all the dumb, self-important rituals of aggression and self-destruction with something like awe—something like *Wow!*—without distance or irony. Much the same way, of course, that Nick took Dean himself.

To the middle-aged moviegoer, it was a peculiar experience—almost as if some implicit contract with the audience was being broken. It was an A movie that *felt* like a B—made for a narrowly targeted audience the way all those zero-budget Republic westerns had been made for the rubes in the sticks. The so-called general audience that A movies were supposedly made for may always have been as much myth as fact (black people, for example, had reason to feel excluded by it), but it was still (whether you knew it or not) one of the things that you went to the movies for—to join it for a couple of hours or more, to visit that commonality. But you saw *this* movie, and you knew it was ending.

Jim Stark (Dean) and his dad (Jim Backus) at the police station
in *Rebel Without a Cause*

But of the two movies that defined the Dean persona for us, the really
swoony, fan-ish one turns out, surprisingly enough, not to be Ray's but
Kazan's. From the first sight of him in *East of Eden* (no wonder those preview girls screamed)—suffering and longing, kicking at the dirt outside
his mother's whorehouse, the lost son—it's clear that as far as the *camera* is
concerned, this kid is going to be adored. Framed throughout in luscious
wide-screen views that make him look achingly beautiful, both defiant
and undefended, offering a face so full of hurt sometimes that it reminds
you of an open wound, Dean's Cal is a genuinely powerful performance.
But it's also, under Kazan's direction, an insistently lovable one. He is
meant to be heartbreaking—and he mostly is. But the insistence makes
you nervous.

Whereas in Ray's film it's Dean himself who makes you nervous. He
even looks different than before—more demonish than elfish, without the
tousled glamour or boyish winsomeness of the Kazan film. He has a mad-
clown face too—as when he's taunting his feckless dad—with the close-set
eyes shining meanly, the inverted V of his eyebrows like a mirror reflection
of the thin, sick smile below. The nastiness—always present as a possibility, but used by Kazan mainly for spasms of theatrical villainy—is nearer
the surface now; the wound is faintly gangrenous. He's still a powerfully

ABOVE: His mother in *East of Eden*—Jo Van Fleet—is cold and rejecting.
BELOW: Bad enough—but in the arms of Ann Doran,
his mother in *Rebel Without a Cause,* his plight looks even worse
(father Jim Backus and police psychologist Edward Platt are at left).

appealing presence, but he is also a disturbing one. Unlike *They Live by Night*—where the young lovers seem on a mostly genteel literary model—*Rebel Without a Cause* gives you the feeling that it really understands about these kids, about their "terrifying morose aimlessness" (as Ray puts it in his research notes); about the peculiar glamour (for all of us) of self-destruction, and the deep erotic charge it often carries—an insight that's in all the details of the marvelous "chickie run" drag-race sequence. *Rebel Without a Cause*—in spite of its gaucherie and occasional mawkishness—offers a complicated experience of both its star and its subject.

A comparison of *Rebel* and *East of Eden* throws light on what Kazan was getting at when he found himself wondering if his friend had been "more of an artist" after all. His film is more coherent, with more variety and consistency of tone, more taste and intelligence in the writing and performing, with an unfailing energy and brio throughout. It's a more dependable sort of entertainment, even in some ways a clearly better movie. But it also, as it goes on, comes close to feeling like a succession of terrific *effects*—and while you go along with it, even feel moved by it at times (the Dean performance especially), it feels curiously empty. And overbearing: an example of what Manny Farber calls "hard-sell cinema," conveying an unearned emotional urgency—characteristic, in Farber's view (in 1957), of directors like Kazan.

When Cal takes his innocent brother, Aaron, to their mother's whore-house to show him what she really is and does, as Kazan described it to Michel Ciment, "Dean not only *showed* his brother to his mother but he threw his brother at his mother"—so that the "reunited" mother and son collapse in a heap on the floor, while the orchestra screams and Cal scuttles away in malevolent triumph. When interviewed by Ciment, Kazan cited this moment as an example of how he would turn psychology into action. Instead of having the three people look at one another in varying states of horror and satisfaction, leaving us to infer their thoughts, he gave them an action that was "especially *a propos* because the brother was a puritan. So Cal says: 'Not only will I show you the shit that you come from, but I'll rub your face in the shit that you come from.' " But the effect is finally as unconvincing as this heavy-handed rationale suggests: worked up and rhetorical more than real. There is a parallel moment of excess in Ray's film, one that's arguably even more melodramatic. It's when Jim attacks his temporizing dad in their living room, knocking him over a couch and landing on the floor with him in a heap, while his mother screams on the staircase. But here the effect is genuinely shocking—it's a moment of real outrage, both between the characters and on the screen. Partly because

Ray's characters live—as *East of Eden*'s do not—in a world where the possibility of *violation,* the violation *between* people, real and terrible and obscene, is always alive. The emotional heat in Kazan's film is just excessive warmth; in Ray's, it's infernal.

In theatre, Kazan was a famously effective audience-grabber, with an instinct for the surefire moment. Even his most distinguished stage work—like *Streetcar*—was famously overwrought, combining the inwardness of the Method with the "outwardness" of Broadway pizazz and calculation. Mostly the plays he took on when he was at the peak of his theatrical success—*J.B., Tea and Sympathy, Dark at the Top of the Stairs,* et al.—all but defined the word "middlebrow." His movies, however, were chancier on the whole and more interesting—often much better than that, in the case of the best ones: *Streetcar* and *Waterfront,* most of *Baby Doll* (1956), much of *A Face in the Crowd* (1957). And as these last two films showed, he had a quality Ray could *never* have laid a claim to: a real comic gift.

But finally you can feel that there is something too *frontal* about even his best and most brilliant work (apart from the two great Brando films)—that even there, even in the nuances, what you feel and experience most immediately is what you get, and *all* you get. In contrast to Ray at his best: *those* feelings, tortured and tangled as they are, can really haunt you.

And by now, with more and more hindsight, it seems clearer than ever that the real achievements of fifties filmmaking were less in the area of the prestige production, where Kazan operated so confidently for a while, but on its edges: where Nick Ray was and pretty much remained—though not where he *wanted* to be.

Thirteen

NICHOLAS RAY

It sometimes seemed, to people around him, that Nick was almost incapable of making the film he'd started out to make—or was assigned to make. In his later interviews, he turned this into a boast: we were "winging it all the way," he'd claim proudly; and that was, of course, part of the reckless-artist image he cultivated. But the boast, like the image, was largely true—and it had mixed results in his work, to say the least. It turned out surprisingly well in *Born to Be Bad* (1950), a minor film he made for his contract studio, RKO, just before doing *In a Lonely Place* for Bogart. A scheming-beauty-on-the-make story starring Joan Fontaine, it was a modest programmer with a smart, better-than-average script credited to Edith Sommer—which Ray, of course, was soon struggling to change. Rodney Amateau, his assistant and friend, described to Bernard Eisenschitz how it typically went during shooting:

> ... Nick would say ... "I hate this scene"—"What's wrong with it?"—"I don't know, I can't get into this scene"—"But you liked it when the guy wrote it"—"No, I'm gonna change the whole scene"— "Wait a minute, you can't change ..." It was a major studio system, and I'd say, "Nick, don't do that, don't get involved with this thing, why don't you shoot the scene, it's just Joan Fontaine, it's just a fucking picture"—"No-ooo, this picture shows the turmoil inside a woman's heart." I said, "The only turmoil inside Joan Fontaine's heart is whether her dressing room is heated in the morning. You're the only one who's got any turmoil ..."

And so on. But soon Nick found himself coming to really dislike his glamorous star. And the movie turns out—happily—to be less about the turmoil in a woman's heart than about the nastiness in her crooked little smile. It's a rigorously unsentimental movie (excepting a ludicrous airfield scene both written and directed by studio boss Howard Hughes), beauti-

Nicholas Ray in the director's chair

fully staged and photographed (by Nicholas Musuraca, who also photographed *Out of the Past*), and with a nice comic tartness, especially in the
way it views the Fontaine character's sweet-kid maneuvers and betrayals.

Bigger Than Life (1956), on the other hand, was a Ray picture that
turned out less coherently. It was an ambitious production, and the first
one on Ray's new (and short-lived) Fox contract. James Mason was both
producer and star. But it was Ray who had first been hot on the original
property, a *New Yorker* science essay by Berton Roueché about an actual
cortisone treatment (then the big new wonder drug) that misfired disastrously for a New Jersey teacher and father.

Ray committed to do the film, and then went off to Europe to publicize
Rebel Without a Cause, just about to be released there. When he got back,
Mason had a completed screenplay—done by two veteran Hollywood
writers, Cyril Hume and Richard Maibaum—ready for him. Ray was predictably unhappy with it (as he would remain through the whole production), and unofficially enlisted his writer friends Gavin Lambert and
Clifford Odets to make changes as they went along. But Mason—less fond
of creative chaos than his director was—insisted the screenplay stay sub-
stantially intact, limiting changes to dialogue within scenes. A concession

Ray's *Born to Be Bad:* Joan Fontaine (center) coming between Joan Leslie
and her super-rich fiancé, Zachary Scott

that Ray took full advantage of: he and Lambert worked on rewrites each
night before the next day's filming, he later said.

And although he and Mason "got along" (it was one of the happiest personal relations of his career, Nick said), it was still a troubled set. The Fox
front office knew that Ray was doing unorthodox things with Cinema-
Scope—shooting crazy angles and bigger close-ups than were then
thought allowable in that process. They also knew that he was changing
the script they had approved. As for Mason, according to Lambert he simply never understood what Ray wanted, or why he was so dissatisfied with
the screenplay. And the movie that finally resulted from all this was a box-
office disaster—a major setback in Ray's career.

Ed Avery (Mason) is an underpaid, overworked teacher in a suburban
public school who has to moonlight as a taxicab dispatcher to make ends
meet. What's more, he wants to keep this extra job a secret from his wife,
Lou (Barbara Rush): "She'll think it isn't good enough for me," he explains
to another teacher. But what she thinks instead—that he's having an
affair—is worse. And yet Ed doesn't even seem to notice that something is
bothering her. He comes home from school and she is in the kitchen,
doing the dishes, and telling him how the water heater has broken down

again: her voice has that strangled sound that controlled anger makes. But
Ed—characteristically—is cheerily oblivious. As he continues to be when
she comments on how many late-night school meetings he seems to have
been going to these days—or when she makes a bitchy remark about a
pretty young woman he teaches with. He's a very laid-back type, treating
everyone with a sort of amused kindliness. He is a fine teacher (we see him
in the classroom)—gentle and patient and reassuring, beloved by the kids;
and to his more excitable colleagues, he is a dependably reassuring presence. And the kind of father to his little son, Richie (Christopher Olson),
that anyone might hope to be or have—fond and close and understanding.
He even has a football trophy he won in college on the mantel—a source of
pride to Richie.

But he sure gets on Lou's nerves—or so we see in at least the early
scenes. And you can see why he would: that unflappable, impenetrable
equanimity of his must be hard to live with. The only sign in Ed of what
might be discontent is the way he seems to have decorated his house with
world maps and travel posters—Rome, Bologna, et al. It would be nice to
get away, he says. But there's nothing to suggest the longing is acute. The
only distress we see in this family belongs to Lou. When Ed comes on to
her at bedtime, she looks almost like he's proposing a tooth extraction.

In this Ray movie, it's a husband rather than a wife (in contrast to the
earlier *In a Lonely Place*) who counsels resignation to their own ordinariness. Lou has just said to him—after an evening at cards with friends
which had featured an animated discussion about vacuum cleaners and
their effect on children with asthma—that she thinks their friends are
dull. But so are we, says Ed, as they climb the weary stairs to bed. "You
are, I am—let's face it, we're dull," he says brightly, as if he were pleased
with the idea. And when she protests, he even insists on it: "Can you tell
me one thing," he asks in the same genial tone, "that was said or done by
anyone here tonight that was funny, startling, imaginative?" But ordinariness can be a burden too; it can even destroy you: as soon as he's made this
last remark (they have reached the top of the stairs), he falls to the floor in
a sudden spasm of disabling pain.

It's startling certainly—and powerful—but it's not quite the bold
metaphoric flourish I just made it sound like. Because the audience has
known from the beginning that Ed is ill with *something* (in the opening
scene we see him gripped by sudden pain in his classroom) and that he is
concealing the fact from Lou, so as not to worry her. Because—and even
though it often *feels* like it is—this is *not* a movie about suburban malaise
(not unambiguously, anyway), but about a man with an illness (never

named) that would have been fatal to him if he hadn't been given the miraculous new cortisone drug. That drug literally saves his life, but it also sends him into a madness that threatens to destroy both himself and his family. It's a movie about how he becomes addicted to this drug—how it becomes for him, as Ray later put it, "a habitual source of grandeur." And whatever might be said for Ed's life *before* the drug—the satisfactions of family life and his teaching vocation—it certainly lacks "grandeur."

But on the manic high the drug gives him, he becomes another person. Instead of the mild, reasonable, self-effacing type we've been seeing, he becomes a take-charge guy, a big shot (he even *looks* bigger, a friend says), overbearing and iconoclastic. The sort of person who *does* say "startling" and "imaginative" things. This new version of him makes its public debut on Parents' Night at his school, when all the moms and dads visit the classrooms to hear from their teachers about their children's activities. As the camera moves through the halls and in and out of the schoolrooms, one young teacher is showing the parents examples of what she calls their children's "little hobbies"—butterfly collecting, comb weaving, and so forth: "We call it sharing," she adds helpfully. But in the next room, as the camera moves along, is the new Ed, holding forth on education before a variously fascinated and appalled audience. He describes the children's watercolors, mounted on the walls around him, as "these grotesque daubs," compares childhood itself to "a congenital disease" which education is meant to "cure," and cites the present stage of someone like the PTA president's little daughter—"a charming creature," he notes parenthetically (the mother being present)—as "roughly on a par with the African gorilla." That's what *he* calls "sharing."

He's become not only a spellbinder but a raving right-winger—a low-rent Bill Bennett. He attacks phonics and progressive education and calls for a return to "the three R's." "We are breeding a race of moral midgets," he declares ringingly—while some of the parents look shocked and others (the most unsavory-looking ones) nod their agreement. "I'm afraid," says one of the scandalized group on her way out, "Mr. Avery hasn't much faith in the unspoiled instincts of childhood."

You bet he doesn't. At home he has gone from a model dad to a mad patriarch, and sets out to re-educate his own little boy, claiming that any untrained child has a natural propensity for evil. Before long, he is dressing all in black and carrying a Bible around, appealing to the Old Testament to justify his fatherly harshness. It's the story of Abraham and Isaac that suggests to him the desperate measure of "sacrificing" Richie to save his soul. And when he catches the kid messing with his cortisone pills, he

Schoolteacher Ed Avery (James Mason) in *Bigger Than Life* is hosting
a Parents' Night—and making it truly memorable.

becomes determined to do the deed, and goes after little Richie with scissors—with Lou frantically trying to stop him. She reminds him of the part
of the story he seems to have missed: "But Ed, you didn't read it all—God
stopped Abraham!" But that doesn't stop Ed. "God was wrong," he
replies—and locks her in a closet.

A movie about cortisone? (It's like Milos Forman's claiming, as he was
given to doing, that his Larry Flynt movie was about the Supreme Court.)
But the fact seems to be that Ray really didn't want to make that *kind* of
movie at all: a semi-documentary with external crises and externally
defined characters, the sort of movie the original screenwriters had given
him (and that Mason was enforcing on him). The more he got into the
project, it seems, the more he felt trapped by it. Even the rewrites weren't
helping that much. "Nick was a fine director," said the co-screenwriter
Richard Maibaum in 1984, "but I thought he muddied things up somewhat." He did his best.

What was the *point* of this movie anyway? Nick couldn't blame the
"wonder drug"—it saves Ed's life. And he couldn't (he regretted *this*)
blame the doctors—the AMA wouldn't allow that, and they were on his
case, so that even the posters for the movie would insist on the physicians'
blamelessness (a figure in the upper corner wearing a surgical mask and

Ed is starting to crash on his drug—and Lou (Barbara Rush)
is trying (vainly) to hold him together.

saying: "*I prescribed it . . . he misused it!*"). But maybe (and Odets was all in
favor of this) he could blame the wife—the heroic homemaker mom, the
one who couldn't be told that her husband was moonlighting at such a
lowly job as a taxi dispatcher. "Ray exaggerated some scenes and diluted
others," said Maibaum, by way of describing the director's process of
"muddying." And so one of the gestalts you begin to see in the movie after
a while is the one that's made by all those troubling little things about
Lou—her irritability, her "niceness," always with its edge of tension and
overcontrol, and most of all, her concern about appearances, even at what
seem like some life-and-death junctures. Her alarm about how it might
look prevents her from getting Ed to a psychiatrist—or even, and most cru-
cially, from calling a doctor when their own doctor is out of town and Ed is
bouncing off the walls at home. What if it should "get around" that he has
"mental trouble," or even that he's back in the hospital again? This reflex
of hers strikes you as both appallingly out of place in the circumstance (it
endangers both her own life and the boy's, as it turns out) and grimly
believable. "What do you think *that's* going to do to a schoolteacher's
career?" she demands of their friend Wally (Walter Matthau) about the
news "getting around." And yet you suppose that she does, after all, have
to think of that, of the family and their livelihood. But whether she is jus-

tified or not, Ray's dislike of her has by now gotten onto the screen. He certainly would *like* to have blamed her. Whatever her virtues, she is still the movie's enforcer of middle-class values and proprieties. "I want her to be boring," he said to Gavin Lambert at one point, "but I want people to *know* I want her to be boring."

And getting at Lou in this way was a way of getting toward the movie he really wanted to make: about suburban angst, about the burden of banality, the falsity and underlying desperation of American bourgeois life. But what he always came back to was this screenplay about . . . yes, a man who misuses his prescription. And who turns finally not into a *contemporary* sort of monster (the kind Lou makes you think of) but into a distinctly pre-fifties, pre-suburban one: a domestic absolute ruler and a religious fundamentalist. So that a movie Ray meant to challenge his audience's complacency with ends up congratulating them on their advancement—or so it would seem.

Nick too was trapped in banality—by this script. And you could almost say he takes the same way out his hero does: through madness. *That's* when his movie comes to life and almost defeats its own incoherence. When Ed loudly bullies the snooty lady clerks in the upscale dress shop, or when he affronts the doting parents with his reactionary views on education in that classroom, the scenes have an unexpected charge of fun and mischief, suggesting how enlivening it might be *not* to be enlightened and liberal, always full of compunction and hesitation and reason, to decide instead, like Jimmy Dean, *not* to be "nice" anymore. It's this anarchic spirit ("an habitual source of grandeur") the movie is deeply, even scarily in touch with at times: the *liberation* of madness, the fulfillment of egomania, the eerie satisfaction of "God was wrong!" *Anything* but this blandness, this ordinariness, this dullness. That poltergeist spirit is there in the most effective scenes, but never examined or explored, never even named out loud.

And yet it's the same old blandness that Ed must be returned to at the end (where else can he go?): the prescription is adjusted, and the last scene shows the three ecstatic Averys embracing on top of Ed's hospital bed, and laughing. One of those false happy endings (as in: can they really *mean* that?) that got more abundant than ever before in fifties moviemaking generally.

The Lusty Men (1952) at RKO was an even more chaotic shoot—going from a story about rodeo riders with Robert Mitchum to a story about a marriage with Susan Hayward and Arthur Kennedy. There were several scripts by several writers before production began, all full of rodeo lore

Nick Ray and Robert Mitchum conferring about—and often
improvising, according to Ray—*The Lusty Men* (original title: *Cowpoke*—
before Howard Hughes renamed it more suggestively)

(again the source was a magazine piece) but no clear central plot. This time
Ray was *really* winging it, he and Mitchum inventing and writing the
scenes to be filmed day by day, with outsiders called in to help them as
they went along. They had decided on a familiar three-stars-above-the-
title plot situation from the studio heydays: "the two guys, dangerous
work, one woman in the middle," as Andrew Solt (one of the outsiders
called in) put it. For Nick, this was more like it—no producer-star like
Mason looking over his shoulder, for one thing. And *The Lusty Men* was a
movie he seemed always to remember with pleasure—not just the happy
result but the happy experience of pulling it off.

It's probably the most *simply* beautiful of all his movies. The feelings of
loss and loneliness, of displacement and yearning, seem as pure and glowing as Lee Garmes's remarkable black-and-white photography. It's not a
western or even a rodeo movie: "This film is really a film about people who
want a home of their own," as Ray described it at Vassar in 1979, only
months before his death. "This was the great American search at the time."
It was also Ray's great American subject—he's the movie poet of homelessness. As in an early sequence here: the Mitchum hero—having "busted

Jeff (Mitchum) and Louise (Susan Hayward) outside the shacks
of the rodeo camp, in *The Lusty Men*

the last three ribs I had" in the rodeo scenes that open the movie—walks
(in long shot) across the empty arena, in the long shadows of late-afternoon
light, his gear on his back, the wind whistling softly on the soundtrack,
newspapers floating and drifting alongside him and a cloud of dust rising
around him, as he comes slowly and limpingly toward the camera, passes
it, and descends into the arena stalls and out—stepping, as it were, into a
montage of time and distance, traveling in a truck, getting off at a country
crossroad, walking under a solitary tree, coming over a barren hilltop, a
series of majestic dissolves and long shots that take him rising into a first
close-up and stopped at a fence, staring at a shacklike, deserted-looking
old house in a scrubby yard. He climbs the fence, sits on it, and contemplates the house. It's the one he was born and raised in, as we soon learn.
He gets down from the fence and goes to the front door. It's locked shut.

The movie's Susan Hayward heroine also wants to find home (she's
never really had a proper one)—to get away from trailer living and from
the rodeo circuit she travels on with her bronc-busting husband, Wes
(Arthur Kennedy). She was the child of fruit pickers, people who never
lived in anything but migrant camps, never a house—as she tells Jeff
(Mitchum), who is hopelessly and quietly in love with her. She tells him
too that when she was earning her living as a waitress in a "tamale joint,"

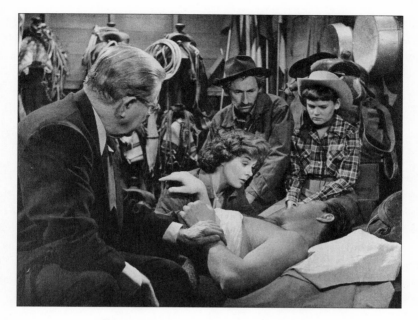

Jeff's death scene—and their only love scene.
(Arthur Hunnicutt is behind Hayward.)

she picked Wes for a husband exactly because he wanted (she thought) what she wanted too—a home and family and "a decent steady life." At least he did until he ran into Jeff, his hero, again—or so she believes. And she holds it against Jeff, too.

She is a powerful woman (Hayward never played pushovers), and fiercely bent on her goals. In the end, she seems an even more relentless upholder of the middle-class ideal than Barbara Rush's Lou (Hayward's name in the movie is Louise). And at a party for the rodeo gang, she goes but she doesn't drink, doesn't even appear to sit down, but stands near a doorway, holding her purse in front of her and keeping an eye on her husband: no danger of his getting much out of line with *her* around. She is exactly—and this is the curious thing—what *this* filmmaker above others ought to hate. Except, as it turns out (she is in fact *very* sympathetic, even moving: you never disbelieve Jeff's fatal crush on her), for that dream of a house she has, her hope of a "real" home, and the ferocity with which she pursues it, redeeming her from the gentility that he really does hate. Beside *her* dream, poor Wes's hankering for fleshpots and freedom seems only trivial and foolish. The only thing in the movie that seems comparable to *her* seriousness is Jeff's unrequited love for her.

In the end Jeff dies of his homelessness—as these odd-man-out heroes often do (he goes back to the rodeo competition out of pride and hopelessness and gets fatally gored). And it was that kind of hero that Ray most identified with.

> *I'm a stranger here*
> *I'm a stranger everywhere*
> *I would go home*
> *But I'm a stranger there . . .*

The lines are from a folk song that Ray collected when he was traveling the back roads with Alan Lomax for the Federal Works Project in the late thirties. He had the hero, Bowie, sing it in an early script version of *They Live by Night*. And he used and reused the song's title ("I'm a Stranger Here Myself") throughout his career: as the title of an early play he wrote, as a line of dialogue for Johnny Guitar, as the title of a 1974 documentary film about his work made by his Binghamton students. It was importantly how he saw himself: "on the road," searching, never fully at home anywhere.

Johnny Guitar (1954) begins much as *The Lusty Men* does, with the hero (Sterling Hayden) in long shot traveling a vast and empty landscape (this is a western, and he enters on horseback) before coming to the door of a seemingly abandoned building. This one sits on a desert expanse, backed against a cliff of redstone and clay and looking as if it were growing out of it. The wind is whistling here too. But the door, when the cowboy tries it, opens to him: on a large high-ceilinged saloon, unoccupied except for two men in green eyeshades, standing by their roulette wheels and staring at him; one of them spins the wheel. It's Vienna's (Joan Crawford's) place—she will presently appear on the balcony—and she is its matriarch. What Johnny will find there eventually is the kind of alternative family that appears so often and so urgently in Ray's work: much the sort of nurturing domestic group that surrounds Bogart's Dixon Steele and puts him lovingly to bed when his work is done in *In a Lonely Place;* or the improvised mom-and-pop-and-son family the three troubled kids in *Rebel Without a Cause* play at in that deserted mansion. "How do you live with yourself?!" cries the tormented cop in Ray's *On Dangerous Ground* (1951). "I don't," replies his partner. "I live with other people." The Robert Ryan hero lives alone—and while his two fellow cops are shown in the movie's opening scenes living nearly as marginally and dingily as he does, in cramped and sour-looking tenement apartments, they are also shown with wife or kids or both: the hero eats by himself while studying mug shots. And he is the only one of the three who won't meet his own eyes in the mirror.

Sterling Hayden and Joan Crawford in *Johnny Guitar*

Robert Ryan is Ray's kind of movie star, specializing in anguish and self-disgust in film after film. With his desolate black-currant eyes, his tightly drawn mouth and strangled voice, he is usually someone divided and conscience-riven. Nick and he were also friends, and of the three movies they made together at RKO, *On Dangerous Ground* is the most ambitious (*Born to Be Bad* and *Flying Leathernecks* were the others). It's a classic noir in part (the best part)—until it shifts styles and plots at the middle, following the original novel (something called—no kidding— *Mad with Much Heart*), and moves to the country, where the blind girl heroine (Ida Lupino) lives. But what comes before all that is pure Nicholas Ray (with no precedent in the novel), devised by him and his screenwriter (A. I. Bezzerides, who also wrote Aldrich's *Kiss Me Deadly*), and taking place in the kind of nightmare city setting that seems to *promise* sudden fissures of sanity in its inhabitants. And especially in Ryan's cop hero, eaten up and unmoored by the daily bitterness of his work, subject to pathological outbursts of violence that leave him undone by self-loathing. The crooks and hoods he deals with seem almost to know about this—and so to invite, in their creepy, insinuating ways, the violence that provokes it: as if they knew that whatever he could do to *them*, they could do worse to him. Is he going to "get rough" with her? a blowsy hooker and potential informer, asks him—hopefully. And he certainly looks like he is—but the scene fades out on his troubled face. A wiseguy little crook he's chased and cornered, now immobilized in a chair but refusing to talk, smiles up at him suggestively, in a sweaty, seductive close-up that seems more sexual than defiant. "*Why* do you make me *do* it?!" cries Ryan, in agony—no doubt he is going to beat this one up too, and badly—"Why do you *always* make me do it?!" And another fade-out.

Violence in Ray's movies (he was noted for it at the time) is not simply sensational, good for a jolt or a shock, but obscene, insidious, queasily alluring—finally more a temptation than love or larceny. That's why, understated and discreet as his rough stuff may now seem (it's often off-screen altogether, as in the two fade-outs above), it *still* feels so disturbing to an audience, and why the final revulsion from it his movies express seems so real and so seriously meant.

It's those invented families who seem needed to control the madness; the real families tend mostly to intensify it. But in Ray's final great (as it seems to me) movie—before his work slipped into the personal chaos it had been so much about controlling—there is no hope of containment or community: there's only repudiation. Among mainstream war movies of the time, his *Bitter Victory* was the first genuinely pacifist one, indicting by implication our one inarguably "just" war, making no felt moral distinction between *our* side's violence and the Nazi Germans'. (As Lenny Bruce once said: " 'Thou Shalt Not Kill' means just that.") That was daring—or might have been if people had gone to see it.

Fourteen

BITTER VICTORY

O ne of Ray's ideas in going abroad to make a movie was to get away from Hollywood. He thought that a European connection, once firmly established, might regenerate his troubled career; by that time he was highly regarded there, especially in France. Gavin Lambert had brought him a French novel about World War II, *Amère Victoire* by René Hardy; an international operator named Paul Graetz had agreed to produce the film version, with major American financing from Columbia; and shooting was scheduled for eight weeks in early 1957 in both North Africa and France. It all seemed propitious.

But the movie that was meant to turn his career around, *Bitter Victory* (1957), all but effectively ended it. It bombed so resoundingly on its first American play dates that Columbia promptly withdrew it and proceeded to re-edit it, shortening it by over twenty minutes and badly distorting Ray's original, then dumping it on the market as a second feature. Much the same thing happened to it in Europe, where each national distributor offered his own mutilation of it—different lengths, different scenes cut or shortened—so that it soon, almost mercifully, sank from sight and memory. For Ray, its failure marked the beginning of a decline, both personal and professional, which he never really reversed.

He was invited to show the original version, shortly after he'd finished editing it, at the 1957 Venice Film Festival. But it won no prizes, and it seems to have perplexed and disappointed even his European fans. Except, of course, for the young *Cahiers* critics, who could hardly (in their style) praise it enough. But their praise—for such aspects as its "abstractness," its lack of "external logic," its "feeling of incompletion" (Eric Rohmer), and so forth—clearly suggests why so many others had a problem with it.

Godard's review was particularly rapturous. (It was there that he made his famous pronouncement "Le cinema, c'est Nicholas Ray.") *Bitter Victory,* he writes, "is not a reflection of life, it is life itself turned into cinema"; he also compares it to the stars—"and the men who like to look at them and

The hopelessness of *Bitter Victory.* The Giacometti-like figures in the background are being led by Curt Jurgens (in white head-covering). He is following the camel and the Arab guide (Raymond Pellegrin).

dream": "How can one talk of such a film? What is the point of saying that the meeting between Richard Burton and Ruth Roman while Curt Jurgens watches is edited with fantastic brio? Maybe this was a scene during which we had closed our eyes. For *Bitter Victory,* like the sun, makes you close your eyes. Truth is blinding." But this sort of effusion was unlikely to help Ray's film anywhere but Paris—*if* there (the French recut and shortened it too). It was simply—more or less since Venice—impossible to see, at least in its complete form.

When I did catch up with it, in the early seventies, what struck me first was its contemporary feeling, its almost Orwellian trenchancy (what we then called "relevance")—at a time when America was still conducting its various proxy wars against the people of Central America, among others (preceding our remote-control Gulf War). Also its originality: Ray—and Ray alone, so far as I know—had explored the subject of that special moral repugnance you feel for the killer who keeps his hands clean. There had been several after-the-fact World War II combat movies that dwelt on the agony of command, the suffering of the one who sends all the others to suffer (movies like *Command Decision* and *Twelve O'Clock High*). But this was the first such movie to suggest that command as a personal situation had its personal advantage—and that it was a contemptible one. Here Nick's bias for "the kids" was *really* paying off.

And the movie deals relentlessly with those questions of authenticity, those anxious distinctions between the real and the fake that formed a preoccupation of the postwar American scene—and that seem to me now one of its most saving aspects. *Bitter Victory* was a European co-production and showed it (that multinational cast, for example), but you could recognize behind it a very American sort of consciousness and concern.

Above all, it's such a terrific *movie.* There are faults and longueurs, of course—as in all Ray's films (as Gavin Lambert observed, Nick wasn't very keen about "structure"—not at all). But the fluency and brilliance of the filmmaking, the easy rich expressiveness of even its smallest details, the power and profundity of its high points—it all could almost persuade you, while you're under its spell, that Nicholas Ray *was* the cinema. The sun, the stars may be a bit much, of course—but the enthusiasm that prompted Godard to deploy them in his review at least becomes comprehensible.

The story is about the conflict between two officers in a British commando unit during the North African campaign against Rommel. The ranking officer, Major Brand (Curt Jurgens) is a professional soldier and a believer in the code and ideals of the military. His subordinate, Captain Leith (Richard Burton), on the other hand, is an intellectual, an archaeologist in civilian life and an unwilling soldier made cynical by the war. He regards Brand and his ideals with contempt. Brand on his side fears the junior officer almost as much as he hates him. And his torment is compounded by the discovery that Leith and Mrs. Brand (Ruth Roman) had been lovers before the war—and that they are still in love. It's on the heels of this revelation that the two officers get assigned with their men to a highly dangerous excursion behind German lines to steal some crucial enemy documents. They succeed, but Leith is killed—with Brand's passive connivance. But Brand is exposed as a coward before his men and his wife. And the mission for which he is promoted and decorated becomes in fact the instrument of his humiliation.

Ray originally intended the role of Brand for Richard Burton, and Leith for Montgomery Clift. Burton was signed; so were the European stars Raymond Pellegrin and Curd (as his name was then spelled) Jürgens—Pellegrin to play the role of an Arab scout named Mokrane, and Jurgens as a captured German officer. But Clift turned the movie down; Ray's next idea for the Leith role was Paul Newman. At this point producer Paul Graetz ("a psychopath who hated directors," Gavin Lambert said, "but we didn't know that at the time") declared that Jurgens, who was then a hot box-office name in Europe, should play the leading role of Brand—leaving Ray no choice but to have Burton play Leith, the *other* leading part. For the role of Brand's wife, Jane, a character whom Ray conceived of as "innocent and *very* English," he wanted Moira Shearer—only to find that Graetz had signed Ruth Roman, an actress who seemed neither remotely English nor specially "innocent," but whom Graetz mistakenly believed to be an important American star.

The problem—in this movie about English fighting Germans—of having the leading English officer played by an almost stereotypical German (accent and all) was "solved," it was hoped, by inserting a line in the script that described Brand as South African. But the casting of Jurgens as Brand caused even more substantive script problems—since he was a notably inflexible and unsubtle actor, whose favorite expressive strategy seemed to be sweating and bugging his eyes. And so the complex "neurotic" figure Ray had wanted Richard Burton to play had now to be modified, in a manner that shifted the balance and relation between the two central characters, and that made the Leith character even more important—often in awkward ways, like the overexplicitness of some of Leith's dialogue. It's as if what Jurgens couldn't act would now have to be said, and mostly by Burton, who seems in the movie almost never to talk to Jurgens without announcing the other man's "meaning" to him—conformity, authoritarianism, cowardice, etc.—or, even worse, describing Brand's concealed thoughts and feelings. "You left me in the desert," Burton says to him as they trek over the sand, "so there wouldn't be any witnesses left to the *real* Major Brand. Didn't you? Therefore my death becomes essential to you. I'm a kind of mirror of your own weakness, and it's unbearable. Isn't it?" No reply from Brand is called for.

The script—after Gavin Lambert worked on it—was passed through several writers, mostly hired by Graetz, working at different times in different countries; some of them, like Paul Gallico, had no contact at all with Ray. It was the Gallico version in particular that Graetz prized, telexing it in bits from Paris to Libya. And on each page as it arrived was inscribed the same message: "Not one word must be changed!" But then it often arrived late. And Ray in Graetz's absence was pursuing his own designs, in spite of the presence on location of Mrs. Graetz, who was there to represent her husband but also, as it turned out, to pursue her affair with Jurgens. And Jurgens himself began to contribute to the script, resisting the now growing unattractiveness of the character he was playing, so that Ray often had to mislead the star about the meaning of a scene to get him to play it at all. And then as the production fell behind schedule, Ray himself began to fall apart: drinking, quarreling with his young Moroccan girlfriend, gambling all night in the casino—where he often lost even when he won, since he had a habit of forgetting which numbers

he played. On the set, he might often lose his confidence—or his voice—
or even, at times, the use of one of his legs. And then there was the
sand . . . which got into everything, no matter what they did and drove
everyone crazy. And so it went.

But the crisis atmosphere seemed to galvanize Nick (as it often did).
And in the middle of it all, he was steadily shaping his film: cutting and
rewriting and improvising with the actors on the set (he got on particularly well with Burton and with Nigel Green). When the production
returned to France, for interiors and retakes of some of the desert footage,
the dissension with the producers went on: Ray argued with them up to
the final shooting days over the film's ending. But at last, after six weeks
in the desert and four in the studio, the production wrapped and cast and
crew dispersed. But while Graetz was writing friends in Hollywood, people like Spyros Skouras at Fox and Jack Warner, telling them *never* to hire
Nicholas Ray again—and while Gavin Lambert was reluctantly deciding,
in spite of his friendship with Ray, never to sign on with him again (he
turned down *Party Girl*)—Ray was still making his movie, working
round the clock with his postproduction crew in Paris to do the final cut.
Best of all, he found a gifted young composer named Maurice Le Roux
(he'd tried to get Shostakovich, but the Russians thought the story was too
"antiheroic") to do the minimal but extraordinary score. And after the
final mix was done, he went to the hospital for a collapse. But he was out
in time to get to Venice with the finished film, and to say when he got
there that in spite of everything, he'd done the movie he wanted to do. It
seems unlikely that he was widely believed.

The most obvious thing about that early scene Godard praised so fulsomely—"the meeting between Richard Burton and Ruth Roman while
Curt Jurgens watches"—is its familiarity. "I want you to meet my wife,"
says Brand (Jurgens), looking smug, and leads Leith (Burton), who is looking confused, across the crowded dance floor of the nightclub to the corner
table where Jane Brand (Roman) sits and sees them coming—looking
stunned. It's the bittersweet three-way saloon encounter (cf. Rick and Ilsa
and Victor Laszlo), one of the most basic tropes of classic Hollywood
romance. But Ray and the actors make you feel the classicism more than
the banality. The scene has an elegance and formality, as well as a banked
excitement, that derives partly from its precedents.

Although it's in black and white, *Bitter Victory* is also in CinemaScope,
the widest of wide-screen processes (2:35 to 1). But instead of using the
width to show all three people at once, Ray mostly cuts between gigantic
wide-screen close-ups of each, as they exchange gnomic remarks and

Ruth Roman is the wife, Richard Burton is the old lover, and
Curt Jurgens is the husband.

charged silences. Leith gazes at Jane, while Brand watches them both—
and Jane, avoiding Brand's eyes, meets Leith's with fake little meant-to-
be-dazzling smiles. They talk about the war—and forgetting things—and
whether that's because people don't really care—and so on. Until Brand is
called away momentarily, leaving Leith and Jane alone.

He left her in prewar London, suddenly and without explanation. And
now she looks more military than he does, sitting erect in her uniform,
while he lounges across from her. Their conversation, hopeless as it is, has a
lovely gravity, showing their different ways of resigning themselves, their
different ways of keeping their dignity. "So you married a major," he says,
casual but dangerous. "So I married a major," she says, with one of her
glassy, nice-girl smiles—as if they were pooling snatches of an old song
they knew. And when Brand comes back and sees them in each other's
arms on the dance floor, their guilty pulling-apart is timed and executed
like another dance step, as they go back to the table, back to the major.

I think Godard was right to pick out this scene. But how to account for
its power? It's not in the dialogue—the lines, often hokey, are little more
than a blueprint for a scene. Godard cites Ray's editing. But the way he
praises it—for its "fantastic brio"—makes you think of a Wellesian display rather than the laid-back style you get here. The cutting is strictly
shot/reverse shot—the standard alternation of standard Hollywood prac-

tice, no more, no less. If it seems inspired, it's because it so exactly suits what interests us in the scene itself: all the nuances of voice and look—especially in Burton's performance, the modulations from malice to tenderness or from regret to contempt that he conveys in a single line or close-up. Leith is a man so steeped in irony that he can be gratified by hopelessness even when he suffers it acutely. And once you see this, Jane's panicked, defended manner becomes even more moving. There is "brio" here, and it's in the cutting rhythm that makes the characters' feeling of painful impasse almost palpable, plugging us directly into their circuit of exchanged looks and looks-away.

One thing that makes the movie feel uncannily accurate about military life is the way it watches people watching people. There are no private spaces anywhere—no domestic interiors for anyone, not even a hotel room. In the desert, too, of course, you're constantly on view—and it isn't much better at command headquarters: a gray network of barracks and offices and gyms and day rooms, connected by bare wood corridors and separated by half-walls and glass. Whenever people meet in the foreground of this setting, the nondescript spaces stretch behind them—not quite in focus usually, but nearly always with someone or other in them, moving or standing or sitting, silently, discreetly, watchfully, or so it seems. A world without walls, and the dominant feeling it gives is of terrible enclosure.

And there's no relief from it. In the outdoor scenes on the desert, Ray uses the "panoramic" wide-screen frame to close down the view rather than to open it up, emphasizing CinemaScope's horizontal narrowing and flattened perspective. No *Lawrence of Arabia* vistas—just sand and sand hills and blank, depthless skies forever: the desert the way you'd see and feel it if you'd been marching across it for a while. And these exterior shots—even more than the interiors at headquarters—seem to push people into the foreground, with flat blank spaces between and around them. In the desert sequences (which are most of the film) Ray uses much longer takes and makes the width of his frame accommodate even more elaborate circuits of looks and glances than he's shown us before. As in the scene where the exhausted commando troop come upon an oasis.

They stagger up to the well and are all about to drink from the wooden bucket when Mokrane (Pellegrin), their Arab guide (he "knows the desert"), warns them that the Germans may have poisoned it. Sergeant Barney (Christopher Lee) agrees: "Poisoning wells is an old German trick," he says. Their prisoner, a German officer (Fred Matter), dignified and authoritative, dismisses this idea out of hand. But he doesn't, we notice, offer to drink. Nor does anyone else in the group now crowded around the well. In the forefront, the sardonic Corporal Wilkins (Nigel Green) is holding the bucket to his chest possessively, with his fixed, slightly mad-looking stare, and his flannel headgear tilted upward like a foolscap. He looks as if he's going to drink. Until he gets—apparently—a better idea. "Who is poisoning wells?" sounds the voice of Major Brand, as he climbs the slope to the well—as usual, a bit slow to join the group. Without answering, Wilkins offers him the bucket. In silence.

It's a stunning piece of insolence. Only Wilkins—who seems both mad and murderous, unpredictable at best, and a smoldering force of anarchy at all times—would be capable of it. And Brand, feeling the expectant gazes of the men crowded around him at the well, looks trapped.

A close-up then, with three heads in the foreground: Brand at the extreme left of the frame; Wilkins at the center, holding the bucket up to Brand and staring fixedly at him; and Burton's Leith at the extreme right, half turned away from the camera and looking, as is everyone else, at Brand, who hesitates, sweating with fear. Then, suddenly and almost convulsively, Brand takes the bucket from Wilkins and drinks from it. Ray holds the shot as Brand lowers the bucket from his mouth. And just as all eyes are turned on him, awaiting the effect, Wilkins (at the center of the frame) turns away—looks front—then right, his head on an angle, bringing his terrible stare to rest on Leith—who is still looking at Brand. Pause: Brand appears relieved. "This water is not poisoned," he announces, regaining his native pomposity. Ray still holds the shot: and Wilkins is still staring at Leith—who now says very softly, with his face still turned away and his voice sounding almost disembodied, "It's too soon to tell." But we are looking at this moment at Wilkins, who is still in the center of the shot looking at Leith—and for a moment it's almost as if that oddly but wittily displaced stare of his had somehow "said" Leith's words. The dislocation is not only unsettling but instructive: the madness is growing . . .

Of course Brand's men *know* about "Jane and Jimmy" and their romance. Or so we assume: it's in the logic of the film that they would. And there have been clues. One night—early in the film—Leith and Jane encounter each other outside the barracks. They don't touch, they merely stand apart and talk quietly. But as they do so, the two soldiers watching them from a distance—Wilkins is the tall one—look on as if they are seeing a romantic movie, the smaller one leaning dreamily against his buddy, in a kind of parody of the yearning they are spying on. It's the only time in the movie that Wilkins doesn't look sinister.

Usually his gaze is a threat, and especially to Brand. Wilkins is the most prominent and the most ominous of all the watchers in the background.

What makes him threatening is not so much things like his being rebellious and murderous as his being knowing and a little nuts. When he tells Brand in the desert that his feet have given out on him and that he can't go on, Brand orders him to stand up, threatening to shoot him if he disobeys. But Wilkins stays put—on the ground, leaning against a rock, and looking up at Brand. "Death for death, I'll take this one," he says into the barrel of Brand's pistol, "—it's quicker." Then suddenly he arches his back and twists to the ground, rolling around in what looks like an epileptic fit—leaving Brand with his gun hanging out, so to speak. You can't give commands to someone who's having a fit, after all—and you certainly can't shoot him, no matter *what* he may say in mid-seizure. What Wilkins is saying is "Jane and Jimmy, Jimmy and Jane," over and over and over again, making kissing sounds with his mouth and tossing about at Brand's feet—while the others look on with innocent faces.

Being in command in this movie mostly means being trapped in the looks of others—and in their unspoken judgments. Brand never passes among these outwardly respectful men without leaving a wake of uneasy, unfriendly glances behind him. And he knows that their judgments of him are contemptuous. That's one reason he drinks at the well. So that even his heroism is a pose, confirming the trap he's in. It can't, after all, escape notice (it doesn't escape Leith's) how ideally suited Brand is to the military mode, with its universal tendency—whether in a war or a weapons system or a barracks inspection—to substitute the successful appearance for the thing itself, the surface for the substance. Brand is the kind of person who sees himself almost entirely in the way he looks to others, who lives in and by what he takes to be their gaze. This too makes it difficult to have Leith around.

You know from the first moment Burton appears in the movie—standing on a chair to adjust a ceiling fan and looking down at Jurgens, who has come for his interview with the general—that Burton is *on* in some special way. "I thought the fan should cool the colonel's head and not the flies on the ceiling," he says. "Yes, of course," says Jurgens, who didn't see him at first—who looks up at him now with distinct unease. Burton looks implacably back—and that's that. It's not much of a scene, but—as with the opening scene of *Camille,* where Garbo, in a closed carriage, receives a bouquet of camellias from an old woman (not much of a scene either)—it makes you sit up, with the sense that you're seeing an actor who's on some special level of excitement and inspiration.

At first Burton seems to turn up the intensity level of the film just by turning up in the frame. As when Brand and Jane, returning from the nightclub, get down from their conveyance in front of the palatial hotel that serves for officers' quarters—only to find Leith has anticipated them. He is standing at the foot of the broad white stone stairway, holding a swagger stick and leaning on his elbow against a pillar. The general wants to see you, he tells Brand. About what? "A little walk in the desert," he says. Causing a minor flurry between the Brands—Jane because she doesn't know what he means, Brand because he does. And Leith looks on: glowing. It's his dissolute-choirboy look—or like some middle-aged version of the magical child, who is still withholding his secret from the grown-ups.

Certainly he withholds himself from her, even though his longing seems fully as strong as hers is. Jane is the one who wants to talk about it, though. "I loved you, Jimmy," she says, as they stand in the barracks doorway, watched by Wilkins and his smaller friend. But whenever she talks like this, Leith looks evasive and canceled. This is the night before the mission leaves. Jane is going inside now to say goodbye to the husband she may never see again—Leith is opening the door for her. "What can I say to him?" she suddenly asks in the doorway. Leith closes the door again and looks at her: this is his kind of question. "Tell him," he says, almost purringly, with flashing eyes and wintry smile, "all the things that women have always said to the men before they go to the wars. Tell him he's a hero. Tell him"—and his lips curl as if were preparing to say an obscenity—"he's a *good* man. Tell him you'll be waiting for him when he comes back. Tell him"—his eyes blazing more than ever now—"he'll be making *history*!" (saying the last word with a literal hiss). He subsides; after this there isn't much to say, and they both know it. He opens the door for her again, and this time she goes through it. Then another door inside: the way to her husband.

Leith's savagery has a kind of elation. It's the satisfaction of actually naming the meaninglessness for what it is—and Burton shows the intoxication of it. Later on in his career, he specialized in cynical, burnt-out heroes, but even the best of these performances—*Who's Afraid of Virginia Woolf?*, for one—seem to me less moving, and less unnerving, than his Leith. Partly because Leith is less burnt-out than burning; his despair has a kind of young man's ardency. Even his exhaustion seems passionate—his insistence on futility almost life-giving. But finally it's Brand himself who really "explains" this paradox—by what he himself comes to be and to mean in the course of the film, and by the sense the film gives us that what Leith sets himself against in the other man is something deeply worth opposing, even being passionate about.

Leith (Burton) gives some marital advice to Jane (Roman):
"Tell him he's a hero."

But the way the movie draws *us* into this passion is wonderfully round-about. On the face of it, Brand would seem almost to be a more sympathetic character than Leith is—certainly a more "human" one. He loves his wife, and though he's willing to risk his life, he's unwilling to kill, even in the wartime cause he serves. In the raid on Benghazi, when he has to sneak up behind a German sentry and stab him in the back, he's unable to do it. Instead Leith does it. Brand admits afterwards that he finds it hard, even after thirteen years in the army, "to kill a man in cold blood." After all, "war is not murder," he says. But, as it turns out, it's just in this area of such seeming decency that the movie makes its profoundest—and angriest—indictment of him.

The crucial point for *all* the meanings of the film comes almost exactly midway through, in the episode where Leith is left in the desert with the casualties. It's the heart of Ray's movie, conditioning everything that follows it—and its intensest point: the sort of movie sequence that goes so deeply into its desolating experience that you think it's reached its limit when it wrenches you onto some new and surprising level of meaning and feeling, touching finally what Eliot calls "the border of those feelings that only music can express." And Le Roux's music is integral to it.

It happens just after the Benghazi raid and the commandos' escape onto the desert with the successfully captured German documents. Now Brand

assigns Leith "to stay behind with the wounded"—a British private and a
German prisoner. Both of them are dying, however—and slowly. So that
it's clear—to everyone except perhaps the man who has given Leith the
order for it—what "staying behind" with these men, beyond all help and
alone in the middle of the desert, must inevitably mean.

And day comes and Leith *is* alone—except for the two wounded men
and several other dead ones lying about—and except for a brief and puzzling glimpse of a distant figure in Arab dress (Mokrane?) climbing a hill,
then turning to look back from its crest. Leith walks among the bodies on
the sand, puts a jacket under the wounded Tommy's head, then sits on the
hood of wrecked jeep and listens to the moaning of the men and the sound
of the wind—clenching and unclenching his fists, knocking a headlight
off the jeep, clutching at the air, and weeping. He reaches for his pistol,
leaps off the jeep into the sand, and—watched by the Tommy—he
approaches the German, a porcine man who tries to show him a snapshot
of his family ("Meine Frau . . . meine Kinder . . .") and even to speak a bit
of English ("We were . . . so happy . . . before the war")—until he sees the
gun, trembling but approaching. "Nein, nein!" he cries. Leith swats the
snapshot out of his hand and kneels beside him in the sand. The man,
though still protesting, opens his mouth like a patient at the dentist's—as
Leith inserts the pistol barrel, and then, pulling his whole body away from
it, in a taut agonized line along his arm that stretches up from the pistol in
the German's mouth to his own contorted face and averted eyes, he fires.

At the sound of the shot, we see the Tommy, watching as before. Then
back to Leith, in close-up—dazed, bleary-eyed, rising and looking with
disbelief at what he's done. Now the Tommy's turn: the pistol shaking
even more violently. "Any family?" Leith asks in a choked voice. But the
man is in torment and just wants it over with: "Don't drag things out!" he
cries, blood running from his mouth. "Do what you've got to do!" And as
the pistol approaches his head (in a high-angle close shot) he looks at it
longingly. But this time, instead of firing, it clicks hollowly. Leith opens
the chamber: empty. The man lets out a cry, turns his face away, and sobs.
By now Leith's situation feels both unbearable and utterly familiar: that
nightmare where you make choices in a horror, and every choice you make
only makes more horror.

Just then, the music—the first soundtrack music we've heard since the
movie's opening titles—which both intensifies the feeling and gives us the
relief of an outside comment on it, however agitated, as Leith, having
decided to try to carry the man now, bends down (another high-angle close
shot, like the approach of the pistol) and pulls him up painfully by the

shoulders, to a sudden, shocking roll of drums. *"Damn you!"* screams the wounded man—followed by a cluster of crashing dissonant chords—as Leith lifts the man onto his back. He staggers forward; the man's trouser seat pushes into a close shot, followed by—as Leith turns again—his face in agony. While those thunderclap dissonances drift into a restless diminuendo—like a shout sinking into a moan, almost as if the movie itself were grieving—then fade, before breaking out again as Leith staggers under his burden and readjusts it, sinks into the sand, turns this way, then that, then staggers on, though it's not clear to *where.* "Put me *down*!" screams the man. "You're *hurting* me!" As of course Leith is—and there seems to be (could there be?) nowhere to go. So that when Leith stumbles and puts the man down and then picks him up again, Ray extends the agony of the moment, the visceral sensation of pain and awkwardness, by cutting *on* the movement (changing focal distance, from long shot to medium)—a kind of filmic rubato that Ray does better (more "viscerally") than any other director I know of.

In this film he often omits the establishing shot (the overall view that lays things out for you)—a way of disorienting the viewer, impelling him forward to the next shot and the next to get his bearings, to see who is where, near whom and what, and so on. Where, for example, is that Arab figure on a distant hill that we've glimpsed twice now? We don't know until now (the third time), when we see him abruptly leaving the hill, going away from us. Cut to a reverse shot—of Mokrane (so it is him) coming down from the hill in the background of the shot, to meet Leith going toward him (and away from the camera) in the foreground, with the man on his back now hanging limp. Another cut on movement, again to the reverse angle, and Leith with his burden staggers blindly forward into a huge close-up, with Mokrane at the left of the frame and turned away from the camera. Leith, his face haggard and streaked with tears, eyes lowered and turning away from Mokrane, reaches his arm across the frame and plants his hand (the other is bracing the man on his back) on the Arab's shoulder, as if to steady himself. "I have been watching you, my friend," says Mokrane—and Leith, unable to look at him, nods blindly in reply.

It's very powerful. Probably we never fully take the measure of Leith's agony in this scene until he gets offered *this* consolation—and accepts it. Mokrane, quite obviously, offers no "real" help, no physical or moral aid—only the report, after the fact, that someone who loves Leith has been looking on at him. The revelation, of course, is how momentous this news *feels,* both to Leith (we presume) and to us: an unexpected reminder how even at the lowest point—in the sort of extremity Leith finds himself in—we do want to be watched by *someone,* want our terrible story to get out to *some-where.* And it's even more moving in this film's special world of uneasy glances and threatening, invasive stares—to be reminded by Mokrane that there's a kind of onlooking that actually sustains us: the God's-eye view, as it were.

Mokrane inspects the man on Leith's back now. "He's dead," he says. Leith nods dazedly—as if to say, of course he *knew* that—and together they lay the body on the ground, Leith sinking to his knees beside it. He bends over and takes the man's head in his hands, stares blindly into the face for a moment, then lets it fall. And the clamorous soundtrack music is silent: only the sound of the wind now. Leith sits back on his heels—in a low-angle shot against the sky—still nodding his head compulsively. "I kill the living," he says, the hysteria rising, then breaking into laughter, "and I save the dead." A plane flies over and they scuttle for cover, using the body as a shield, and the sequence ends. Later on, when they surprise the company by catching up with them in the desert, Brand is horrified at what Leith tells him he has done—to "the men you left me to kill." "I left you to *save* them," replies Brand, in quite genuine distress.

The point is that Mokrane may have been watching, but Brand was not—and *will* not. That is finally what the movie asks us to see as counting most heavily against him—and contributing most heavily to Leith's contempt for him. And to ours: once we have been inducted into Leith's agony, Brand's innocence of it feels simply unacceptable. In this movie, "war is not murder" *only* if you don't *look* at it. The sort of killing we do get to see—close-up and hands-on and even intimate at times—is, Leith says, what "makes the soldier." It is also, as he adds, what destroys him—as he is finally destroyed. Earlier on, at Benghazi, when he seizes Brand's knife and plunges it into the back of the German sentry, he does it with an intake of breath and an agonized face that makes it look more like suicide than ambush. Whatever the context, Leith is, after all, doing something terrible when he takes this man's life—"in cold blood," as Brand puts it. But he's also registering it—*looking* at it, suffering it.

It's not at all that Brand can't "kill," or even can't collude in killing if he has to, in spite of his loss of nerve with the sentry. It's rather that he can only do what Leith calls "the approved killing at the approved distance." That distance—and the unconsciousness that goes with it—is one of the privileges of command. Brand's "decency"—his sense of himself as a duti-ful and humane man—is of a terrible and familiar sort: the kind that doesn't prevent you from participating in the general indecency and inhu-maneness around you, even from giving the orders for it. It only prevents

Major Brand (Jurgens) and Captain Leith—near the end
of their "mission"

you from noticing—and from bearing the burden later of having noticed.
Which means in the end that you may be capable of anything. Brand too is
a killer, as it turns out.

First he kills Leith, though indirectly—by failing to warn him when he
sees the scorpion crawling up his trouser leg. Then he shoots Mokrane,
who has pulled a knife on him in an attempt to avenge Leith. But all this
melodramatic event, in the latter half of the film, feels oddly detached
somehow, almost foreordained. It's as if—after Leith's agony of futility in
the desert—something in the spirit of the movie itself had been broken.
Though Leith is still taunting and challenging Brand—in the self-
destructive way that finally brings on the death he's been wishing for. And
Burton still seems lit up from inside, like some curdled, sardonic holy
man; but his passionate, half-elated quality is gone, replaced by something
colder. As in the wonderful moment at "Crown City," the ancient desert
ruin where the troop has stopped for a rest. Burton is inside one of the
excavation's low, narrow tunnels. With a younger officer behind him, he is
inspecting the wall, touching the ceiling. "I can't make it out," says the
officer. "Berber, I think," says Leith, the former archaeologist, his hand on
the ceiling. "Tenth century. Built, I suppose, to protect themselves from
Arab invasions." He scans it with his eyes; he pats the wall in a curiously
moving gesture, almost as if he meant to console it. He withdraws his

hand—regretfully. "I'm not very good in this period," he says, his eyes still scanning the ceiling, his voice soft and distant: "Too modern for me . . ."

This scene, like a lot of others—as Bernard Eisenschitz, Ray's exemplary biographer, reports—was improvised on location by Ray and his actors. Ray's assistant director on the film, Edouard Luntz, recalled that Ray was "always underneath the camera" during shooting—"so as to see the looks people gave," Luntz said. "The looks on their faces were the most important thing." Godard praises Ray in this movie for getting us to see the spaces *between* things: "What lies between the objects and which becomes an object in itself." But it's the spaces between *people* more than objects, I'd say, that Ray transforms and makes magically palpable—in those powerful circuits of exchanged looks and looks-away he's gotten us to watch so intently. There is a particularly bold example of this in Leith's final, "posthumous" appearance.

The morning after the scorpion bite, Leith is mortally ill. And Brand announces to him that they will be obliged, according to their orders, to leave him behind: nothing can be allowed to jeopardize the safe delivery to the British of those stolen German documents. But just as the troop is getting ready to depart, a sandstorm blows up, and Leith pulls Brand to the ground to save him from walking into it. When it passes, Brand struggles up from under the sand and turns Leith over: he is dead. The men start to gather round solemnly, when there is a commotion over the hill behind them. Trucks from headquarters are arriving to rescue them. And while they are all running to greet the vehicles—cheering and sliding down the sand, hugging each other and dancing—they forget, it would seem (Brand included), that they have left their German prisoner unguarded and alone with the mailbags containing the documents.

In a more conventional film, this might be a point of high suspense—or of savage irony. Here it is noted without emphasis—the filmic equivalent of a shrug. What dominates our attention from now on is a remarkable recurring close-up of the dead Leith. The first time we see it is just after Brand has turned him over—and it's a stunner. For the first time in the movie he looks conventionally glamorous: clean-shaven, the pitted skin looking lustrous and smooth, his hair blowing gently in the wind that bends the clump of desert grass above his head, and his wounded eyes closed. He looks transfigured, but this time by a light from *without*—since this is clearly a studio shot, in rather jarring contrast to the location footage. Like the suddenly recurring soundtrack music, it's an intrusion from the outside. But it begins to feel right, even to make a kind of sense, when we notice that around Leith's mouth is the subtle but clear suggestion of a smile.

So the men welcome the trucks—with Le Roux's apocalyptic dissonances (the same ones we heard over the dying Tommy) crashing onto the
soundtrack. The music doesn't so much undercut the jubilation as seem to
suggest a kind of coldly detached view of it. And Ray keeps his camera at
such an impersonal distance from the commotion that we can't really tell
one celebrating commando from another. The close shots here are reserved
for the dead Leith—and now the German officer, a grizzled, square-jawed,
shrewd-looking man, with one arm in a sling from his shoulder. His back
is to us in his first close-up, as he watches the commotion; then he turns
front, looking at something offscreen—which turns out to be (in the next
shot) that close-up of Leith, his look of serene triumph seeming even more
marked than before. Then a medium shot of the German which shows us
that he is standing right next to those abandoned mailbags. In close-up
again, he looks toward Leith (we never see the two of them in the same
shot), frowning fiercely and working his jaw. Then, taking a grenade from
his jacket and pulling the pin out with his teeth, he kneels (in the next
shot) and plants it among the mailbags. And as it goes off (we almost don't
hear the explosion over the music), Ray cuts—astonishingly—not to
Brand and the men, nor back to the German, but to Leith's death mask.
It's surprising—until you realize that the German has by his action
reduced Brand's mission to the meaninglessness that's been lurking in it
from the beginning—that he's really fulfilling Leith's vision of futility.
And clearly Brand, kneeling before the smoking ruins of the documents as
his men scramble to put out the fire, knows whose victory it is. He too
"exchanges" a look with Leith—whose transfigured close-up ends the
sequence.

Now he has to go home to Jane—in the movie's "epilogue," as Ray
called it (which was entirely cut, astonishingly enough, from some of the
released versions at the time). We see her first (after the fade-out from the
desert) in a corridor back at HQ, in her uniform as always, and holding a
clipboard in front of her, trying to learn from the general's adjutant if
there's been any news of the unit. Then they arrive. But the focus of the
scene is on Roman, standing in the doorway and scrutinizing the men as
they jump from the trucks and pass in front of her. By the time her husband appears—the last of them—she knows that Leith is not with them.

In a way, we've been waiting to see her again. Just before Leith died,
Brand asked him if he had any message for her. Leith replied: "Tell Jane
she was right and I was wrong" (referring to the way he alone broke off
their affair). Jane has much the same importance for the film as she does for
these two men. Unlike them, she is direct and honest and uncomplicatedly
serious. What Ray lost in Moira Shearer's Englishness, he gained in Ruth

Roman's gravity and solidity, in the intent, ominous sharpness at the center of her big dark eyes. *Her* gaze is the one that Brand really lives in, it's clear; and you know that if *she* could see him as a hero, or at least not a coward, he might perhaps survive. "I'm proud of you," she tells him in the doorway—and it's dreadful, because her eyes slide over him as she says the empty words. And he *still* has to tell her about Leith's death. He takes her arm and they move inside—among the training dummies.

These dummies, Gavin Lambert said, were all Ray's idea. They are both the first things we see in the film (appearing under the titles), and the last. They hang from the gym ceiling in rows suspended two or three feet off the floor. Since we never get an overview of the space, we're not at all sure how many of them there are, but there *seem* to be dozens—or more. They are like one disturbing figure replicated indefinitely: limp and gray and cloth-covered, with an unformed fetal look—arms tapering to points, a pinhead with an inverted T to mark the face, a heart outline on the chest, square shoulders and narrowed torso. In earlier scenes they were mostly in the background of shots, mostly just hanging there, other times being "assaulted"—with jumps, punches, stabbings and karate chops, and loud accompanying cries—by the trainees. In these later scenes, however, they are mostly in the foreground. And they look throughout like *symbols* of a rather oppressive kind—which they are (Leith calling Brand a "stuffed dummy" at one point, and so on). Mostly, however, they are simply presences—and, like the desert, or the actors, charged with a primarily mysterious force.

"I suppose you'd like to know what happened to Leith," says Brand, walking her away from the camera. Yes, she would. They stop and turn to each other, but he is looking now at the men who are assembling, at the general's order, among the mannequins and the exercise gear. There is a pause. "The men think I killed him," he says, still looking off. Now there is no pause: "*Did* you?" she says gravely, in a close-up. We are still looking at her looking at him when he says: "I wanted to save him but it was too late." Close-up of Brand now: watching his words register. Then back to her: her eyes, still fixed on him, fill with tears. She lowers her head and turns away. Brand watches her as she walks out of the frame. She arrives—in the next shot—at one of the hanging men: she is just at its waist, with the arm hanging down into the frame near her face. It turns in the air, toward her. She takes the "hand" in hers and starts to cry on the gray cloth. Brand, towering over her, comes into the frame behind her—they are both facing the camera. And in the exchange that follows he lies to her about Leith's last words to her, saying that the wind had drowned them out: "I suppose he *would* have said, 'Tell Jane I love her' "—and then, taking Leith's dog tags out of his shirt and giving them to her, he adds: "Those would have been *my* last words too." Now the general enters: "Where is the hero of Benghazi?" he calls out—and the men come to attention. It would appear that enough of the documents survived the fire to avoid canceling the award ceremony.

And it goes smoothly, though it's very dispirited. The men look surly and disaffected, muttering like a potential lynch mob as they assemble. Brand, at attention before the general, looks grim and desperate. And the general's speech sounds mechanical and unconvinced. Wilkins, with his unyielding stare, has moved into Brand's former place in the frame behind Jane and the dummy—which she is still holding on to, still crying. For Brand it's the being-naked-in-public dream, where everyone sees what no one seems to notice. The men despise him and the general is noncommittal. A dream, but also business-as-usual in the army: an empty ceremony, an undeserved commendation. "I have the authority and pleasure," intones the idiot general, over a tortured close-up of Brand, "to award to the man who led you, Major David Brand, the Distinguished Service Order." At this point, and in the silence that follows, Jane looks up at the face of the dummy, relinquishes the arm, and walks slowly out, her footsteps sounding as she goes. Wilkins, still behind the dummy, turns to watch her go. A few more pompous words, and the company is dismissed. Brand stands where he is, alone—as the men mutter and wander slowly out. Wilkins is the last to go, pausing in the doorway to nod knowingly at Brand.

For the first time in the film Brand is alone—with no one looking at him. Beside him in the frame is a mannequin. And for a moment at least he has the dignity of confronting his own emptiness. Then, with an angry, violent jab, he pins his medal on the dummy, setting it swinging. And before going out, he looks up at its face—just as Jane had done: the film's last "exchange" of looks—except for the one *we* exchange, so to speak, with the mannequin in close-up (the final shot of the film), turning in the air, with the medal in its "heart."

There is no escape from futility in this shattering and unrelenting film. Finally there's only the option of facing and naming it—of walking out, slowly and firmly, on the public ceremony that disguises it. It's a bleak alternative, but it is certainly something—as the smile on Leith's death mask suggests.

Joan Bennett in Max Ophuls's *The Reckless Moment*

PART THREE

THE MOVIES

*I am neither a reader nor a writer of didactic fiction,
and . . .* Lolita *has no moral in tow. For me a work of fiction exists only insofar as it affords me what I shall
bluntly call aesthetic bliss, that is a sense of being somehow, somewhere connected with other states of being where
art (curiosity, tenderness, kindness, ecstasy) is the norm.*

— VLADIMIR NABOKOV

As one grows older art and life become one and the same.

— GEORGES BRAQUE

Fifteen

THE FIFTIES

Oreone of the most curious things about Rodgers and Hammerstein's *Oklahoma!* (the movie, 1955), it always seemed to me, was that the malign force threatening Curly and Laurey, the hero and heroine, is neither outlaws nor Indians, rustlers nor cattle barons, railroad men nor crooked sheriffs, none of those nemesis figures of power that we knew from other westerns, but rather someone quite powerless: Jud, the hired hand who lives in a mud hut out back, where he looks at the dirty pictures he gets by mail order and yearns after Laurey. But since he is poor, friendless, and personally revolting, the heavy-breathing conflict between him and the others, all those laughing, dancing celebrants of the Way Things Are, seems strangely pointless. Until you realize that it's the simple—and nearby—existence of someone like Jud, even the thought of him, that is threatening to Curly and Laurey and their friends. (The man never even bathes!) And more important—for all the rest of us—to Rodgers and Hammerstein themselves.

The times belonged to them, it seemed to a lot of us, more than to anyone who was only making movies. You couldn't escape *them* the way you could a movie: their songs, all those hymns to radiant normalcy, all that self-willing cheeriness, came at you from every direction. "Oh, What a Beautiful Mornin'," "It's a Grand Night for Singing," "I Enjoy Being a Girl," "I'm in Love with a Wonderful Guy," "There Is Nothin' Like a Dame," "This Was a Real Nice Clambake" ("We had a real fine time . . .")—not to mention "Happy Talk" ("Keep on talkin' happy talk . . ."). Only in *Carousel,* the richest of their shows—though among the worst of their movies (in 1956)—does the fierce declarative contentedness take on a conditional note ("If I Loved You," "When I Marry Mr. Snow," "What's the Use of Wond'rin'," and so on). But then, as if to make up for that, it all comes to an end with that resolutely nondenominational hymn of "belief," "You'll Never Walk Alone."

But all this unconvinced "happy talk" embodied the larger spirit of those hollowly triumphalist times. America had won the war and survived it (as we usually do) uniquely intact. We had begun to rule the world, but without really wanting to. That's how we saw it anyway, being used to believing in our national innocence. And now, that innocence seemed to be paying off. In the fifties, Americans were more prosperous than we had ever been before, more upwardly mobile, more hopeful about our own and our children's futures. Barring a nuclear war, of course—which almost all of us believed to be likely somehow, without ever *quite* believing it (at least until the Cuban missile crisis). The Communist threat at home seemed more like a theological problem than a real one, since there wasn't much material evidence for it. But to those who actually worried about it, that of course *was* the evidence.

Living in fifties America—to the young man I was then, anyway—was in many ways like living in a public absence: like a public space that's suddenly emptied out, a theatre after closing, or a classroom after school. The emptiness could feel liberating, but it could also make you feel blank and vaguely nostalgic. The war was the big event we had grown up with. Even though, as the people on the "home front," we experienced it mainly through the movies—with all their appeals to heroism and idealism, all their stokings of national grievance and indignation. Tinny and unconvincing as these appeals mostly were, they made their impression. It was mainly at the movies that we learned to associate American life with high purpose and challenge, with the emotion and great communal experiences of the war and, before that, of the Depression and the New Deal. Later on, when we arrived at Eisenhower's America, it felt like a movie that was over. And yet here we were—still on the set.

That feeling only intensified for me once I got drafted for two years in the army (1955–57). It was after the Korean War; and that had been a war (unlike the one before it) that *no one* wanted to pay much attention to (unless they had to) even while it was going on. Though our NCOs in the army, who'd actually been in that war, most of them, liked to refer to it in their training sessions with us, it was the Second World War whose set *we* were on. For us, that was the big reality behind all the daily small ones we had to go through: the barracks and mess halls and PXs, KP and mail call and guard duty, imperious COs and crusty first sergeants, and so on—we'd seen it all, even been through it all, at the movies we'd grown up with. And it was the vestiges of that great glorious wartime past, clinging now to all these locations and routines, that somehow made the army, in spite of everything, even your detesting it (as I did), a place you sort of half wanted to be—or, more exactly, to have been.

Even in the fifties—when the army that had once been the American male's rite of passage, the "democratic" army that "everyone" had to serve in for a while, was over with. Now only the negligent or the unlucky, it seemed (deferments were widely and easily gotten), got drafted into it. And the traditional sort of "war games" they put us through in basic training, with gas masks and bayonets and live ammo going off just above our heads, felt like some historical re-enactment, as unreal as playing cowboys-and-Indians again—not only because it was peacetime then, but because that really wasn't the kind of war anyone expected our country would ever again have to fight. Some time after that, they sent us to a guided missile site in New Jersey, to become part of the nation's all-important radar defense rim. *That* was more like it—or should have been.

It was called the Nike ground-to-air system. And it seemed like another game. Because we knew by then—arriving in New Jersey from our training in Texas—that we almost certainly couldn't hit anything with *our* Nike missiles, since we'd failed to hit the dummy targets they'd sent up for us during our final tests in the New Mexico desert. This caused a lot of consternation, especially among our commanding officers. But the non-happening quickly became a nonfact, expunged from the records, as we all supposed, allowing us to be shipped without delay to our permanent New Jersey assignment. There, under the pressures of army routine, and in the direct vicinity of all that expensive and complex equipment, it was the fiasco in the desert that began to seem unreal.

But that wasn't all. I was assigned there to the orderly room, and my principal job was to keep and update (they had been neglected by the previous man) fake records. My job title was Training and Information NCO, and I had to keep track of each enlisted man's attendance at daily and weekly classes of various kinds—except that there were no classes of *any* kind going on, and I had to make it all up. Since the regulations required daily training for every man on site, they also required training records. And those at least were easier to provide (the only time they took up was mine). These records were then periodically inspected—checked for their currency and "accuracy"—by officers who had to know as well as I did (we were a very small outfit) that they were a fake. But then of course our officers were inspecting them not for themselves but for the officers above *them*—the inspectors of *their* inspection—and so on upward. At some point, you supposed, someone was fooled.

The officers in our outfit never joked about any of this, the way we did—so it seemed. Being officers—and unlike us—they had to pretend to be deceived, maybe even to themselves. The burden of command. All *we* had to do was go through the motions. For us what was disgraceful was to take being in the army at all seriously, or to work at it too hard. What we did work at, even compete with each other about, was *not* working—often a harder job than the actual work might have been, because you wanted not only to foil the system but to fool it. The difference between fucking off and fucking up: there were no points in the contest for getting caught at not doing your job. *That* was just incompetence, provoking pity, at best, or disgust. (The all-time champion for us was the corporal in the supply room, who was always being commended by our captain for his diligence and who spent all his day, as the rest of us knew, off post with his wife.)

Essentially we were all (even the corporal) powerless, of course, with all those feelings of lost autonomy, even identity, that the army so famously gives you. But at the least, we found out, we could speak lies to power. That time was probably the closest I've ever come to the experience of the black American (a more common one in that pre–gangster-rap era) who learns to be good at "putting on whitey"—whose acquiescence is a form of contempt, even a kind of power.

All this was much like our relation to the movies in those days—and to the power *they* had over us. We "put them on" too, so to speak, often going to them just to make jokes and break one another up—especially in college, where such jeering expeditions were widely popular. And they were a lot of fun provided you brought the right wise-ass friends along, and if you picked the right movie. But they could easily get out of hand, too. I remember, on a 1953 Saturday night in Ann Arbor, the almost hour-long roar of hilarity and derision that filled a packed theatre at something called *The I Don't Care Girl* with Mitzi Gaynor. College-town movie houses may still have pandemoniums like that, but I doubt it, now that the movies themselves (now *made* by wise-asses) make jokes about their own emptiness and make more noise themselves than any live audience could (quelling the rabble by leading it).

It's embarrassing to me now to think of some of the movies I made fun of then—almost anything by Douglas Sirk, for instance (though I probably wouldn't even have known his name at the time). But what was important to us was less a matter of being "right" than of being dissident, publicly defying the power of the movies, and the depressing cultural consensus they represented. It was not just *funny* to talk back to them—it was exhilarating, speaking *truth* to power this time, taking a stand against the engulfing banality. We hadn't yet heard of camp, but *our* mockery was not so lighthearted as that term sometimes suggests. That outbreak of sustained hilarity in the Ann Arbor movie house had been full of anger, the whole thing nearer to a riot than a merry crowd—an uprising of insulted and injured: a *fifties* sort of student riot.

In Terry Southern's comic novel *The Magic Christian* (published in 1960) a super-rich eccentric, Guy Grand, devotes his time and fortune to inventing and carrying out, for his own amusement, elaborate jokes on the great American public, no expense spared. He buys a first-run downtown movie house where he shows all the biggest hits, but not without altering them in some way, subtly but enough to disturb and upset the audience. Inserting, for example, into a scene of domestic idyll between Mr. and Mrs. Miniver a three-second close-up of a glinting sharpened pen knife in the hands of Mr. Miniver.

He makes an even more inspired alteration in *The Best Years of Our Lives* when he shows that popular film. His change occurs, you are told, in a romantic scene on the front porch between the amputee vet whose hands have been replaced by prosthetic hooks and "his pretty hometown fiancee." The vet is wearing "a brave smile" and the girl's eyes are shining "with tolerance and understanding" as they sit together on the porch swing. But the heartwarming moment "was interrupted by Grand's insert: a cut to below the girl's waist where the hooks were seen to hover for an instant and then disappear, grappling urgently beneath her skirt. The duration of this cut was less than one-half second but was unmistakably seen by anyone in the audience not on the brink of sleep . . ." Who couldn't, of course, believe their eyes. The rest of the movie then proceeded without change, "without incongruity or surprise," but hardly anyone could follow it now. Had they really *seen* that? And some people would sit through the movie again to find out. But at the next show Grand would always run the original, unimproved version, without the insert.

This joke of Southern's became sort of famous among the people I knew. It was directed against the sort of movie we especially hated, and I knew the joke long before I read Southern's book. I'd seen *that* movie, of course, just as everyone else had. It was the kind of well-intentioned success, both acclaimed and popular, that could make you feel hopeless about goodness, the "social criticism" never seeming as strong as the complacency underlying it. And *The Best Years of Our Lives* became a kind of model for the "serious" films that followed it, as Hollywood began taking on more and more tough and troubling subjects—mostly to turn them into kitsch. As with Stanley Kramer's *The Defiant Ones* (1958), where America's race problem was figured in two convicts, black and white, chained together as they escape from prison: enemies at first, comrades at the end, each competing to sacrifice himself for the other.

These "controversial" movies were always, of course, apolitical. One absolute taboo (surviving to this day in something like Mike Nichols's *Primary Colors*) was to suggest that there were *political* problems, let alone political remedies. In MGM's *Trial* (1955), the town's racists want to fry the Mexican-American boy accused of murder, but the left-wing radicals, who only want to use him to stir things up for their own propaganda, are just as evil. The movie's heroine, Dorothy McGuire, is its expert on radicals, being herself a repentant former Communist. "Did you ever wonder why lady comrades were always so unattractive?" she inquires of the hero, Glenn Ford, who apparently hasn't. She tells him anyway: the Party tells them sex was unimportant, so they never buy or wear makeup.

Fifties "issue" movies offered many such insights: that Communists were mentally ill or else lacked love (McGuire again), or that they were really "just out for themselves" like everyone else. Like the Broadway actor who is a secret Party member (Dean Martin!) in Hal Wallis's *Career* (1959)—the same movie where the actor hero (Anthony Franciosa) is advised by the heroine (Carolyn Jones), who is also his agent, not to resent the people who have mistakenly blacklisted him so that he can no longer get a job, since they are patriots who are working for us all. He hadn't thought of that, it seems.

But at least in one area the new "maturity" was an unquestioned gain. The old Production Code pruderies about sex, more strictly and absurdly enforced during the war years than ever before, were being more and more successfully challenged, so that even by 1950 it had become possible (if you were Elia Kazan, anyway) to make a movie of *A Streetcar Named Desire*—not without a fight but without entirely compromising the original play.

But if movies got franker, they also got dumber, it seemed, in other ways connected to that. The sins and terrors of the gothic small-town melodrama—as in 1941's *Kings Row,* for instance—turned with the new candor into the soap operas of "repression" and "maladjustment," the homiletic culture of mental hygiene, as in 1957's *Peyton Place.* And it seemed like a decline—as if the movies were becoming more "honest" and "grown-up" only by telling us new and less obvious lies. Certainly they were getting less grandiose in many ways—as in their versions of the happy or uplifting ending. For example: the suffering heroine of Susan Hayward, recurrent through the postwar years, goes at the end of her movie from an act of maternal sacrifice in 1950 (*My Foolish Heart*) to a triumphant singing comeback in 1952 (*With a Song in My Heart*) to a TV appearance as the subject of *This Is Your Life* in 1956 (*I'll Cry Tomorrow*)—

striding down the theatre aisle to the stage and the cameras and the wit-lessly grinning emcee awaiting her (Ralph Edwards as himself) as if she were undergoing a heavenly ascension, or at the least a coronation, as the music swells and the movie ends.

The postwar years were a time for movie breakthroughs, and one of the pioneers was Stanley Kramer, who made the first Hollywood movie about antiblack prejudice, *Home of the Brave* (1949), as well as Brando's debut movie, *The Men* (1950), about the rehabilitating of paraplegic war vets. At first Kramer was only a producer (*Home* was directed by Mark Robson, *The Men* by Fred Zinnemann), and one of the new independents. But the studios—facing nothing but troubles now—were impressed by his success, both critical and (to a lesser extent) commercial. It was a new idea (to them) of a prestige picture: combining a bare-bones budget with a hot cur-rent subject. Columbia signed him and gave him his own production unit. There he turned out three or four films a year, on the same enlightened and "controversial" lines for the most part: like *The Sniper* (1952), about a sex criminal (who kills from a Code-enforced distance—with a long-range rifle!); *My Six Convicts* (1952), a "warmhearted" look at penal reform; *The Wild One* (1954), about juvenile delinquents, again with Brando; and so on. He varied such socially conscious stuff with budget-minded movie ver-sions of cloying, middlebrow Broadway plays like *The Happy Time* (1952) and *The Four Poster* (1953), with Rex Harrison and Lilli Palmer.

But almost none of Kramer's Columbia movies made any money (the reviews weren't so good, either) until the last and biggest one, his produc-tion of *The Caine Mutiny* (1954). Independent of Columbia after that, and now directing as well as producing, he made another "big" film, also from a best-seller, *Not As a Stranger* (1955), about doctors in training, and with five name-above-the-title stars (Mitchum, Sinatra, Olivia de Havilland, Gloria Grahame, and Broderick Crawford). This combination of multistar casts and serious issues set the pattern for the rest of his career—even when the result seemed incongruous. Ava Gardner and Gregory Peck, with (nondancing) support from Fred Astaire, in a movie about the nuclear apocalypse—why not? Once again from a big best-seller, *On the Beach* (1959)—and it too made money.

In spite of his beginnings as a modest innovator, and his political liber-alism, Kramer was soon reminding people of the most risible excesses of the old Hollywood titans—he was turning into the liberals' De Mille. At any rate, it was in some De Mille–like fit ("So they want a funny movie? I'll *give* them a funny movie!") that he seems to have conceived *It's a Mad Mad Mad Mad World* (1963)—a movie distinguished by all the wit and comic skill its title seemed to promise, and then some: probably the unfunniest and most ponderous, certainly the longest (three hours and twelve minutes), the widest-screened (Cinerama), and the most many-starred (over thirty—count them—Buster Keaton to Jerry Lewis), slap-stick comedy ever released. But it was a success (not good days for comedy then). And it had Spencer Tracy, top-billed, in it too—the star who had become for Kramer a sort of guarantor of worthwhileness, almost invari-ably cast in the producer-director's most ambitious films. Most notably, *Judgment at Nuremburg* (1961), inflated to "epic" scale (three hours and ten minutes) from a rather modest TV original, set mostly in a courtroom, and comprised of a series of flamboyant star turns—by Burt Lancaster, Richard Widmark, Marlene Dietrich, Maximilian Schell, Montgomery Clift, and Judy Garland—each performed under the brooding Solomonic scrutiny of "Judge" Tracy. It was, like most Kramer productions, a painfully well-meant film—even perhaps down to his casting of two famously dissipated, now dramatically debilitated movie stars as Holocaust victims. While you might want to think that Kramer was the only one who could have believed that was a great idea, he wasn't, of course: both Clift and Garland were nominated for Academy Awards. (The movie's screenwriter actually got one and accepted it "on behalf of all intellectuals.")

"When I was in Hollywood recently," wrote the critic Dwight Mac-Donald in a 1960 *Partisan Review,* "I was told by one of the most intelli-gent younger directors, Stanley Kubrick: 'The reason movies are often so bad out here isn't because the people who make them are cynical money hacks. Most of them are doing the very best they can; they really want to make good movies. The trouble is with their heads, not their hearts.' This was borne out by the film I was there to write about, a mawkish travesty of Nathanael West's *Miss Lonelyhearts* that was written and produced by Dore Schary with the noblest intentions." Schary (the producer of *The Next Voice You Hear*—see pp. 73–74) and *his* intentions had more impact on Holly-wood even than Kramer's—mainly because Schary ran MGM for eight years, 1948 to 1956. (*Lonelyhearts,* 1959, was one of his last movies and a flop.) He too was a liberal (openly supporting Adlai Stevenson for presi-dent twice, and even opposing the Hollywood blacklist—before giving in to it), and his career followed a similar trajectory to Kramer's: from a beginning in low-budget "quality" filmmaking to a climax on the heights. But the heights were a troubled place in the fifties, filled with panic about declining receipts and audiences. Part of Schary's attraction for the MGM bosses was that his career up to then had *not* been associated with opulence. Quite the contrary.

Heading MGM's low-budget unit in the forties, he gained a reputation for cautious daring, as well as for launching such stars as Lassie and Margaret O'Brien. He left to work for David O. Selznick's company, and then (briefly) for RKO. His biggest hits in those years tended to be with anodyne suburban comedies that had mildly topical subjects: a politician's maid runs for Congress against him (*The Farmer's Daughter,* 1947); Cary Grant encounters the new teen culture (*The Bachelor and the Bobby Soxer,* 1947); a city couple (Cary Grant again, with Myrna Loy) move to the suburbs (*Mr. Blandings Builds His Dream House,* 1948). But Schary's deepest enthusiasm was for the sort of production, low-budget and "controversial," that he began his job at RKO with: Edward Dmytryk's *Crossfire* (1947), a stylish noir thriller about a raving bigot (Robert Ryan) who murders a friendly Jew (Sam Levene). It was the first movie to talk openly about anti-Semitism, even beating Zanuck's more expensive and prestigious *Gentleman's Agreement* to movie screens that year. *Crossfire* was just the sort of movie Schary could make at a minor-league, loosely run studio like RKO—until Howard Hughes bought the place. The reputation for quality and mild innovating that had recommended Schary to a Selznick made him unacceptable to Hughes. This was when he took on the production-chief job at MGM, sharing the power (at first anyway) with Louis B. Mayer himself.

He wanted to do good things there, and to some extent he did, though almost never were they the films he "personally produced" (*Washington Story, Go for Broke, Plymouth Adventure, Dream Wife,* et al.). One exception was John Sturges's *Bad Day at Black Rock* (1955), a contemporary western on the model of Kramer's *High Noon* (1952)—an action film that also denounced racism, blending suspense and social significance in the same way *Crossfire* had done (with the same villain as well: Robert Ryan as the raving "Jap hater").

Mayer hated Schary's movies and his influence (which was growing) on the general studio output. Schary, he said, made "propaganda pictures." Mayer liked shlock, but not the "meaningful" shlock that Schary liked. The old lion's ideal of entertainment, as was well known, was the Hardy family series. Now *that* was "family values": Mickey Rooney clowning, and Judy Garland singing a song or two, and always those audience-tested "man-to-man talks" between Andy and his bemused, benevolent dad, Judge Hardy (Lewis Stone). Schary's version of the same thing was more like *The Next Voice You Hear* or, even worse, *The Boy with Green Hair* (color prejudice). Mayer's kind of taste, of course, made more money than Schary's ever would. It also, arguably, made better movies, at least on balance.

But the legendary mogul's day was past. When he demanded in 1951 that the board of directors choose between him and Schary, they chose Schary. Probably only Mayer himself was surprised. His Hardy family, after all, was a dream of *small-town* America. Schary's fantasy was more up-to-date—more suburban: Mr. Blandings Builds His Dream World. The MGM he presided over and shaped was in some ways more enlightened than Mayer's, but it was also blander and duller—the old man's vulgar gentility replaced by Schary's more middlebrow kind.

But there were still, thank God, those terrific thrillers (before color and CinemaScope, among other things, did them in). The kind of movie (we could identify it long before we learned to call it noir) that almost seemed to redeem the creeping smarminess of the rest: tough-talking and tough-minded, unsentimental and unpretentious, these wonderful "suspensers," as *Variety* called them—movies like André De Toth's *Pitfall* (1948), Jules Dassin's *Thieves' Highway* (1949), Robert Aldrich's *Kiss Me Deadly,* Phil Karlson's *The Brothers Rico,* Don Siegel's *The Lineup* (1958), et al. These movies, more than any other kind, seemed to deliver us from all the piety and upbeat and cheeriness, from the self-importance of the social-issue movie and from the self-absorption of the Method kind. They seemed to put almost the same sort of value on skepticism and sharp wit and lively talk as the great prewar comedies had done. And in the fifties it became clearer than ever before that the pleasure they gave us was connected to their hardheadedness, their adamant refusal of pathos. *That* had defined them almost from their beginnings: "Maybe I'll have some rotten nights after I've sent you over," said Bogart to Mary Astor in 1941, "but that'll pass."

But even these movies got softer in the fifties. Like John Huston's *The Asphalt Jungle* (1950)—which seemed at the time almost a kind of turning point. An A picture from Schary's MGM, it had a B-picture look, grainy low-contrast photography, and no stars except Sterling Hayden, who was hardly a major one. It was a hit, nonetheless, helped by reviews that hailed it for its novelty, for its unprecedented "realism." But what seemed *most* novel about it in 1950 was the way it had changed the usual noir toughness into a sentimentality about missed chances and blighted lives, into heavy dumb ironies about fate, and the numbing perception that crooks are people just like us, really—the "little people" line so favored by Hollywood populism (Huston's co-screenwriter, Ben Maddow, was *that* kind of writer). The movie had some power, but it was the kind you could regret subjecting yourself to: these crooks were *so* winsome, coming on nasty but then showing how "human" they really were: a doting new dad (Anthony

Marie Windsor and Sterling Hayden in Stanley Kubrick's *The Killing*

Caruso) showing snapshots of his baby; a kitten-loving hunchback (James Whitmore); a horse-loving southerner (Sterling Hayden) concerned, southern-gentleman-style, with his "honor"; and so on. (Louis Calhern's crooked lawyer feels the least clichéd, partly because of his wonderful scenes with Marilyn Monroe as his baby-doll mistress.) There is even a dimwit, golden-hearted tart (Jean Hagen), in love with the hero (Hayden). The noir claustrophobia (tightly framed shots from low angles in dark, low-ceilinged spaces) is inflected here with a morbidity that only gets underlined by the achingly slow pacing of each scene and by the hokey humanism.

Six years later Stanley Kubrick made his first important and mainstream movie, *The Killing* (1956), co-writing the script with Jim Thompson (from a novel by Lionel White). And Kubrick clearly knew (as you might expect *he* would) where the real life of the noir style still was: in its astringency and toughness, its shrewdness and cold, offbeat glamour. He reminded us, too—in this brilliant, harrowing and darkly funny movie. And he did so by practically remaking the Huston film (which he admired)—only doing it better, as Orson Welles observed (to Peter Bogdanovich). Both movies are about gangs planning and pulling off elaborate heists. Both starred

Hayden; in both he's involved with horses—in love with them in the Huston movie (even dying poetically in their midst at the end), plotting to shoot them (a racetrack heist) in the Kubrick. And although the Kubrick film is also filled with picturesque, lovable-type losers—a dimwitted girlfriend (Coleen Gray), a chess-playing wrestler (Maurice Oboukhoff), a puppy-loving gun dealer (Timothy Carey), even a patient, invalid wife (Dorothy Adams)—they are as coldly viewed as the movie's bad guys are. And they are, for the most part, enormously appealing. At least partly because their "humanity" isn't insisted upon—as if it needed to be. The sense that it *does* with the characters in the Huston movie is what gives that film some of its unintended (presumably) creepiness.

Sixteen

THE RECKLESS MOMENT

Jean Renoir, languishing in Hollywood in 1949 (he'd made five films there during the war years and just after), wrote to his good friend Ingrid Bergman to console her about the recent disaster, both artistic and commercial, she'd had with her grandiloquent *Joan of Arc* movie (1948). What the misfortune should teach her, Renoir said, was that "in art only the form counts." "Dear Ingrid, we had many amusing arguments together and I was the first one to defend, stupidly, the importance of 'great subjects.' I wasted a large part of my life by becoming uselessly busy with the 'significance' of my pictures. . . . Today, I regret not having busied myself with the endless ant-like work of small, cheap pictures of a definite style, like 'westerns' or 'murder' stories."

If, as it turned out, it was too late for Renoir in Hollywood to act on such an insight (he had already made, in 1947, his final American film, *The Woman on the Beach,* and was left even more dissatisfied with it than he had been with the other four), it wasn't for others there. While the Method and the postwar "message" movie seemed to be getting all the attention, something else, less noticed, was going on in Hollywood: the old-fashioned genre movies (westerns especially) were showing a renewed, even unprecedented vitality.

Renoir's words now seem almost prescient—today when you may argue that the 1950s movies that have worn the best were the ones that were the least "serious" and ambitious, the ones least involved in "significance" and "great subjects." Many veteran directors took the freedoms that the collapsing studio system (and their own past records of commercial success) allowed them to immerse themselves more deeply and personally, more idiosyncratically, and more exclusively than ever in genre movies, with their recurring structures and "definite styles": Ford and Hawks in the western, Hitchcock in " 'murder' stories," producing eccentric masterpieces like *Vertigo* and *The Searchers* and *Rio Bravo,* among others.

"The great filmmakers always tie themselves down by complying with the rules of the game," wrote Godard ("I have not done so," he added, "because I am a minor filmmaker"). And Max Ophuls's great noir movie, *The Reckless Moment* (1949), is surely a case in point. It's a conventional noir with a twist: the *femme* here is *fatale* to the hero because she is respectable *instead* of criminal. But beyond that, this modest and not-very-thrilling thriller is one of the most moving and powerful films ever made about the modern American family. Renoir might have been talking about it when he wrote in the same letter to Bergman that one of the virtues of the genre movie was the standardization it imposed—because "in a structure that is always the same, you are free to improve what alone is worthwhile, the detail in human expression."

James Mason is a blackmailer who falls in love with his victim, Joan Bennett, an upper-middle-class suburban housewife. It all starts when Bennett's spoiled teenage daughter, in a quarrel with her middle-aged boyfriend, a lowlife and a crook named Darby (Shepperd Strudwick), accidentally kills him, pushing him off the upper landing of the family boathouse, leaving the body impaled on an anchor in the sands below. Mother to the rescue: to save her daughter and protect the rest of her family—comprising a teenage son, an absent husband who is working overseas, and a live-in father-in-law—Lucia Harper (Bennett) resolves to hide the corpse, dumping it from an outboard boat into the waters outside their Southern California home, all by herself. She even gets rid of the anchor—so that when the body is discovered (it soon is, of course) there won't be anything to connect it with with the Harper family.

Except, as it turns out, some ardent letters the daughter, Bee (Geraldine Brooks), had written to the dead man, which have now fallen into the hands of his fellow crooks. One of them, an Irishman named Martin Donnelly (Mason), has turned up (almost a half hour into the movie) in Lucia's home. He's waiting for her, standing in the shadows of the room they call the library, when Lucia gets back from her shopping, still carrying the groceries in her arms.

At first (the maid has let him in) she has no idea who he is or what he wants. But you'd think she was visiting *him,* the quiet way he takes over the room, and the situation. "Do you mind?" he says, as he steps past her to close the louvers on the room's slatted doors for privacy (only the upstairs rooms in this house seem to have real doors). They both remain standing, and he is still in the shapeless black overcoat he wears throughout the movie. He tells her about the letters (he calls them "writings"), shows them from across the room, even reads a choice passage (Bee declaring her passion) out loud in his lilting Irish brogue, holding the paper over a lamp on a nearby desk. It's a melodramatic moment, and he is in command of it. Until Lucia's boy, thirteen-year-old David (David Bair), bursts in on them, with brash, nasal-voiced excitement about the unknown body the police have just found nearby. That breaks the spell. So does an ensuing commotion outside the room—a squabble on the stairway between brother and sister. Lucia runs out to quiet them, leaving Donnelly behind, nonplussed, standing over the desk, holding the "writings" rather limply in his hand, looking after her—in the background of a low-angle long shot. In this shot, the room seems quite dark—except for the spot by the lamp where he's standing, engulfed by shadows, while the sounds of family echo off, in another room. And it's in a version of this same shot—repeated a few moments later when she leaves him abruptly again—that you first notice the very tall Christmas tree looming in the darkness in back of him. "You don't know how a family can surround you at times," Lucia says to him in a later scene. "No, I don't," he replies softly.

That exchange, in fact, takes place the next day. They are seated in the front seat of his car (he is at the wheel), drifting across the water on a ferry taking them from Balboa Island, the coastal enclave where she lives, to the mainland—and he is already looking calf-eyed at her. She is trying to explain to him, while looking straight ahead, why it is really impossible for her to raise five thousand dollars, the blackmail demand set by his boss, so quickly. She lights another cigarette (she's a chain smoker) and he remarks softly, almost sheepishly, that it's bad for her. "What?" she says, rather sharply. "You smoke too much," he says, turning his eyes to the front and looking off, his arm resting on the steering wheel, as they drift on the water. She turns and looks at him—she almost never looks at him directly—as if to say, "What are you about?" Not that she cares. She tells him she needs to stop at the drugstore when they dock, to make a phone call she couldn't make at home. He takes that for progress.

That is, he thinks she's calling about the money. But when the scene in the car dissolves into a close-up of Lucia in the phone booth, wearing her glasses now, she is talking to her sister Edna, about "taking" Bee for the holidays (getting her away from the local publicity about the killing), and Edna is resisting: "But Edna . . . she *isn't* hard to manage, Bee isn't *like* that." Then the operator wants more money, and Lucia has no change left. She tells Edna to hold on and leaves the booth, winding her way through the narrow aisles, crowded with merchandise and Christmas decorations, of the apparently empty store (a long lateral tracking shot), looking for a clerk—until she comes to the front door, where Donnelly waits outside. "I need some change," she says breathlessly, backing away and holding her

Lucia (Joan Bennett), with the help of her genial and clueless
father-in-law (Henry O'Neill, in the yachting cap), entertains
the blackmailer, Donnelly (James Mason).

hand out—"I'm in the middle of a phone conversation"—while he fum-
bles in his pockets and follows. In this awkward fashion they move back
down the aisles together—Donnelly fumbling and muttering ("I have
some dimes, I think," as coins clatter on the floor), Lucia holding her hand
out ("I'll need another quarter")—until they reach the booth. She deposits
the coins, resumes her conversation, and closes the door on him.

And he's embarrassed. Looking stranded again, in a long shot and an
incongruous space, just as he did in her library—with voices murmuring
off, the store apparently no longer empty. He stands sheepishly, with his
hands in his overcoat pockets, looks around uneasily, then walks slowly
back (another long tracking shot), past some browsing customers, a stock
boy, the displays, toward the front of the store. There's a folksy-looking
clerk now at the front counter by the cash register, and they chat amiably.
There are questions about "Mrs. Harper's order" (is it two or three tooth
powders?), which Donnelly can't answer. But he sees some "preventive"
cigarette holders on display ("Less Nicotine! Less Tobacco Stain!") and
buys her one, paying for it separately and putting it with the things on her
list (she will return it later, thinking it was the store's mistake). And when

she comes back from her phone call, she too seems a bit uneasy. "Did you remember to put in my father-in-law's razor blades?" she asks the clerk—and Donnelly echoes (also to the clerk): "Did we?" As they leave, he gathers up the bags and opens the door for her—they are both uncomfortable now under the clerk's curious gaze. "Goodbye, Mrs. Harper—goodbye, Mr. . . . uh . . . ?" No answer. But it's clear why he wonders about Donnelly. In this lovely, gently comic scene, Lucia—without thinking or meaning to—has reduced him to the motions of a husband. The crook and the housewife.

When they are back on the ferry in the front seat of his car again, the opening shot, framing them together in a tight low-angled close-up, emphasizes his threat and control. He's in the foreground, turned toward her and away from us, the bulk of his head and shoulders filling most of the frame—with one arm resting on the steering wheel, the other extending toward her along the back of the seat. As usual, he is looking at her, and she is looking straight ahead, her face and shoulders framed and held in the V-shaped curve of his overcoated arm. He wants to be assured that she will be getting in touch with her husband—about the money. "I told you I can't do that," she says. And now the camera view is reversed, looking past her toward him. She is in the controlling foreground, turned away from him, in resolute profile, while he looks at her with stricken eyes. Her husband, she says tightly, can't be reached. "I wouldn't think," says Donnelly mildly, "there was anyplace that remote." Still gazing at her profile. "He's traveling," she says. "You can cable him on a boat," he replies slowly, turning his gaze away, looking slowly down along his arm and then up at his hand on the wheel. "Or a train," he adds—dreamily, almost as if he might drift away on the words. At that moment she turns on him, starting up suddenly in the frame, her back nearly filling it (the camera lurching slightly forward to underscore the movement): "What do you expect me to *say?*" she says angrily. " 'Send money, I'm being blackmailed'?!" And above her upraised shoulder—which blots out his lower face, landing on it like a blow—we see his startled, distressed eyes, fixed on her with hurt and alarm. She subsides and sits back again, looking straight ahead again. But you think she can't have seen what *we've* just seen—i.e., those eyes of his—and not been sort of reached by it.

· But of course she can. She has her own troubles—most of them right now owing to him. She tries to downplay the incriminating letters: "Children"—her way of referring to Bee—"dramatize things so much." But he reminds her the police aren't likely to see it that way. And he maintains his gentle, steady insistence that she get the money now—somehow. His boss, a man named Nagle, he says, won't wait. But she doesn't believe there is a Nagle—"You're on your own, you might as well admit it," she says scornfully. "We're all involved with each other," he replies, "one way or another." Then adds: "You have your family—I have my Nagle." It's *not* a comparison she appreciates: between her family and "this Nagle—*if* he exists." And she wouldn't be trying to raise the money at all, she insists, if it weren't for the shock it would be to Bee if the whole thing came out. "She's lucky to have a mother like you," he says rather wanly. "*Everyone* has a mother like me," is her brusque reply, looking straight ahead. "You probably had one, too."

As a matter of fact, he probably did—as we later find out. But the way he is looking at her now—at her implacable profile—only conveys his despair. Lucia's last words suggest not so much a failure of imagination as a refusal of it. And this exchange between them makes for one of those moments of sardonic recognition the movie is so rich in: her complacency is all at once funny and awful and entirely believable. After all, isn't such a view of things (aren't people the same everywhere?) one of the things you moved to the suburbs *for* in those days—to have and sustain such comforting "thoughts," undisturbed? And it's not the only instance in the movie where her solipsism, her familiar suburban-domestic self-enclosure, will simultaneously surprise and not surprise us. *The Reckless Moment* is about that self-enclosure. But it's even more deeply and originally about Donnelly's attraction to it.

Because if Lucia is certainly not the mother that "everyone has," she is, equally certainly, the mother that some changeless part of everyone—that part that's still motherless—will always want. The person who really *promises* you it will all turn out okay: who not only finds the body but hides it, and tells you not to worry (as Lucia so tirelessly does), to go to bed now, to take a hot-water bottle, to get ready for dinner, and so on. What she offers and provides is all the comfort of the *ordinary.* That other *can't* have happened, can it? Not when dinner is waiting—how could it? "I hope I never have to go through anything like that again," says Bee, with her usual note of entitlement, just after the fateful struggle at the boathouse. "You won't have to, dear, I promise you," says Lucia—with such resolve and authority that even *we* almost believe her. Her commitment to the "normal" course of things, to the sustaining surfaces of everyday life, is never less than impressive. "Roll down your pants and button your jacket, David," she says to her son as she docks and ties up the boat she has just dumped a man's body from. "Just *once,*" she adds (is it too much to ask?), "I'd like to see you fully dressed."

This sort of thing could be played for laughs—in another sort of movie.

But here it's offered with the same straight face that Ophuls maintains throughout. And that also characterizes his heroine. Not that *she* doesn't have trouble with it sometimes. "They'll find the *letters!*" cries Bee, unaware there's already someone in the library using them for blackmail. "No—no, they won't," says Lucia, hands clasped in front of her, the inevitable cigarette between her fingers. "No one will find anything," she says—and the close-up as she says this tells you just how much, of strength and will, this reassurance costs her. Before the inevitable next thought— "Get ready for dinner, dear"—as she goes to confront Donnelly again in the library.

It's her job to reassure them, after all—not just the kids, but Grandpa too (Henry O'Neill), so futile and good-natured, pottering about in his yachting cap. And especially she mustn't upset the "Tom" we never see, the husband and father who remains so helplessly far away (a European engineering project). When one of her letters to him gets a little out of control, she tears it up and begins again: "to tell you how much I love you." "You don't know how a family can surround you," as she says—but you're never sure she herself knows just *how* surrounded she is. Just how much she is bounded by their innocence—by the incessant questions ("Mother, where are you going?" is the first spoken line in the film), by the ignorance she is committed to keeping them in. If she can't stop the bad things from happening, she can at least try to keep them from being noticed once they do—she hopes. "Whatever happened to that man has nothing to do with you," she tells Bee, quite falsely, after the newspaper story breaks. "So please put it out of your mind." All this may seem retrograde, but it's also something more: something that belongs to that atmosphere of sustained care and concern that the movie defines as "family"—and that Donnelly, when he visits, looks on at so hopelessly. And it *all* depends on her.

But in Joan Bennett's deep, quiet performance, Lucia has none of the consciousness of victimization that might make her intolerable. "Do you never get away from your family?" Donnelly asks her. "No," she says, after a pause, as if the idea were almost new to her. And when he later suggests that she is "quite a prisoner," she replies without hesitation: "I don't feel like one." The movie sees her as one, of course (and all the more for her not knowing it), but you never supposed *she* would. If Lucia is extraordinary in any way, she is certainly not interested in knowing about it herself. But for us and Ophuls, Lucia has the peculiar glamour of someone whose heroism is no big deal to her ("*Everyone* has a mother like me")—she's achieved selflessness without the curse of being aware of it.

Later in the movie, in her attempt to get the blackmail money, she goes

"Whatever happened to that man has nothing to do with you," says Lucia—to her daughter Bee (Geraldine Brooks), who has just seen the newspaper. Behind the glass, in the out-of-focus background, Sybil, the maid (Frances Williams), watches—as she does throughout the movie.

to one of those no-questions-asked loan companies in the city, climbing a long and dingy stairway to the office. There she is "taken care of" by a Mrs. Loring (Kathryn Card), a dowager in a tasteful black dress with an incongruous tropical-looking flower in her graying upswept hairdo, and an impeccably gracious manner for condescending to her applicants. Something she now does with Lucia—who is embarrassed and uneasy, saying she wants to "make a loan" instead of get one, and so forth. While Lucia squirms in a close shot, as she sits in front of Mrs. Loring's desk, the latter's disembodied face floats serenely above her in a reflection on the glass partition behind. There is a hopeless pause when Lucia finds herself staring almost stupidly at a vase on the desk with a single rose in it: "I grow them in my garden," says Mrs. Loring complacently, in answer to a question that hasn't been asked. And then proceeds herself to make, sweetly and almost pityingly, just those inquiries Lucia had hoped to avoid, like "the purpose of this loan" and how exactly Lucia plans to repay it. Her jewelry, Lucia hazards. Mrs. Loring, heaving an invisible sigh and tearing Laura's application form in two, expresses her regret that the company has "no pawn-broker's license." "State law, you know," she adds helpfully, as she rises to signal that the interview is ended.

This awful woman is a variant of Lucia herself, of course—of the genteel-matron type. And utterly different: she helps us to feel again what we genuinely like about Lucia, who is incapable of the sort of self-satisfaction and pleasure in power over others that Mrs. Loring shows. Lucia is too forth-right, too serious, too unpretending. She is Joan Bennett, after all—a very unsentimental sort of actress. Bennett was one of those thirties women whose authority on the screen (Stanwyck is the pre-eminent example) came from their seeming so powerfully *sensible.*

Though never quite a major star, she was a firmly established one: audiences expected to see her sort of regularly and did more or less, for over two decades. By the time she made this movie, she was thirty-nine and had been starred in over sixty others, beginning with *Bulldog Drummond* in 1929, being rescued and romanced by Ronald Colman in the first primitive talkie where the dialogue (largely thanks to Colman's way with it) seemed more an asset than an intrusion. (She had been recruited from the New York stage, where she had appeared with her legendary father, Richard.) A pretty doll-like blonde in those days, she was mostly cast in ingenue roles (she was Amy in Cukor's *Little Women* in 1933) until she dyed her hair black in the middle of a 1939 movie called *Trade Winds* (her character was fleeing the cops). After that she would never be blond again. As a brunette, she turned out to look remarkably like Hedy Lamarr—and not just to her press agents. Though she had none of Lamarr's Viennese languor: Bennett was too American for that, too sharp-eyed and alert, with a distinct colloquial performing style. And in spite of a faint upper-class accent (casually broadened A-sounds) and a finishing-school upbringing, she had shown—even as a blonde—a real if underused affinity for playing tough, funny broads: as a wisecracking hash slinger in Raoul Walsh's *Me and My Gal* (1932), opposite Spencer Tracy as the mug she loves, or as cop Cary Grant's mouthy girlfriend in *Big Brown Eyes* (1936), also by Walsh.

But as a brunette at the end of the thirties she seemed newly and excitingly sexy—which was also the intended effect of her noir roles for Fritz Lang: the ingenue reborn as a femme fatale. Not only for Lang but for Renoir (she worked with good people) in his *The Woman on the Beach.* And the same year (1947), in Zoltan Korda's *The Macomber Affair,* opposite Gregory Peck and Robert Preston, she was the definitive incarnation of the Hemingway bitch-wife, making bitter side-of-the-mouth gibes at her weakling husband. But it was just this tart-tongued quality of hers that somewhat worried Ophuls. Robert Soderberg, one of *The Reckless Moment*'s two young screenwriters (Henry Garson was the other), remembered that Ophuls made them write and rewrite "every damned line she had in the picture so that her delivery of it wouldn't come out tough."

It never does—and "tough" would be exactly wrong. What Ophuls is drawn to in Bennett's Lucia is something at the least more mysterious than that. His camera watches her almost raptly, but at an appropriately respectful and meditative distance—unlike Hitchcock's close scrutiny of *his* heroines: his hovering, foreboding, possessive camera. Ophuls maintains a medium-shot separation and a reflective angle (slightly above eye level) as he tracks after or alongside of Bennett. He was, of course, known for his elaborate and extended tracking shots; but his camera travelings in this movie have none of the surge and grace, the serpentine and dancelike patterns with which he follows his "European" heroines: Danielle Darrieux in belle-epoque Paris (*The Earrings of Madame de . . .* , 1956) or Joan Fontaine in a studio-built Vienna (*Letter from an Unknown Woman,* 1948). This heroine belongs to modern, middle-class America—for Ophuls a place of right angles and linear movements, straight ahead for preference. It's surely no accident that the least right-angled person in this movie— Mason's conflicted and self-despising blackmailer—is a foreigner.

Over the course of his movie Ophuls shows Lucia going through, in and out of, a variety of public settings—a hotel lobby, a bank, a pawnshop, a post office, a cocktail lounge, and so on. He omits establishing shots, so that we enter these places with her. And she is accompanied, for the most part, by ambient sounds alone (there is hardly any musical underscoring in this film, even at the big moments), often intricately layered, with traffic and bustle and snatches of overheard conversation. But he's never more intent on her than in those moments when she's moving around her house, especially those times when she is between rooms and encounters: on the stairs, in the hall, on the way to the door, walking and thinking, then setting her face for the next question, the next lie, the next intrusion on her thoughts—on the stairway landing calling up to quiet the children, then lighting a cigarette, gathering herself together over it, while a distant banjo (David in his room) thrums tunelessly in the distance. It's extraordinary how absorbing these moments (there are a great many of them throughout) always are—when "nothing happens" except Lucia's walking and thinking and pausing. The intensity of her concentration, along with her isolation on the screen, draws you in irresistibly.

The movie, produced by Walter Wanger, was based on *The Blank Wall,* a short novel that had appeared during the war in the *Ladies' Home Journal,* by Elizabeth Sanxay Holding, a writer (though forgotten now) Raymond Chandler had called "the top suspense writer of them all." The novel is intelligent and compelling but less ambitious than the movie turns out to be. The movie follows it closely, reproducing its situations and much of its dialogue, but it changes emphases and meanings—especially those that have to do with Lucia. In the novel, which is narrated by her, she is altogether more self-aware, more conscious of her own provincialism, and not at all so complacent as she is in the movie. Ophuls's Lucia is more complicated, often in painful ways—as you're bound to feel, I think, in the climactic scene between her and Donnelly at the bus station.

She meets him there by prearrangement—she's supposed to bring the money. But she's failed to raise it: she's just tried the bank, the loan company, even a pawnshop (where she hocked her jewelry). She's come to "believe" in a Nagle by now—that he exists, that is. And that Donnelly is her friend—who would, as he's told her, pay Nagle off himself if he could. They are now less like crook-and-victim than confederates in crime. And she is looking straight at him at last: intent and wide-eyed and frightened, amid the indifferent noisy life of the terminal (what follows here are the most complex tracking shots in the film).

She is telling him that she couldn't get the money, but he cuts her off. Good news: they've got the man who killed Darby; she and her family are off the hook. Her first reaction is dismay—he's the wrong man, she says. Donnelly concedes the man may have been framed, since he is a well-known, much-disliked crook—Donnelly knows him, it seems. But what does it matter? The important thing is she's been saved. So has her family. She starts to protest again when he takes her by the arm and pilots her through the crowd to the lunch counter, where he gets her a coffee. They go back through the people to an out-of-the-way bench, in front of a closed Travelers Aid counter. She sits compliantly while he stands over her. She has a little net veil on her hat which she lifts to sip from the paper coffee cup. He is behind her; she looks off and talks, distractedly. But he interrupts: he wants to know how she can be so certain that the man they've got *didn't* do it. "Don't tell me *you* killed him?" he says with a smile. Well . . . yes, she did, she says. He doesn't believe her, of course, and tells her never to repeat that claim to anyone again: think of the family.

Now her bus is announced over the public address. She looks at him and rises heavily, and they walk slowly, silently at first, side by side, toward the gate—the camera following their backs now, watching them from behind: her fur coat and little pillbox hat, his square-shouldered black overcoat—as the loudspeaker voice, booming and cantorial, slowly intones her

Lucia and Donnelly at the bus station

departing bus's stops, like a dirge: "Bus for Hermosa, Manhattan Beach, Long Beach, Newport, Laguna, Balboa . . . now loading." Donnelly speaks again as they walk, softly, consolingly, above all reminding her of her family. "But he's innocent," she protests—if weakly. "All right," answers Donnelly, "so he's innocent of this, but he's guilty of a hundred other things, so it doesn't matter." They stop, turn, and face each other, with bowed heads, like a priest and his penitent. He is talking to her urgently now: she must not sacrifice her family "for a man that's no good, that deserves what's coming to him. If he gets it for this it's the only good thing he's done in his whole life . . . You're not dealing with the kind of people *you* know, you're dealing with the kind of people *I* know."

It's a major moment—Buñuelian even, in its quiet sardonic force. The movie's deadliest irony yet—that the single real enemy to her self-enclosure ("We're all involved with each other . . .") is now its champion and defender. Those "others" ("the kind of people *I* know") have nothing to do with her, after all, or with her family—he sees that now and he's urging *her* to see it. And she's giving in. It's a moral dislocation—even a shared madness—stronger than anything up to now in this film; and it feels monstrous.

And yet Lucia up to now has never been so sympathetic, so simply appealing as she is here: unbending to him at last, looking and listening and intensely aware of him, she has learned to trust him and to doubt herself. But this complication in our sympathies only makes the scene more appalling—and more moving, as it goes on. It's a measure of the difference between the movie and its source that in the novel Donnelly urges the same course on Lucia (even in the same words) but there she rejects it out of hand, firmly and unhesitatingly. For the novel's Lucia to let another person, whoever he is, be (in her words) "punished—executed—for something he didn't do" would simply be wrong, "a sin" (not a word you could easily imagine the movie's Lucia invoking). "You have to do what's right, no matter what comes of it," she tells Donnelly, and so they both forget about it in the book. But not here.

Now Donnelly looks even taller than usual next to her—as they turn their backs to the camera once again and resume their slow, reluctant progress to the gate, Donnelly leading, Lucia slightly behind but still at his side. You can see his new manner even from just looking at his overcoated back: fond, husbandly, gently condescending. Lucia, looking up at him, looks diminished, submissive. His voice is round-toned and lordly now, the melancholy lilt all but gone. As always, he calls her "Loo-*see*-a" (everyone else says "*Loosh-ya*"). "It's the right thing to do, Lucia—the right thing," he says, making a gesture that looks from the back like hitching up his belt with his forearms, American-hero-style. He says he'll "have it out" with Nagle now, since the letters have become worthless; he'll get them and return them to her himself. But then she asks him—just as she is about to go through the gate to her bus—not to come to the house with them. "I'm sorry, but—" she says nervously, and breaks off. But he understands, of course—the lordliness a bit quashed by this, as she goes out and leaves him alone in the shot, looking after her. After a moment, he turns and goes up a ramp to the exit, the camera still following, slowly.

Lucia arrives back home like someone pursued, getting out of a local taxi ("Good night, Mrs. Harper") in the dark, pushing through her garden gate into a close-up, then down the lane (the camera tracking in front of her) through foliage and shadow and wind into the light cast from inside her house, and onto her porch—where Sybil (Frances Williams), her intrepid black maid, is waiting for her. There's a man to see her, Sybil says, named Nagle, waiting in the boathouse. Lucia goes first into the house to cope with the family—who greet her with their usual mixture of need and alarm: where has she *been?* "We've been worried sick about you," says Father-in-Law. Bee is sulking, and David needs a dollar to go to the movies. Bee is refusing to go along, in spite of her date with "Owen." "Oh, but you *should* go, dear," says Lucia. "Owen will be terribly disappointed." She sits at the dinner table but she can't eat. Father-in-law, still hovering over her, expresses his concern, and she responds with the kind of lie she is so used to telling: there is nothing wrong with her except that she misses Tom. She is still trying to get Bee to go to the movies: "I'll give you my fur coat—it looks lovely on you." Father goes to bed. Bee soon relents and puts on the fur coat ("Wait a minute, Bee, I want to roll down your sleeves"), stepping out the door with David, who has gotten his dollar ("Take it—but *one,* not two"), with Lucia back on the front porch waving them off. At last. Now to the boathouse. She lights a cigarette. Sybil is standing in the front doorway behind her. Nothing needs to be explained to Sybil, it seems. "Do you want me to go with you?" she asks. No, says Lucia, as she goes determinedly off, her hands with the cigarette clasped at her waist.

Nagle (Roy Roberts) is a scary man. He's beefy and gimlet-eyed, he calls her "Duchess," and he threatens her with the letters again. But "they've got the man who did it!" she exclaims. He's been cleared and released, says Nagle. "Then I'm going to do what I should have done in the beginning," she says—namely, go to the police. But that option gets dramatically precluded, for the moment anyway, when Donnelly unexpectedly bursts in on them (he's been tailing Nagle) and the two men fight. They are on the floor, and Nagle is stabbing Donnelly in his side with a broken bottle and trip-hammer motions of his arm from the floor—which only seem to stop when Donnelly, the one on top, has at last choked him to death. He rises from the deed dazed, arms dangling like a puppet's, while Lucia looks on in silent shock and horror.

She comes forward, half staggering, looks down at the dead man, then at Donnelly. Mechanically, and still not speaking, she puts her hand inside his coat (he even *fights* in that overcoat) on his chest, where the blood is. "You need help," she says numbly—then withdraws her hand and walks toward the door, in the same thought-stricken mode, hands clasped in front of her, that we've so often seen her in by now. Except that this time she's in a state of shock. Another body at the boathouse . . .

Now she *is* going to call the police, she says. "I'll tell them it's my fault, not yours, that you did it for me." They won't believe her, he says. He stops her in the doorway, taking her by the arm. They are both moving like sleepwalkers now. "I'll get help," she protests, "you're bleeding." But he holds on to her in the doorway, her back against the outside wall, her face turned toward the house and the call to the police—she doesn't move. Then he turns to go back to the body—he has to get rid of it, he says—and she pulls him back by the lapel of his coat and puts her hand inside it again. He presses his hand on hers over the wound. This choreography of clutchings and pullings and turnings-away is very powerful. It's not only the first time that Lucia touches Donnelly; it's the first time that she's touched anyone in the movie—except the corpse at the beginning.

They lean against the wall and he holds her hand to his chest. And as he talks—about his misspent life, his regrets, his feelings for her—she begins to sag beside him, her head hanging, in shame and sorrow, sinking lower and lower as he goes on. It's not love they've achieved (there was never much hope or question of that) but complicity. And the unresisting way Lucia now accepts their intimacy—

Another body in Lucia's boathouse (Roy Roberts on the floor)—and Donnelly is wounded.

like the direct way she put her hand on his wound—reminds you of what's appealing about her in spite of everything, as well as what's sort of awesome: her matter-of-factness in the face of enormity. But she is also someone who lives more than half-averted from her deepest, strongest feelings: just as she is so poignantly now with him, outside the doorway—both holding on and turning away at once.

And she has the same half-averted relation to someone else who is crucial to her life. As we are reminded when she finally pulls away from him to go to the house, to get something to dress his wound with. "Mr. Donnelly's been badly hurt!" she says to Sybil—who has, of course, been waiting for her to come back. Instructing Sybil to get bandages upstairs and not to wake anybody and to "*hurry,* Sybil—please!," Lucia crouches on the kitchen floor looking in a cabinet for the brandy when she is suddenly wracked with sobs. But only momentarily: she's on her feet again with the brandy bottle as Sybil comes downstairs with the first-aid kit. "Can't I come with you?" says Sybil. Again Lucia declines. "You better take your coat!" Sybil calls after her.

You come to register Sybil in this movie by a process that almost re-enacts Lucia's own relation to her. She is a small, late-middle-aged woman with alert, kind eyes and graying hair. At first you notice her not much more than the Harper family seems to. She is simply, discreetly just there—in the background usually, always busy, vacuuming, answering the phone, making dinner, putting groceries away, smiling to herself, and so forth. "Part of the family," it seems—the easy, natural way she scolds the children, for example, or enters into a happy family event, like those phone calls from Europe that Tom makes. Of course, Lucia will inevitably close a door, with Sybil on the other side of it, when talking "private" family things.

But in fact, as you soon come to realize, Sybil knows everything. What's more, Lucia—on some unadmitted level of herself—knows that she knows. Their understanding doesn't require words. And it's finally no surprise at all—for you or for Lucia—when Sybil becomes her employer's able and unquestioning confederate in this final crisis over Donnelly, and over the new body to be got rid of. It's in the latter cause that Donnelly disappears now, driving off with Nagle's corpse just as Lucia gets back to the boathouse with the first aid. The two women drive after him, Lucia at the wheel, Sybil beside her, observing sadly that she has always liked "Mr. Donnelly." That, too, is no surprise.

Because Lucia has a more reciprocal human connection—in some ways a deeper and more genuine one—with her maid and her blackmailer than she does with her family. Sybil and Martin (as Lucia now calls him) are *her* grown-ups, as it were—the only ones in her life she doesn't have to protect and lie to, the ones *she* can depend on—in the special loneliness of family life.

The two women finally arrive at the place where the wounded Donnelly's car has gone off the road into a ravine. Lucia clambers down and finds him pinned beneath the wreckage. She crouches beside him—puts her face against his and weeps helplessly, despairingly, into his shoulder and hair. But he sends her away: she will "spoil everything," he tells her (she must think of the family, of course) if the police who are on their way find them together, with Nagle's body on their hands. She protests, but she goes: "Come on, Mrs. Harper," says Sybil to her, with a firm, quiet authority," *I'll* drive." And so she does—with Lucia, in shock again, beside her. At home, they learn the news of Donnelly's death over the radio, and of his final confession to *both* killings, Darby's as well as Nagle's. The Harper family is finally in the clear.

This was Ophuls's fourth and final American movie. He was almost seven years in Hollywood, arriving in 1941 with wife and son, before he got his first directing job. Unhappily, it was for Howard Hughes, who quickly fired him. But then he was hired by Douglas Fairbanks Jr., to whom he'd been commended by Berlin friend and fellow émigré Robert Siodmak, who was still riding high in Hollywood. The movie was *The Exile* (1948), a swashbuckler with Fairbanks as English king Charles II hiding out in seventeenth-century Holland. It was little noticed at the time. Ophuls's next was in many ways his luckiest. *Letter from an Unknown Woman* (1948) would become the most famous and widely praised of his U.S. movies: a tearjerker with Joan Fontaine, set in a lovingly re-created turn-of-the-century Vienna. His next two films had contemporary American settings and stories. *Caught* (1949) was James Mason's American debut (his postwar British films had made him widely known here), but it disappointed his fans, among others. Instead of the tormented, sexy villain-heroes Mason had become known for (he was the Svengali music master who slammed the piano lid down on Ann Todd's fingers in *The Seventh Veil,* a huge art house hit, in 1945), in Ophuls's film he is an idealistic slum doctor, contending for the love of shopgirl Barbara Bel Geddes against her mad millionaire husband—who was modeled on Howard Hughes and played by Robert Ryan (the role Mason *should* have played, according to many reviewers at the time). It's a kind of chamber film, full of charged intimate encounters in darkly lit interiors, but with a leaden script by Arthur Laurents, and with almost none of the feeling for American life and experience that Ophuls's next, *The Reckless Moment,* would so remarkably show.

This was the movie that he meant to be his really *American* one, at last—about contemporary American life, confronting American audiences on the ground of their own experience. This time he had the help of two smart screenwriters, Soderberg and Garson, who had been hired by Wanger, the producer, for their experience writing a relatively sophisticated CBS radio show about upper-middle-class family life, *Junior Miss* (spun off from a Broadway hit show, derived in turn from Sally Benson's *New Yorker* stories). What Ophuls might not know about the movie's suburban milieu, the writers would.

And one of the most extraordinary things about Ophuls's movie—in spite of the intensity of focus on two main characters—is how richly it evokes the life around them, even to the people you see only in passing: like Mrs. Loring with her garden-grown rose, or the suspicious but whistling ("Home on the Range") pawnbroker, or the curious, rabbity drugstore clerk ("goodbye, Mr. . . . uh . . . ?"), or, more prominently, Darby himself in his early scene with Lucia in the hotel bar—with his aging seducer's nerves, his anxious freeloader's way of smoking a cigarette, closely and furtively, as if someone might say it wasn't his, and watching all the exits as he talks.

One of the nicest early scenes shows Lucia, shortly after she's dumped Darby's body, standing in line at her local post office behind an officious and impatient neighbor, Mrs. Feller (Ann Shoemaker), who simply cannot believe that she hasn't wrapped her package well enough to suit the post office—not when she did the best she could, as she informs the man behind the window. "You might have done the best you could," drawls the bespectacled clerk in reply, "but your best is none too good." She looks at him (he looks nearly blind): what she expects from the post office, she tells him, is "delivery—not philosophy." She turns to Lucia behind her: "Lucia, doesn't it look all right to *you?*" "Oh, I think he'd know, Catherine," replies Lucia, with her characteristic reasonableness—while at the same time straining to overhear a conversation between some postal workers about the newly discovered corpse in the bay.

That postal clerk who excites Mrs. Feller's impatience is like one of Preston Sturges's recurring minor players (I first thought it was Sturges's favorite, Harry Hayden—I was close: it's Harry Harvey, according to the cast list): round and bespectacled and laconic, of an indeterminate middle age, sounding when he talks just the right folksy-acerbic, friendly-weary note. The whole sequence, in fact, is like something out of a Sturges movie: in the faces and sounds and sense of teeming local life, in the mix of amusement and enchantment at the busy, tough Americanness. And it all seems effortless.

The two directors had been friends, as well as mutual admirers. Ophuls had been a regular at the Players Club, Sturges's outrageously convivial restaurant on Sunset Boulevard. Marcel Ophuls, Max's son, himself a major filmmaker, told me that his father often said that Preston was the funniest man he'd ever known—something Marcel resented at the time, since he thought his father was the funniest man *he'd* ever known. Sturges—after screening Max's 1932 Austrian film, *Liebelei,* and being duly impressed—had gotten Ophuls his first Hollywood directing job, at the new independent production company that Sturges had started with Howard Hughes. The film was *Vendetta,* adapted from Mérimée's *Colomba* and designed to showcase Hughes's newest female "discovery," Faith Domergue (later in *Where Danger Lives* opposite Mitchum—see p. 13). But both Ophuls's job and his friendship with Sturges ended unhappily—with Sturges, the movie's official producer, in one of his now more frequent madman phases, usurping Ophuls's control of the movie itself, then being forced by Hughes to fire him and take his place as its director. Which Sturges did—until Hughes fired *him* shortly after. (The completed movie, a famous mess, credits Mel Ferrer as its director: it was no help to his career, either.)

What seems to me most Sturges-like about *The Reckless Moment* is less the minor players than something central: the stance the whole movie takes toward its heroine, and toward the sort of American life she embodies. Like Donnelly, its hero, it's half in love with her, while it also views her with a detachment that's quite beyond him. It's just this feat of clarity and balance that reminds you of Sturges: of all his awful-but-wonderful heroes and heroines, like Henry Fonda in *The Lady Eve,* or Betty Hutton in *The Miracle of Morgan's Creek,* who also embody representative American types of innocence and solipsism. Ophuls and Sturges have a common propensity, in their different ways, for seeing ordinary American life (to which in their own lives they were both outsiders) as prodigious. But where Sturges gives us absurdist farce, Ophuls offers a sustained quiet irony.

Farce was better box office. *The Reckless Moment* was a commercial nonstarter. None of Ophuls's Hollywood movies had been moneymakers, but this one was a simple disaster. After a harrowing early preview (the usual story), Columbia judged the movie such a certain loser that (much as they would do later with *Bitter Victory*) they dumped it on the market to play off on double bills at flat rentals (a hundred dollars a booking!), and the U.S. audience Ophuls had hoped so much to make a connection with was lost to him for good. By the time the movie was released he was already back in Paris, where he had made most of his pre-Hollywood pictures, and where he now stayed to make his final ones: *La Ronde* (1950) and *The Earrings of Madame de . . .* (1953)—probably his two most famous films—as well as *Le Plaisir* (1951) and *Lola Montès* (1955). He died in 1957, at fifty-five.

At a 1995 press conference on Long Island, Robert Altman described himself as being one of those Hollywood moviemakers who work "underground" (Manny Farber's word too), the ones who *know* "how to work their art and not get caught." That precisely describes, it seems, what Ophuls was consciously up to when he was filming *The Reckless Moment.* From his experience in Hollywood he had concluded that you could get away with making a good movie as long as you didn't attract the studio's attention while you were doing it. In some ways it's the most conventional of his four Hollywood movies, the one that sticks most faithfully to the accepted patterns of structure and storytelling. Yet it's also the movie he had the fullest final control of: he was fast and efficient and not at all "difficult" in the way an arty European director was expected to be. He loved the American studio professionalism and all its resources of skill and technology. And he had learned (he was an enormously charming and good-humored man) how to handle the studio bosses. In any case, he seems to have won nearly every important argument about this film, successfully resisting the inevitable attempts to coarsen or broaden it—even by his two talented screenwriters, who wanted a more overt, *Casablanca*-like romantic exchange between Lucia and Donnelly when they say their final goodbye at the car wreck. And Harry Cohn wanted "a Stanwyck scene," as he called it (i.e., a big emotional outburst), for Bennett wherever they could get it in. But Ophuls (sometimes with producer Wanger's support, sometimes not) got his way each time. He made a genre movie that played by the rules of the game while aiming at depth and nuance and consistently avoiding the simplistic and obvious. Paying attention to "what alone is worthwhile," in Renoir's words, "the detail in human expression."

But seeming as it did such a *familiar* sort of movie, it left audiences wondering what had happened to them at the end—or rather *not* happened. Where *was* the "Stanwyck scene," after all? And why did the big melodramatic climaxes—like Donnelly crashing the car (it happens off-screen)—seem so uninflected? Most of all, what were they supposed to think of *her*? Usually, for such a maternal figure, the clues were clear and uncontradictory—but not here. Because you're bound to be aware, even early in the movie, that you're seeing Lucia without the intrusion of stereotypes, the customary ways of seeing (and judging) such a character. The saintly, self-sacrificing mother, or the devouring matriarch, or the neglected wife ripe for adultery—those three were pretty much the options at the time. But Ophuls's heroine both evokes them and eludes them at the same time.

And she can be a sort of problem even for an audience today—who are also used to clearer options for recognizing and judging a central character. Although the movie *places* Lucia exactly and often stingingly (as when we hear her reminding Bee that her parents never wanted her to go to art school because of "the sort of people" she'd be "exposed to" there), it was not meant to be, nor was it, an art-house film: it never patronizes her nor places us, as the enlightened audience, in what Pauline Kael (objecting in a review to the smug tone of Terence Malick's *Badlands*) calls "the ugly position of feeling culturally superior to the people on the screen."

On location, Max Ophuls (in the beret) eats al fresco
with his stars, Mason and Bennett.

In the final sequence (she and Donnelly have just parted) Lucia is alone
in her darkened bedroom, lying facedown on the bed and weeping. Sybil's
voice through the door tells her that "Mr. Harper" is on the phone from
Berlin. Lucia gets up, staggers toward the door, and goes slowly down the
stairs to the hallway phone—surrounded, as usual, by excited family.
Except, momentarily, for Bee—who rushes in from another room to tell
Lucia, as she reaches the middle of the stairway, that Donnelly has died
(the news broadcast on the radio) and confessed to two killings. "Oh, Bee!"
cries Lucia—like some small animal's squeal of pain—staggering, then
straightening again and making her way to the phone below. Once again it
is time not-to-worry Tom. She takes the phone from her son, pitching
backwards slightly, and begins to speak, her voice breaking but in control:
"Tom—we mailed your Christmas packages. . . . We're going to have a
blue Christmas tree"—Bee's preference—". . . Everything is fine, except
we miss you terribly. . . . Yes, Tom . . . ," gradually declining as she speaks
until she's sitting down, Ophuls's camera descending with her, until
you're looking at her finally through the thick banisters of the stairway, as
she sinks under the weight of these comforting words to Tom, and the
music and the end title rise together.

This final image of her—behind bars, as it were—makes a nice black-

comic fade-out. What's surprising about it is the sudden (relative) explic-
itness. It's as if the filmmaker, with this witty summarizing image, were
suddenly "speaking" directly to you, here at the end; as if you were suddenly, if momentarily, alone with him, the way you can be with a poet or
novelist or painter. But then not so surprising. Movies, especially smart
ones, were beginning to seem less interested than they had been in including all of us in their effects. If Hollywood movies—still the most popular
in the world in those postwar years—were changing fundamentally, it was
in their changing relation to the great audience they still attracted. Even
mainstream movies were no longer the dependably *public* sort of experience
they had been. In the best of them, the signals from what Altman calls the
"underground" of them—the place where the "art" gets made—were getting clearer and louder.

Seventeen

ROBERT SIODMAK

B ut they weren't supposed to get through at all, those signals. Not in the *movies*—where the so-called invisible camera (the invisible direc-tor, too) was the rule. "Technique" was supposed to be unnoticeable. Hol-lywood movies were no-nonsense realistic affairs, built on a foundation of what the French named "the American shot" (*le plan Americain*)—that is, the plainest and most direct one, at eye level and a medium distance—along with camera movements that were discreet and underplayed (one reason Ophuls with his virtuoso tracking shots made them nervous) and the sort of cutting that was so "logical"—that is, in its steady alternation of the shot-reverse-shot—that it too was unnoticeable (the invisible cut): all in the service of telling the story, *not* showing off the director. "The man who made that picture was camera crazy," wrote one audience member on his reaction card after the unhappy first preview of *The Magnificent Amber-sons*—and that was exactly the kind of comment that made studio bosses panic (it was quoted in that spirit to Welles by the then-boss of RKO, George Schaefer). If the audience is thinking about the camera or the per-son behind it, then they are *outside* the movie—and so what was all your hard work *for*?

Being a stylist in Hollywood in those days (there were, in fact, a lot of them) was a little like being a Communist or "fellow traveler": it was bet-ter not to be named. "If they notice how it's directed, it's badly directed" was the director's public credo, repeated in interview after interview, and never more dependably than by filmmakers who might be suspected of not believing it—people like Lang and Siodmak, for example. But most aston-ishingly of all, by Orson Welles himself. "Whatever they're aware of is your failure as a director," he declared to Peter Bogdanovich—adding that he never admired the kind of director *he* was accused of being. The sort of filmmaker that he personally preferred, he said, was someone like Marcel Pagnol (*The Baker's Wife* et al.), "who just turned the camera on . . . and when they ran out of film they cut."

249

Incredible. But then no doubt many of them really felt this way. Maybe even Welles—at least during interviews. As Marcel Ophuls (Max's son) once said to me, "The virtuosos don't admire the virtuosos." He was talking principally about his father and his attitude toward Welles and *Citizen Kane.* He thought it was "arty," Marcel said—and that was one of the worst things Max could say about someone's movie. The kind of American movie the senior Ophuls relished was more like Raoul Walsh's *Gentleman Jim* (1941), a knockabout Errol Flynn vehicle depicting the early days of boxing: he and his young son (as the latter recalled) went to see it three times together when they were living in Hollywood.

It was *Citizen Kane,* of course—also in 1941—that offered Hollywood the most blatant and overt challenge anyone had seen yet to the received wisdom about the invisible director and camera: a *show-off* movie if ever there was one. But it was also a prototype of the film noir. With its doomed hero, its shadows and angles and deep-focus chiaroscuro, its combination of ominous atmosphere and wised-up talk, its extended inquiry into the past and its fractured chronology, with multiple flashbacks and witnesses—it had every noir requisite except a violent crime. And Welles would supply that later, in subsequent films like *Journey into Fear* (1943), *The Stranger* (1946), and, most notably, *The Lady from Shanghai* (1948)— the latter in particular exploring even more hallucinatory possibilities of the style. Even though it was meant to be a Rita Hayworth vehicle, coming shortly after *Gilda,* it offered a version of her (shorthaired and vicious) that neither her studio nor her fans wanted to see.

But it was a success compared with his next and final foray into the Hollywood thriller: *Touch of Evil* (1958). Beginning with the famous three-minute traveling shot under the opening credits, the movie's bravura of execution—hectic, fragmented, overheated—is relentless, even arbitrary, as if the whole idea were to keep goosing things up (as when Welles straps the camera onto the hood of an open sports car and then sends it, and us, hurtling backwards down the narrow street while the driver, Charlton Heston, relates plot information to a companion). In some ways it's Welles's most reckless movie—pushing his style to the furthest extremes. It was too much for audiences in the fifties, sinking out of sight nearly as soon as it was released. And even today, its odd, exacerbated, self-referring methods, at once highly wrought and overwrought, can seem both unnerving and unresolved. But generally it was the Europeans who had to be watched, who were the ones most likely to commit artiness, in the view of most old Hollywood hands. Like writer-producer Nunnally Johnson, who wrote, in a 1951 letter to a friend, about turning down an invitation to a screening of Robert Siodmak's latest movie (unnamed, but probably *Deported*): "I told him no, because I knew I wouldn't be able to see anybody on the screen. It's a waterfront picture, and if there's anything one of these European geniuses like it's an opportunity to shoot everything in the dark, with people appearing in silhouette behind piles of stuff on the dock . . . The foreigners like rain too . . ." He needn't, however, have worried about *Deported*—which was shot plainly and listlessly, on location in Italy (the neorealist bug), by a growingly discouraged Siodmak, nearing the end of his American career. And it was evenly lit throughout.

Although the sort of movie Johnson evokes here sounds more like Marcel Carné's *Quai des brumes* than *Woman in the Window* (which he himself wrote and produced, with Lang directing), the noir movie look was not French but German—just as its most eminent early practitioners were: Siodmak, Wilder, Preminger, Lang. The expressionist look was already familiar to their American audiences, mostly from "arty" early talkies like John Ford's *The Informer* (1935); but in the bleak deep-focus thrillers of the forties, it became even more stylized: ominously tilted frames, planes of light and shadow far into the background of the shot, stark single-source illumination, low-angle shots of drab low-ceilinged rooms, high-angle shots of deserted rain-slicked streets, the sort of compositions within the frame that either loom over you portentously or pitch you forward uncomfortably—and into the dark.

And though this look may have suggested to some the preciosity of "European geniuses," the talk that usually went with it was irreducibly American—tough, wisecracking, unillusioned: German expressionism out of the UFA silents, now crossed with the sound of Hammett and Chandler and their pulp-fiction successors. And it was surprising, really, how well the sound and the look went together.

It was the film noir that licensed, so to speak, the stylization in Hollywood movies. It even preserved Wellesian formalism when Welles himself was debarred from practicing it. And even when that license began to run out in fifties noir, it was being renewed by other filmmakers in other modes, notably in the quasi-operatic melodramas of Nicholas Ray and Douglas Sirk, of Robert Aldrich, Vincente Minnelli, and Samuel Fuller, et al. And because of just such filmmakers, Hollywood in the fifties passed through a baroque mannerist stage—not much commented upon at the time, but which has turned out to be nearly that movie decade's most interesting development. More than its vaunted new realism.

It was in the fifties, it now seems to me, that you first began to notice how certain movies that you loved—like *Vertigo* or *The Searchers*—felt remarkably like listening to music did. (Welles's movies, said Truffaut, "unroll before the eye the way music moves in the ear.") Such movies felt like a concert experience more than like a play or a novel one—the sort of feeling you already knew from films like Dreyer's (*Day of Wrath* and *The Passion of Joan of Arc*) or Eisenstein's (*Ivan the Terrible, Part One*): hypnotic movies that you could see again and again, and that only became more powerful, the way great music does, the more you "heard" them. But that, clearly, was "art." Still, what you had from Hollywood sometimes—especially if it was from Hitchcock or Welles (both of whom compared themselves to composers in their interviews)—could feel like that too.

But Hitchcock was the only functioning director there who was bold enough to assert to his interviewers that he never cared about "story" in *his* movies—whatever else those others said or did about it. He *always* put style above content, he claimed—or so he said when he was having hits instead of flops (he was less boastful after something like *I Confess*). He never cared what a movie of his was about, whether the story was "good or bad, you know"—any more than a painter cares about whether the apples he is painting are "sweet or sour." Style is everything in a movie, just as it is in painting or music. He only wished he could write the whole movie down beforehand, "in the same way as a composer writes all those little black dots from which we get beautiful sounds"—and let somebody else "conduct," presumably, so he wouldn't have to go on the set at all, an activity, as he told us, that he found generally unrewarding.

Whether you swallowed all that or not, it more than hinted at what many felt was an almost crippling drawback in Hitchcock's work: its impersonal and overdetermined quality, what Welles (who was not a fan) called "a certain icy calculation." To many people, Hitchcock's talent seemed to go more into playing games with his audiences, springing his traps and surprises on them, including that jokey "personal appearance" he made in every film (there he is!—invisible director, my ass), than it went into making fully coherent or humanly believable movies. He was too much a prankster and too much a technician (making a movie without cuts in reel-long continuous takes, as in *Rope,* or one that takes place entirely on an inflated raft at sea, as in *Lifeboat,* and so on) to be taken altogether seriously.

It was partly because of all this that reviewers welcomed Robert Siodmak the way they did: as "the new Hitchcock," and the improved one as well, for many of them. Dubbed by *Time* as "the new master of suspense," fulsomely and lengthily profiled by *Life* in 1947, he made thrillers that were more "psychological," less gimmicky and improbable than Hitch-

Robert Siodmak (at right, pointing) directs his friend Charles Laughton (center) in *The Suspect*. (Eve Amber is the young woman at left, with Dean Harens partially visible next to her.)

cock's, more grounded in character and dramatic logic—altogether more in key with the postwar seriousness. For a time, he seemed to make more of them than anyone else, and his influence on the noir style was major.

When he first arrived here he was already—like his friend Ophuls—an established European director: first in his native Germany, where he became well enough known to be denounced as a Jewish "corrupter of the German family" by Goebbels himself; then in France, where he fled in 1933, making movies there with stars like Chevalier (in *Pièges*, 1939, the original of Sirk's *Lured*) and Louis Jouvet and Harry Baur. When France fell in 1940, he came to Hollywood—where he was, like most of his exiled compatriots there, quite unknown. But Preston Sturges (just as he would do later for Ophuls with Howard Hughes) intervened for him at Paramount. *He* hadn't heard of Siodmak, either, but he told the Paramount bosses otherwise, and Siodmak was signed as a contract director, in the B-picture unit—his first assignment being something called *West Point Widow* (1941). When the producer complimented him on his willingness (unexpected in a European genius) to follow orders, he replied—so he told his *Life* interviewer—"I don't argue because I don't care. This picture isn't good enough to be known as a Siodmak picture. It will only be known as a Paramount picture."

Under contract at Universal, where he spent most of his American career, he first made an above-average Dracula movie (with a script by his brother Curt) and a soon-to-be camp classic, *Cobra Woman* (1944), with Maria Montez playing good and bad twin sisters on separate tropical isles—and with such total conviction that she was "Method acting before its time," Siodmak later said. But the movie was a hit. And he followed it with *Phantom Lady* (1944), a true "Siodmak picture" at last (produced by Joan Harrison, who had worked with Hitchcock for many years) and a surprise success that made people remember his name. He was then assigned to a noir film that would star the studio's biggest and most profitable star, Deanna Durbin, to be produced by Felix Jackson (né Joachimson), another distinguished émigré from the Berlin theatre and movie world (also Durbin's fiancé at the time). The movie, *Christmas Holiday* (1944), would be an attempt to vary the star's wholesome teen image by presenting her in a heavy dramatic role with a sordid milieu, as a "hostess" in a joint who is married to a killer.

The girl herself had all but singlehandedly saved Universal from bankruptcy eight years before this, when she appeared unheralded (as the publicists would say) in the singing lead of *Three Smart Girls* (1936). She was fourteen—and "the spirit and personification of youth," as her special 1938 Academy Award citation read. By 1944, she had made thirteen highly profitable and mostly well-reviewed Universal movies (they never loaned her out), all of them more or less cut to the formula of the first one. But the early Durbin pictures were surprisingly sophisticated, taking place against fantasy backgrounds of glamour and wealth, closer to the world and style of thirties screwball comedy than to the down-home tear-jerking mode that MGM, for example, reserved for *their* teen "sweetheart," Judy Garland. But Durbin's personality was dryer than Garland's, her screen persona had more dazzle than warmth; and the studio molding of her star image had been nearly as much directed to the audiences abroad (she was immensely popular in England and Europe) as to the ones at home. And unlike Garland, who was from the beginning a consummate and versatile musical performer, Durbin was more a recitalist, seemingly content to stand still making pure and pretty soprano sounds, with secure, metallic high notes and a luscious, almost creamy middle range, in a minimum of three songs per movie. Though for a child star she matured very successfully, going—as Ephraim Katz's *Film Encyclopedia* puts it—"from a peppy adolescent to a starry-eyed romantic beauty," she remained the girl-

Deanna Durbin—*before* the dance hall—in Siodmak's *Christmas Holiday*

ish type. Reviewer Graham Greene, a grudging admirer, complained about the excessively "virginal" atmosphere of her early movies ("the awkward age has never been so laundered and lavendered"). And later on, the studio too began to feel a problem about this. She had been "kissed," of course (in 1939, by Robert Stack in *First Love*), but more was needed in that direction. She was still their number-one box-office asset, and time was running out: by 1944 she was already twenty-two.

Christmas Holiday, with Siodmak directing, was what they decided to do. It was a prestige production, both louche and classy. Gene Kelly was borrowed from MGM to co-star (in a nonmusical role). Herman J. Mankiewicz, not long after his Academy Award for *Citizen Kane,* supplied the screenplay. (He even gave them something *Kane*-like: a labyrinthine structure and a fractured chronology.) He adapted it from a somewhat scandalous Somerset Maugham novel, in which a callow, smug young Englishman visits a Paris brothel, where he meets a whore known as "the Countess" and by listening to her story Learns About Life. In Hollywood Maugham was a certified Major Author; and in all the ads for the movie the possessive of his name was ahead of and as large as the title (like Coppola's *Bram Stoker's Dracula*). And the excited press releases went out. Deanna Durbin, the *New York Times* announced, was to play a serious dramatic role: "a somewhat tragic entertainer in a cheap roadhouse, whose past involved a shattered romance with a murderer husband." The film, it was promised, would follow "the Maugham story as closely as a shifting of the locale from Paris to the United States and the Hays Office purity rules will permit." The "roadhouse," as it turned out, became in the film a dance hall—the sort of movie setting that all grown-up audiences would recognize as the accepted euphemism for a brothel (cf. *From Here to Eternity, The Revolt of Mamie Stover,* et al.). As a result of this custom, real, unambiguous dance halls in movies had all but disappeared.

The movie was a sensation, and a box-office hit, in many places almost tripling the receipts of previous Durbin pictures. But *Christmas Holiday* was the hit that no one seemed to *like,* judging from the outcry that greeted it. It was so bleak—for Durbin fans especially (they *still* don't want to remember it: it's the least shown of all her films, and rarely even mentioned in present-day accounts of her career). And it had, as Gene Kelly recalled later, script problems from the beginning that were never really solved (Mankiewicz was near the end of his tether by then: this was his last important screenplay). But for Durbin fans the main problem was exactly what the studio had been so proud of and yet so nervous about: her new image. Even the publicity stills told people what they had done to her: showing her against a wall, her head thrown back into the shadows, her face distressed, the trampish eye shadow on the clown-white skin, the décolleté black silk gown. It was a transformation, as more than one reviewer said, comparable to when Garbo first talked. But for audiences, who certainly wanted to *see* it, the experiment was too extreme. As Bosley Crowther (a well-known propriety upholder) wrote in the *New York Times:* "It is really grotesque and outlandish what they've done to Miss Durbin in this film . . . like watching a sweet schoolgirl performing the role of Sadie Thompson"—and so on. Durbin's *next* movie, released the same year (and quickly) was called—with grim but unintended aptness—*Can't Help Singing.* She wore a wig of long blond curls and sang in a hoopskirt in front of the Grand Canyon in Technicolor—more than ever the prisoner of an image and a career she had come to detest. *Christmas Holiday,* she would later say with some bitterness, had been her favorite film. Just four years and seven pictures, later she took the money (she had been the highest-paid woman in Hollywood) and ran—to marriage and family life in France, where she still lives, retiring from public life with a finality that no star of comparable eminence (except Garbo) has ever quite matched. Judy Garland once told the following story on herself to Gore Vidal: after a specially triumphant concert she'd given, on a whim she phoned her old

Yvonne De Carlo in *Criss Cross*

friend from early days to tell her about it. "Are you still in that asshole business?" replied Durbin.

But if Durbin had violated her metier, as it seemed to so many, with *Christmas Holiday,* Siodmak had found his. The movie showed him in total and brilliant command of the Americanized Germanic thriller mode, of the noir stylization and aestheticism—too much so for his audiences, perhaps. But today it's a still an astonishing film. And it didn't hurt his career at the time that it made a great deal of money, more than *any* other Durbin film had or would.

Two more Universal thrillers followed, both domestic dramas: *The Suspect* (Charles Laughton murders his domineering wife) and *The Strange Affair of Uncle Harry* (George Sanders murders his domineering sister), both 1945. Modest, low-budget movies, but elegantly produced (the latter by Joan Harrison) and among his best, they were smart and intense enough to make an impression and to confirm his growing reputation. Then came the peak of his Hollywood career: three big hits in a row, all thrillers: *The Spiral Staircase* (for Dore Schary and Selznick, 1945), *The Killers,* and *The Dark Mirror* (both 1946). Then it began to fall apart: Universal gave him a generous new contract, promising him more freedom and money, but only at the price of his first doing a script he disliked, from a romantic best-seller about a troubled concert pianist (*Time Out of Mind*, 1947). It was a calamitous failure, both for him and for the studio. His next two pictures were thrillers again—*Cry of the City* (1948), on a loan-out to Fox, starring Richard Conte, and *Criss Cross*, back at Universal with Burt Lancaster and Yvonne De Carlo. These last two were arguably the richest and deepest films he'd done, at least since *Christmas Holiday*, but Siodmak seemed to be souring on Hollywood. In interviews he was beginning routinely to complain about his identification with the thriller genre. It had all been just an accident, he said: nothing to do with his own inclinations or talents. But he still made another terrific one: *The File on Thelma Jordon* (1950), with Barbara Stanwyck as a murderous con woman. And he went on to other genres, but not successfully. First came an all-star superproduction at MGM—a Dostoyevsky adaptation with Ava Gardner and Gregory Peck, *The Great Sinner* (1949), so ill conceived and soon so out of control that (according to Peck) Siodmak started to ride his camera crane up to the soundstage ceiling and stay there, to get away from the chaos below ("He'd mutter, 'Up, up, up! . . . And Ava and I would grin at each other and say 'There he goes again' "). Then he refused to do the retakes that Schary had demanded (more love scenes), and he was replaced (uncredited) by Mervyn LeRoy. Nothing could prevent the movie, however, from being a flop.

As were the next two he did: a Jeff Chandler movie about a retired gangster returning to Italy (*Deported*, 1950) and a semi-documentary about a labor struggle in a New England textile plant, resolved when the true benignity of the bosses—the main one is played by Dorothy Gish—is finally understood by the fractious workers (*The Whistle at Eaton Falls*, 1951). But his next one was a big hit: *The Crimson Pirate* (1952), filmed on location in Ischia. But for Siodmak that success was purchased at the cost of a steady public and private humiliation by its producer and star, Burt Lancaster. "What is going on [in Hollywood] is a kind of anarchy," he told a reporter in 1959. "It is terrible. Most of the big studios are little more than leasing organizations . . . The stars are in charge. These egomaniacs who want to direct and write and act and produce." He left America in 1954 ("No, Hollywood did not give me up. I gave *it* up"), back to Europe to resume his career there, first and primarily (he hoped) in Germany, then in the muddled nowhere world of international co-productions. "I got out of Germany the day after Hitler came to power," he said in 1959. "I got out of France the day before war was declared. I got out of Hollywood the day before CinemaScope came in." But he soon found that CinemaScope and all the rest, including the anarchy, had followed him, and by the mid-sixties he was saying he would return to Hollywood ("I'm longing to go back"). But he never did. And though he went on making movies, he never regained the reputation he had enjoyed in America. "He was a genius," said his brother Curt. "He pissed it away."

For a noir specialist—and unlike Lang or Hitchcock—Siodmak is notably unsadistic. But he has a rich feeling for transactions of personal dominance. As in *Cry of the City:* Richard Conte, with his glittering gambler's eyes, is a hood on the run who has a talent for seducing people into helping him even when it's hopeless. Marty (Conte) is under arrest for killing a cop and has been badly wounded himself. But even flat on his back and chained to a hospital bed, he is still exerting control, not only over the prison infirmary nurse (Betty Garde) with the slouched shoulders and sad bulldog face, who has a kind of appalled crush on him ("Miss Pruett, would you see if it's close enough?"—asking her to feel his face after he's been shaved), but over all the other characters who are out to control *him:* the cops who come to grill him about his girl, or the lawyer who visits to offer him a crooked deal and to threaten him when he balks. Niles (Barry Kroeger), the lawyer, has a velvety voice, wet, thick lips, and a trace of jowls, and when he moves, he tends to swagger a little, but tentatively, unsteadily; he is *nervously* crooked. Siodmak stages their infirmary confrontation with great elegance—with the lawyer circling the bed while Conte watches him from below, smiling brightly up at him till he hears the threat against his girlfriend, then reaching up and trying to strangle him, with such fury that he nearly does. Later, when he breaks out and goes to the lawyer's office, he kills him by stabbing him through the back of his leather desk chair.

In this world of circling predators, it doesn't do to let *anyone* get behind you. We realize Marty has achieved a kind of parity with the burly, spooky masseuse whose parlor he's in when he reaches up his arm and stops her from getting behind his chair. That encounter is later on, when he is wounded once again and near the end of his strength, slumped in his chair, his head lolling backward as it did in that hospital bed. But he never stops working his charm. When he isn't menacing, he is almost childishly seductive—not calculatedly, but like some feral-eyed pet animal. As the enormous masseuse (the unforgettable Hope Emerson)—towering above him as she always and inevitably does—says: "You're a cute little man." That's before she succeeds in getting behind him in order to throttle him by the neck—then thinks better of it and carries him to bed on the couch instead, patting his head and tucking in his blanket, like a big girl and her dolly.

Marty on his back with big people looming over him is the central

"You're a cute little man": Hope Emerson and Richard Conte
in *Cry of the City*

metaphor of the movie. Though he gives always an impression of coiled and
dangerous power, he is also "a cute little man" who has to maneuver with
his vulnerability. His co-star, Victor Mature, on the other hand, playing the
cop named Candella who pursues Marty so relentlessly, is a large man, not
at all "cute," with his dark handsomeness and clotted, sleepy eyes, his
broad, lumbering frame. Siodmak is as alert to the incongruities between
the two men as if he were staging a comedy of manners. And their interaction in the scenes they share, fervid as they are, has a comic richness of nota-
tion: Mature's heavy, unrelieved moralism (Candella has no other motive for
tracking Marty so implacably—except for the bad example Marty gives to
his little brother) opposed to Conte's quicksilver charm and the unstop-
pable enthusiasm his character brings to his own cause, utterly lost as it is.
When Officer Candella observes that the reward of his work as a cop, however poorly paid it is, is that he at least "sleeps at night," "*Yeah,* but in some
cheap room," says Conte brightly, quickly, and triumphantly—as if scoring
an unanswerable point. As in a way he has . . . He *is* the life on the screen,
after all.

Siodmak is a virtuoso of such mordant contrasts. As in *The Strange
Affair of Uncle Harry,* when George Sanders comes to visit his sweetheart,
Ella Raines, in her apartment, to talk yet again about the troubles being
made for the two of them by his domineering sister. Siodmak frames the

lovers in an unmoving medium shot, as Sanders sinks into an armchair and Raines, following him, sits on the chair arm beside and above him, leaning against him. They both look off into the distance. He has to tell her this, he says—while she protests tenderly ("You don't have to say it, darling"), putting a hand on his shoulder and resting her cheek on his head. But as Sanders talks on, getting more and more emotional—this dim, private man unburdening himself, telling her how their love has changed his life and given him hope ("I owe everything to you")—Raines, her head above his, begins to look more and more troubled. She hears something in his words that he himself is unaware of: his disabling self-pity. Until he reaches the end of his confession ("Somehow I feel . . . I'm going to be happy . . ."), whereupon she rises out of the frame and leaves it—leaving him alone in it, as he is looking off, smiling tearfully at his own feelings. It's a beautifully shaded, quietly devastating moment.

It's also probably the best leading performance Sanders ever gave—the one where the usual chilly detachment seems to have a whole human dilemma behind it. Raines is wonderful too (first "discovered" by Howard Hawks, she never appeared in a Hawks film but was in four of Siodmak's). She's a *dashing* female type (the Hawksian preference)—gallant and glamorous, dressed in mannish shirts and ties and deep-pocketed skirts, the kind she can plunge her hands into when she is confronting a head case like Harry's sister Letty (Geraldine Fitzgerald), with her fussy genteel manners, her seemingly helpless insidiousness. Siodmak gets some of his nicest effects from the incongruity between them: Deborah's (Raines's) steady-eyed attentiveness to Letty's darting-eyed expostulations. Letty hardly ever looks up and directly at anyone—and Fitzgerald gives the character's eyes such terrible energy that you guess she almost *has* to keep them lowered, not to give herself away. Even with Harry—at least when she's not seducing him to her will—she tends to keep them hidden. But when she raises them in triumph and shows him their *real* malignancy—in the movie's penultimate scene—you can believe he won't recover, that she's truly destroyed him.

"I am interested in character above all else," said Siodmak in 1959. And certainly his movies like this one bear that out. And if he had been drawn to "gangster scripts," as he called them, somewhat inaccurately, it was because the genre "lends itself to deep exploration of character and motivation." And he enjoyed actors—if not stars. Geraldine Fitzgerald remembered him in 1990 as "highly articulate" and "very amusing, very jolly and jokey"—a smart, funny man who reminded Nunnally Johnson of a gnome ("I spent a good part of an evening with old Robert Siodmak the other

The Strange Affair of Uncle Harry: George Sanders, Geraldine Fitzgerald,
Ella Raines, and Moyna MacGill (Angela Lansbury's mother)

night. He was so cute I thought he was going to leap on my shoulder . . ."). Ethel Barrymore called him "the only *movie* director who gave
me the same feeling I had when working on the stage." He got on especially well with the notoriously difficult Charles Laughton—two men of
culture, and they became good friends. Laughton was notorious for all the
ways he had, once a movie was under way, of subverting both his own performance and the director's control. But on *The Suspect,* Siodmak had managed from the start to allay the actor's anxieties and got from him in return
one of his most beautifully nuanced screen performances, even (remarkably
enough) a quite restrained one. Whereas Hitchcock—with his quite different approach to actors' anxieties—two years later set off all Laughton's
alarms working with him in *The Paradine Case* (1947) and elicited one of
the actor's most scenery-chewing, camera-hugging appearances.

But then *The Suspect* had a smart, well-written script (by Bertram Mill-
hauser), like most of Siodmak's successful movies—and unlike his breakthrough hit, *Phantom Lady,* which had a lame and absurd one. The only
vivid and coherent character in it (who is also the murderer) is a roaring
and outdated cliché: a mad artist with a facial twitch. This figure had been
imported into the original material (a Cornell Woolrich pulp fiction)
because producer Joan Harrison wanted a rich, big part for Franchot Tone,

Thomas Gomez and Franchot Tone in
Phantom Lady

whom she admired, and who would give the picture at least a nominal star for the top billing (over Ella Raines and Alan Curtis, the two leads). But the impact of the Tone character is to make an already preposterous story seem even more so, and more threadbare. *All* murderers are insane, insists the philosophical cop, Thomas Gomez, who really likes to talk to this artist guy, never seeming to notice how agitated the man gets whenever people talk about insanity in front of him—as Gomez often does, and very heatedly sometimes. "Do you think the Borgias were *normal*?!" he demands rhetorically—and there is the sound of something hitting the floor offscreen. It's Tone—who up to this point has been having facial spasms in his mirror—now fainted dead away.

Was Siodmak joking? (It would be hard to improve the comic timing of that off-screen fall.) Having the kind of amusement he later suggested he had from the filming of *Cobra Woman*? ("Silly but fun," he said.) Impossible to know. But the feeble script was clearly a problem—which he seems to have addressed by emphasizing certain formal elements and set pieces. It's in these that you can locate the excitement of this first real "Siodmak picture."

The heroine (Raines) is on the trail of an unknown murderer, trying to save her wrongly convicted boyfriend from the chair—and now she finds herself sitting at a bar, staring silently at the bartender. Her idea is to unnerve this man (Andrew Tombes), whose perjury has helped to convict the boyfriend. She is sitting at the extreme end of the crowded bar's vertical line, keeping the bartender in her implacable gaze, and he is growingly nervous. Later when he leaves, she follows him—walking after him down dark rain-washed tenement blocks, shown in a high-angle long shot with a lamppost in the foreground, to an elevated station. He climbs the stairs, followed by the sound of her heels on the metal as she comes up after him. Separately they cross the platform, walking in and out from under pools of light from the lamps overhead. Stopping, she deliberately places herself near the platform's edge—with the now quite confused and panicked little man coming up behind her. She faces toward us, into the camera, but the way her eyes move we know she is "looking at" him all the while—while he is thinking, as we can also see, about pushing her off onto the tracks. A long, unmoving medium shot as they stand there in silence. The bartender frowns and adjusts his tie. Then a new arrival: a portly, discouraged-looking black woman in a floral print dress enters the turnstile and walks exhaustedly—in a long, lovely lateral tracking shot—down the wooden platform. Back to Raines at the edge, and offscreen the train now arrives, with grinding wheels and brake sounds. But all you see is the light from the windows passing across her face, and a great gust of air which the bartender turns and faces into almost thoughtfully, his tie lifting in the air to one side as he leans with his body to the other and the train comes to a stop. The thought and the danger are over.

The movie's most celebrated sequence (it got its own photo layout in *Life*) was the after-hours jam session that drummer Elisha Cook Jr. takes the heroine to (he is another of her perjury suspects). Raines has improbably disguised herself for this event as a gum-chewing floozie ("I'm a hep kitten!") in a black satin dress. The session is in someone's cramped basement rooms and it is under way explosively when the two of them get there. The screen too explodes once Cook joins the group on his drums, crosscutting objects and faces in a flurry of tilted frames and off-balance angles and distorting close-ups—cutting from the inside of a horn to the sight of a madly jiggling foot to the drummer's sweating and wild-eyed face in what looks like orgasm throes as Raines stands in front of him and urges him on. But this episode—more like something out of a late UFA silent, like E.A. Du Pont's *Variety,* than a Hollywood feature—is perfectly discrete, having no bearing on the plot before or after, no consequence outside itself. Still, it was the thing people remembered from the movie: an exercise in style.

Ella Raines masquerading as a "hep kitten" for Elisha Cook Jr.,
in the acclaimed jam-session sequence of *Phantom Lady*

Not, of course, the kind of moviemaking Siodmak—or indeed anyone
but Hitchcock—would endorse in his interviews. But Siodmak would
always cite *Phantom Lady* later on as a favorite among his movies—not surprisingly, perhaps, since it brought him his first great success in Hollywood. *More* surprising was the way he could be relied on to dismiss
("potboilers") much better Siodmak pictures like *Criss Cross* and *Cry of the
City.* "Not my kind of film," he said about the latter (to John Russell Taylor in 1959), when so obviously it was, if you judge by the film itself. "I
hate locations," he explained (some of it was shot in New York City—just
as some of *Criss Cross* was shot in 1949 Los Angeles), because, he said,
"there's so much you can't control."

And there was so much, more and more as the fifties began, that Siodmak felt he couldn't control in Hollywood. Like those megalomaniac
stars—and the collapse of the studio system itself, with, for all its drawbacks, the order it had imposed and the largesse it bestowed. "You know,"
he said, "the pattern of film production is changing. Once it was so *extrav-
agant.* Someone made a suggestion, and they all said: 'We'll try it' . . . But
no longer. The important thing is to bring the picture in on schedule."

That combination of experiment and control was crucial for him. He was a "psychological" storyteller, and a consummate one—but he was also a formalist, out of the expressionist tradition, a sophisticated artificer who was feeling more and more impinged on by the semi-documentary styles that were forcing filmmakers off their studio sets and onto the uncontrollable streets. Not that he didn't try to get with the program—even doing, before he left for good, that disastrous labor-strife movie in New England. But in the end, of course, it was his noir work and its Americanized expressionism that would have an impact on the mannerist moviemakers who came after him.

Eighteen

CHRISTMAS HOLIDAY

The script that Herman Mankiewicz supplied for Siodmak's *Christmas Holiday* had some resemblances to his Academy Award–winning *Citizen Kane* screenplay. It has the same skewed chronology, the same overlapping flashbacks; and entering it is a bit like stepping into a labyrinth (one of Welles's favorite movie metaphors), mostly because it begins so far away from its main story and characters. It's almost fifteen minutes before the star and central character appears or is even spoken of. In the meantime, there are (the opening scene) an OCS graduation ceremony (even a speech); a scene in the barracks with a young lieutenant (Dean Harens) getting a Dear John wire from his fiancée; a passenger-plane flight through an electrical storm; a forced landing in New Orleans; and the soldier getting a room at a hotel where people are all but sleeping in the lobby (it's wartime and it's Christmas Eve). In the hotel bar he meets a friendly, half-soused newspaperman, Simon Fenimore (Richard Whorf). You got troubles? I'll take you to the Maison Lafitte, says the newspaperman. What's the Maison Lafitte? "It's a—well, let's face it—it's a kinda joint a little way outa town."

It looks like a *Wolf Man* outtake when we get there: a crumbling porticoed mansion in a raging night storm, overarching trees bent by wind and rain in the foreground of a long shot, as the two men emerge from their car and struggle through the storm onto the front porch. But inside the entrance hall, it's light, with a Christmas tree by the door at the foot of a stairway, and a crystal chandelier overhead, as a maid in cap and apron takes their coats and lightning flashes through the windows, while a Dixieland band rides and rollicks on the soundtrack. And after all the neutral, generic places we've been looking at before this (from the parade grounds to the hotel room), getting to this one—lush and lively and tacky all at once—makes you feel the way a good song does when it finally gets to the chorus. *Now,* we know, we're really at the movies.

And there is a marvelous, Ophuls-like tracking-and-panning shot that follows the two men as they make their way through the place—Simon leading, with his drunken, loping walk, around tables, past pillars and paintings and potted plants, onward into the roadhouse dimness, with a long lighted bar in the far background. Simon seats the compliant lieu-tenant at an empty table and goes on through the club, the camera track-ing alongside him. So much goes past in this brisk, complex camera movement that we don't quite take it all in. But we get the impression of a hot place having a slow night: small groups of women in evening gowns sitting and standing around, lounging, chatting, buffing their nails, a bunch of sailors at the bar in the back, a black maid talking to a couple in a corner and so on—it all goes by as Simon shambles along, stopping briefly at a table to talk to two of the women, while two others, dancing together, go by in the foreground, as he goes off right, then turns and veers—the camera now tracking backward in front of him—onto the dance floor and crossing it, past a shadowed table in the foreground with three more women sitting around it, their backs to us, as the woman near-est us (the one with the barest back) rises, dropping a chiffon handkerchief she's been holding onto the table. Simon now leaves the shot (exit right), the camera stopping at last and panning slightly to watch the woman walk—full figure, sexy black silk gown—around a table, past a couple on the dance floor, toward the bandstand. She steps onto it, turns, and starts, in the far background of the shot, to sing. It is, of course, Deanna Durbin.

And what a jolt that was at the time. There are accounts of audiences gasping out loud at the early showings. And it has an impact even now to anyone who knows who "Deanna Durbin" was (and still *is* on the Ameri-can Movie Classics channel). A 1939 Cole Porter lyric ("When Love Beck-oned" from *DuBarry Was a Lady*) speaks of "sweet suburban ideas / You know what I mean, Deanna Durbin ideas." But the girl-woman we see here certainly entertains no such ideas: she looks depressed, a bit irritable, and tough. And the shock compounds with her commencing to sing—fac-ing the dance floor, settling herself on one hip in that décolleté body-molding gown, arms hanging at her side, and still situated in the background of the shot (the camera hasn't moved to follow her; it's just watching her from where it stopped). Her singing is impassive, laconic, almost sullen—like a vocalized pout. Instead of the soubrette coloratura her audience was used to, there is this feline, eerie, small-voiced sound, with the hint of a growl behind it, and an inertness that makes it fall like a dead weight on the accented syllables of the song:

Spring will be . . . *a little* late . . . *this year* . . .

Not that anyone seems to be listening to her. They have other things on their minds (more activity now, more women and men), so what the hell? She sings—it's clearly part of the job description. And the first cut away— from this elaborate traveling-and-stopping shot that had begun with Simon and the lieutenant's entrance—is not to a close-up of her but to one of the lieutenant at his table alone, *not* listening, waiting for his guide, Simon, to come back.

One of the effects of all this is to involve you in the strategies of the movie itself. You're not only aware of the sequence's skill and stylishness, but you're even more aware of how risk-taking it is: taking the star's first song number, which is also the occasion of her much-overdue first entrance—not to mention presenting her like *this*—then throwing it all away. Undercutting it, just as Durbin's singing seems to undercut the wonderful Frank Loesser song (written for the movie), with its witty lyric and its "lovely, finely fashioned melody" (Alec Wilder). Loesser, of course, hated what they did to it. And it goes on—now you see her close up—

> *A little late arriving*
> *In my lonely world over here . . .*

in three-quarters profile at frame right, facing onto the dance floor; it's a glamour shot (highlights on her hair and the black silk of her gown), but one that's composed to evoke something about the way she inhabits this place and her role in it—i.e., off to one side and toward the back even when singing. The small band accompanying her (percussion and brass) includes the rotund trombonist at her elbow, beyond him (in brighter illumination) the piano player at a white upright with carved cupids on it. There is a half-wall behind the band, and above and behind that a stairway, with a traffic of girls and waiters with trays. A blonde standing and drinking by the piano bends and kisses the pianist; the trombonist looks on and smiles. A girl on the stairs beckons the two girls behind her to follow her up, and they do. The trombonist lifts his horn and plays:

> *For you-oo have left me . . .*

Another girl rushes onto the bandstand, confers with the blonde over the head of the piano player:

> *And winter continues cold . . .*

Another shot of the lieutenant, still bored. Another long shot, angled over the crowd toward Durbin singing in the background; in the foreground is

Jackie (Deanna Durbin) dancing with the lieutenant (Dean Harens)
in *Christmas Holiday.* This is the Durbin look that shocked and
dismayed both the *New York Times* and her biggest fans.

the shadowed profile of an aristocratic-looking elderly man, with a
Vandyke beard and a pince-nez, sitting alone at a table near the bandstand.
But then the blonde leaves the bandstand, and the camera pans to follow
her as she walks onto the floor, where it *then* picks up on an entering waiter
crossing the floor in the opposite direction, carrying a drink on a tray to the
elderly man's table. There some silent bargaining takes place: the man
indicating the singer with a movement of his head, giving the waiter a card
and some money; the waiter smiling and bowing, then disappearing in
back of the half-wall behind the bandstand. Durbin is finishing her song—

> *Yet time . . . heals all things,*
> *I shouldn't cling to this fear . . .*

and now comes her first solo close-up—

> *It's merely that Spring . . .*

with a slight lift of the head, a shift of the eyes—

> *. . . will be a little late this year.*

And she's done. Now the band hots up, Dixieland-style. (It's the jazz band, and not her singing, that seems to be the real event.) She is just stepping down when the waiter calls her ("Jackie!") from between the little curtains in back. She turns, walks back between the trumpet and the trombone, takes the card from the waiter, and goes off, turning it over speculatively as the band plays and she strolls back across the floor to her table—which is just behind the elderly man's. He sits turned away as before. She passes the card without comment to the very tough-looking brunette opposite, who hands it in turn to a younger girl passing their table, who takes it and goes to the old man's table, only to be turned away impatiently (all this takes place in dumb show under the jubilant, break-out music). While the brunette, having handed off the card, turns and lights a cigarette from the table candle, smiling as she does so across at Durbin, who has picked up her handkerchief again and slumped down into her chair, her back to us again, facing away toward the band—who are now hotter than ever. But the real dazzler in this sequence has been Siodmak's orchestration of it— his control of all the disparate elements.

This sequence seems almost as virtuosic as something from Welles (though more quietly so), the way it orchestrates so many sights and sounds and details, pulling them all together into a gathering effect. And it gives the kind of pleasure you often got in good noir movies—of suddenly coming across something so *smart,* so confidently and powerfully so, that it makes you sit up with excitement. The whole scene is like an inspired jazz riff, teasing and playing with the familiar "melody"—the introduction/entrance of the star. And the familiar background: one of those great raffish saloons the movies always did so well. And so you want to see *this* one, of course, all you can of the Maison Lafitte—and you do. But then you also want to see *her*—and you do—and you don't, it seems. There's always so much distraction going on all around and behind her, and there's no telling where that camera will go to at any moment, after a blonde or a waiter or whatever. And while you're sort of dazzled by all of it, it's not till it's gone by that you may realize how much of nuance and detail you've been prompted to take in (it's the kind of moviemaking that makes *you* feel smarter), and how offhanded it's all been—like the band, and like her singing.

Her name is Jackie Lamont, we learn, and Simon introduces her to the lieutenant—calling her (with his usual sneering intonation) "the star of our little entertainment." Jackie and the lieutenant dance, and when she learns that he is going to midnight Mass at the cathedral she asks him to take her along, with surprising urgency. So that the next big set piece takes place in church.

It's a surprisingly prolonged one—six minutes or so—alternating long shots of the cathedral interior, the congregation, and the altar, with close shots of the boys' choir and the two principals in their pew at the back of the packed church. She is kneeling and he is standing beside her next to a pillar. It's the old-style Solemn High Mass, of course, all in Latin, and with the three priests facing away from the congregation and toward the altar throughout. It's all too impassive and even newsreel-like (it was, as it looks like, the real thing, shot in a real L.A. church) to strike you as "beautiful" in the way that movie church services, especially lavish ones like this, usually are: swoony and lyrical and kitschy. The emphasis here is on the remoteness and mystery, even the impassivity, of the ceremony—and on the *music:* the boys' choir, the priests' chant, the liturgical song-and-response of the Kyrie Eleison, and the joyful "Adeste Fideles" hymn that breaks out at the communion service.

And yet you wonder why it goes on so long. Until the moment (at the communion) when Jackie starts to weep out loud and then more and more convulsively. Watched by the concerned lieutenant, she falls to the floor by his feet, sobbing and burying her face in her hands. After a moment, she gets obscured by his quietly and gallantly taking a step in front of her, the skirt of his topcoat coming between her and the camera like a curtain. She's withdrawn from us again—just as in a sense she's refused to sing for us.

After the cathedral, they go to an all-night diner she knows—where she tells him, as they sit at the crowded counter, that she hadn't been crying for the reason he might think (guilt over her way of life at the Maison Lafitte, presumably) but because of her disconnection from other people that the service had brought suddenly home to her. This is a *second* un-Durbin-like look now—she is mannishly dressed but with too much makeup, in a belted trenchcoat and fedora-like hat tilted rakishly over one eye—but it doesn't seem unsuited to her. Later on, she describes herself as "a gentleman" ("in my own little way"), and it's almost startling how right that sounds.

Her real name (a true Deanna Durbin one) is Abigail Martin, she tells him, and she is the wife of Robert Manette, a convicted murderer now serving a life sentence. The lieutenant has never heard of him, and so she commences to tell him her story. It's the beginning of the movie's first flashback; and it introduces, on a slow dissolve, the Deanna Durbin image you expect, innocent and wholesome, but also ripe and luscious, asleep in her canopied bed. It's one of those quilted bedrooms Graham Greene complained about in Deanna Durbin movies: the virginal organdy-curtained-

Jackie and the lieutenant at midnight Christmas Mass

and-covered American girl's room. The camera moves in a slow dreamlike track up to the sleeping Abigail as Jackie in the diner talks on the soundtrack. What we don't know at first is that this idyllic room, with its American teen-mag aura, is an appendage to a very different sort of place: an old and dark and guilty house, a home for family secrets—for which this fantasy room is like a kind of afterthought, not even meant to be convincing. It even has its own separate entrance, a porch and a flight of stairs from the courtyard to the door, through which this sleeping beauty's prince now appears, coming in from under the moonlight. But he's come from having killed a man—as Jackie now tells us—unknown to Abigail.

Robert (Gene Kelly) plays at being boyish, pleading excuses for his "terrible hours" as he comes to her bed, promising "never, never to do it again," and covering his eyes with his hand. He gets a glamour close-up too, as lush and gleaming as hers—but its effect is unnerving. With his arch manner, his sharp nose and pointed chin, his smile and gleaming eyes and black cap of hair forming the widow's peak on his forehead, he's uncannily like the Mephistopheles of nineteenth-century illustrations. No sooner have you formed this thought than Abigail puts it in to words— "Devil!" she says, as he tries to get her to relent and smile, and just before she falls into his arms.

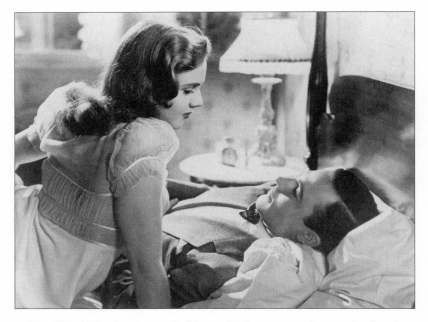

"Devil!": Abigail—the *pre*-Jackie—with her wayward young husband,
Robert Manette (Gene Kelly)

She discovers his crime the next day. As well as his gorgonlike mother's collusion in it: she burns his bloodstained clothes while Abigail looks down on her from an upper window. And when Robert asks Abigail to lie for him when the cops come ("My life may depend upon it") she realizes that she loves him enough to do it, to do anything for him.

But by this point in her story, Jackie has missed her last bus back to the Lafitte. Since it's Christmas and there are no more rooms, the lieutenant offers to share his hotel suite with her. The next morning she tells him the rest of her story, thus beginning the movie's second and much longer flashback—which starts before her marriage to Robert, and with a sequence that deliberately reminds you of the cathedral Mass: another public ceremony, but less austere, less remote, and putting us at less of a distance from the heroine's emotion. It's an orchestral concert, a great hall filled to capacity, and the piece is the Liebestod from *Tristan und Isolde*. (At the insistence of music director Hans Salter, the studio doubled its usual thirty-six-piece soundtrack orchestra.) "He always liked listening to music," says Jackie in the hotel room. "That's where I first met him . . ."—as the familiar strains of the Wagner music begin to rise under her voice, and the hotel room scene dissolves to the hall.

As the cathedral sequence did, this one, too, begins with a long shot of the "altar"—but from much higher up and farther away, making the brightly lit orchestra under the proscenium arch look jewellike on its stage. But instead of a cut away, this opening shot begins to move (a camera crane)—first turning slowly in midair until it's facing toward the galleries instead of the stage. And then it begins to climb with the rapturously climbing music—up and up, three, four, five levels, moving closer in on the spectators at each one, until—on the music's first great resolving chord—it reaches the topmost gallery, with Durbin and Kelly, under the ceiling, sitting next to each other. Now a second resolving chord: the film cuts back to the orchestra, from even higher up and farther away—approximately *their* level, that is. Now close-ups of them, separately and then together, looking maximally beautiful: Durbin, moist-eyed and leaning back in her seat, her head moving just perceptibly, in rapt response to the beauty of the sound; Kelly, leaning forward intently, absorbed and grave and contemplative—as different as possible from the smirker in her bedroom. And the music's great concluding diminuendo is matched to an extreme long shot, from the back of the balcony, of the orchestra far below, the angle pitched so vertiginously downward that it seems to lay out the whole place between—with listeners Durbin and Kelly, in the front row of the gallery, sharply focused in the middle distance, surreally outlined against the great drop and gap between them and the stage, seeming to float there in their separate absorptions. And at that moment, this image—like a held breath—seems nearly on the same order of the wondrous as the fading music does. (Woody Bredell was the photographer.) Stillness—and applause.

They meet and talk going out, and he asks her to the next concert—an all-Beethoven one. He says he has some passes for that upper gallery, but when they go, they're on the main floor in the expensive seats—betraying his eagerness. The views of the orchestra now are close ones: a flurry of quick eye-level shots of conductor and various players keyed to the resounding opening chords of Beethoven's *Coriolan* Overture. Then a sudden cutaway—startling and funny—to a tearoom ensemble playing (as a fatuous-looking violinist turns into the camera) not *Coriolan* but "Always," and very soupily. This is the place they've gone to after the concert. And Irving Berlin's "Always" (written in 1925 and a familiar standard by this time), as it turns out, will be *their* Liebestod. And "their song," as Robert now dubs it. It's also what they play and sing together later on—for Mother . . . *after* the wedding.

"The first six months we were married," says Jackie in her voice-over, "we kept completely to ourselves—Robert, his mother, and me." This disconcerting enumeration segues into her first rendition of "Always"—with Robert at the piano in the parlor, Abigail standing behind him, and Mrs. Manette (Gale Sondergaard) in a nearby rocking chair knitting. As Robert plays noodlingly, Abigail hums, putting her hands on his shoulders, and sings the song's rarely heard verse—

> *For the longest while,*
> *I'd forget to smile—*
> *Then I met you . . .*

—with its wistfully winding and arching tune, the words' homely Berlin-style elegance ("the longest while") and wit (*forgetting* to smile). Getting to the familiar chorus, she folds her arms around his shoulders, and sings into his ear in her softest, creamiest soprano ("I'll be loving you / Always . . ."), the two of them in the darkly shadowed foreground at screen right, in extreme close-up, while Mrs. Manette is in the brightly lit background, in sharp focus, rocking and smiling and knitting (she's got him staying home at last). What's striking about this tableau (another arresting deep-focus composition) is how *separate* these deeply entangled people remain—lapsing into themselves as the music goes on: Robert thoughtful over the piano keys, Abigail clinging to him without looking at him, Mrs. Manette kvelling in the corner.

"And then," says Jackie on the soundtrack, "actually overnight everything changed." The next night Robert has murdered Teddy Jordan, his bookie, and is soon arrested and charged. The cops come to search the Manette house, and Abigail hides the evidence they're looking for (Jordan's stolen money). In spite of this demonstration of her daughter-in-law's loyalty, Mrs. Manette turns on her, accusing her of failing Robert—of closing her "eyes to what it was all about—what *he* was all about—selfishly, just so you could be happy . . ." When Abigail protests—"There was no way for me to know"—Mrs. Manette lays out her indictment: "You should have known. You weren't blinded because you had to be—you *wanted* to be. It might have hurt to know that . . . Robert is what he is. But if you had been willing to be hurt for his sake you could have helped him . . . It's I who love him. Because I'm willing to know all about him and keep *on* loving him!"

The trial follows. Robert is convicted of first-degree murder and sentenced to life. Abigail and Mother leave the courtroom and move swiftly past the reporters and through the corridors of the courthouse—Siodmak's camera tracking in front of them, the soundtrack music pounding. Suddenly Mrs. Manette stops and turns to Abigail: "You killed him!" she cries, and slaps her squarely across the face. As the flashback fades, Abigail-now-Jackie is standing against the wall in the lieutenant's hotel room, touching her face where the slap had landed, and repeating her mother-in-law's words.

She feels guilty still. And it's that guilt, we soon learn, that's impelled her to the Maison Lafitte—out of a feeling that if she degrades herself sufficiently, she will somehow atone for the degradation in Robert that she refused to confront or even to acknowledge until it was too late. As if now doing penance for that Barbie-doll bedroom, for her own willfully prolonged innocence ("What's a bookmaker?" she asks Robert, when he first tells her about Teddy Jordan)—for being "Deanna Durbin" too long. Of course, the idea that innocence can be culpable is an insight that's at the heart of noir itself, though rarely so clearly stated as here. But then that turns out to be more or less the problem: in this film it's more stated than enacted, more an idea than a realized meaning.

Still, the Mankiewicz script is superior, it seems to me, to Maugham's repellent little novel, and the nasty-fastidious tone with which the book maneuvers its complacent bourgeois Englishman in Paris (the lieutenant in New Orleans in the movie) into learning the customary Maugham lesson about the squalor of love. The whore of the novel, known as "the Countess," is the original of the Durbin heroine, and tells roughly the same story about her past and her marriage, including the mother-in-law; and many of the events of the novel (like the midnight Mass and the heroine's crying jag) reappear with altered meanings in the movie.

We all knew, said Gene Kelly in 1990 (in a telephone interview), that the script had unsolved problems. Certainly Siodmak knew: Kelly remembered him as responding by concentrating his efforts on the picture's "mood," making do with the screenplay he had, from a still quite important screenwriter (both the ads and the credits on the screen featured Mankiewicz's name prominently). The "problems" are less with the flat, sometimes bathetic dialogue (Jackie, a character says, "has that one-man look in her eye") or the stock characters (the good-hearted madam, the cynical drunken reporter, the domineering mother, et al.) than with the script's failure to develop the themes it touches on. It was a sort of dramatic necessity, probably, to leave out all details of Abigail's transformation into Jackie, but it's something else altogether to leave us in the dark about the crime and the criminal himself. Mrs. Manette accuses Abigail (the scenes I quoted above) of choosing not to know that "Robert is what he is"—and that would be a more telling accusation if *we* knew what he was. He's a gambler, we know, and chronically out of work. And finally a murderer—although even that event, apart from the fact that he did it, remains remote and unreal. The explanations of the same central event in the novel—Robert is a drug dealer and his victim a homosexual on the make for him—could not of course be offered by a Hollywood movie of the forties. And this made for some spaces in the movie's plot and coherence that Mankiewicz seems mainly (even lazily) to have left blank. This irresolution at the heart of the action left the audiences feeling almost as put off as the transgression of Durbin's innocence did.

In the climactic section—after the flashbacks are over with—Robert has broken out of prison (another remote and unreal offscreen event) and learned that his young wife, far from "waiting for him," has become a worker at the Lafitte. With the cops on his tail, he forces Simon at gunpoint to take him there: he's going to use the gun on Jackie, he says. The lieutenant, worried for her after the jailbreak news, is at the Lafitte too now, at the bar, talking with Valerie, the madam (Gladys George), telling her how much Jackie's life story has educated him about his own life (he's given up the idea of paying back his ex-fiancée for *her* infidelity—since "the heart has its reasons," to quote both Pascal and Woody Allen). Valerie is pleased, since Jackie is a favorite of hers ("that one-man look"). But wait—"Jackie's getting ready to do her number," says Valerie—and then: "There she is." This is the kind of movie where the real excitement begins not with the lovemaking or the shooting but with the music.

First you see her from across the dance floor—as before, her "entrance" is like an afterthought, in the distance, with people getting up to dance in the foreground between her and us. The place seems really crowded, unlike the way it was Christmas Eve. Jackie exchanges a whispered word with the piano player, who then performs an introductory roulade as she crosses in front of the band and leans against a fluted pillar to one side of them. And she starts to sing—it's "Always" again, in a languorous rhythmic dance tempo, accompanied by piano and bass alone. She is wearing a more modest version of that earlier black gown—with a rounded rather than plunging décolletage, shoulders, and short sleeves.

Berlin's "Always"—as in the joke about Wagner's operas—is better than it sounds. Like a lot of Berlin's songs, it's almost numbingly simple on its surface but complicated and troubled beneath, containing that characteristic Berlin "dislocation" between words and music that critic John Rubins so beautifully described in his Berlin centenary essay (*New York*

Review of Books, June 16, 1988)—a contrast here between the song's cheery, dumb lyric and its "restless, spasmodic melody" with its "disturbing modulations" and "undercurrent of anxiety." And in *this* performance, by Durbin and her accompanists, the "restless, spasmodic" undertone is in the forefront. She sings it almost mournfully, like a blues—with a high-humming Mildred Bailey sound. The band when it kicks in carries the restlessness and jocularity; Durbin carries the lament: with her heart-struck torch-singer look in close-up, lots of lip rouge and eye shadow, leaning back against the pillar, the hand of the bass player moving in the light behind her. This conjunction of song

Jackie sings "Always."

and image is so seductive that you're sort of jolted by the first dramatic cutaway: plunged suddenly into darkness and quiet behind a door opening slowly onto the light and sound of the club, the silhouetted backs of two men emerge against the light of the big room—Simon with Robert (we presume) behind him, holding a gun to his back. A reverse angle: Simon, facing us and alone, stepping into full view, standing uneasily in front of the door. Jackie singing, again in close-up—her eyes closed now, in the singer's absorption, her head moving (the way it did at the Wagner concert) from side to side against the pillar, the humming sound in her voice now even higher and bluesier:

> *Days may not be fair*
> *—Always . . .*
> *That's when I'll be there*
> *—Always . . .*

But then, before she can finish, Simon from the doorway catches her eye, as if to say "Robert is here." She breaks off, surprisingly, leaning forward and smiling, then sweeps off the bandstand and out of the frame—as the band finishes the song for her, bursting into a raucous, horn-blasting Dixieland that accompanies her (in the next shot) as she rushes into and through the shadow and crowd of the dance floor. It's as if the infectious music propels her, with the tracking-and-panning high-angle camera following the path she cuts through the dancers—until she emerges again in front of the door, Simon, a grim-faced doorman, to one side of it. She comes to a stop, her back to us, on the music's exultant concluding downbeat, hesitating before the door as Simon looks on. Then she goes in.

Now she's in the darkened room; and this part of this final sequence is quite another sort of experience than what we've just been having, though no less artful or consciously designed. In a way, since it's centered around Robert and his gun, it's a conventional sort of showdown scene. Except that what Siodmak does with it—while you're still on a high from the scene before—is anything but conventional or predictable.

What happens is simple and direct. She embraces him eagerly; he is hostile and sneering. She tells him the place is surrounded by cops, so they will have to hurry if they're going to get away—but they'll need money and so forth. When she turns away, he grabs her, throwing her violently up against the wall, and accuses her of betraying him. Pinned against the wall in the dark, she follows his angry words with wildly darting eyes. She tells him that the Maison Lafitte has been her way of degrading herself, of being close to him, of sharing his imprisonment: "This is *my* prison . . . I've been holding on to you all this time." He is, not surprisingly, unconvinced by this (though clearly *we* are meant to be). The madam and the lieutenant are in the room with them now, as well as Simon, but Robert still has the gun and is on the point of using it when the cops get the drop on him from a window and shoot him down. He is dying and she holds him in her arms, as the Liebestod rises on the sound-track. "You can let go now, Abigail," he says to her tenderly—and dies. As the lieutenant repeats these words to her ("You heard what he said. You can let go now, Abigail"), she rises and walks slowly, as if entering a dream, to the window, where she looks up with shining tear-glazed eyes at the clouds and the stars in the night sky. And on this image of the night sky, as the Liebestod swells, the movie ends.

Well . . . you can see they had a problem. Bosley Crowther, in his unfavorable *Times* review, claimed to see in this final scene "the suggestion . . . that the young widow and the soldier will take it up together from there."

Jackie against the wall, facing Manette on the lam and with a gun (Kelly at right, his back to us). At left, in the door, are the reporter (Richard Whorf), the lieutenant, and the madam (Gladys George).

But although that may indeed have been the original idea (an audience certainly would have expected it), Siodmak does all he can to defeat it, it seems. What we see instead of a promise of any redeeming romance in the future is the heroine transfigured on the spot, having a kind of epiphany by herself—this whole final sequence a battery of expressionist effects and stunning close-ups. Anything but a predictable sort of ending.

One thing Siodmak does here—more extremely than before in the movie—is to turn his two leads into photographic objects. Kelly's death mask, for example; or Durbin trapped against that wall—evoking the torch singer against the pillar we've just seen, but a sinister version of her. When you first see her pinned there, with her head and shoulders pressed back against the floral-patterned wallpaper, her face is startlingly like a mask: clown-white skin, overrouged lips, dark thick brows, and even thicker eye shadow. The amount of mascara noticeably varies from shot to shot, according to the dramatic intensity of the moment. Just as Kelly's face, noticeably stubbled when he's playing the thug, becomes (like Burton's death mask in *Bitter Victory*) radiantly clean-shaven when we see him dead.

Even more striking is the way Siodmak (and his cinematographer, Woody Bredell) deploys shadow. When Robert crowds her up against the wall, it's his shadow that seems to violate her the most. The darkness he casts on her fills most of the frame, forming a top-to-bottom diagonal across the frame, so that all you see is her panicked right eye, deep-set and mascaraed and shot through with fear—like an equine eye just before it starts to roll—as she pleads with him, telling him again that she loves him, to no effect.

The cutting becomes equally stylized: a barrage of different, dislocating angles. Especially once the perfunctory shoot-out with the cops (two or three gunshots and it's over) is done with and Robert has died. Jackie, kneeling by him and cradling him in her arms, lets him slowly down to the floor on the music and on the same movement rises to stand. But this movement of hers is shown in a classical montage, which both fragments and prolongs it, showing it from different angles successively, achieving a deliberate sort of Eisensteinian momentousness. And then as she walks to that open window, it's shown through a similar series of disorienting close shots, each one so breathtakingly lit and framed that you experience the movement in a succession of gasps, as a heightening and quickening, consonant (once again) with the excitement of the rising music.

And it's exciting partly because it's so crazy—so audacious. If this odd movie works in the end—as I think it does—it's not because its heroine's character makes anything much more than the most minimal sense required, but because she becomes an essential part of that powerful aestheticizing strategy that Siodmak has imposed on the production. She has been central to it from the beginning, of course—just as "Deanna Durbin" herself has been. But it isn't until this ending that she's transformed by it: each glimpse of her, each moment, each gesture and cut becoming a kind of "accompaniment" to the musical exaltation. And we "believe in" that transfiguration of her in the end because Siodmak has involved us in the process that arrives at it, in all those "musical numbers" that have led us up to it.

For the fact is that all the most vivid and compelling moments in this movie have involved either performing music or listening to it; at the Lafitte, at the cathedral, at the concert, at the piano in the Manette parlor. It's an extraordinary range, and a daring one—from a new Loesser song to a Latin liturgical song-and-response to Wagner to a Berlin standard to Wagner again—richer and more suggestive than the movie's writing ever is. And there's some way in which it all comes together—from worship to jazz, from love-death to American-style wisecrack (that late-coming "spring"): all about coping and transcending in different ways. And it's that range of differences that gives the movie its feeling of riches. It's the heroine's relation, through vivid and convincing imagery, to each one of those different "songs" that gives her her "character." That, and her relation to Deanna Durbin, of course.

Siodmak has staked his movie here not so much on solving the problems of the script (supposing he had the power to do so, as he well may not have had) as on pulling off these set pieces, these musical "numbers." It's the same tour-de-force approach he used more sparingly on *Phantom Lady.* At its most successful, this kind of moviemaking can remind you of all those great American (now "classic") musical shows with less-than-great books—*Show Boat* and *Pal Joey,* among the greatest before Rodgers and Hammerstein, *Gypsy* and *Follies* after them—shows in which the defining moments and the intensest life are less in the action of the script than in the reflections on that action that the "song numbers" give us. Where the numbers depend on the dramatic writing, but not much at all on how good or bad it is.

So that in the end *Christmas Holiday* is not so much a movie about a doomed and tragic love—though it takes such a love as a given—as it is a film about the power of a ceremony or a concert or a terrific song or even a night sky to transfigure your experience. "I've been alone as long as I can remember," says Jackie to the lieutenant early in the movie. And at the end (Bosley Crowther notwithstanding) Jackie is more alone than ever. But she has moved into the hieratic fulfillments of the movie itself—which has all but forsaken conventional moviemaking, or even (one could argue) narrative conviction, and left her and us looking at the sky and listening to the Liebestod.

The effect is saved from "artiness" importantly by Durbin herself, and by the way the movie has dramatized her—from her first stirring appearance, singing "Spring Will Be a Little Late This Year." What she does there, it turns out, controls the rest of the movie; more than that, it expresses something at the heart of American noir, and of American popular song. Just as there is a generic little girl's face, round and pretty, with deep-set eyes and traces of baby fat, in the hardboiled young woman's, there's an inadvertent wistfulness in her singing here, impassive as it is. Durbin was twenty-two. And this grown-up version of her has an authentic sadness—an earthbound quality just the opposite of the soprano rapture she was otherwise identified with; even her back and shoulders look sad in this early scene. But it's a sadness so settled and uncomplaining that it also gives her a kind of dignity—the sort that goes with a heaviness of

spirit and a *real* toughness ("Are you still in that asshole business?").
"Jackie" embodies that same blend of jauntiness and disconsolateness that
Loesser's wonderful song gives—as so many classic American songs do.
Loesser (as I said above) thought they'd trashed it; but you realize instead,
watching and listening to Durbin here, that her offhand way of singing it
is a way of singing just such a song very fully. (She did a soprano-rapture
version of it on the recording, and that *really* trashed it.) The inertness of
her voice seems to let the song itself carry her along, while she stays apart
from it. She's a performer who knows the value in this sort of hovering,
this withholding of self or part of it in the act of performance itself, this
retaining a kind of speculative distance—much like the distance the song
takes on the pain it tells about, rising out of discouragement into
metaphor ("And winter continues cold . . ."). But not rising very far, when
Durbin's heroine sings—making a sound less like a lifted voice than a
raised eyebrow. Like the unmelodious title singer in Frost's great poem
"The Oven Bird"—who "frames in all but words . . . what to make of a
diminished thing," the sort of bird who "knows in singing not to sing."

Nineteen

ORSON WELLES

It was this *Christmas Holiday* kind of filmmaking—formalized, unre-solved by conventional standards, intensely " stylish," and so on—that Orson Welles had done more than anyone to bring about in Hollywood. In spite of its box-office failure, *Citizen Kane* in 1941 became the single most influential movie on *other* American moviemakers since Griffith. And even when it first opened, it was greeted with the best notices that anyone could remember. It was a new birth of the movies, a new art form, said reviewers; the best film he'd ever seen said John O'Hara in *Newsweek;* Hollywood's "greatest creation" to date, said *Time.*

But to some of the more serious movie critics of the time—the ones we still read now, that is—to Manny Farber and James Agee, to Otis Ferguson at *The New Republic*—Welles's achievement in *Kane* was deeply suspect. Their objections to it were as much moral as aesthetic: the movie is a phony, too fancy to be the real thing they valued in movies. "The old flow-ing naturalistic film," as Farber described it, concerned "with narrative, character, and action for their own sakes." Or as Ferguson put the same point, with rhapsodic insistence: "story, story, story." Farber argued that *Kane* had "almost no story," something that would have been perfectly apparent if Welles had been content to tell his story in the *old* way; in that smoothly flowing line that Farber admired in the mid-career movies of Howard Hawks and Raoul Walsh, or with the "skillful anonymity" that he praised in Nick Ray's *The Lusty Men.* Welles's pretentious "shock-happy work," he wrote in 1952, had "anticipated everything that has since become fashionable in American films."

> Oddly enough . . . [*Kane*] made little impression at the time on Hol-lywood's veterans. Only in the 1950's did the ghost of *Citizen Kane* start haunting every A picture out of Hollywood. Before the advent of Orson Welles, the most important thing in motion picture tech-nique had been the story, the devising, spacing, and arranging of

Orson Welles, on one of his *Citizen Kane* sets

shots into a plot line that moved easily from one thing to another. Welles, more concerned with exhibiting his impudent showmanship and his deep thought about graft, trusts, yellow journalism, love, hate, and the like, fractured his story all along the line, until his film became an endless chain of stop effects . . . a succession of fragments, each one popping with aggressive technique and loud, biased slanting of the materials of actual life.

Farber is right about quite a few things here (as he usually is), it seems to me. It's the overcontrolled, overdetermined aspect of *Kane* that can make it feel oppressive at times, that can even turn some audiences off it altogether. But when Farber complains about Welles's "impudent showmanship," he seems to me to be complaining about just the aspect that redeems what he's objecting to—at least for most of us. It's the movie's showing-off that makes it feel so slangily and happily American, that takes the smell of "culture" off the stylization and fanciness. "More fun than any great movie I can think of," says Pauline Kael (notably less puritanical than her critical predecessors); and Welles's "impudent" style functions a lot like the fast, funny talk in the tough thirties comedies she says the movie comes out of: the breakfast-table montage that traces the stages of decline in Kane's first marriage, for example, or the *March of Time* parody at the movie's beginning. Or the scene of Susan's debut at the opera— shown in that now famous traveling shot that rises with the opera house curtain and the strangled high notes of her first aria, up and up into the stage gridirons, the voice growing fainter, until you reach a catwalk with two stagehands looking down over the railing, one turning to the other and holding his nose.

Nevertheless . . . "Because of its congestion of technical stunts, it fails to move us," said one (otherwise favorable) review. You're left cold by it, Otis Ferguson said, "even while your mouth is still open at its excitements." And many who admire it even today (it's routinely cited as the greatest film ever made in international critics' and filmmakers' polls) will describe it as a triumph of form over substance, as a dazzling artifact.

Certainly it's not the kind of movie where you have a direct powerful experience of story and character "for their own sakes," the sort of thing Farber and Ferguson invoke against it. There is too much "art," too much of the filmmaker, between us and that. But it *is* some kind of powerful experience. And among its *most* powerful moments are the ones where we are most conscious of the mediation of the movie itself—those "excitements" Ferguson alludes to. But now that we've got used to *Kane,* so to speak, having lived so many decades with the fact of it, with its reputation and reshowings, its accomplishment doesn't seem so puzzling: it's become clear to nearly everyone that it's exactly those "stunts" and "excitements" that *do* move us—those great tour-de-force sequences where the passion of the filmmaking becomes as much an event on the screen as the story and characters, and inextricable from them as well.

At the end, for example, when the investigating reporter Thompson (William Alland) is having a final, unhelpful interview with Raymond, the butler (Paul Stewart), as Xanadu is being emptied and closed down (they are both at the foot of the grand staircase as the workmen move in and out around them), the camera lifts off and leaves the two men, taking off on its own, launching onto its majestic traveling overview of all the treasures and junk that Kane has left behind in the estate's vast warehouses, tracking inexorably past and above crates and boxes, over statues and paintings and furnishings, *things* seemingly without end, one slow overhead traveling shot dissolving slowly into the next one, and so on and on. Until reaching a little clutch of belongings from Kane's childhood home—toys, wooden chairs, an iron bed, a sled, and so forth—and a blazing open furnace with workmen pitching things into the fire, among them a sled. The camera tracks downward and into the flames—in time to see the word "Rosebud" just as the fire melts the paint and the music swells on the soundtrack. Another series of dissolves puts you outside the building, and then the Xanadu gates, looking at the No Trespassing sign that began the movie, and now ends it.

What's crucial here is the way Welles's movie, with its characteristic "technical stunts," makes all this happen to us. For example, the mingled solemnity and excitement of that first camera lift-off, as it starts on its magisterial survey of Kane's goods. It feels not only right but deeply satisfying here at the end that the camera should go off on its own. *Kane* is a "private eye" sort of movie where the movie itself becomes the detective, posing larger questions than Thompson the journalist (whose face we never even see) ever could. At the end, then, we're alone (at last) with the movie itself—and with the Rosebud revelation, as the fire obliterates the secret forever, concealing it from everyone but us, sealing our compact with the movie—making it, so to speak, "our secret." And that furnace shot is still thrilling even when you know it's coming—as nearly everybody does by now. *Citizen Kane* feels like a "great movie" importantly because of the deep and complex ways it involves us in itself *as a movie,* not only with its spirit but with its filmic strategies.

But it wasn't Welles's favorite: he always said *that* was his mutilated masterpiece *The Magnificent Ambersons* (1942)—a much quieter, less showy and overtly dazzling film. But it's here, according to Welles (talking to biographer Barbara Leaming), that he achieved "the greatest tour de force of my career"—namely, the great Amberson ball, near the movie's beginning.

It "was the last of the great, long-remembered dances that everybody talked about," says Welles's narrating voice on the soundtrack—over an extreme overhead long shot of the Amberson mansion, windows alight and carriages arriving, as the camera descends, the screen dissolving to a close shot of the front entrance. A great gust of snowy wind opens the massive outer doors and propels the camera forward and inside, following the thickly upholstered backs of a man and a woman, scarves billowing, clutching their hats and each other, moving past the uniformed men at the doors into the splendid reception hall, as the enormous crystal chandelier sways and chatters above them in the wind from the doorway. Reverse

The Magnificent Ambersons: Tim Holt as George Minafer; Dolores Costello as Isabel, his mother; and Joseph Cotten as her old beau, Eugene. This is the beginning of the great Amberson ball.

angle: from far inside the hall, with couples running past a towering Christmas tree, and elegant black footmen taking coats and giving directions, and the three Ambersons themselves, all three generations of them, receiving their guests near the door. And the camera moves slowly toward them, past the tree and under the chandelier—which now looks not only grand but a little ominous. Just as the mansion interior, in all its massive, overbearing solidity, with its carved woodwork and black walnut staircases and stained-glass windows, seems to offer a comment on all the bustle and high spirits, looking at once festive and funereal. And the musical underscoring—a soft, plaintive melody for strings—has the same elegiac sound we've been hearing in Welles's voice-over. So it comes as no special surprise that the film dialogue you can make out in this tracking shot, amid the bustle and competing sounds, seems to be about cemetery plots.

"I suppose that's where they'll put the major when his time comes," says the chin-whiskered old coot now being received by the Ambersons, prompting the major (Richard Bennett) to abandon his post, walking off in sudden conference with a servant—leaving behind his daughter, Isabel (Dolores Costello), and her son, George Minafer (Tim Holt), to receive the next guest, who turns out to be her old beau, Eugene Morgan (Joseph Cotten). (It was his back, and his daughter's, that we saw at the beginning.)

For the beautiful Isabel and the widower Eugene it's a deeply felt reunion. The son, George (he is and will be the problem), is feeling something else, looking on and frowning. Not that *they* notice: "This your boy, Isabel?" says Eugene, beaming at George over her head, clasping her hand in his—as she looks up at him (in her own close shot now) with an answering radiance. The words they exchange here sound as rapturous as they are conventional: she introduces George, Eugene asks after Wilbur, her husband, but she thinks he's in the game room at the moment. "He never was much for parties," she says, with her seraphic smile, as if she were giving him some marvelous present. "Remember?" she adds, still smiling, as if to say: "Of course you remember, we *both* remember, and isn't that wonderful too?" As he seems clearly to think it is. And so on. The fullness of feeling that imbues the whole sequence is already remarkable here, at this early stage. And it goes on like this: as the great ball goes on, and all the major characters of the major family groups, Ambersons and Minafers and Morgans, walk and talk and dance through the crowded rooms, as they mingle and connect and depart and reconnect, all in a succession of exhilarated long-take moving shots, with the camera tracking backwards in front of them. It's one of the most purely elated sequences in all of movies—yet always with that undertone, suggested by the chandelier and the opening music and the gravely tracking camera, of time and loss.

Young George is very taken with Eugene Morgan's daughter, Lucy (Anne Baxter)—if not at all with her father ("that queer-looking duck," as he calls him)—and Lucy strolls on his arm through the party, taking place on all three floors of the great Amberson mansion, going up the crowded stairways to the main ballroom, with its orchestra and dancers and lavish buffets. The young couple's conversation (this is their first meeting) is full of oddities, missed connections, and gentle ironies—most of them being Lucy's, at the expense of George, who is revealing to her with almost every word he utters his extraordinary complacency and snobbery. But Lucy's initial disapproval gives way gradually to a mixture of amusement, genuine interest, and final puzzlement. All the while, she never relinquishes his arm.

The others have gathered around a punch bowl, with their long-absent friend Eugene at the center of the attention and cheer. There is the major himself, flanked by his two grown children, Isabel and her brother, the Honorable Jack Amberson (Ray Collins), a U.S. congressman with the shrewd but hearty manner of a deservedly respected public figure. Also Isabel's spinster sister-in-law, Fanny Minafer (Agnes Moorehead). And joining them in his usual recessive and unnoticeable way is Fanny's brother, Wilbur (Don Dillaway), husband to Isabel and father to George.

At the punch bowl, Ambersons and Minafers and one old friend:
Major Amberson (Richard Bennett); Eugene Morgan; Isabel and
her recessive husband, Wilbur (Don Dilloway); his spinster sister,
Fanny (Agnes Moorehead); and Isabel's brother, the Honorable
Jack Amberson (Ray Collins)

The major jovially reminds his son-in-law of the way he "got" Isabel: when
Eugene, the leading contender for her hand years ago, got drunk and dis-
graced himself—an accident with a bass viol. And you can tell from the
delighted way they all react to this (all but Isabel, who blushes) that it is a
favorite family story. Now Fanny interjects that Wilbur not only got
Isabel but "kept her." It's a somewhat dissonant note, typical of Fanny
(who has a long-standing crush on Eugene herself); but the group style and
the atmosphere of powerful conviviality, public and personal, accommodate it easily. They are all so glad to have Eugene back again—even
Wilbur, his erstwhile rival in love, seems to be. And Eugene now declares
gallantly that there is one thing and only one that could make him "for-
give that bass viol" for spoiling his chance with Isabel—and that is his
daughter, Lucy, he says, pronouncing her name just at the moment she
strolls into the foreground of the frame on George's arm, smiling and half-
turning to her father as she passes, at the sound of her name on his lips.
And that half-turn (like so many of the details here) is very beautiful: a

sudden unexpected image for just the way her father's love, down even to its simplest gesture of awareness, sustains her—even in passing, as it were. The open and untroubled tenderness between Eugene and his daughter—their simple pleasure in each other—offers a visible contrast in this sequence to Isabel's anxious love for her son, George. Just as *that* contrasts in turn with the fullness of her radiance toward Eugene, her old love.

But this is just what a big, opulent party *should* be—with fancy dress and open hearts, ritualized but intimate, full of people's excitement at being with each other in a crowd. And the sequence takes its power a lot from the way Welles (the radio veteran) gets his main actors to *sound:* with that peculiar brimming quality, close to *tears* of happiness, that people get in their voices at the top of their feelings. "I judge a scene by how it sounds," he told Peter Bogdanovich. "I think the sound is the key to what makes it right." And the sound in this scene grows steadily more exciting, the whole thing reaching a kind of climax in the dance.

Old friends reunited, Eugene and the Honorable Jack Amberson have been standing on the sidelines of the dance floor together, chatting in front of a huge mirror reflecting the couples whirling by. Now, after a brief pause, the orchestra strikes up a rousing ragtime tune, and the two men walk forward, the backward-moving camera tracking in front of them: Eugene walks briskly, leading the way; "Goodbye," he says to Jack, who is at his elbow, just keeping up. Eugene announces that he has this dance with Isabel—which seems to delight Jack even more: "Eighteen years have passed," he says, "but *have* they?" But then he remembers "poor old Fanny"—has Eugene danced with her yet? "Twice," replies Eugene, smiling and touching Jack's arm in reassurance, then turning to look toward the two who have just entered the moving frame and are now walking beside them, Isabel and her husband, Wilbur. They are all coming forward now on the surge of the music and the heightened feeling, walking together: Isabel at the center, Jack and Eugene on either side leading her onwards, with Wilbur (characteristically) lapsing to the rear. Jack is now almost beside himself with happiness: "By gosh!" he exclaims. "Old times are certainly starting over again!" Eugene replies over his shoulder, drawing Isabel toward the dance floor: "Not a bit! There *aren't* any old times. When times are gone, they aren't old, they're dead—there aren't any times but new times!" And with this he takes Isabel into his arms and into the dance, as the ragtime music rises irresistibly and carries them off, the camera following them.

No times but new times—that's crazy, of course (especially in a movie as lovingly about the old times as this one is), and hopeless. But the craziness only makes it feel more infectious and jubilant; the hopelessness only makes you laugh—on the sudden rush of music and movement and feeling that Welles brings off here. Not only by the way he builds to this dance, but by the way Cotten says his lines, his voice full of that brimmingness I mentioned (he does it better than anyone else), rising with the ragtime music like a singer-actor saying the words that lead into his big song number, leading here instead to his sweeping Isabel onto the floor in his arms on the rollicking ragtime beat. Costello, a very stately woman, looks literally carried away by him and, instead of losing her stateliness, seems to take flight with it—leaning back against his encircling arm behind her, her head and trunk thrown back, drifting and careering on his and the music's movement, as they wheel and rock, the camera receding before them, across the floor among the other couples—and then out of the frame.

But this extraordinary and extended take hasn't ended yet: just as Eugene and Isabel sweep out of the frame in the middle distance, George and Lucy, still strolling, enter it in the foreground. There they stop—the camera stopping with them—and turn to each other, their faces in close-shot profile, with George's partly (and disturbingly) shadowed. The couples on the dance floor go by behind them. Lucy asks him what he's studying in school—"college," he corrects her. Just a lot of "useless guff," he tells her. "Why not take some useful guff?" she asks. Because, he answers, he doesn't want to become someone like the young men he sees around him at this party. "Look at them," he says—and so she does, turning her face into the camera, with an expression of some puzzlement. He explains: "Lawyers, bankers, politicians—what do they ever get out of life?" She is still looking. "What do they know about *real* things?" he says—now *he* is looking at them too, but his face, unlike hers, is half in shadow. "What do they ever *get*?" he says—but this time it sounds like a real question, almost plaintive, as if he'd really like to know (standing in his shadow) the answer to it. Lucy turns now and asks him what he himself wants to be. "A yachtsman," he replies brightly—what else? She gapes at him disbelievingly as the band's ragtime beat rises suddenly on the soundtrack and sends them bouncing and wheeling across the dance floor away from the now stationary camera. Eugene and Isabel dance by again in the foreground, and the scene ends in a dissolve.

George's bow-off line ("A yachtsman") lands like the punch line in a blackout sketch (or a radio scene just before the bridge music rises). Like *Kane, Ambersons* is structured as a series of sketches, or set pieces (see Manny Farber above: "an endless chain of stop effects . . . a succession of fragments"); but *Kane* has a jokier tone. The flippancy here is sort of unexpected, and it makes you feel something you don't altogether want to. The joke on George seems to reduce him to an idle-rich-boy cartoon, contradicting the complexity and richness of sympathy you feel everywhere else in the scene.

But the movie's George *is* something of a cartoon—more than he is in the novel, from which this dialogue is taken verbatim. His snobbery in this scene, like his self-satisfaction, is so crude, so untroubled by experience or intelligence. And the rather dim presence of Tim Holt (the first preview audiences especially objected to *him*) would seem to compound that impression. Some people, like Welles scholar Robert Carringer (who has reconstructed and published Welles's original shooting script), argue that Welles himself should have played George, just as he had two years earlier in his radio adaptation of the novel (*The Mercury Theatre on the Air,* in 1939). Welles claimed he was too old for the role; but Carringer points out that he was only three years older than Holt (twenty-three when he played it), and concludes that Welles was avoiding George because of the character's dangerous closeness to himself—that George's mother fixation, with all its Oedipal reverberations, was too threatening a parallel to that part of Welles's own family history (his feckless father's absence, his powerful mother's dominance) that he was trying both publicly and privately to reinvent, portraying his childhood as "normal," that is, happy and untroubled.

But surely Welles would have avoided in any case any role that called for him to seem boyish: *that* was an image he'd been struggling against almost since he had really been a boy. And while his King Baby looks had never been a help in that struggle, his voice had been. It was one of the richest, fullest, wisest, most purely grown-up voices people had ever heard. And it's that voice that he uses to such marvelous effect in *Ambersons,* commenting and narrating in the words from Tarkington's own narrative ("And now Major Amberson was engaged in the profoundest thinking of his life . . ."). But when he played George on the radio, he used a joke voice, whiny and adenoidal and full of mock-childish inflections, like radio's Henry Aldrich (always impersonated by a grown-up actor), then so popular. It's a terrible performance (it survives on tape), fatally condescending to the character.

How he *might* have played him in the movie, of course we'll never know. In the novel, Tarkington says that George has the air and manner of "a deity"—and you know Welles could have managed that, all right (as he does in *Jane Eyre,* 1943). Just as clearly as someone like Tim Holt couldn't have—*if* it had been asked for. (Holt had a career as a juvenile, but he was never quite successful as a leading man, except in the Poverty Row westerns he soon ended up doing almost exclusively.) What *was* asked for is suggested by the long, unmoving take that shows George at the kitchen table wearing a bib and talking through a mouth stuffed full of his aunt's pie while she quizzes him nervously about his mother and Eugene. This George is not only infantile and intransigent but thick: the hero as slug. So it's a little surprising when the most intelligent other characters call him "interesting," as they repeatedly do: "my interesting nephew," says Jack; and "ever so interesting," says Lucy, even at their first meeting.

But they aren't exactly wrong, either: he *is* interesting—though it may not be immediately clear to you how or why he is. Till you become aware that the movie's asking you to see him in a way that transcends those categories that might allow you to dismiss him, or to see him as *merely* foolish and spoiled and childish and so on. You don't, in any case—and it has to do with that "What do they ever *get?*" question he asks at the ball—the way Holt says it and Welles stages it—with that grain of real puzzlement behind it. Welles is attracted to that puzzlement—and means you to be too. Somewhere, after all, George seems capable of real bafflement, even awe, in the face of things (after all, what *do* they ever get?), in spite of his willfulness.

But that willfulness ("set in his ways," as the old phrase has it) begins to seem monstrous as the movie goes on. Wilbur has died and the widowed Isabel grows closer than ever to Eugene Morgan; there begins to be "talk," and that horrifies George—who then, unknown to his mother, informs a bewildered Eugene that she no longer wishes to see him and slams the Amberson mansion door in his face. Welles then shows George at an upper window, as he watches the shocked and confused Eugene walk away from the house and get into his carriage at the end of the driveway. This virtuoso shot is one of the movie's most *Kane*-like effects: the frame is nearly filled by George's now massive face and head, but as it's reflected, a bit insubstantially, on the window glass through which the camera is looking out at the departing Eugene, who becomes a minuscule moving figure (*quite* substantial) at the bottom corner. It's a stunning image, striking you both with its artfulness and with its revelation: of George's dumb, mad willfulness and the power it gives him, the simple terrible power of that massive "head" of his.

Jack hears about this incident and goes to Isabel to tell her, as gently as he can, what "Georgie" has been up to. Brother and sister confer together in a downstairs parlor behind closed doors, when George appears on the stairway and starts down to interrupt them (presumably). But Fanny—

who first incited George to make trouble and now feels guilty for it—hisses at him from an upstairs landing (the camera tilting upward to show her leaning over the railing) and hurries down to stop him on the stairs. "Jack's telling Isabel the whole thing, and you stay here and let him tell her!" And so they squabble on the stairway, in one of the movie's most harrowing scenes. "It's *indecent!*" cries Fanny at one point (referring to their quarreling like this—"like squabbling outside an operating room!"). And everything that Welles can contrive here makes you feel the force and rightness of the word: the unsettling shadows and low angles, the ominous low music, the vertiginous levels of the staircase, and, most of all, Fanny herself—in all her pain and remorse, her shrill-seagull voice almost splitting apart with hysteria (she is *trying* to whisper), clutching and pulling at George ("You let go of me!" "I *won't*—you come back here and let them alone!") as he stands above her in profile, implacable, snub-nosed, almost fetal, like some sinister idol. "Leave her *alone!*" cries Fanny, out of a suffering that now comprehends Isabel as well as herself. George may be no more than the "young fool boy" he otherwise seems (as Eugene calls him in a scene from the ball that was cut), but his willfulness, his stubborn refusal of knowledge and sympathy ("a boy with the pride of Satan," Eugene also says of him), has a moral weight that this scene registers as almost literally unbearable.

But he's not a villain. He turns out—if too late to undo the suffering he's inflicted on his mother and Eugene—to be quite a decent, even selfless person, once he's had his "comeuppance" (as Welles's narrating voice calls it), and we watch him on his knees, from a distance and in shadow, praying for forgiveness. If George is a sort of monster before that, he is a mundane and familiar one—obsessed and selfish and trapped (like most of us) inside his own (capacious) head. And the film is clearly more intent on offering that perspective on him than it is on taking us *inside* that head. For Welles, that would almost have been a presumption; but it was exactly his refusal to do that which so puzzled his audience. There are, for example, *none* of the expected Freudian glosses (even a Shakespeare character on most occasions gets those) on George's obsession with his mother or on hers with him. The movie feels, even looks, like it *should* be a "psychological melodrama"—but it's not. Just as that quarrel on the staircase looks like it ought to be about a murder, at the least, instead of a threat to intrude on someone else's private conversation.

RKO must have expected, or at least hoped, that Welles would give them a more conventional sort of movie this time. The novel, after all, had been a 1918 Pulitzer Prize winner, in the always popular genre of the fam-

On the Amberson stairway: Tim Holt below, Agnes Moorehead above—
and about to come down

ily saga, by a famous and still popular writer. And Welles's screenplay was
not only a faithful rendering of the book (except for his final scene) but an
almost verbatim one. And yet the movie that resulted was even more off-
putting to audiences than *Kane* had been.

There were those now famous and disastrous previews—especially the
first one, in Pomona, when Welles himself was already in South America,
shooting an even more ill-fated project (*It's All True*). Studio head George
Schaefer sent him the bad news by urgent special delivery:

> In my 28 years in the business, I have never been present in a theatre
> where the audience acted in such a manner. They laughed at the
> wrong places, talked at the picture, kidded it, and did everything that
> you can possibly imagine. I don't have to tell you how I suffered, espe-
> cially in the realization that we have over $1,000,000 tied up . . . I
> queried many of those present and they all seemed to feel that the
> party who made the picture was trying to be "arty," was out for cam-
> era angles, lights and shadows, and as a matter of fact, one remarked
> that "The man who made that picture was camera crazy."

Welles's original version had been over two hours long, but even his partisans at the studio (his friend Joe Cotten among them) judged the movie unplayable at that length. So the running time at Pomona had become 110 minutes. But after the response *there,* it was again re-edited, with scenes radically rearranged, for the second preview at Pasadena, where it became somewhat longer again (117 minutes)—but fared not much better with the audience. Finally the studio removed the picture from the control of Welles and his people altogether and recut it themselves, reshooting some scenes and adding an entirely new ending (the present one), bringing the whole thing down to just 88 minutes. As a result, more than forty minutes of Welles's original movie was eliminated and lost. "They destroyed *The Magnificent Ambersons,*" Welles would later say (more than once), "and the picture destroyed me."

By the time this final studio version (now the only one we have) reached theatre screens in 1942, it was playing on double bills with *Mexican Spitfire Sees a Ghost,* the studio having given up on it ahead of time. They were wrong, of course; but it seems unlikely the general audience of the time could have warmed to the movie much more than those preview audiences had—less because it seemed arty than because it seemed, on top of *that,* sort of pointless. *Citizen Kane,* after all, had announced itself from its opening shots as something riddling and unorthodox. Whereas *Ambersons* was a conventional linear narrative telling a conventionally absorbing story of love and death and family fortunes—the stuff of the *most* popular movies of all, of *Gone With the Wind* and *The Godfather.* But as one of Welles's more unsympathetic early biographers (Charles Higham) observed about it, the movie has "no clear emotional binding thread," no character "to identify with," no character development except in "hectic glimpses" (cf. Manny Farber on *Kane,* above). Once again, the familiar accusation: audiences might be "intrigued" by *Ambersons,* but not "moved." Welles, it seemed, had made another "cold" movie—and this time, a depressing one as well (in spite of the studio's happy ending), without even the amusements and razzle-dazzle and wisecracking exuberance of his first one.

But far from being a cold movie, *Ambersons* is an extraordinarily fond and generous-hearted one. It's the atmosphere of overarching benignity, its mixture of unsparing shrewdness and tenderness toward its characters, that gives the movie its feeling of depth and amplitude, that binds together all those "hectic glimpses." But Welles had done the same thing with the people in his movie this time as he'd done with those in *Kane*— i.e., kept us at a distance. That's what Truffaut was talking about when he described Welles's movies as "anti-psychological."

Take, for example, the celebrated "answer" to the riddle of Rosebud in *Kane.* Pauline Kael, happily susceptible though she is to most of that movie's devices, resists that one—calling the sled revelation at the end "phony" and "banal." People who *like* it, she says, "go for the idea that Rosebud represents lost maternal bliss and somehow symbolizes Kane's loss of the power to love and be loved." For that matter, even Welles himself disdained it later on, and even managed at one point to attribute the whole thing to Mankiewicz (answering, when asked about the latter's contributions to the script: "Everything pertaining to Rosebud belongs to him"). He was less mischievous in his later (1969) account of it, and probably more honest. "We were desperate," he said, and needed a gimmick; Rosebud "was the only way we could find to get off." "It's a bit corny," he added, "it manages to work but I'm still not too crazy about it."

The line he took about it in 1941, when the movie opened, was, of course, very different. In a press statement that year he sounded exactly like one of those "lost maternal bliss" interpreters that Kael would later describe. "In [Kane's] subconscious," said Welles, the sled "represented the simplicity, the comfort, above all the lack of responsibility in his [childhood] home, and also it stood for his mother's love . . ." Because Kane "has never made what is known as 'transference' from his mother. Hence his failure with his wives." And so on.

You suppose he was kidding, or at least having some fun seeing the newspeople write that stuff down. And most of all at the time, he was after stories to throw them off the Hearst track that had caused him and his movie so many problems, ways to persuade people that Kane was a deeply conceived *original* creation. And they always liked that sort of what-it-*really*-means explanation—just as we still do ("Wasn't the symbolism terrific?" I recently heard someone say coming out of Ang Lee's *The Ice Storm*).

But if Rosebud does manage to work, as Welles concedes about it, it's not, I think, because it conveys "lost maternal bliss" or "Kane's loss of the power to love," let alone his failure to make "what is known as 'transference,' " but rather because the surprise feels so right when it comes, seeming to come out of the logic and feeling of the movie itself. Kael is right, it seems to me, when she objects to the reporter Thompson's final speech in Kane's mansion—when he tells Raymond, the butler, that it probably doesn't matter that he's failed to identify Rosebud, because "no word can explain a man's life." You really do wince at that line, but less, I think, because it sounds like a cop-out (as it does to Kael) than because it's telling you something you don't really need to be told by now—namely, that

Kane is unknowable. The closer we get to him, the more remote he becomes; the more we learn about him, the more finally mysterious he seems, even to escaping the personal relations that have preoccupied Thompson's search. Just as the movie itself has finally escaped them. As has been widely noted, *Kane* is not a "humanistic" sort of film: unlike *Ambersons,* it really *is* "cold." But more even than that: there is something at its heart that calls *personal* relations into question.

When Thompson interviews Kane's lawyer and friend Bernstein (Everett Sloane), the latter suggests to the reporter that Rosebud might have been "some girl." Is it really likely, responds Thompson, though respectfully, that "Mr. Kane could have met some girl casually" and then remember her "some fifty years later, on his deathbed?" Bernstein, rather imperial behind his desk, replies—as Welles's camera tracks slowly in on him: "Well, you're pretty young, Mr.—er—Mr. Thompson. A fellow will remember a lot of things you wouldn't think he'd remember . . . You take me. One day back in 1896, I was crossing over to Jersey on the ferry, and as we pulled out, there was another ferry pulling in, and on it there was a girl waiting to get off. A white dress she had on. She was carrying a white parasol. I only saw her for one second. She didn't see me at all, but I bet a month hasn't gone by since, that I haven't thought of that girl . . ."

This was his favorite scene, Welles told Bogdanovich in 1976—simply "the best thing in the movie." And Mankiewicz had been its sole author, he said: "That was all Mank." Perhaps so—but it's one of those scenes that now seems to us definitively and irreducibly Welles's. It couldn't easily evoke, or even occur in, a movie by anyone else.

For me, it's not lost mother love or remembered innocence or other such plausible generalities, not even what we saw early on of Kane's boyhood, that the Rosebud ending evokes most strongly and inevitably: rather, it's this story of Bernstein's about this girl on the ferry whom he never knew or saw again or forgot. The kind of memory, like Kane's Rosebud, that we all have, negligible but inexpungible: the kind that seems to "make no sense," and that makes up much of our conscious lives. A memory that's important, even intelligible sometimes, to *us*—but being incommunicable in the end (who cares anyway?), only confirms our final aloneness. And it's that isolation that Welles is finally describing in these films. The *real* noir element—like the noir heroine herself, both appalling and seductive at once.

That's the theme he had ended his *Ambersons* movie on—with Eugene visiting Fanny in an old people's boardinghouse, and both of them talking past one another out of their separate isolations, in a relation no longer per-

The lost final sequence of Welles's *Ambersons:* Eugene visits Fanny
at her boardinghouse.

sonal in any but the most automatic ways. This was the only sequence in
his movie and screenplay (the script and some stills survive) that had no
basis in the novel, was even a radical departure from it—the only sequence
that was solely Welles's own. But it was too grim, too disturbing for the
studio, and they trashed it, refilming and replacing it with a more conventionally upbeat one of their own—it was their most damaging mutilation.
And their ending, ironically, was close to the novel's (Tarkington, after all,
was a more successful popular artist than Welles ever could have been).

One of the great pleasures of Welles's final Hollywood film, *Touch of
Evil,* when it first came out (and almost as quickly disappeared) in 1958
was in how smart it seemed, especially near the end of *that* movie decade,
when noir was already dying out, and particularly the kind of noir Welles
made, in his black-and-white baroque style, turning nightmare into high
spirits and playfulness. It reminded you forcefully of his *The Lady from
Shanghai* ten years before, that other thriller with spectacular set pieces
that he seems to have made up from almost nothing to start—and turned
into box-office poison. But *Touch of Evil* was even more outrageous in some
ways (and even more of a box-office flop), more baroque and virtuosic,

more jokily self-referential—full of mostly disguised and unbilled star turns by Welles's friends, producing little who-*was*-that? jolts in the audience. Joe Cotten as the coroner was easy to spot, in spite of a Fuller Brush mustache (the unmistakable voice); so was Mercedes McCambridge, as a menacing leather-clad gang leader (the voice again)—both of them unbilled. And there was Zsa Zsa Gabor, billed, as a strip-joint hostess (because the movie's producer, Al Zugsmith, wanted a friend of *his* to be in it too, once the guest-star game got going during shooting). And then there was Dennis Weaver's wild comic turn as a lunatic motel night clerk (a Shakespearean fool, Welles later called him), registering all the madness and horror the movie itself means to convey—and quite relentlessly does.

And yet doesn't, too. The horror feels less real, though even more emphatic, than *Psycho*'s, by *another* jokester: more Guignol than haunted-house. Its peak is reached in the episode of Welles strangling a man in a fleabag hotel room, first pulling him down from the wall he's been trying to climb, then leaving him behind so the drugged Janet Leigh can wake up next to the corpse's engorged tongue and bugged-out eyes. The sequence is shocking and thrilling, it's so lurid and nerve-jangling (helped by the music and cutting) and over-the-top. But it's horrifying in a way you don't take quite seriously (as on some level you do take the shower scene in *Psycho*).

The movie stars Welles himself, as Sheriff Hank Quinlan, a bully and a racist, a border-town cop who has a history of flouting the law he also enforces by planting fake evidence on the people he "knows" to be guilty of murder (and he's usually right). In the course of the movie he becomes a murderer himself, attempting to frame the straight-arrow honeymooners, Mexican DA Mike Vargas (Charlton Heston) and his wife, Susie (Janet Leigh), for the killing of a local petty gangster named Grandi (Akim Tamiroff)—the corpse in the hotel room.

Quinlan is a bad man; but he has, like everyone, his reasons. We learn about them as the movie goes on: his battle with alcoholism, his overweening professional pride. But most important and most exculpatory of all is his undying anguish over his brutally murdered wife, done in by someone he now calls "the last killer that ever got out of my hands." He's been framing the rest of them ever since. "Drunk and crazy as you were when you strangled him," says his sidekick, Menzies (Joseph Calleia), after discovering that Quinlan has murdered Grandi, "I guess you were somehow thinking of your wife, the way *she* was strangled." "I'm *always* thinking of her, drunk or sober," growls Quinlan. "What else is there to think about?"

Anyway, you don't exactly believe all that, or *dis*believe it. It's only "motivation"—not the sort of thing this movie makes you feel is very urgent. But the fact is, Welles insisted in his 1958 interview with *Cahiers,* that Quinlan, in *spite* of his "detestable" beliefs and actions, "has a heart." Maybe so, but what the movie makes you feel about him is mostly something else. In spite of all the gestures toward "humanizing" him that are present in the dialogue, the tendency of the movie's imagery is in the opposite direction: making him look (and feel) more monstrous, more grotesque and inhuman, as it goes on.

His huge face looks more like something on a chalk cliffside than living flesh: the only life it shows (apart from some sweat now and then) is in the mean, rheumy little eyes. To his own 270 pounds, Welles added 60 pounds of body padding as well as false jowls and a Doonesbury nose. When Quinlan first appears, arriving at the scene of the opening explosion, he doesn't so much "get out" of his car as totter and bulge from it, until he's onto the ground—where the camera seems to be too, looking up at him. He walks with a cane ("my game leg"), heaving his great bulk along with its aid across the yawning black spaces of the moldering Mexican border town (really Venice, California). But this impairment only makes the creature go faster, it seems: the others (even athletic-looking Vargas) almost have to run to keep up with him; and cameraman Russell Metty's wide-angle deep-focus photography makes even the act of crossing a street look preternaturally swift and imposing, even momentous. Quinlan is a nightmare figure. And even among the other such figures who populate the movie—the jittering Grandi with his constantly slipping toupee, the motel night clerk with his little dance of terror, the lesbian tough with her Groucho eyebrows ("Lemme stay—I wanta watch"), et al.—Quinlan stands out, if only by being bigger, taller, and fatter than any of them.

But nothing in the movie quite matches the visual hyperbole of his death scene—when he gets gunned down (while trying to shoot Vargas) by his dying partner, Menzies, and falls backward into the sludge and garbage of a polluted canal, floating away on its surface. The movie may *tell* us about his murdered wife and blighted ambition and so on, but what it *shows* us is more like this: a human blimp drifting dreamily and terribly on a pool of slime. Now *that's* an image that's hard to compete with.

And even when Welles *seems* to be offering a more conventional characterization of Quinlan, the effect is in fact of something else, more unexpected but unmistakably Wellesian. For one wonderful example: the scene where the sheriff and his men are searching the apartment of the murdered man's daughter, Marcia Linnekar (Joanna Moore). Vargas is there, too, looking on rather suspiciously, as Quinlan is third-degreeing the man who has become his favorite suspect, Marcia's Mexican lover, Sanchez (Victor Milan). But Quinlan has also sent one of his men out to get him some coffee—who now arrives, carrying a covered paper cup. "Oh, there's my coffee," says Quinlan, interrupting his interrogation of Sanchez, taking the cup in his hand, standing in an entranceway between rooms, but then turning in alarm and looking offscreen right, where the cop who brought the coffee has just exited the frame. "Dincha bring me any *doughnuts?*" says Quinlan, his voice breaking slightly on that last word—as if, you know, really . . . doughnuts were too much to *ask* for? And not only *that:* "Or *sweet* rolls?" he says, in an even more plaintive voice, the incredulity growing with his awareness. And the hesitation, just a beat or two, before "sweet rolls" is specially nice, letting you know that the hunger the man is speaking out of here is really—or almost—too much to name. No—what it *is,* it's that life (that sucker!) has done it to you again: brought you coffee without doughnuts, or *even* sweet rolls. It's unbearable. But then "life," as it's called, goes on: he resumes his accustomed bullying persona, hectoring the now terrified Sanchez, wising off to the ever moralizing Vargas, and so forth. He even drinks the coffee. But that escaped sound of heartbreak still lingers in your head.

It's a "characterizing" moment, of course (reflecting comically on Quinlan's weight, his infantilism, his being an ex-drinker on the wagon, though soon to fall off, and so on); but like other such moments in Welles's movies—like Bernstein's speech about the girl on the ferry—it has a generalizing force that outstrips the specific ones, seeming almost to detach itself from the character, to be less in the end about explaining or describing than recognizing him in some inspired, unexpected way: the way a single magical image or turn of phrase can bring a poem to life for you. It's the sort of coup that prompted Truffaut to describe Welles as a lyric artist attempting to be a narrative one—a poet trying to write prose, and failing. As he does in this movie's occasional feeble attempts to "motivate" its characters ("How can I leave here until my wife's name is clean? Clean!" cries Vargas, just when the movie needs him to stay and audiotape Quinlan) or to impose coherence on its own convoluted action—which is at its most persuasive precisely when it's most disorienting.*

But it's the movie's pervasive feeling of semi-seriousness (another thing

---

*The much clarified, recently restored version greatly diminishes its power, it seems to me. The original studio cut, however much Welles may have resented it, is the one (there have been several over the years) that works best.

it shares with *Lady from Shanghai*) that has impelled some people to describe it as camp. And among the reasons for calling it that, none seems stronger than "guest star" (billed) Marlene Dietrich's utterly improbable appearance as Tanya (pronounced "Tanna" in the film), a Gypsy fortuneteller-cum-whore, running a cozy one-woman bordello on the Mexican border, in a black wig and Gypsy costume—which she had retrieved for the occasion, according to Welles, from the Paramount warehouse (it was left over from her postwar "comeback" film, *Golden Earrings,* ten years before). And she appears here, of course, bearing with her for the audience a whole extraordinary movie career, then nearing its end, as well as a highly public friendship with Welles himself (he used to saw her in half for the troops during the war). Tanya was an almost minuscule role (by star standards), and yet Dietrich would say, and repeat, till the end of her life that it was the best thing she'd ever done: "I've never been as good as I was in that little teensy part."

Yet it was all a kind of afterthought: one old friend to another ("You can't *know* how close we were," Welles said to Bogdanovich), written for her by Welles only after she'd told him she'd do it ("We were well along before I even thought it up," Welles said) and filmed in a single night, sunset to sunup, on the California location. And Welles was as effusive about the result as Dietrich. As he said to Bogdanovich: "I think all that Dietrich part of it is as good as anything I've ever done in movies . . . Really, Marlene was extraordinary in that. She really was the Super-Marlene. Everything she has ever been was in that little house for about four minutes there."

It all begins magically—outside the little house. After the noise and neon of Zsa Zsa Gabor's strip club, Sheriff Quinlan and his crowd of cops and cronies have stepped outside into darkness and quiet, into the center of an empty wind-whipped square, with litter flying in the air around them, and the dim far-off sound of a Pianola. "Huh?" says Quinlan, straining to hear. Then, turning to the camera as the sound rises: "Tanya's still . . . open for business?" he says to himself, as realization dawns, looking offscreen toward the house, then coming forward, toward the sound of the Pianola—it's one of those memorably eccentric line readings (the rhythmic pause after "still") that Welles the actor will often give to a nostalgic meaning. Tanya is from Quinlan's past. And just as important—or even more so—from ours too.

He goes up onto her porch, as a crumpled paper flies in over his shoulder ahead of him, under the fretwork arch outlined in the dark above his head. He goes inside the low-ceilinged house, into the tacky, cluttered,

Touch of Evil: Quinlan (Welles), hearing the Pianola,
comes toward it and Tanya's porch.

cozy-looking parlor, with its fringed lampshades and framed mementoes
and diffused light. Dietrich, in her motley Gypsy costume and black hair,
first appears in the background of his point-of-view shot, emerging out of
a doorway to an inner room. Then, in a close shot, she is standing in the
near doorway and looking at him—smoking a cheroot, exhaling a cloud of
smoke, giving him her unnerving fixed gaze (does Dietrich ever blink?),
the one that tells you that you have her full attention but *never* tells you
quite what she's attending *to.* "We're closed," she says at length, still staring (the two of them are never—except once very fleetingly—together in
the same shot), while Quinlan in close-up stands between hanging lampshades and looks back at her with a sort of querying roguishness. Which
gets no response. She goes out again and comes back carrying a pot. "You
been cookin' at this hour?" he asks. "Just cleanin' up," she answers indif-
ferently. His close-up again: "Have you forgotten your old friend?" he asks.
This doesn't do it, either: "I told you we were closed," she says. "I'm Hank
Quinlan." The gaze she turns on him now is wide-eyed and unambiguous.
She looks him up and down, then says, gravely: "I didn't recognize you."
She turns to go: "You should lay off those candy bars," she says. "It's either

the candy or the hooch," he replies—and she turns back to look at him again. "I must say," he says, "I wish it was your chili I was gettin' fat on . . . Anyway *you're* sure lookin' good." "You're a mess, honey," she replies matter-of-factly.

And the audience laughter that invariably greets this line—as well as "lay off those candy bars"—is partly made of relief. She's said it, and that means Welles himself has said it, and so gotten *us* off the hook, as it were. But not entirely. Because Welles's Quinlan seems not just a grotesque sort of character turn but a projection of a powerful self-disgust, and that makes you (as it's meant to) uneasy. Tanya and Quinlan trade a few more risqué-nostalgic observations—about her Pianola, and again her chili ("It may be too hot for you"). But she knows nothing about the explosion at the border crossing that he's investigating, and he departs, reluctantly—going back to the rest of the movie, and its plot.

When he returns to Tanya's place at the movie's end, his own situation has become desperate, with Vargas now the hunter on his trail and getting near the end of it. Quinlan sits alone in Tanya's cluttered, overstuffed parlor, getting drunk, while the Pianola (a close-up of it here, with a tilted framing) plays loudly. Tanya is at a table in the other room, doing her accounts, we learn, with her tarot cards next to the ledgers she's working on. Quinlan staggers in, lurching forward with his great bulk and scattering the cards with his hand, demanding that she read his future for him. Then a pause: "You haven't got any," she says, looking up at him, in a tilted-frame close shot of almost stunning gravity and beauty. "*Huh? Whatta ya mean?*" he demands. "Your future's all used up," she says slowly, drawlingly. Then, compassionately: "Why don't you go home?" Tanya's open compassion for him here is a new note in this film, and it's moving. Of course, Hank should go "home"—whatever that is to him (there's been mention of a chicken ranch): it's where you want to *be* when you're finally at the end of things.

But Quinlan doesn't do that. Instead he goes outside with Menzies, who has been wired by Vargas to get the goods on him. And the two men, with Vargas following surreptitiously, go out into the night landscape with its chiaroscuro of oil derricks and junk piles and crumbling bridges arching over sludge-filled canals: the place where Quinlan gets killed by Menzies, who does it to keep him from killing Vargas. (Menzies too dies—shot by Quinlan.)

Tanya—apparently having heard these shots—runs out of the night to the scene, calling "Hank!" as she passes the open car where Vargas and Susie, reunited, are embracing, just before leaving the movie altogether

"Your future's all used up": Tanya (Marlene Dietrich) among her ledgers and tarot cards. Quinlan—coming toward her again—is the shadow at right.

("I'm taking you home," says Vargas, "—*home!*"). Tanya arrives just after Quinlan has died, in time to see him floating on the canal. Vargas's lawyer friend Schwartz (Mort Mills) has also arrived and stands next to her in a two-shot that has them both in three-quarters-face looking off left, at the canal (presumably) and Quinlan's grotesque remains. "Isn't someone going to come and . . . take him away?" asks Tanya, with just the suggestion of a shudder in her voice. Soon, replies Schwartz. Then this—as they stand looking off—

SCHWARTZ: . . . You really liked him, didn't you?
TANYA: The cop did. The one who killed him. He loved him.
SCHWARTZ: Well, Hank was a great detective all right.
TANYA: And a lousy cop.
SCHWARTZ [*smiles and turns toward her*]: Is that all you have to say for him?
TANYA [*still looking left, as the Pianola music rises on the soundtrack*]: . . . He was some kind of a man. [*After a pause:*] What does it matter what you say about people? [*She turns toward the right and leaves the frame.*]

This famous (or infamous) valedictory speech of Tanya's has a curious effect. People like me who find it moving are always going to be startled when an audience, as it often will, reacts to it with laughter. But it's easy to understand why people do. The scene is an ambitious one—raising, even changing, the stakes in the game we took the movie to be playing with us up to now. Welles scholar Tony Comito, for example, speaks of the line's "portentous emptiness," but then suggests that that may be "part of the joke" (Welles's, that is), adding parenthetically that much "remains to be discovered about the effectiveness of such famously 'awful lines.' " (So it got to him too.) Pauline Kael calls it (after—significantly—misquoting it: i.e., "What can you say about anybody? He was some kind of a man . . .") "either one of the the worst lines ever written or a parody of bad writing—the funeral scene in *Death of a Salesman*."

But the impact of Tanya's line seems to me almost the opposite of *Death of a Salesman*'s bad writing, with all its cringe-inducing sentimentality about the Little Guy ("out there on a smile and a shoeshine," etc.)—itself not far from Dore Schary's version of it. For one thing, Quinlan is no Little Guy: he's a bad and awful one. And the power of Tanya's "eulogy" for him comes from a complex of meanings and effects, of more or less importance. For example, it doesn't hurt exactly (it wipes *me* out) that the Pianola sound, with all its gathered nostalgic-romantic reverberance, starts up on the soundtrack for the final time under Tanya's "some kind of a man" words. Or that the speech itself takes us by surprise, and yet (like the Rosebud revelation) feels entirely right (the next surprise) when it comes, making the rest of the movie—for me—fall into place behind it. Or that Dietrich says these words so movingly, combining a sort of Mother Courage–style indomitability with an almost infinitely pained tenderness. "I think I never said a line as well," she said years later—and she had reason to feel that way. If nothing else, it's certainly Tanya's tenderest moment in the movie, except for the time she asks Hank why he doesn't go home. But *that* was "only personal," as Gatsby says. This isn't.

And it's surprising as well because it's an emotional note that would seem to be mostly beyond the range of this show-off, smart-ass, campy movie; but also *not* surprising, because it shows the kind of beneficence that has been lurking in the wings all along, you realize—the kind that's been implicit in the movie's god's-eye view of character and event. Tanya's openness "for business," her sexual availability and largesse, are clearly and plainly quite impersonal matters. So finally is her affection for Quinlan— something less like "love" than a clear-eyed, all-embracing sorrow. The character is Dietrich, after all, and could be nobody else. Dietrich in excelsis: the "Super-Marlene," as Welles called her—near the end and at the peak of her odd and remarkable career as a star, and as a fixture of our moviegoing lives and memories. What she is (it's clearer than ever now) is an archetype of the noir woman, and an antithesis—in benign form—of all the Susies and Janets, the Debbies and Shirleys. The noir heroine as seeress-Gypsy-fortuneteller: she knows (as the Susies do not) about fatality.

In interviews Welles tended to defend Quinlan: in spite of his "detestable" character, he said, "I have to like him." Why? "Because he loves Marlene Dietrich . . ." was the answer—one that might surprise you until you stop to think about it, that loving the "Super-Marlene" might not be *altogether* such an easy matter. Tanya is a truth teller ("Your future's all used up"), even in her way a humorist ("You're a mess, honey")—unlike, you suppose, the late, much-beloved Mrs. Quinlan, whose death ("What else is there to think about?") has been offered in sentimental exculpation of both Quinlan's crimes and his weight. But it's his love for Dietrich, in all her implacability, that we really believe in.

In this final scene it's almost less what Tanya says than what she *declines* to say that makes the point: namely, her steady and repeated rejection of Schwartz's invitation to be fondly reminiscent ("You really liked him, didn't you?"), even sentimental ("Is that all you have to say for him?")—her refusal to offer anything remotely *like* what Mrs. Loman says over Willy's grave, for example.

After all, what *does* it matter what you say about people then? Tanya's question is unanswerable. Quinlan, like Kane, has escaped all the "answers." But the point is strong enough for Dietrich to steal the movie with it, here at the end—saying "Adios" to Schwartz and to the camera, walking slowly away, down the empty highway and into the darkness, to the ever more stirring sound of the Pianola. So *that's* where we've been going, is what you feel then (unless you feel like laughing, I suppose). All the hyped-up technique and headlong violence and parade of human grotesques, all of it moving toward just the kind of odd serenity behind a flamboyant facade that Dietrich herself has always embodied for us, with her peculiarly detached sort of tenderness and concern. Roughly the same stance that Welles the moviemaker has aspired to—in his attempts, however partial they may finally be doomed to be, to get beyond the merely personal, the simply "psychological."

Twenty

JOHNNY GUITAR

Like Welles and Hitchcock, Nick Ray loved tour-de-force set pieces. And one of his best is in *Johnny Guitar* (1954)—the big romantic scene, nearly halfway into the movie, between the two leads, Joan Crawford and Sterling Hayden. Like the piano bar scene of *In a Lonely Place* (see pp. 148–150), it has the structure and feel of a song number—though this time without a song.

First, the "verse." Vienna (Crawford) is the boss of a big empty saloon and gambling joint built into the side of a red rock hill on a big empty desert (she's expecting the railroad to come through and make her rich). It's the middle of the night and she can't sleep. The sequence begins as she comes down the stairs from her upstairs bedroom to the barroom below, wearing a crimson nightdress and a dark purple cape. She pauses to give an idle spin to one of her roulette wheels, then heads toward the kitchen. Cut to the kitchen interior: showing Johnny (Hayden) there, slumped in a chair by the cook-stove, staring into his whiskey. He's come back to her after a five-year absence, but he hasn't gotten the reception he clearly hoped for, so now he is brooding and boozing alone. As we hear her footsteps approaching, the camera moves slowly in on him. It stops when she appears in the serving window just behind and to the right above him; she leans forward on her arms on the ledge, like a portrait on the wall. She looks at him from there; he looks at his whiskey.

And even for this artful movie, it's an artfully composed shot: the frame-within-a-frame, the subtle shadowing of rich autumnal colors, of copper pots (hanging from the stove's tin roof) and suede (his jacket) and deep red (her nightdress), the whole effect anchored by and centered in the wasted faces of the two stars, in the collapsed lines of Hayden's mouth, in the grim set of Crawford's, looking inward at their own bitterness even when they're looking out. And so they begin to talk, idly—Crawford in her frame, Hayden below in his slump—and with their usual (up to now) testy inflections, about not sleeping and bad dreams and whether drinking

Johnny Guitar: Johnny (Sterling Hayden) broods and Vienna
(Joan Crawford) repines—neither of them can sleep.

really helps (he says yes, she says no), while the string section on the soundtrack noodles along dreamily under the voices (Victor Young's score).

Now the "chorus." You know it's arrived when you hear—as it enters softly on the soundtrack—the movie's lyrical, epically melancholy big tune (borrowed from Granados) with its guitar obbligato, its yearning rubato rise and fall. As Johnny says, slowly and mournfully, still staring into his whiskey: "How many men have you forgotten?" like the opening of a ceremony. She doesn't answer at first. She leaves the window and enters the kitchen through the swinging half-door beside it, appearing in front of him, leaning with her hip against a countertop and looking down at him. Then replies solemnly: "As many women"—a beat or two—"as you've remembered." And you know you're at the movies *now . . .* This exchange doesn't exactly make sense (why should she forget and he remember; why not the other way around? And would it make any difference?), but that won't bother you if you recognize the opening notes of an aria, the familiar movie sound of relaxing into rapture. From this point on, the filmmaking becomes so kinetic and exhilarated that you're swept along regardless. The talk is important, of course, but more like lyrics, closer to song than sense.

Johnny leaps to his feet. "Don't go away!" he says, cornering her. "I haven't moved," she replies coldly. Looking up at him with her laserlike stare, she is partly in shadow now, a half-lighting that highlights the fierce eyes and crimson-slash mouth, as well as the low-cut bodice. He towers above her (Crawford hardly comes up to his shoulder), and he looks as a result all the more vulnerable and outmatched. What he wants from her now, he says, is for her to tell him "something nice." "Lie to me," he says, "tell me all these years you've waited." "All these years I've waited," she repeats, mockingly—and her anger grows as he goes on ("Tell me you'da died if I hadn't come back," and so on)—until she's had enough and smashes the whiskey glass out of his hand, shattering it against the wall. He thinks *he* had it rough? What about her? She offers to tell him how she made her money while he was away, but he won't let her. "For every board, plank, and *beam* in this place . . . ," she chants dolefully, as she strides rhythmically to the left and looks up and around at the "place," the camera panning with her, while Johnny continues to protest against hearing. "You can't shut me up, Johnny—not anymore," she says, but falteringly, as if she were relenting a bit, and on the brink of tears. She is framed now, in her red-and-purple deshabille, in front of the blue-brown wood of an enormous old wine barrel behind her in the shadow, the right backdrop for the sound of old sorrows. "Once I would have crawled at your feet to be near you," she says, with breaking voice; then turns, the music on the soundtrack swelling mournfully, into a reverse shot, coming urgently forward into the camera, then stopping, Johnny now behind her. "I searched for you in every man I met," as her tears brim and the music rises.

That's enough encouragement for Johnny. "Look, Vienna," he says, with a sudden if rather determined ebullience, "you just said you had a bad dream. We both did, but it's all over!" And on another upsurge of the music, he pulls her by the hand through the swinging doors, into the big outer room, the camera following, tracking backwards just above and ahead of them as they go down along the bar, Johnny talking her along all the way: they are back at the Aurora Hotel, he says, they're having a drink, they're celebrating, the band is playing, they're getting married. Until they get to the end of the bar's length ("So *laugh*, Vienna—and be happy") and he throws her out, as a dancer does with his partner, and propels her forward into a close-up: "It's your wedding day!" On this he pulls her back, toward himself—as she comes forward (toward us) and then halts and turns, into a reverse shot over his shoulder. And Ray cuts on the exact moment of her turning, on the transformation in her face from alarm and confusion to joy and relief as she rises radiantly into Hayden's arms. "I *have* waited for you, Johnny," she says." What *kept* you so long?" Kiss and fade-out.

It has almost the same sort of impact as the end of a great Astaire-Rogers dance does—of a triumphant romanticism. But here it's less the impact of the "dancing," such as it is, than of the filmmaking—and the way these two rather lugubrious people are swept up in it, even transformed by it, by its brio and exhilaration. *They* are also what give it poignancy, of course; and even Crawford in this movie, as absurdly imperious as ever, is unexpectedly moving. They are, in their perverse sort of way, a deeply convincing couple—as old lovers, meeting after long and bitter separation. There is something weak and soft and yielding in Hayden's very attractive male presence, something finally and determinedly evasive—just the sort of thing to baffle and outrage Crawford's fierce intentionality, her steel-trap resolve and decisiveness. And because of that, we can believe in their wanting each other very much—and also in their not getting what they want, not easily anyway. Equally believable is the energy of exhaustion that brings them together at last.

Johnny Guitar is known by now as a famously crazy movie. Not that it didn't seem loony at the time. "This preposterous Western," as Gavin Lambert described it in 1954, with its air of "fascinating, portentous lunacy," is full of excesses of every variety: outsize performances, ludicrous formulaic situations and dialogue, outrageous action—including a famous gender-bending gunfight at the end, between the two leading women. It all seemed at the time like one of those aberrations in mainstream moviemaking (who let this one escape?) that were happening more and more with the decline and disarray of the studios. Still, it was—to most people's surprise (including Ray's)—a hit. "The atrocity *Johnny Guitar* is finished and released," Ray wrote to his close friend Hanna Axmann, "to dreadful reviews and great financial success. Nausea was my reward . . ." But not his only one: it was the receipts, not the reviews, that impressed the suits at Warner Bros., the ones who would soon okay his *Rebel Without a Cause*.

And the French, as you might expect, adored it. The "preposterous Western" would become for them the locus classicus of Ray's cinematic genius. In Godard's *Pierrot le Fou* (1965), for example, the Belmondo hero tells his wife he's let their maid off three times that week just because she was seeing *Johnny Guitar* over and over again and so "getting the right education." And soon, it would seem—very soon—even Ray himself was

An atmosphere of "portentous lunacy" (Gavin Lambert): Vienna,
in her gunbelt, is flanked on the right by the "Dancing Kid"
(Scott Brady), on the left by the kid named Turkey (Ben Cooper).

persuaded, and began to talk about "the atrocity" with some of the same
enthusiasm its European admirers did. In spite of the torture—excessive
even by his standards—that it had been to shoot it, owing mainly to Crawford, its mad, tippling star.

Even though her long career was in decline, Crawford was still the main
commercial element in the package of his clients that the agent Lew
Wasserman had put together and peddled to Republic studio. The other
elements were a screenplay from a pulp novel (both by Roy Chanslor, a
specialist in quickie western scripts) written for Crawford (it was dedicated to her), and the services of Ray as both director and producer (later
on, he and Philip Yordan, another Wasserman client, who was said to have
"a Jungian memory" for old movies, rewrote the Chanslor screenplay). But
the effective "producer" of the movie, once they were all on location in the
Arizona desert, became Crawford herself—with her endless discontents
and threats to walk out, especially whenever she thought that Mercedes
McCambridge, the only other woman in the cast, was outshining her. (At
one point, according to Ray, Crawford stole McCambridge's clothes from

her cabin and strewed them across the highway to the airport.) Nor did she get on any better with her leading man, Hayden—who took the occasion of the movie's premiere party to announce on TV that he planned never to work with "Miss Crawford" again. Ray would later claim that he often stopped his car on the way to work to vomit, the tension on the set was so bad.

It shows on the screen. At first Vienna seems to take no notice of Johnny's arrival below in her empty saloon (see p. 194). She emerges from her room, on a landing under the eaves at the the top of the stairway, only to lean over the balcony railing and give an order to the croupier at the roulette table: "Spin the wheel, Eddie." Why? Eddie responds, as the wind howls outside—there's no customers. She tells him to spin it anyway, and he does. She likes the sound, she says—and goes back to her room, where she is entertaining a railroad man, pouring tea for him in front of a bust of Beethoven on a stand in the corner (she is musical).

"Never seen a woman who was more like a man," says one of the dealers working for her below. And you sort of get that point from her clothes too: black shirt and breeches with a blue string tie, along with her close-cropped hair. Soon, she is strapping on a gun belt, while the hapless railroad man looks on at her, to go out and face down the fractious bunch that's just come in—a group of those townspeople who want to run her out of the place, led by the malevolent Emma Small (McCambridge) and McIvers, a rich local rancher (Ward Bond). They burst through the doors followed by a gang of men who throw a body on top of the billiards table: it's Emma's brother, who has just been killed in a stage holdup. And they accuse Vienna of hiding the robbers who they say killed him, her friend the Dancing Kid (Scott Brady) and his men (who are not, in fact, the ones who held up the stage). Vienna draws her gun and holds them off from her stairway, displaying as she does so her talent and relish for angry speech-making: "Down there I sell whiskey and cards. All you can buy up these stairs is a bullet in the head. Now *which* do you want?!" The "boys" choose the whiskey, but Emma, their leader, is not so easily diverted. As the men disperse around the bar and Vienna slowly descends her stairway, Emma comes suddenly to her side, looking up at her with puppyish eagerness. "I'm going to kill you," she says softly, showing her gleaming little teeth. "I know," Vienna replies wearily, as she reholsters her gun, "—if I don't kill you first."

And it's only just started. This whole opening sequence, inside Vienna's churchlike (high-ceilinged and cross-beamed) saloon space, goes on for a third of the movie's length, some forty minutes of successive and intersect-

Vienna, on her stairway, confronts the posse from town: the views
from below (above) and above (below). In both, Emma
(Mercedes McCambridge) is the woman at the center of all the men.

ing fights and clashes and quarrels, of put-downs and face-downs and challenges. *Johnny Guitar* is almost like a Kabuki western, full of ceremonial
standoffs. Now the Dancing Kid and his gang enter, coming down for a
drink from their silver mine in the mountains; and so confrontations ensue
between them and Emma and her crowd. Then between the Kid and
Johnny. Then Johnny is challenged to a fistfight by the mean and nasty
Bart (Ernest Borgnine), who is an obvious Bad Guy, even though he's with
the Kid, who is mainly a Good Guy. There's also a clash between the Kid
and Emma—and between Vienna and almost everybody: it's those orders
she keeps giving them all ("*Play,*" she says to Johnny, handing him the
guitar over her shoulder). Even minor figures get in on the discord and
contention—like McIvers, and the marshal (Frank Ferguson), and Turkey
(Ben Cooper), who is one of the Kid's men, and who really *is* a kid, callow
and adolescent. And he has a crush on Vienna.

It's this effect that Vienna has on men (even boys) that burns Emma the
most—that and the fact that Vienna and the Kid have been sometime
lovers. Emma has the hots for the Kid herself, in spite of her also wanting
to kill him (as she does at the end), because, as Vienna puts it, "he makes
her feel like a woman" (Emma is severely repressed). The Kid is still in
love with Vienna, who still loves Johnny, who loves her too, even though
he's been away for five years because he didn't want to "settle down." And
so it goes. A touchy crowd.

But what keeps this opening sequence—all forty minutes of it, like an
anthology of movie clichés—from becoming tiresome (as it very nearly
does)? Partly, it's the subtle but steady stylization that Ray has given to
it—in the rhythms and accents of the movement and cutting, the group-
ing and regrouping of actors, the choreographed action. Including a
lovely sort of pas de deux—of advance-and-retreat-and-advance-again—
between Johnny and Vienna after the others have left, their movements
accompanied by their hieratic dialogue, less like talk than an exchange
of song titles: e.g., Vienna's "When a Fire Burns Itself Out (All You
Have Left Is Ashes)"—or her "He Wasn't Good, He Wasn't Bad (But I
Loved Him)."

And earlier on, a *real* dance happens—between a most unlikely couple.
The Kid, who appears to be pleasantly aware of Emma's tormented crush
on him, suddenly grabs her—after winking at Vienna—for a brief impul-
sive whirl around the floor, accompanied by Johnny on his guitar. This
humiliates Emma, of course (as it seems intended to), and by the dance's
end even the Kid regrets it. This is one of those moments when Ray's stylization is not at all subtle, but declares itself openly. As Johnny strikes the

concluding chords of the song, the "dancers" come to rest, freezing in a tableau of shame and discomfort: they have swung apart, Emma, stiff and straight-backed, rocking back against his arm, her eyes shut and her clenched, gloved hands lifted to her lower face and covering it; the Kid both holding her and looking away from her, his left arm behind her waist, his right one extended and pointed down along the line of his averted gaze as he hangs his head in shame. They walk apart—"I'm sorry, Emma," he says softly, as the others, after this musical diversion, resume their wrangling.

A striking thing in the way Ray shows the dance is how little (a few quick cuts) he actually shows us before that final held pose: how little we see of Emma's humiliation, how much of the people watching it and reacting. Vienna tries to stop it, looking alarmed and making a move toward the Kid as soon as she sees what he's up to (the wink he gives her is a clue), but too late. Johnny, as he plays his guitar, looks on with seeming—and characteristic—neutrality. As the couple sweep by him, the boy Turkey looks interested at first, in his first reaction shot, but then sheepish and embarrassed in the second one. But next to him, in the same two shots, mean and nasty Bart discloses a growing and prurient pleasure. As you'd expect.

These carefully registered distinctions are important ones to this movie. What makes the Kid's treatment of Emma so troubling is that it's so *slyly* mean—the sort of personal violation that only a Bart (or an Emma, we can probably assume) could actually enjoy watching, something that even the Kid, who inflicts it, has to turn away from at the end. But this is also just the sort of nastiness that always seems to be threatening in the movie. It's the disturbing undertone that animates the formalism—just as those ritual standoffs we've been watching have all in their different ways been strategies *against* humiliation, keeping the nastiness at bay. If just barely: it's there in Emma's obsessive hatred of Vienna (that sly little smile, "I'm going to kill you," and so on) throughout. That's one reason that admiring accounts of the movie almost invariably laud its "perversity" and "kinkiness" (one *New Yorker* account, unsigned, even invokes Krafft-Ebing!), classifying it as a noir western. And that was certainly a common enough variation of the genre in the fifties, as in the popular westerns of Anthony Mann.*

---

*In his black-and-white *The Furies* (1950), for example, the Barbara Stanwyck heroine is not only incestuously attached to her father, Walter Huston, but so possessive that she hurls a scissors into the face of his intended bride, scarring her hideously.

In any case, both the seething undertone and the surface stylization suit Crawford, the leading player. It seems safe to say that this was not—in spite of its director's usual proclivity—a Method sort of shoot. Mercedes McCambridge would later tell Ray biographer Bernard Eisenschitz that Nick never at all, surprisingly enough, talked to her about her character or performance. And Nick liked *her.* It seems unlikely he could have had much more rapport with Crawford, who was already well advanced into the unwitting self-parody and ringing falsity that had sometimes marked even her youthful performances. With a starring career dating from the twenties, she had by the fifties become as much a fixture of our moviegoing lives and memories as Dietrich. And Crawford made ten times more movies.

To her credit, she rarely asked us to love her. When she did, she became more unlovable than ever—in her beseeching, don't-kick-me style. Mostly she played smart women—that was her type, more or less. But she never seemed on screen to *be* very smart, and so she was often ludicrous. Still, she was always vivid, and had enormous authority whatever she did, compelling the camera, and most of her audience, even when she was bad. The directors who'd made her look good, giving her not only luminousness but some appearance of depth—from Edmund Goulding (*Grand Hotel,* 1932) to Otto Preminger (*Daisy Kenyon,* 1947), among others—had mostly toned her down. But that was not an option, for Ray or for her, with *Johnny Guitar.*

But Ray finds many ways in the movie to make her angry presence (getting angrier, as it seemed, with each terrible movie she made—like *Torch Song* and *Queen Bee,* just before and after this one) intelligible, even sympathetic. This, after all, is a movie where everybody on screen seems to be fuming—where the heroine has to bully and battle her way even down her own stairway. After all, it's tough enough to begin with not to be a man (a woman makes "one mistake" and she's a tramp, she says to Johnny). But then to be stuck with him on top of it, a man who won't even act like the hero he's supposed to be ("I'm not the fastest gun in the west," he says to McIvers and the gang—though of course he is), who isn't even comfortable saying his lines half the time. And *then* to have Emma in her face—not a man but a demon version of herself. *Another* woman with a gun and a grievance: it's too much. No wonder she's furious most of the time.

And yet her job, it seems, is somehow with her iron will to control all the fury around her. "I won't have killing," she tells Johnny later on when things have really hotted up, and she even sends him away because she thinks he's "gun crazy." But Emma *will* have killing. Once she's put on a long black dress and gone to a funeral (her brother's), she is careering through the movie like some unleashed satanic force, leading a nighttime posse to Vienna's place, where they expect to find the Kid and his gang, who have just robbed the town bank. What they find instead is probably this movie's single most jaw-dropping scene—Vienna's coup de théâtre.

It begins with offscreen music in the night air—a piano playing the movie's melancholy Granados theme—as the posse rides up to the place. Emma hardly waits for the horse to stop before she jumps off it, running up to the closed doors—where she hesitates (as the piano sounds louder) and turns into a close-up, spreading her bent arms like condor wings, and looking back at the others: aren't they coming? Then she turns again and pushes at the doors, which open magically, allowing the camera to move over her head inside and past her—where Vienna sits at the far end of the room on a stage in a long white dress, playing the piano against a wall of red rock. (Her saloon, as it appears, is built into a mountainside.)

Emma's men—twenty or so, all in black like her (the funeral)—enter slowly, behind her. They are understandably a bit dumbstruck. Emma is center front of the ranks, with the marshal and McIvers on either side of her. At the rear a few men peel off to search the place—the others, with Emma in the lead, advance slowly, wordlessly, toward the extraordinary sight and sound before them. Vienna plays on imperturbably, erect on her piano bench, without even a glance in their direction, punctuating her playing here and there with heavy fortissimo chords, in angry accompaniment to the movements of the searchers as they dash and clump about the place, her controlled response to the outrage of this invasion. When the marshal starts to speak, she answers him above her music. The posse, as they creep forward, have formed into a flying wedge, Emma and the two men at its apex—as if responding to the show in front of them with a more modest one of their own. (Ray even lets us see the men who've been searching as they return and scuttle hastily into their places in the back row.)

Vienna, as she reminds them, has no reason to run or to hide from them. "I held up no bank," she says as she plays. "Every man here knows that. I don't *have* to rob banks. All I have to do is to sit here and wait for the railroad to come through. And that is what I intend to do." More fortissimo chords: more protest from the others—as Ray shows the invaders now in a menacing low-angle shot, standing under the saloon's great chandelier, Emma front and center, smiling her little smile again. They require that Vienna show them the way to the Lair, the Kid's hideout cabin high in the mountains. She refuses, indignantly. "We won't take that," says the marshal. *That* tears it: she crashes her hands down on the keyboard and springs to her feet, coming to the front of the stage. "And just *what* do you think I've been taking from you?!" she demands, eyes blazing. She goes on: "Who *are* you? And you? And you? To break into my home—with your angry faces and evil minds? . . . *Why* have you come here? I knew you would—but why? I robbed no bank, I held up no stagecoach—but you're here again. I know when I know you know I'm innocent. Yet you stand there in your funeral clothes—like vultures waiting for another corpse! . . ."

They are transfixed—as we are. But just then—just when she really has them—there's a crash and a moan, and the wounded Turkey, whom Vienna out of pity has been hiding, is discovered. This is the end point—as well as the high point—of Vienna's "theatre," her attempts to control the chaos and evil by formality and artifice. Now everything explodes. And Emma takes over. Vienna and Turkey are hustled off to the lynching tree, while Emma stays behind just long enough to shoot down the great chandelier (so often raised and lowered at big moments by Vienna), setting the place afire, conjuring the flames like a witch, then rushing outside and turning into a close-up that shows her orgasmic glee against the inferno behind.

They hang Turkey. And Vienna very nearly—the men can't do it: "Not a woman," says the hangman. "You'll have to do it yourself, Emma," says Vienna, astride a horse, hands tied behind her and the noose around her neck. Emma does it—since she has to (there are some things even an Emma might consider unwomanly). But Johnny, concealed above, cuts the hanging rope, so that the horse who is meant to ride out from under Vienna carries her off instead—to freedom. It's like a sleight-of-hand trick, and it's the beginning of the magic—which now takes over the movie.

The reunited pair descend below the ground, into the mineshaft under the burning saloon (setting her dress afire—Johnny puts it out), and come out into the sunlight, into the woods, submerging themselves in a stream and swimming across it, then stepping across a rocky sparkling brook to the other side—in a beautiful long shot that shows Vienna stumbling and falling, caught and steadied by the immensely tall Johnny, where she looks at once bright (her red shirt) and strong and vulnerable (she is so small)—passages through fire and water, bringing them finally to a waterfall, streaming in a long narrow cascade from bluffs high above, hiding an opening through the rocks. It's through that that they enter into the domain of the Kid and his gang and ascend to the Lair itself, a cabin perched high in the mountains against open sky.

Emma and her lynch mob set fire to Vienna's saloon.

And there they enter—as often happens in a Ray movie—a mock domestic world, where something like family life gets re-created. The conflicts and squabbles don't end, of course; it's just that they become more mundane, even comic—less about life and death than about who makes the breakfast. "You have any eggs?" asks Vienna, who's promised Johnny a meal. "Yeah," the unhappy Kid replies. "*Get* 'em," she says, in her usual way of giving an order—while Johnny (in *his* usual way) sits silently at the table. "Let *him* get 'em, he's eatin' 'em!" retorts the Kid. And so it goes: bicker, bicker. There is even a mock gun-pulling contest between the two boys—which "Mother" allows, and even rather enjoys (Johnny, her favorite, wins). But in the meantime—in case everybody's forgotten— *Emma* is coming, and something has to be done. "Let's *try* to work together—just *once!*" says Vienna, more hopeless than peremptory. She's fixing her tie—the one that goes with her yellow shirt—in the mirror.

It's extraordinary. It's as if a kind of sanity has been restored, a kind of reality. Life up here, on the empyrean heights, seems closer to farce than to

Vienna in the Lair, tending to her Lost Boys: keeping the peace (above)
and cooking the breakfast (below). (And she took a *lot* of trouble with
her tie as well.) After facing down the Kid, Johnny fetches her the eggs,
while the Kid, between them, seethes (no one cooked *his* eggs).

Emma shooting and killing the Kid—just before Vienna kills her.

melodrama. Even when in another part of the Lair the sneaky and traitor-
ous Bart (about to join forces with his natural ally, Emma herself) suddenly
kills the sickly but loyal Corey (Royal Dano) with a blow to the head, he
caps the shocking act with a laugh line: "Some people just don't *listen!*" he
says peevishly over the body.

Finally *Johnny Guitar* seems as much about exhaustion as it is about
rage—very much a movie about being middle-aged and a bit played out.
As Vienna tells Johnny, as she makes his breakfast: "We've both done a lot
of living. Our problem now is how to do a little more." And the spirit is
catching. "I've had enough of this killing," says one of the posse to
McIvers, as they mill around on the rocks below the Lair (Emma has led
them through the waterfall at Bart's signal). "So have I," says McIvers, and
adds that this fight is really between the women—"and it has been all
along." And that's the way it all finally plays out: rigid with anticipated
pleasure, like a walking hard-on, Emma moves up the hill to her fulfillment, toward the entrapped Vienna, even shooting the Kid through the
head when he attempts to stop her; reaching the cabin at the summit, and
being gunned down from the porch by Vienna herself (the men just
watch—these women can get crazy).

So ends the madness. Vienna throws her gun down, Johnny helps her down the mountainside, and they both walk through the posse—who are dumbstruck once again, this time shamefaced as well. The pair go back out through the waterfall. And the film's concluding image is a long shot of their final exultant embrace standing in the rocks and water, flinging themselves into the clinch, the kind of all-out gesture that conveys the special freedom-in-control that has characterized the whole movie.

And yet it's not camp—it never feels less than entirely (if oddly) serious. Even when the obligatory title song breaks out (a fifties movie custom—though it usually happens over the opening credits instead of the end, as here). It seems that the Granados-derived theme actually has words, and they are sung by Peggy Lee (she also wrote them). As Johnny and Vienna descend from the mountain and pass through the men in black:

> *Whether you go, whether you stay—*
> *I love you . . .*
> *But if you're cruel, you can be kind,*
> *I know . . .*

Then, over the final clinch, the key change and heightening:

> *There was ne-ver a man like my Johnny—*
> *The one they call Johnny . . .* Gui-*tar!*

But that's not exactly right—*is* it? Oh, well. He's certainly a nice guy—so why not? Anyway, its *not* being "exactly right" is what makes it feel right for the end of *this* movie—it confirms that final "absurd unreasoning happiness" that, as Graham Greene put it, only the *movies* at their "most fantastic" can leave us with. And it's appropriate certainly—in its inaccuracy—to a movie that at once subverts and sustains its own romanticism.

It's that double-exposure effect that Ray imposes on the people: a hero who's not exactly a hero, a heroine who's not exactly a heroine, a woman who is "more like a man," a villain who is more like the heroine's double, and so on. It's a fairy tale, of course—even if amended to be for and about grown-ups—where the witch is less a malignant plotter than a terrifying improviser, and where Snow White has seen some rough times, which doesn't keep her from shaping up the dwarfs in their lair or whatever else she has to do. Truffaut, on the other hand, compares it to "Beauty and the

The final clinch: Johnny and Vienna in Arcadia

Beast"—Beauty being Johnny, of course. In any case, it's a fairy tale where the evil force is not so much strange as uncomfortably recognizable—in the seductions of ugly feelings and violent acts. Emma, it's very clear, has more fun than anyone else in the movie. And she simply has to be killed, that's all—so that the shuddering revulsion she also inspires can give way to the light and freedom of the ending.

If anything, *Johnny Guitar* is, it seems to me, an anti-noir western. And its overall shape is roughly the one that belongs to that tour-de-force sequence I described at the beginning of this chapter—where Johnny and Vienna go from recriminations to release to a rousing romantic triumphalism. "So laugh, Vienna—and be happy. It's your wedding day!" *That* too is not exactly right. But it doesn't matter.

Ray's baroque and eccentric western is surely one of the most rigorously aestheticized movies ever to come out of mainstream (more or less) Hollywood. But in a way, that shouldn't have been so surprising, given Ray's record. This formalizing, aestheticizing tendency was one of the elements that set his version of the Method movie apart from others of the time. It's apparent even in his first movie, *They Live By Night* in 1948, with its painterly compositions (in black and white) and its choreographed movements—not to mention an ending scene that's an almost startling parallel to Siodmak's ending of *Christmas Holiday* four years before (I have no idea if Ray ever saw that film, but it's not unlikely that he would have). The scenes are alike not only in content (heroine with dying hero), in action (she kneels by his prone body, holds him, then rises and walks away), but most strikingly in the fragmented Eisensteinian cutting that conveys her movement. In *Johnny Guitar,* however, there are no such effects: Ray's stylization here is in the staging—his mise-en-scène, as the French have named it—not the montage. But the artifice is more radical. If Ray got away with it—as he did, since the movie was a hit—escaping both front office and audience disapproval, that was importantly because it was so clearly a *trashy* sort of movie. One of the commonest ways for a filmmaker to get away with the fancy stuff (and especially in the fifties) was to do this sort of over-the-top pulp material. It was almost like a license to commit artiness. Welles, of course, *didn't* get away with it, since his pulp films got shunned too; but he tried, certainly. And so—more successfully—did a lot of others, directors like Sam Fuller, Robert Aldrich, Douglas Sirk, among the most notable.

"I set out to break every goddamn rule there was to break in a western," said Ray later on, in his full macho-artist mode. When the fact is, it seems, that he had set out to make the best of a bad situation, once he got into it: something he had done before, and would do so often again, with varying results. He thought of himself, with reason, as an artist beleaguered and often defeated by constraints—by the studios, the audience, the system, and so forth. But it seems unlikely he could have functioned even so well as he did *without* those constraints. Like most Hollywood directors of the past that we think of now as masters of one sort or another, he was stimulated by those limits too—his gifts and energies focused by them, as they might never have been otherwise. What he yearned for, like all romantic artists, was freedom. But there is no suggestion in the little of it that he finally got (his final completed film, highly personal and made with his students at Binghamton, turned out an unhappy mess), or in the movies he planned and talked about without making (a film with Norman Mailer and porn star Marilyn Chambers, a mixed fact-fiction movie about the Chicago Seven trial, etc.), that "freedom" would have suited him.

Chesterton once wrote that the essence of any painting is the frame. It's the sort of old-fart observation that Nick would probably have resented—applied to himself, that is, and coming from somebody else (he could be pretty orotund himself). But his troubled and aborted, finally triumphant career, I think, more or less bears it out.

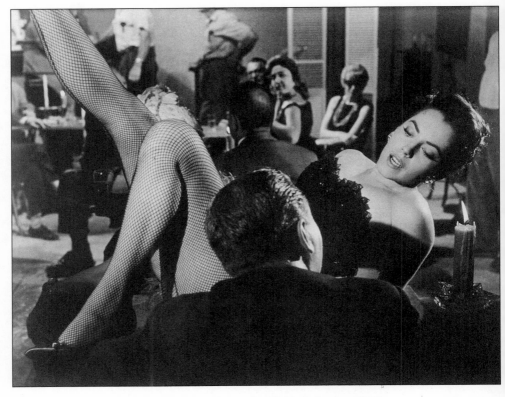

Susan Kohner in Douglas Sirk's *Imitation of Life*

PART FOUR

THE MOVIEMAKERS

Nothing is more exhilarating than philistine vulgarity.
— VLADIMIR NABOKOV

I'm not thinking about returning to France . . . In Paris I would have a much better situation than here, but I admit that the old world scares me a little. Seven years spent in a country put together by immigrants and where one rubs shoulders with all races, all accents, all religions, has made me quite indifferent towards questions about which I was once passionate. There is one thing about which I am pretty sure: that "progress" has been an error . . . One of my friends wrote a play about Galileo which has been much talked about in this town. My opinion is that the Church was very wrong not to burn this dangerous innovator swiftly, and that things worked much better when the earth was flat.

— JEAN RENOIR (HOLLYWOOD, 1947)

Twenty-One

RETROSPECTIVE

Interesting man," said Nick Ray when I told him I was planning to interview Douglas Sirk on my trip to Europe in the summer of 1977. I don't remember his saying much else about Sirk in that conversation, beyond indicating his great respect for the man's work and regretting his own unfamiliarity with a lot of it. But he was right: Sirk *was* an interesting man. Just as Nick himself was—though in very different ways.

I knew Ray only passingly, and in the last years of his life. The first time I laid eyes on him was in 1975, when he made a personal appearance at the First Avenue Screening Room, a small New York "art house," with the first showing of a documentary about his career, made by some of his former students, *I'm a Stranger Here Myself.* The theatre was packed, with people overflowing into the aisles—not just the cultists but some recognizable celebrities, most notably Ray's old friend and mentor, John Houseman. Nick had been away for a long time, and it was an electric occasion—surviving even the hour or so he kept us waiting for him to appear. When he did, he briefly introduced the documentary, then took questions afterwards.

He looked ghastly—ravaged and sick. But with his black eyepatch, his tall, gaunt frame, his craggy face and head of curly white hair, the effect was a theatrical one too. He talked softly, a bit disconnectedly. He seemed high on something—so did some of the audience, especially that part of it he'd brought with him, his usual crowd of young acolytes. But the movie went over well: it had extended clips from his films (including the *Johnny Guitar* love scene), and they seemed thrilling even out of context. But a sense of disaster, as I remember, never quite lifted—even through the postmovie question period, which seemed to bring him to life. But the next event on the program was the showing of his newest film, one that he'd been making collectively, over the last two years, with his students at Binghamton—*You Can't Go Home Again,* it was called (a Nick Ray kind of title). He was still re-editing it, he said, and some footage was missing.

Nick Ray in 1975 at the First Avenue
Screening Room

But there was enough of it—running through the theatre projector that
night in fits and starts (the film kept breaking)—to show how hopeless a
project it was. Nonlinear and "experimental," full of arty tics and mod-
ernist flourishes, it was also "real." That is, Nick played himself playing
director to his students, just as the students played themselves, real names
and all. And there was a lot of it about how they were being morally cor-
rupted by the movie we were watching—*as* we watched, as it were—and
by Ray their director.

At one of the pauses for repair in the projection booth, the lights went
up and Nick was at the front of the audience again, explaining what was
happening and apologizing for the delay; then just standing—what else to
say? . . . He looked down at the front rows, which were still filled, though
people toward the back were drifting out. "How do you like it so far?" he
said softly, almost wistfully—the lifelong kid. The question was so simple
and direct, and under the circumstances that made it sound bizarre, even a
little grotesque. But disarming—like a disguised whimper: let me *out* of

here. Somebody gave him an answer, inaudible to the rest of us. Nick listened, and looked thoughtful. And the lights went down again. Eventually.

It wasn't until two years later that I met him. I was showing *In a Lonely Place* to an audience at the New School, in what was then their Fifth Avenue movie house, when one of the ticket-taking students at the door rushed back to tell me she'd been told that Nicholas Ray himself was here. He was with his usual entourage of four or five young people, including Susan Ray, his wife. And they'd come on an impulse, he said—prompted mostly by Susan, who hadn't seen the movie, or at least not seen it lately; I'm not sure which now. But I remember how exciting the surprise visit was—to everyone. I announced him to the audience before the movie, and he answered questions afterwards—very gracefully. Then he returned two weeks later to do the same when I showed *Johnny Guitar.* And both nights we talked afterwards in a nearby diner—with the entourage, silent mostly but seemingly content. I got the feeling they followed him everywhere. Some of them were from his Binghamton film class.

He was clearly in better shape than he had been two years before. It was a time when he was kicking both drugs and alcohol, and going to AA meetings. And the cancer that would end his life only two years later hadn't yet been diagnosed. (He died in 1979, at sixty-eight.) And I was soon drawn—very willingly—into the drama of Nick's aborted career, becoming one of a number of people (as I gathered) who were already working at it. *My* idea for him was to get him together with Balanchine—who was at that time, I'd been told, growing more receptive to the idea of ballet *movies,* of filming his company and dances. I even wrote Mr. B. a letter (he was reputed to be a special fan of American westerns, and I invoked *Johnny Guitar*). It was delivered by photographer David Lindner, with his backstage access, to one of the dancers to hand on. And in the meantime, I went with Nick—who was more admiring of Balanchine's work than he was familiar with it—to the New York City Ballet one night, an all-Balanchine program, including the wonderfully witty and ebullient *Stars and Stripes.* I remember that because Nick registered a concern afterwards about what he took to be its jingoistic flavor. Not very promising, I thought at the time. But in any case, there was never any response from Balanchine or anyone else. Nick began teaching at NYU and at the Actors Studio, classes in acting and directing. And it was one of his NYU filmmaking classes that I was visiting when I told him about my impending interview with Sirk.

What the two men had most strikingly in common, of course, was their latter-day "rediscovery"—the revaluation (thanks to the auteurists and to

Douglas Sirk (left) directing Lana Turner and John Gavin (right background) in *Imitation of Life*

Andrew Sarris) of careers that had been largely ignored or derided when they were happening a decade before. And Sirk's Hollywood career had looked even more deplorable than Ray's did—mostly consisting of glossy kitsch tearjerkers and Rock Hudson action films in color at Universal, the sort of assembly-line pap that sophisticated audiences avoided and reviewers routinely panned. He turned out two to four a year, until the end of the fifties, and never lost money for Universal, where (after a brief postwar "prestige" period) low-risk, low-budget filmmaking was the rule: the very model of a dependable and compliant (unlike Ray) studio hireling—who, because of the auteurists and their influence, would become later known as a kind of subversive artist, working in the belly of the beast, a director who by his ironies regularly undermined the kitsch affirmations of his own movies.

Not that such an idea of him wasn't appealing on the face of it. Like having a *real* Guy Grand (*The Magic Christian*), in Hollywood: not just in the projection booth making his mischief, but on the set and behind the camera! But then it hardly seemed likely. Especially when I thought of the two Sirk films I *had* seen when they first came out, *Written on the Wind* and *Imitation of Life,* his two biggest successes—both, I thought, just unredeemably bad.

But then, some twenty years later, I started seeing *Imitation of Life* again. Not all at once but in fragments, and in black and white, at a time before going to bed when I had the habit of turning my TV on to a local Late Late Show, which had a habit, it seemed, of showing this movie. And

I began to wonder if I wasn't seeing what the auteurists meant about it. By the time I saw the whole movie again, in a real theatre on a real screen and in its original color, I was pretty much converted. Not only because some of it (especially the scenes with the black mother and daughter) now seemed to have so much truth and authentic power (a lot of it didn't—like the scenes with the white mother and daughter), but because my awareness of even a possible ironic intention seemed to transform the movie for me. As it had, it seemed, for the audience around me, who were responding to it in a way no imaginable fifties audience could have: being alert to and amused by every hollow ring in Lana Turner's multicostumed leading-lady performance, for example, just as I was being. We had become an audience for the "Sirkian subtext," as it was called. And we were no longer (as we had been years before) jeering alone. *This* time even the director was on our side.

Still, I knew (I hope) that it wasn't *that* simple—nor could it be. Then I saw *Written on the Wind* again, and I was moved by that film too. I couldn't put it into words, why these Sirk movies now felt so important to me. But it's exciting to change your mind when you're finding new ways of seeing old experiences. Like *Imitation of Life*—where Sirk, as it now seemed to me, had taken a kind of movie, the sadomasochistic tearjerker, that I'd always experienced as an oppression and turned it into something altogether larger and freer, something both cool and powerful, sardonic and emotionally full. More than that, it seemed as if he was showing you not only another way of connecting to his audience but also to his formulaic materials, a way not only of turning threadbare trash into interesting art (plenty of filmmakers had done that before) but of doing that and still *leaving* it trash somehow. For me, it was almost like a new idea of what an artist might do, of how he might speak to you.

So I got the idea I wanted to speak to him. And the idea was much encouraged by Jon Halliday's remarkable and fascinating *Sirk on Sirk,* a book-length record of Halliday's 1970 conversations with the director in Lugano, where Sirk now lived—and where I now (seven years later) wrote him to ask for an interview. He replied immediately and graciously, inviting me, in his highly formal English, asking only that I *not* bring a tape recorder: "Take as many memory notes as you wish—I'll gladly demonstrate the utmost patience in this respect—but the mechanized device of a recorder has always been irritating to me, the inevitable consequence being something lacking in spontaneity." So I went from Paris to Lugano that summer (1977), and spent three days with him, talking about his life and work—almost two decades after he'd abandoned America and his

Hollywood film career, and four decades after he'd fled Hitler's Germany, with his Jewish wife, actress Hilde Jary.

He'd wanted when he was young to be a sea captain, one of his oldest friends later told me—he'd been in the German Naval Academy during the First World War when he was eighteen. And you could see him in that role, I thought, even at seventy-seven: on the ship's bridge scanning the horizon, a tall, lordly man with ice-blue eyes and an erect bearing. And so glad to have an *American* visitor, he said—to talk English again with an American; it had been a long time since he'd done that. And he wasn't at all sure now that he'd done the right thing in leaving America so finally (he'd never been back again), and he missed it deeply, he found. But of course he is still an American citizen—as he assures me in the living room of his and Hilde's apartment on a mountainside high above the tiny Swiss city and its lake. Lugano is only made tolerable to him and to Mrs. Sirk because they can spend so much of the year away—in Munich in the fall, where he teaches at the university, and Locarno in the late summer, where he is involved in the film festival. Right now in his leisure he is studying Latin again. And rereading Hegel. Because, he says, "no one ever reads Hegel finally."

For above everything—as I knew from the Halliday book—Sirk is a European intellectual, of an old-fashioned academic kind. Now once again he is working at what he loves: "For twenty-five years, I was grazing in arid pastures in this respect." And he tells me a story about the incredulity of a librarian at UCLA in the late 1940s when he asked for a copy of Euripides.

He thinks perhaps his happiest time in Hollywood was those years in the San Fernando Valley in the early forties when he and Mrs. Sirk (mostly Mrs. Sirk, he emphasizes) ran first a chicken farm and then—when the chickens at last defeated them—an alfalfa farm. That was before he got fully back into the movies again. No, he had, oh, friends in the movie business—oh, acquaintances perhaps—not even that really. There was George Sanders—an exception—he moved in with the Sirks and stayed for a year. The only "real" friends he and Mrs. Sirk had in Hollywood were the people they got to know, farmers and the like, when they first settled in California. And now—back in Europe—it's a *quality* in America that he misses the most: "the simple creative generosity that you find in some ordinary Americans." They would have gone under with their farm if it hadn't been for the unsolicited help of some more experienced farmer-neighbors. "Now that kind of thing you would not find in Europe. There, if some foreigners went bankrupt on their farm, they'd say, 'Good—they didn't belong here anyway!' "

"Creative generosity" did not distinguish the German colony in Hollywood, however. That extraordinary collection of exiles from Nazism—
such figures as the Manns and the Reinhardts, Werfel and Lang and Brecht
et al.—was not just an identifiable group: being a German in Hollywood
was a way of life in those days. What bothered Sirk most about the expatri-
ates was their "spite" about America, which amounted in conversation to a
group obsession, almost a madness. "To talk constantly about how uncul-
tured, how awful and ugly America was—and they saw nothing, nothing
at all. Oh, but no one *here* knows Dante, they would say—this often from
people who themselves had never read Dante; I can tell you they hadn't.
No, no, soon I stayed away. I had to stay away from their spite." Then he
smiles—a change of tone: "And you know what that spite did for them?"
Pause. "They thrived on it!" He laughs. "They absolutely thrived. Probably it saved them all, you know."

Sirk was a wonderful talker, even in an English he said he was rusty at,
with his air of irritable kindliness. His favorite modifier—after "goddamn"—was "what-do-I-know," used just before some word choice that
was invariably apt or as a rough equivalent of "and so forth." Although he
certainly had his vanity, he had, it seemed to me, a surprising lack of ego-
tism. About the films—if not about his own latter-day eminence, which
he clearly valued and enjoyed—he showed some ambivalence, sounding
almost dismissive. "*Magnificent Obsession* has never been one of my favorite
pictures." "A whole picture which I kind of liked—though the *script* I
didn't like too much—was *Written on the Wind*": that was the closest he
came to an endorsement. He hadn't watched most of them since he made
them, he said. Why not? "Because you don't like them. Because you get
depressed." I see, I said—and I really did, though that wasn't quite what I
expected him to answer.

But he *had* read his new critics (he even read one of them *to* me, translat-
ing from the German), including Fassbinder, of course, who had done
more than anyone else—indeed, was still doing it—to promote Sirk's late-
blooming reputation. ("Not one of us," he wrote, "not Godard or Fuller or
me or anybody else, can touch Douglas Sirk . . .") They had become
friends—however unlikely a pair they might otherwise have seemed. Sirk
told a story about him and Hilde arriving by appointment one day at Fassbinder's apparently unfurnished Munich apartment and being left to sit on
the floor (not easy to imagine) until their host appeared from another room
almost an hour later, without explanation or apology.

Unlike Ray, who sometimes liked to discomfit his interpreters with a
no-I-never-meant-*that* kind of response, Sirk (more like Hitchcock) was
steadily obliging, as I judged from his other interviews—happy to suit the

predilections of his interviewers and alert to their cues as well. And though he was invariably moderate about his own films, he could be quite the opposite about the intentions behind them, their origins and influences—discoursing to Halliday, for example, about the impact of Emerson and Thoreau on *All That Heaven Allows,* or Euripides' *Alcestis* on *Magnificent Obsession.* Or comparing his situation at Universal to Shakespeare's at the Globe (he, too, had to please a popular audience, and so on). I'm sure he had such thoughts when he was *at* Universal, quite a lot (it was one of the ways he got through his assignments there, I imagine), just as I suppose his distance from the films made it easier—especially before admirers—to invest them with such theorized majesty. But that was the sort of line I wanted to avoid.

And he took that cue, too, it seemed to me—*very* readily. He had, after all, his own kind of down-to-earthness, his own bullshit detector, what he thought of, I'm sure, as his "American" side, preserved along with the citizenship, impatient of cant and pretension and sanctimoniousness and "what-do-I-know"—all that. As we went on he became more expansive and relaxed, though he complained vaguely of a headache once, and canceled one meeting. But that was a small interruption; and we continued, as he spoke more and more movingly and often humorously not only about his career but about his experiences of Germany and the Nazis, about his at-homeness in the America outside Hollywood, and so on.

But when I sent him a prepublication copy of the interview (it appeared in the summer 1978 *Film Comment*) he wanted to disown it, wiring me instantly, and clearly upset. He had other reasons to be, as I learned later: the headache was the first sign of a clot behind the eye, which left him partially blind in the end. His concern at the time about the interview was that he thought it too informal, too colloquial and unbuttoned—"too gabby" was his phrase for it. Soon he had rewritten much of it—just as he had done, I learned, with the Halliday interview. But the result this time, I thought, was really unhappy: he had wanted to stiffen the whole thing up a bit, to give it the appropriate appearance of seriousness and intellectual heft. But he had only, in my view, made it ponderous—not at all like the lively conversations I remembered. I told him I thought the changes would only falsify those conversations, and that I felt obliged to stick with the original—which was published with an introduction registering his objections. In the end, he was pleased. He had been "overly cautious," he said, because of earlier interviewers. ("I reread your interview and think it splendid!" he wrote me later.) And we were friends to the end of his life.

In some ways, as I thought later on, it was like his movies: letting go without wanting to let on. My warmest memories of the Lugano visit are about his openness and generosity—qualities that I went on finding in his letters after that—even in his first letter, inviting me, and in his warmth when he met my train. I was right away his friend, as he put it then. Now he was insisting that I was to be his and Hilde's guest—at a hotel he had chosen, since their apartment was so unfortunately small. I protested, with thanks—but I couldn't have that, I said. No, no, he said, it was all in his hands, all arranged. And he drove me to a local lakeside hotel, where I stayed the next three nights.

There were signs after that, however (I no longer remember what they were, but I remember registering them), that he wanted to let himself off the hook about the hotel, and yet felt he couldn't. And even though I was still protesting, I wasn't doing it firmly enough to allay his anxiety. Or so it seemed to me afterwards. We were both caught: he wanting to do something rather grand, and me wanting him to do it; we *both* wanted him to be the sort of unstinting magnanimous figure he had in his head, the one he'd started to enact, and that I might later report about. In any case, it finally developed—to my horror—that he was going to "take care" of the hotel bill not by paying the hotel (which I had already done) but by paying *me,* producing, while we were sitting in the front seat of his car waiting for my train back to Paris, a fistful of paper money, which ended up, when I refused to take it, scattered on the car floor (he had put it on the dashboard in front of me) and which I then had to scoop up and return to him—to his immense and very visible relief.

"Douglas was *stingy,*" his old friend Irene Heymann told me with a laugh some years after his death. "*God,* was he stingy!" But what struck me at the time, and especially afterwards, was how much he wanted *not* to be, how much discomfort he felt at not being able to carry through on his big gesture. But like a Chekhov character, he simply couldn't. Though he did run some risk that I might actually take the money; I think he was never sure—really sure—that I might not. It was an acutely embarrassing situation for both of us. But in the end—at some distance from it—I guess I found it more appealing and finally sympathetic than simple openhandedness would have been: the painful and familiar human bind of having larger impulses than you can act on.

At the last minute, because of Douglas's health, he and Hilde had to postpone their intended visit to America in 1978. But they did come in December 1979, for a celebratory return, to be feted on both east and west coasts. Here in New York there were tributes at MOMA and Goethe House and City College, scheduled appearances at repertory venues like the Thalia. But it was a little too much for him, and he had to cancel the latter date at the last minute, when I arrived at his hotel room to pick him up. I was delegated to take his regrets back to the audience at the theatre. But there was still time, and the three of us—Douglas, Hilde, and I—sat rather gloomily together in the hotel room, the only quiet time I had with them on that visit. It was then that he talked—for some reason I can't remember—about how his first wife (I hadn't heard of her before, or found her in any of his bios) once tried to kill him, entering the empty and darkened orchestra of a Berlin theatre and firing a gun at him while he was on stage rehearsing the cast. Really? Hilde was nodding her head in the background—*it's true.* (She had been there, apparently.) The woman was mad, Sirk said, and she became a fanatic Nazi Party member. And she had had a son by him. Oh, yes? (The Sirks were childless.) What happened to him? I asked. Sirk said he wasn't sure but thought he had died on the Russian front. Then I had to go—no time to ask the obvious questions, even if I'd felt I could have.

But this was less like Chekhov than Nabokov—the gun-wielding madwoman, firing out of the dark at the stage illusion, the disappearing act of both mother and son, and so on. But that was the artist that Sirk had come more and more to remind me of. Nabokov (who had also retired to Switzerland then) had like Sirk been both visitor and citizen, an observer from another place who was wedded to the landscape of fifties America not only by circumstance but by an unexpected quirk of temperament, and by fascination and love. Sirk and Nabokov, in their different ways, are both artists of the magical deceptive surface—with a common ability to make us experience the banality of our American lives, their look, shape, and sound, as if it were a mystery, a puzzle, a deadpan joke.

Twenty-Two

WRITTEN ON THE WIND

A mong other things, movies seemed to lose their sense of humor in the fifties—a worse development for some of us than the out-of-focus Eastmancolor or the empty palaces. Before this even Hollywood's biggest successes, the most broadly popular movies of all—like *Gone With the Wind,* like *Casablanca*—had been marked by wit, skepticism, a core of tough-mindedness. That was what "the movies"—at their best—had meant to us then: an eagerness to be either vastly amused (as in screwball comedy) or deeply chagrined (as in film noir) by the outrageousness of our American lives. But in the fifties that eagerness seemed to vanish: the anguish was no longer just an undertone, the controlling spirit no longer dry and knowing but upset, fretful, overwrought and overdone. Where the movies used to wink at us, so to speak, now they were shouting and grimacing—melodramas like Sirk's *Written on the Wind* (1957), for example, one of the decade's big hits.

And the uproar begins even before the opening credits do—with a dramatic long shot of a yellow roadster speeding in the nighttime distance down a desolate blue ribbon of highway past a forest of oil derricks rising in the sky. The car—sleek, open, low-slung, a hot canary-yellow—zooms up to and past the camera with a roar, scattering whirlwinds of dead leaves in its wake, as the soundtrack orchestra plays a low, ominous ostinato. A reverse shot next, of the car going away—past a towering black skyscraper with a big red letter H (for Hadley) flashing on and off at the top. Then a close-up of the driver, Robert Stack, uncorking a bottle with his teeth. The car—in long shot again—speeds through a small business district, down an empty Main Street, and out; then turns off the road into a tree-lined driveway winding and leading to a white-porticoed red brick mansion, as the foreboding music relaxes and segues into a lilting jukebox strain that we recognize as the inevitable "theme of the movie" (Victor Young again).

Then a startling tilted close shot—from the ground looking up—of the car in front of the house, easing to a stop almost on top of the camera now, fender and hood all but filling the frame, while at the top right corner of the screen we see Stack getting out, and above him the mansion's upper windows. This close-up effusion of yellow chrome feels like the visual equivalent of a shriek—except that just at that moment the Four Aces on the soundtrack launch into the movie's languorous, woozy "title song" ("A faithless lover's kiss / Is written on the wind . . ."). And that's even *more* startling—there is such a disconnection between the dreamy, dumb sound of the song and the precise glamour and kinetic sweep of the visuals.

The credits unroll. First the four above-the-title stars are introduced in separate shots beside their names, as each reacts to the roadster's arrival: Rock Hudson looking disturbed at a window, Lauren Bacall languishing in bed behind him, Stack outside draining his bottle and staggering forward amid blowing leaves, Dorothy Malone watching him at another window. Stack then enters the great house, leaving the door open behind him and those inescapable leaves whirling in after him as he lopes brokenly in a panning shot across the black parquet of the entrance hall. He goes into the first room to his left. Then we are outside the house again, just beyond the portico and its columns, looking at the empty room through the open door—at the foyer's gleaming black floors, the grand staircase at its far end, the elegant crystal chandelier. Then at the top of the staircase (an extreme long shot) Malone appears, in a negligee, coming swiftly down and gliding across the reflecting floor like a skater, stopping with her hands and ear to the door Stack has just disappeared behind. She too goes into the room. The leaves blow and scatter across the empty hall. Then a high-angle view, looking down through trees, of the yellow car, parked and empty, in the driveway. Then another straight-on view from outside looking into the hall: no movement at all now, except the shadows of wind-tossed tree branches on the white columns of the portico; no sound, either (the music has stopped, and the credits are done), except the wind. Another high-angle shot of the car and driveway. A pause, and a gunshot. Stack (you presume)—just his trouser legs in medium view—comes onto the porch and drops his gun. Then in the far background of the repeated driveway shot—the roadster in the middle plane, blowing trees in the foreground—he staggers off the porch and falls face-forward. Cut to Bacall in nightgown standing at the open window above amid whirling curtains, then fainting and falling to the floor. The leaves of a desk calendar flip backward and the flashback story begins.

This opening under-the-credits montage introduces you not only to the movie's dominant imagery—the dead leaves, the roadster, the mansion and its foyer, the horizons of oil derricks, the desolate roads and streets,

Written on the Wind: the blowing leaves of the movie's climax and beginning—
and Kyle Hadley (Robert Stack) with a gun

etc.—but to its characteristic devices: like that visual rhyming of blowing
trees and whirling curtains inside, or the way it shows us a key event like
Stack's collapse on the porch with some overweening object (the roadster
in this case) in the fore- or middle ground, coming between us and it.

Sometimes those objects *are* the event—or very nearly. Like all the
shades and textures of things in Bacall's Palm Beach hotel suite—the one
she's never seen before, and that Stack, in his attempt to seduce her, has
reserved for her, to her surprise and dismay (she hardly knows him): mauve
walls and golden screens and white rugs and blue moonlit waters on view
from the windows and terrace. As she moves slowly into the room—Stack
and Hudson observing her reaction from the doorway—the camera moves
laterally alongside her, disclosing as it goes a champagne bottle and
gleaming silver bucket, a burst of purple orchids amid white posies, a
bowl heaped with apples and bananas, and finally (against the wall) a pro-

fusion of small-bud magenta flowers rising and spilling from their vases. It's these red flowers that Bacall stops at—in her quandary, turning her back on them. But you notice she sways a bit—leaning into them with her back, looking judicious, before moving away. Nearly all the flowers in the movie are like that: radiant, effulgent, chorus-girl flowers—even a funeral wreath we see later on, blown skittering across a driveway, with its shiny black ribbon against the rich, vivid fir-tree green.

The inanimate objects in this movie are not portentous, as they usually are in Hitchcock. What they are instead is intensely *present*. Like that yellow roadster, or those ceaselessly nodding oil pumps (like grazing pterodactyl heads) that often turn up at the sides of the screen in exterior shots. The *things* in the movie get your attention even when they don't seem to be calling for it—even when they're not foregrounded or otherwise highlighted. Not because they seem "so real"—we don't normally, for example, see colors at such an intensity as they have here, in Russell Metty's Technicolor photography—but because they seem so powerfully sensuous, so intractably material. And they are everywhere . . .

It's sort of a shock, then, when this effect first happens to a person—when a human figure is objectified in the same way: when Bacall—who is now married to Stack and on her honeymoon—arises from their bed and moves her sleeping husband's pillow to make him more comfortable, disclosing the revolver concealed beneath it. What gives this revelation its impact is the seeming tactility of everything in the shot: Stack is on his back, sleeping deeply, his face turned to the left, his upper body exposed to the waist, the smooth-skinned, deeply tanned flesh against the blue-tinged whiteness of the pillow and sheets; and Bacall, at screen right above him, standing in shock at her discovery, holding the pistol with its blue metal barrel and pearl-white handle in the palm of her hand over the brown form below. And yet while Stack's character looks almost alarmingly *embodied* here, heavy and inert and scarily exposed, Bacall is made to look almost bodiless, chic and gaunt in her diaphanous but concealing nightgown. And throughout the movie, with its insistent materiality, she becomes an almost *abstract* sort of presence. And a distinctly uncomfortable one, moving warily through it all, as she does through that hotel suite.

Lucy (Bacall) works for the Hadley Oil ad account in New York. Mitch Wayne (Rock Hudson) is a geologist working for Old Man Hadley; he is also best friend of and unofficial watchdog to the Hadley son, Kyle (Robert Stack). Mitch brings Lucy to "21" to meet Kyle, who has flown himself and Mitch all the way from Texas to have the steak sandwich there.* Both men are drawn to Lucy, but it's Kyle who makes the play for her, while Mitch looks on unhappily (his role through much of the movie). They fly to Palm Beach, where Kyle springs that hotel room on her, stocking it with expensive presents. But she is not that kind of girl—though she's tempted, she admits—and she leaves. Kyle follows and stops her at the airport. She's fallen in love with him, she confesses—and he with her. So they get promptly married—in Acapulco—leaving Mitch behind, disapproving ("Your torch is showing," someone says to him). The father, Jasper Hadley (Robert Keith), having been assured by the trusted Mitch that Lucy is no golddigger, is happy about the marriage, seeing some hope in it for salvaging his dissolute son.

But the wildest member of the family is the daughter, Marylee (Dorothy Malone), and she is no friend to her brother. Openly contemptuous of him, she is equally hostile to the new wife. And she is desperately in love with Mitch, who is unresponsive, who cares for her "like a sister," as he tells her. Since she can't have him, she sets out to have every other male in town, it seems, most of whom work for her father. She grew up with Mitch: by a curious arrangement between his dad and Jasper, Mitch was raised with the two Hadley children. And almost their happiest memories now (Kyle's and Marylee's at least) are of those childhood days "by the river" where they used to play together ("our own private world"). "Mitch, let's go down to the river," Marylee says to him, just after he's rescued her from an overpersistent date. But she has to go alone—and when she does, it's only to remember how much in love with him she's always been, and how happy the three of them were back then. She does persuade him to picnic there later on. And it's the only untroubled encounter we see the two of them have. Even Mitch, it seems—resolutely grown-up as he is—is not immune to the spell of "the river." "How far we've come from the river," is his final telling rebuke to Marylee at the movie's end.

None of this is especially convincing as written. The screenplay is schematic enough at times to seem like a plot outline. Dialogue references to "the river," mostly unelaborated, have the regularity of TV commercials. And there isn't much apparent interest in the psychology of these people, much as they might seem to invite it. Mitch and Lucy are mostly lay figures, conventional hero and heroine types. The "villains," of course—Kyle and Marylee—are more interesting. But they are also flat, vivid, posterlike figures, suiting the movie's look and style, and, for *us* at

---

*The steak sandwich John Travolta orders in Quentin Tarantino's *Pulp Fiction*—with its fauxfifties diner—is called "the Douglas Sirk."

least, as much identified with their own intense materiality as the objects around them are.

Marylee is luridly provocative—but there's something blurred and out-of-focus about her prettiness: it's too defiant, too anxious even. And she never lets up: she looks sidling and sinuous even sitting still—"keeping her motor running," as one of her pickups instructs her to do. But unlike her suffering brother, she does seem to enjoy herself—never more so than when she's embarrassing her family. Like the night the cops bring her home, with Hadley Senior at the door: she goes up the big staircase without a word, trailing her stole and swishing her tush and smirking triumphantly all the way—then slipping behind the door into her room looking as if she meant to burgle it.

Marylee saunters and Kyle lopes. And while she looks challenging, *he* looks and sounds tormented—with his strangled voice, his boyish curly hair and granite chin, most of all in his suffering, haunted eyes. He has a rocking stride when he walks, an air of unconvinced macho, and a slant-shouldered angle that's most extreme when he's most upset—or humiliated, as he's made to feel after an early barroom brawl with one of Marylee's oil-worker studs. Kyle is defending the family honor, supposedly, but he gets knocked down and it's Mitch who has to finish the fight for him, with Marylee as a delighted onlooker—happy when Kyle is losing, even happier when her hero, Mitch, wins. Fighting for *her,* she hopes ("So you *do* care?")—but no such luck.

She goes out in disgust, in her high heels and sexy red sheath dress, going through the beaded malacca curtains, then pausing in the hallway behind them (in one of the movie's most memorable shots), standing against the wall and looking back. Kyle follows her, mortified, with his tilted lope—then stops (in the same shot) in front of the curtains and turns, issuing a final threat to the unconscious man on the floor, Mitch and the bartender standing over him: "I'll kill him!" Kyle says in the foreground, with Marylee behind, in a figure-molding half-light. It's a very Sternberg-like shot (the beaded curtains alone)—a director Sirk admired. He uses saturated color here the way Sternberg used high-contrast black and white: for a noir effect—in the bluish shadows, the back- and side-lighting of both figures, and in the ambiguity of their interaction. "A whiskey bottle's about all *you'd* ever kill," says Marylee through the curtains. Not replying, Kyle turns and looks at her, looking at him—then plunges through the curtains, sending them swaying and chattering behind him, and goes past her and out. She stands for a moment, looking at the others, then goes slowly out after him: his licensed torturer.

As you'd expect, she's a hot dancer—doing the mambo in a long black dress with a plunging bodice at a big Hadley soiree. Doing it with Mitch, in fact—until he gives up chucklingly and quits the floor. No surprise *he* can't dance—sometimes it seems he can hardly move (unless he's fighting), he's so big and tall and towering over everyone, so eponymously Rock-like. But Mitch is in a painful bind through most of the movie, not only disapproving of Kyle but committed to watching over him, even when he marries the woman Mitch loves. All he can do about *that* is look on at it, and continue to rebuff the insatiable Marylee—and he disapproves of her, too. "You've not only got your axe buried in Kyle's head but you're grinding it too," he tells her, accurately enough. "You should be huntin', not broodin'," his outdoorsman dad says to him. But Mitch's situation doesn't seem to call for much *beyond* brooding—until it comes time to beat up Kyle and save Lucy. And in the end, he seems as ill at ease in this movie as she does. (You don't see either of *them* around beaded curtains.)

Mitch, of course, is the son that Jasper Hadley would like to have had—as Kyle well knows. But what about Jasper, the estranged and powerful father? He's someone impressive, we are told—a man of such stature and authority that his son despairs of living up to him or even pleasing him. But this titan is played by an actor who looks more like a purse snatcher—or a gutless small-town sheriff (a role Keith actually did play in *The Wild One* with Brando)—and who has apparently been directed here to confirm just such impressions, counterindicated as they may be by the script.

But *all* the dad figures in this movie are a little fishy. Mitch's father, Hoak, for example (Harry Shannon)—we hear about him ahead of time too: Kyle tells Lucy that he's a local legend, a great white hunter, a throwback to Daniel Boone, and so on. Then we see this lumbering, portly, nasal-voiced old fellow who is clearly most at home seated on his front porch. And the Hadley family doctor (Edward Platt), who first implies to his patient Kyle that he might be sterile by barking at him irritably that "there's nothing wrong with *Lucy*" and then walking off with his drink to rejoin the party (being given by Kyle)—and who later confirms the bad news ("The tests we took show—well, a weakness") over Cokes at the local drugstore under a banner that says BUY QUALITY DRUGS HERE. (What tests?)

But the sort of unease such figures inspire permeates the movie. Especially its quieter scenes, like the first meeting between Jasper and his new daughter-in-law. Sirk's pacing of this scene in Jasper's office is strangely hesitant, the polite, banal exchanges ("Have you been out to the house?" "Yes. It's beautiful. And it's *home*." And so on) are offered so slowly and gravely that they begin to sound ambiguous—even Pinteresque. As do the interactions in a later scene, in the Hadley library during the big party, when Jasper, with Kyle looking on, gives Lucy the present of a jeweled necklace. "Oh, *thank* you, Dad," she says, giving him a sort of air kiss, then turning and tipping backwards so he can fasten it around her throat. Kyle wonders aloud if "the poor husband" doesn't get a kiss too. Of course he does—and she bestows it sweetly, darting a nervous glance at him when he jokes about "the stork," then turning to smile on Dad again. She goes to a wall mirror to look at herself and her gift. She is very pleased, of course—until Kyle joins her in the reflection, when again she looks fleetingly uneasy, but turns and smiles. A bit later Kyle will see her slow-dancing with Mitch, the two of them alone on the parquet, looking dreamy and close.

But Lucy—in spite of the invidious suggestions of such scenes—is neither mercenary nor unfaithful, but is, on the contrary, staunchly, even exemplarily loyal to her deeply troubled husband. But though such suggestions about her seem not to be in the script, they *are* in the scene as directed. They are, in fact, just why he cast Bacall, Sirk told me in 1977: "Because she has this ambiguity in her cold face. She has almost a designing quality at times. And people asked me why I didn't cast a nice sweet American girl. But I wanted what Bacall has. She has this wavering light about her—and she is not a lover. The whole relation between her and Stack remains ambiguous then."

Kyle and Marylee, on the other hand, are enemies of the ambiguous, attempting to defeat it at every turn. "Haven't you learned to hate Marylee as much as I do?" says Kyle to his wife—who really doesn't want to pursue *that* subject at the moment. She and Mitch are sitting with the drunken Kyle at the country club bar: they are on the shared mission of finding out (for Jasper as well as themselves) what's made Kyle start drinking again (he is too ashamed to tell his wife about the "weakness" diagnosis), after he's been so good for so long. "So you'd like to know my secret?" he says—and pauses. Mitch leans forward expectantly; Lucy stares intently. "My secret—" he says slowly, then another pause—"is not to *pour* the vermouth, but just to *pretend* you're pouring . . ." And he collapses in helpless and delighted laughter onto the bar—while Mitch and Lucy exchange a hopeless look above him.

They should only know (as they soon will) what Marylee is up to now (she declined the invitation to join them at the country club). *Her* roadster is red, and she drives it through the usual landscape of oil derricks rising against a dishwater-blue evening sky, turning off the highway into the

"Because she has this ambiguity in her cold face" (Sirk):
Lauren Bacall as Lucy, with Rock Hudson and Robert Stack—
in Kyle's private plane

wooden carport of a ramshackle gas station. And the ensuing scene is in a distinctly Sirkian mode, combining the ravishing and the creepy.

As she pulls up to the gas pumps (they have big red "H"s on them), the camera looks down at her from the eaves of the carport, and a shadowy uniformed figure in brown walks toward her. "Fill 'er up?" he asks (predictably) and goes to the pump at the back of the car, taking the gas hose down—as the camera begins slowly to descend, as if magnetized by that car: which is not only intensely red but seems in the hazy air of the evening half-light to be giving off *waves* of red like heat. Then a low-angle close shot: from the front of the car, looking up and over the curves of undulating red metal above the dashboard at Marylee behind the wheel, against an expanse of that desolate ashy sky, as she teases and flirts with the gas jockey (they've recognized one another from high school days), her white-gloved hand on the leather of the passenger seat moving slowly and sensuously up and down, while the faceless guy (he's still in shadow) "fills 'er up" behind. As they chat, both their voices—his especially—have a ghostly, disembodied sound: she wants to know when he gets off work and he answers that he'll close up right now. The next time we see the red car it's outside a squalid-looking roadside motel.

The cops bring her home—along with the poor garageman. These cops routinely report to old man Hadley, and so they do again. That very same night Lucy brings Kyle home, dead drunk and draped across Mitch's shoulders. It's all too much for Jasper. While Lucy puts her husband to bed, Mitch tries to console (rather feebly) the old man (as well as preventing him from shooting the garageman). Upstairs Marylee, looking pleased with herself, enters her room, going to the window to watch the cops drive off. She lights a cigarette from the fireplace, takes her framed photo of Mitch in one hand, and with the other turns on her phonograph, eliciting a sudden blast of jazzy mambo music ("Temptation," no less). Downstairs, Jasper climbs the staircase to bed. And as he does so, more and more wearily, Marylee dances, more and more wildly: Sirk intercuts the exultant, demonic dance with the elderly man's slow, heavy ascent, and finally his fall and death at the foot of the stairs—in the movie's most famous tour de force.

More jolting than that first blast of music, as the sequence begins, is Marylee's sudden seizurelike movement, arrhythmic and grotesque: kicking her shoes off onto the thick carpet, Mitch's photo in one hand, a cigarette in the other, she comes pitching and shuffling forward, head thrown back and bosom thrust forward, arms and elbows pumping galvanically. Then she whips around, reversing direction, and goes in back of the frosted-glass perfumery cabinet—which is just behind that vase of lascivious red antheriums in the foreground, with their protruding yellow pistils—and strips, putting the framed photo on top of the cabinet and kicking away her dress, still dancing. Cut to downstairs: Mitch and Jasper still in the library, hearing the distant music. Back to Marylee and the mambo at full volume: she's in a black undergarment now, and dances behind the cabinet again, putting on what turns out to be a negligee of red chiffon—through the cabinet's frosted glass it looks almost like she's bursting into flame. Cut to Jasper trudging up the stairs, the music loud and louder—as the crosscutting between the two scenes gets steadily more rapid and agitated. And the views of Marylee (as her father toils upward) in more and more furious motion—her *Totentanz*—become more like mere glimpses, fractured and discontinuous, of her grinding butt or flailing limbs, body parts in motion and streaming red fabric, bursting out and onto the close-up low-angled camera; in one quick view of her, full-length but headless, she seems to be rushing bacchante-like right at it. And reaching the top of the stairway, Jasper staggers, pitches back, and tumbles to the bottom, as Mitch runs to his aid and Lucy comes onto the landing above. In her room, Marylee falls backwards onto a couch, the music crescendoing, as she scissor-kicks her legs in the air under the swirling red chiffon, holding her hands over them like a puppeteer. While old dad lies dead below.

All this is apparently telling us—fairly loudly—that Marylee is not just a nympho (her usual designation in descriptions of the film) or a tramp or a spoiled rich girl, but a rather seriously bad person. Unlike her brother, who has killed his father with inadvertence, out of his own desperate weakness (that image of him hung across Mitch's broad shoulders), Marylee does it out of a more active intention, a more serious malevolence, it would seem. But then the pure outrageousness of the sequence really undercuts that point, making it impossible to feel such a conventional moral judgment of her, even if it's the (at least partially) intended one. The scene is too thrilling, too much fun to watch: the audacity of it can make you laugh out loud with satisfaction and pleasure. You certainly can't feel much about Hadley—he's been too "ambiguous" for that, and too much (in spite of the buildup he gets earlier) a nullity, in the movie and in his daughter's life (in fact they appear together in the same shot only once in the whole movie: when the cops bring her home and she goes wordlessly past him to her room). What you feel instead is a kind of collusion with Marylee's recklessness—and her ruthlessness. *She's* not afraid—unlike Kyle—to "kill" the dad, or to dance on his grave. We never see her mourning the loss, or feeling guilty—as we do Kyle.

But—she makes you nervous, all the same. She inspires apprehension, just as Kyle does—"these two degenerated kids," as Sirk (in his nicest slightly off-balance English) affectionately called them when we talked. Marylee is hell on her family, but she's no femme fatale. Far from it. "I'm desperate for you, Mitch," she tells the love of her life—and he turns uncomfortably away, or else looks uncomfortably straight ahead. She's sexy enough in these scenes with him, but also more than a little embarrassing—if only because they are always so hopeless. And that doesn't keep her from repeating them, and then rolling with the inevitable rejection. "Still the idiot boy," she says, almost good-humoredly, as he rises and leaves her—and then she goes off and dances. She's sort of indomitable. But like her brother, Kyle—though in a different way—she seems very exposed.

It's after the funeral, after the mourning wreath has been taken down from the front gates, and the survivors are at the table in the formal Hadley dining room. But not Kyle: drunk again probably, or God knows what; at any rate *very* late for dinner. They sit plunged in gloom and silence, as the tactful black butler circles and serves them: Lucy at the foot of the table, the head empty and waiting for Kyle, Mitch and Marylee across from each other at the sides. Marylee is eating her shrimp cocktail (the other two are not touching theirs) and seeming to enjoy it. "It's rather pleasant here without Kyle, isn't it?" she says brightly. They ignore her (*they* are very worried about him). Then there's the sound of his car in the driveway—and he comes lurching amiably in to the room to join them, grinning hugely. "*My,* you're a dandy group!" he says to the stone faces around him. They ignore that too.

He sits in his place, facing Lucy at the other end, and begins by refusing the shrimp cocktail ("Bring me a cocktail I can *drink*"). He looks at the others (who have clearly been *waiting* for him). Then, with a look of irrepressible sudden delight, grinning, squirming on his chair, curling in on himself with the great joke of it, he says: "I suppose you're wondering why I brought you all here tonight?" Mitch and Lucy do not laugh. "Now if the lights would only go out!" says Marylee, still showily enjoying her shrimp.

They're just like children really: acting up at table, talking back, giggling and making dumb jokes that are funny only to *them,* and so on. But now the distinctly grown-up Lucy—sleek, suffering, serious—rises and approaches her husband; she has something she wants to speak to him about, in private (she is pregnant). "Come upstairs, Kyle," she says, going behind his chair, putting her hands on his shoulders. "Do you wish to confess?" says Kyle, but looking apprehensive now (*that* joke wasn't so funny). With her arm around his waist, she leads him gently out of the room. "Amusing, isn't he?" says Marylee, as they pass, to Mitch. *"Very,"* comes the sepulchral reply.

Lucy supports her sozzled husband gently and inexorably up the staircase. He tries more joking on the way. But they keep going up; and she looks so solemn, he's getting frightened. And so he babbles away—about giving a party or going back to Acapulco, or to Palm Beach. Then they've reached the landing, heading toward their room. "Whadda you say to Palm Beach?" he says urgently, grasping her hand and sitting down on a hallway chair. "It'll be fun, like turning back the clock!" Still she doesn't answer, but draws him to his feet, moves past him, and opens the door to their room. He sways a little, steadying himself with an arm against the doorframe: "Palm Beach. I like that. It's got meaning, it's got signif—" But she is inside the room now and drawing him after her: "It's got meaning," he says, hopelessly, and goes—

Into the half-darkened foyer. He goes by her and crosses the screen, staggering, into a shadow, leaning with his elbow against a chair back, turning to her in a strange, insinuating, almost feminine movement, framed against a backdrop of eerily glowing, translucent rose-tinted cur-

Mitch (Hudson) and Lucy (Bacall, at head of table) have been waiting for him, and Kyle (Stack) has just staggered in—drunk again. Marylee (Dorothy Malone) has *not* been waiting—but enjoying her shrimp.

tains: "Are you sure your husband's out of town?" he says, in a mournful voice, from out of his shadow. And she walks past him (the camera following her), through darkness, to a table lamp, turning it on, two dusty-rose soft chairs on either side, a silken gold Chinese screen behind it. "Sit down, Kyle," she says gently—ominously. They both sit in the chairs—with now a bowl of the most improbably glowing oranges between them.

These oranges, of course, don't "mean" anything, but they get your attention. And all the unsettling details of what's just preceded them, in the couple's walk up the stairs and entry into the bedroom—those strangely glowing curtains, the oddly displaced, oddly mournful sexual note, the atmosphere of languor and insinuating dreaminess, and so on—seem to come together over them, like the ingredients of a magical spell. Kyle is not only like a child—in the care of his watchful and maternal wife—but like a magical child, casting a spell to ward off the evil now about to strike. Sirk takes you *inside* that spell here—the magic is infectious.

He's been doing that all along, of course—so deftly that you've hardly been noticing (the oranges are a tip-off). You might say the whole movie is enthralled. That's why all those intrusive luminous objects between you and what's going on never *seem* intrusive—why they feel more substantive than irrelevant and decorative. From Kyle's yellow roadster to Marylee's red one, from the whirling dead leaves to the Palm Beach hotel suite brimming with gifts and colors, Marylee's perfumery of frosted glass and the panting red-and-yellow antheriums, to all those different and transfiguring curtains (the beaded ones at the barroom, the roseate ones in the bedroom), and so on. It's a *world* of magical objects (only "the river" when we see it looks unmagical—like a cheap Universal set), projections of the picture's two "secret owners" (as Sirk called Kyle and Marylee), and only they seem truly at home in it. As we know, they most of all want their childhood back. And in a sense the movie *gives* it to them—though it's a poisoned gift.

When Lucy tells Kyle she is pregnant in this scene, he reacts first with disbelief, then with anger ("You shouldn't have done that to me!")—assuming that the child is Mitch's. And when he accuses her, she stands up, shocked and incredulous at what she's hearing—but she has risen into a shadow that hides her face. She has, in fact, fallen in love (undeclared) with Mitch by this point; but like him—like Jasper too, and all those others—she holds back and holds in, guarding her secrets, controlling her pain. While Kyle and Marylee let it all hang out—too much. They are like the Method actors of their own lives. And in the same way this movie is like an aesthete's tribute to self-expression, to the theatre of raw emotion—an aesthete who sympathizes. "The director's heart," Sirk told me, "is with the two doomed people." But he keeps his distance.

Kyle flies into a rage, rushing at Lucy and knocking her to the floor. Hearing the commotion, Mitch rushes to intervene. There's a scuffle—and some very Sirkian inflections. Mitch, also in a rage, has grabbed Kyle from behind—on the way to throwing him out the door—and now swings him suddenly around, passing his face in front of the camera, so close up that it seems almost a collision between face and camera. The effect is over in an instant, but it's still memorable—a moment in which Kyle's humiliation seems almost unbearably exposed to us and present, as if Sirk were suggesting that this abasement was almost too painful to look at. "Get out before I *kill* you!" shouts Mitch at the departing Kyle, ordering him out of his own house—while the soundtrack music pounds. And the silent, mortified Kyle lurches blindly down the great staircase—his Quasimodo walk—across the foyer and out the front door. But instead of following him toward and then out the door, Sirk's camera turns away at the foot of the staircase, watching the defeated man's ignominious exit—instead of looking directly at it—through a mirror on the wall, hanging just above an end table and a vase of autumn flowers.

Upstairs after dinner: Kyle's rage at Lucy when she tells him she is pregnant

But turning away, I think, can be one of the most powerful movements a camera will make. And it's a particularly moving gesture in the middle of such an overblown movie. Yet even that overblownness has been a kind of turning away, putting us at an aestheticized remove from the characters and from their pain. But our sense of that pain is never less than real and acute. And the formalist strategies by which Sirk mediates it—turning pulp into ceremony—can often seem (as here) like a kind of tact, an expression of benevolence, the sympathy all the more telling because its form is so respectfully indirect. "Sirk," wrote Fassbinder, "has made the tenderest films I know: they are the films of someone who loves people and does not despise them as we do."

But neither that indirection nor the tenderness it expresses could work without wonderful people on the screen, without Stack and Malone and what they bring to their roles, the way they express the warring levels of pain in each character—in Kyle's anguished hopefulness, Marylee's demonic will. And they connect with us too because of what the movie has made them represent: that peculiar, specially American (to a European's eye, at any rate) relation to our imagined lost innocence, and to the magic spell of childhood.

Sirk avoids the time-honored way of dramatizing this relation, which in

Marylee (Malone at left) at the inquest, waiting to testify—
as Mitch and Lucy look on anxiously

movies past normally involved some early or flashback scenes of the golden childhood days, with child actors standing in for their grown-up characters. But there are no golden days for Kyle and Marylee in this movie, only their yearning for them. And they are not, kidlike as they are, James Dean– or Marilyn Monroe–like figures, those cultural icons of then and now who seem to have preserved against the heaviest odds their specifically childish integrity. For the Hadleys it's truly lost (the only set in the movie, as I said above, that looks glaringly fake is the river one). And the only way they can get back to "the river" is by dying, it seems—as Kyle finally does, promising to wait there for the others, for Mitch and Marylee. "What are we doing here, Mitch?" he says before he expires. "Let's go down to the river where we belong." And that sense of being bewilderingly out of place in his own life, as if it were something he'd been exiled to, is probably the deepest note in Stack's performance (Sirk told him, Stack said, to play the torment, not the drunk). It's the sort of panicked consciousness that Marylee seems exactly to be resisting. At least till the end.

Earlier on, after having been thrown out by Mitch, Kyle comes back with a gun, intending to kill him. This is the episode that we saw in truncated form under the opening credits. Now, instead of staying outside the house, we follow Kyle into the library, where he confronts Mitch with the pistol. Marylee runs down from upstairs (as we saw) to stop him. She rushes at him, and in the struggle over the gun Kyle is shot. Mitch goes to him and holds him. Then he staggers onto the porch and dies. But it's in this scene that we see Marylee's powerful will collapse at last—and that look of terror that has always seemed (you recognize), like a double exposure, to be the face beneath the perpetually challenging one she's worn up to now, appears without intervention. She really does look like a frightened little girl.

It's not her last transformation. The melodrama has another act: Mitch is suspected of murdering Kyle. And Marylee (more desperate than ever now that Lucy is free to marry Mitch) threatens to testify at the inquest that she saw Mitch do it *unless* he agrees to marry her.

She is dressed in black at the hearing, her hair pulled back into a knot in back under a huge black hat with an enormous flat and circular brim, like an old vinyl record with the center cut out. She sits alone, slumped in her chair, looking grim and severe—and inscrutable. And she is now, understandably, the focus of Mitch's and Lucy's anxiety and suspense, as they sit together across the room from her. On the witness stand under questioning, however, Marylee exonerates him completely, telling of the accident just as it happened. And accounting for Kyle's extraordinary behavior when the coroner asks her about it, she merely replies that her brother was "sad . . . the saddest of us all"—joining herself with him at last, no longer fighting the recognition, and lowering her head slowly as the scene fades out, the black brim of her hat descending across her face like a curtain slowly lowering. It's the emotional climax of the film, and it's genuinely moving. And it's no surprise to you by now that that hat seems to have almost as much to do with it as Malone's acting does.

·

Twenty-Three

DOUGLAS SIRK

Of the people I talked to about Sirk after his death in 1987, Irene Heymann was the only one who had been a close personal friend. And a longtime one: they had known each other from their early days in Weimar Germany to and through their Hollywood years. Heymann arrived there in 1942 and worked for some thirty-five years as personal assistant to super-agent Paul Kohner. She was still at her desk there when I met her at the Beverly Hills offices in 1992: a small, round, bright-eyed woman, now dependent on a mechanized chair, a lively and delightful talker—and a thoughtful one, often pausing to consider before she spoke in her small, quiet voice. "I don't think," she said, after one of those musing pauses, "Douglas was ever a very happy person . . . I think it was a kind of disappointing adventure in Hollywood for him." In spite of his success there? I asked. "I don't even know if he *cared* for great success," she replied. Then added: "He *loved* being a stage director. He would have been head of the Berlin State Theatre if it hadn't been for Hitler . . . Douglas was kind of an intellectual snob in a way. Not that his movies really showed it . . ."

He lived modestly, she said, and kept aloof from "the Hollywood crowd," letting his devoted wife, Hilde (it was clear that Heymann never cared much for *her*), front the world for him and handle all the business there was. "Douglas was a cold fish in many ways. Not a warm person—though he *thought* he was." He was really "a little cynical" about people, she thought, but "of course he had been done by a lot people very badly." His friends in the movie business tended to be the writers—like Salka Viertel (Berthold's wife, Peter's mother, Garbo's friend and screenwriter). "Salka had acted for him in his theatre at Chemnitz. He was very friendly with her." But he never was part of her famous salon of German émigrés (the Manns, the Reinhardts, et al.) that met regularly at her house on Maberry Road. Could they, I asked her, have been snobbish about the kind of movies he did? She laughed. "No, that wouldn't happen—anybody who worked and made money was *very* favorably regarded." Douglas was simply not "terribly social." Unlike his friend Robert Siodmak, who was less of an intellectual, and who "definitely belonged to the 'inside Hollywood' group." But Siodmak was a very charming man: "very lively, very funny." Another pause. "Douglas could be funny. But he always thought if he was going to be funny he'd lose some of his dignity. He was *awful* stiff. I used to make fun of him about that . . . He used to call me 'the porcupine,' because, you know, if something happened, all my little things would stir up . . ." A smile and another pause. "We were good friends," she said softly, fondly. (Of course you were, I thought: *he* was a porcupine too—though more in disguise, I would guess, than his prickly little friend.)

Sirk was much warmer and friendlier on his sets, she said, than he was in his private life: "He worked *awfully* hard with actors, and they gave performances for him they never repeated." Robert Stack and Rock Hudson ("a dear man") both "adored" him. Hudson in particular was like a hero-worshiping student around him: "There was a lot of the teacher in Douglas—he liked to hold forth."

The former Sirk actors I talked to around the same time as the visit with Heymann were warm admirers still, and with a common point of remembrance: in one way or another he was like a father. To Barbara Rush (in four of his films) he was kindly and indulgent ("like a papa bear"); to Susan Kohner (in *Imitation of Life*) he was stern and demanding; to Juanita Moore (in the same film) he was doting and endlessly solicitous. The only actor I talked to who seemed not to have liked him was (the rather *un*daughterly) Claudette Colbert (in two Sirk films), when I interviewed her in 1984, mainly about Lubitsch and Sturges. She looked almost startled when I also asked about Sirk—then made a little face. "Dour man," she said, and changed the subject. (She said a lot more about Capra, whom she also didn't like.)

But it's only recently—through Tag Gallagher's article on Sirk in *Film Comment* (November–December 1998)—that I learned more about that mysterious son Sirk had alluded to so elliptically the last time I saw him. According to Gallagher, the boy was eight when Sirk was permanently barred, on the grounds of his remarriage to a Jew, from any contact with him. More extraordinary: he then saw him again at the movies. The son, raised as a Nazi, became—as Claus Detlef Sierck—a top child movie star in Germany. Until he grew up and then was drafted at the end of the war for the Russian front, where he became officially missing in action. Sirk returned to Europe after the war to search for him—with no success—and kept the whole story more or less private while he lived.

Sirk himself (born in 1901, as Detlef Sierck, to Danish parents in Germany) had been more fortunately a young man in the cultural ferment of Weimar. Both gifted and energetic, he was by turns a writer (publishing a translation of Shakespeare's sonnets at twenty-two), a painter, a journalist, moving in circles of figures like Brecht and Weill, being a friend of Max Brod's, studying art with Erwin Panofsky at the university. But it was the theatre that he was really drawn to, and where he made his early reputation as a brilliant and protean young director in state theatres at Hamburg, Bremen, Leipzig, and so on—until the Nazis stalled his Berlin appointment. Then he went into picturemaking.

In his three years at UFA (1934–37) he made eight features for them, including an Ibsen adaptation (*Pillars of Society,* 1935) and a musical in both German and French versions (*Das Hofkonzert/La Chanson du souvenir,* 1936). But his biggest popular successes were the two pictures he made starring a stolid, rather heavily smoldering Swede named Zarah Leander, appearing as a sort of echt-Dietrich, singing sexily and living bravely in exotic locales: Australia in the first, *Zu neuen Ufern* (1937), and a Germanic sort of Puerto Rico in the second, *La Habanera* (1937). Leander quickly became the Third Reich's biggest box-office draw, and Hitler's own favorite star. But by then Sirk was gone—even before *La Habanera* had premiered in Berlin. On the pretext of scouting locations, he and Hilde had gone instead to Rome. And from there—helped, as he told it, by some sympathetic trickster nuns (Nabokov again)—he made it into Switzerland. A year of European wandering and occasional work (he directed a feature in Holland) followed. In 1939 the couple embarked for Hollywood: Warner Bros. had hired him to write an American version of his hit *Zu neuen Ufern.* But the project came to nothing in the the end, and left the Sirks to their failing chicken farm—until 1942, when he signed as a screenwriter at Columbia. He was not, however, allowed to direct at first. It's not hard to imagine why: "One of my dearest projects," he told Halliday, "was to make a picture set in a blind people's home. There would just have been people ceaselessly tapping, trying to grasp things they could not see . . ."

Not even his émigré friends—active independent producers like Seymour Nebenzal (producer of Lang's *M*) and Arnold Pressburger—would spring for *that* project (he'd done a screenplay, he told Halliday). But they did hire Sirk to direct (on loan-out from Columbia), and the films he made for them were, as he later said, "totally European": *Hitler's Madman* (1943, about Heydrich and the Lidice massacre) and *Summer Storm* (1944) for Nebenzal, *A Scandal in Paris* (1945) for Pressburger. They were modestly budgeted films and, by American standards at least, rather arty and offbeat

Douglas Sirk on the set of *Lured* with two of the stars,
Lucille Ball (left) and Cedric Hardwicke

ones. Even so, one of them—*Summer Storm,* based on Chekhov's novella *The Shooting Party*—was a surprising box-office success, due mainly to lurid ads featuring a sexy Linda Darnell, an actress who up to then had been typed by her home studio (Fox) as an alluring innocent, as the virginal alternative to Rita Hayworth (*Blood and Sand*) and Dorothy Lamour (*Chad Hanna*).

There wasn't much that ads could do for *A Scandal in Paris,* however. "Based on" the memoirs of François Eugène Vidocq, a nineteenth-century con man and crook who became head of the Paris police (George Sanders as Vidocq), with its stylized Bloomingdale's-window look, its relentlessly "witty" dialogue and epigrammatizing hero, and an adultery plot that seemed less titillating than nutty (e.g., the cuckolded husband disguised as a peddler prowling after his young wife with cages of twittering song-birds on his back; a villain impaled on a Chinese carousel; and so on), it was too much for the home audience. But it remained a favorite of Sirk's. "In fact if you talk of art," he said to me in 1977, "I consider *A Scandal in Paris* my best picture." In fact we *weren't* talking of art, but this was a movie he wanted to praise—as well as its screenwriter, Ellis St. Joseph, whom he described as a friend and, more sourly, as the only person he met in Hollywood who knew who Kafka was.

His next two movies, though, were in the noir vein, and both close to astonishing: generic, even formulaic materials transformed by pure film-making brio and by Sirk's rapport with his actors. The first one, *Lured* (1947), was a remake of Siodmak's 1939 French film, *Pièges,* the last picture he made before fleeing Paris ahead of the Germans. In Sirk's American remake Paris becomes London (and Maurice Chevalier becomes George Sanders), and Lucille Ball (a real Sirk chum, according to Heymann—he called her "LuBall") is the American chorus girl who consents to be a Scotland Yard decoy to capture a serial killer, confronting the various suspect-creeps—from Hollywood's still wonderful roster of familiar character players (Alan Mowbray, Boris Karloff, Joseph Calleia, Cedric Hard-wicke—not to mention Charles Coburn and George Zucco on the police side)—that the plot throws in her way.

The next one was a Claudette Colbert vehicle, *Sleep My Love* (1948), for Mary Pickford's new independent production unit. It's a "suspenser" about a trusting rich wife who thinks she is going mad when it's really her gold-digging husband who is doing it all to her, slyly plotting her destruction and death. Sirk came to the overfamiliar plot eight years after George Cukor (*Gaslight*), four years after both Jacques Tourneur (*Experiment Perilous*) and André De Toth (*Dark Waters*), among others in between, and outdoes them all, it seems to me, redeeming the utterly predictable scenes and events by a fully imagined strangeness. Colbert's role—as the woman in peril—is, though elegantly played, generic, but Don Ameche as her murderous husband is a wonderfully pious, aggrieved sort of villain. And Robert Cummings, as her would-be lover and savior, with his talent for looking suspicious (something that undermined a lot of his *other* leading-man performances), with his button-bright eyes and faintly smirking mouth, is specially fine as he listens brightly to the unctuous Ameche smarm away at him in the requisite concerned-husband manner.

But as often with Sirk, it's the secondary characters you remember best. Especially the husband's two co-conspirators: Hazel Brooks as Daphne, his mistress, a svelte, lacquer-haired young woman with a burning stare; and George Coulouris as the half-blind photographer who is hiding her out in his home and studio, squinting at her through bottle-thick lenses (*"Look,"* she says—and he blinks at her swimmingly). Daphne is mostly to be seen—in a negligee, indolent and irritated—on some elevated level above the others. "Come down, Daphne," pleads the besotted Ameche (she is lounging on the photographer's modeling platform). But she rarely does,

George Coulouris, Hazel Brooks, and Don Ameche
play the evil conspirators in Sirk's *Sleep My Love.*

even for him—and almost never at all for the couple who are her hosts: not
only Coulouris but Queenie Smith, as his nattering, adenoidal little wife,
who is not privy to the criminal plot, and who never seems to notice how
garishly sexy-sinister (not to mention unfriendly) is the houseguest she
calls "Daf-uh-nee," with undiscouraged affection, throughout.

Sirk's noir style, in these two immensely entertaining thrillers, is sort of
like noir *mit Schlag*—more Vienna than Berlin, at once rigorous and lush:
ornate interiors, oblique angles, diagonal lines reaching into the deep-
focus background, through doorways, down hallways, in mirrors—frames
within the frame, and then frames within *them.* And yet at the same time
the mobile camera, constantly reframing, sustains a sense of forward movement, both within scenes and between them. Like Ray, Sirk cuts on movement, and he often "rhymes" the concluding action of one scene to the
opening one of the following scene—"my gliding cuts," as he called them.
Like Hitchcock and Welles, he makes movies like music: a linguistic point
he would invariably make to his interviewers was that "melodrama" originally meant "drama with music."

After this, Columbia actually let Sirk direct—two films which he
would later disown because of studio interference (though one of them,
Shockproof with Cornel Wilde, certainly has its moments). "I was com-

pletely fed up with Harry Cohn," he said. He got out of his Columbia contract and spent almost a year in Germany again, returning to the U.S. in
1950, where his friend Nebenzal asked him to direct an American remake
of *M,* with David Wayne in the Peter Lorre role. Sirk, wisely, declined
(Joseph Losey didn't).

What Sirk did instead, as it happened, was to form an independent production unit of his own, with his friend Rudi Joseph and (more importantly) Charles Boyer, to make a movie version of a play both Boyer and
Sirk admired: Emmet Lavery's *The First Legion*—a Broadway failure in
1934 but an ongoing success in theatres throughout Europe. The movie is
about a faculty of Jesuit priests at a California seminary who are confronted
by a fake miracle, and then finally by what may be a genuine one. Boyer is
the devout and skeptical priest who exposes the original fake, and Lyle
Bettger—with his burnished android looks—is the agnostic doctor who
has perpetrated it. Barbara Rush plays the hopelessly crippled girl (a boy
in the play) who rises and walks at the end, just before the fade-out.

The First Legion (1951) was the last—and arguably the finest—of Sirk's
pre-Universal movies. Religion, he said later, was "one of my constant pre-
occupations" ("even though I haven't been to church in decades"). Once he
had even written a religious play, he told Halliday, but he hadn't been
"entirely happy with it," adding: "You know, in a way, I think everything
is about religion: it's about the unknown things in men." *The First Legion*'s
screenplay, credited solely to Lavery, was in fact rewritten by Sirk with his
friend Irene Heymann (both uncredited). And while it's never quite
inspired, it's intelligent, even astute—remarkably without any of the fake
piety or booster-style religiosity that seemed required at the time for a
movie that featured one or more Catholic priests, let alone (as here) nearly
a whole cast of them. But the production *was* "watched," Sirk told Halliday: "The Jesuit fathers . . . were on the set the whole time, scrutinizing
every line and implication . . . I think it could have been a sharper picture,
more clearly in focus, if they hadn't been there."

But once again, if the writing isn't inspired, the filmmaking is. The
movie has a grace and fluency that are even beyond Sirk's two noir films
before it—a controlled lyricism, in Robert De Grasse's crystalline deep-
focus black-and-white photography (De Grasse had done Astaire-Rogers
movies at RKO). It was filmed entirely on location (Sirk, in contrast to
Siodmak, loved location work) at a real and historic California mission: a
complex of Spanish baroque buildings around a courtyard, which is filmed
most strikingly in low angles, with the camera looking up at skies, spires,
faces, the action taking place either in cramped interiors like the cell-like

backlit rooms where the priests live and work (there are no studio shots at all), or in grand spaces like the courtyard or main chapel or the community's vaulting common room. There is an almost continuous sense of space opening up before the camera, a kind of spatial flowering and straining upward, like the paralyzed girl's attempts to lift herself in her chair. And there are moments of almost Wellesian brilliance and power.

Like the ambiguous circumstance of that first "miracle"—the sudden rising to walk of the elderly Father Sierra (H. B. Warner—the famous Christ of De Mille's *King of Kings*), who has been bedridden for three years. The episode begins with the priests all assembled in the high-ceilinged common room, which is ringed—like a courtyard—by an open landing. There is a stairway to the landing and the upper rooms at the far end of the common room. Just to the left of the stairway and on the floor below the landing, a portable movie screen has been set up. A visiting missionary priest from India (Walter Hampden) is showing the home movies he made there. The lights are dimmed (though the landing is still lit), the projector whirs in the silence, the light beam passes through the darkness over the heads of the audience; and on the screen, in the far background of this long shot, there is the image of another long shot: the grainy, flickering silent image of thronging Indian crowds surrounding a ceremonially garbed elephant as it moves slowly among and above them. A vision of milling and lumbering and apparently directionless "progress"—what is it anyway? "Indian holy men capture the soul by capturing the imagination," intones the missionary at the projector—unhelpfully. The projector whirs steadily: a long shot again of the length of the room and of the far-off movie picture of the crowd milling and the elephant toiling along above it—and above *that,* on the landing, a shadow appears, then a man, the old priest (you presume), staggering along the railing. The priests below rise into the projector beam, then rush toward the stairway. Then a closer shot of movie and landing: the elephant coming into clearer focus and toward us, just as the frail old priest turns the corner above and begins to descend the stairway. He is ecstatic, convinced that he has seen "the blessed Joseph" in a vision that has restored his legs. It's really—as you guess—the agnostic doctor (Bettger), visiting his patient, who has restored them, and who then, as a malign private joke, lets the priests and others take it as miraculous.

The men all gather around Father Sierra on the stairs, on different levels (a favorite Sirk blocking). Only the skeptical Father Arnoux (Boyer) stands a bit apart. The doctor—with his aggressive disbelief and all the power that gives him over these others—stands above them all, coming up slowly behind at the height of the excitement. Arnoux alone is looking at *him.*

The First Legion: Charles Boyer (left) as the skeptical Jesuit, Lyle Bettger
as the atheist doctor, and H. B. Warner as the dying priest—
who will soon be "miraculously" brought back to life and health

The psychological duel between these two characters—between faith
and disbelief—is the core of the movie. And faith, of course, carries the day
at the end—when the girl who is a *real* paralytic staggers to her feet in
front of the mission's altar. But even here, at the climax and peak of the
film's inspirational bent, there is something detached and finally reserved.
It's not a religious movie—in spite of Sirk's announced preoccupation with
the subject—in the sense, for example, that Bresson's *Diary of a Country
Priest* or even Buñuel's *Nazarin* can be said to be the works of religious
artists. Sirk's relation to the material is a little like his relation to America—being drawn to the possibilities without ever quite believing in
them.

At the end of 1950 Sirk signed an exclusive contract with Universal,
arriving at the studio at almost the same time his friend Siodmak was
departing it, in discouragement. But it was by that time—like most of
Hollywood—a much diminished place. After an experiment with classier
product—from '46 to '49, just the period when Siodmak had flourished
there—the studio had reverted (with a management shakeup) to its tradi-

tion of low-budget, low-risk programmers. The Universal specialty, it seemed, had become "knock-offs" of the other studios' more prestigious and successful originals, as well as of their own (three successive versions of *Back Street,* for example, and each one dimmer than the one before)—featuring stars who were either past it by that time or who had never quite been there at all, and who nearly always made an unhappy contrast to the originals: e.g., *The Spoilers* (1955) with Anne Baxter instead of Marlene Dietrich, *My Man Godfrey* (1957) with June Allyson instead of Carole Lombard, *When Tomorrow Comes* renamed *Interlude* (1957) with Rossano Brazzi and June Allyson replacing Charles Boyer and Irene Dunne. It was also the home studio of Ma and Pa Kettle, of Francis the Talking Mule, of Tammy, Gidget, "tits and sand" actioners, B and C movies in Technicolor, and Audie Murphy westerns—the sort of factory-made stuff that was aimed at the lucrative "undiscriminating audience," as it was then called.

All the studios, of course, aimed regularly at a fairly low idea of audience taste and intelligence; but Universal aimed lower than any of the rest of them, more steadily and unashamedly—and achieved as a result a steady profitability, when the bigger studios around them were flailing and floundering in spite of their Academy Awards. And Universal was still able, as those studios no longer were, to "raise" its own new young stars, to train and promote "discoveries" like Tony Curtis and Piper Laurie and Sandra Dee and many others less notable (George Nader, Mari Blanchard, Julie Adams, et al.). The "teen stars" at Universal were a specially wholesome lot, even for the fifties. They never suggested (as the Brandos and Deans had done) the glamour of nonconformist behavior: they were as much designed to reassure the parents (*and* grandparents) as to please the kids.

And this, improbably enough, is where Sirk would spend the rest and—even more improbably—the *best* of his filmmaking career. He was there eight years (he made twenty-one movies for them, *apart* from some uncredited salvage jobs), until (in 1959) his failing health—that and "the kitschy scripts," according to Irene Heymann ("Billy Wilder or John Huston never got *that* kind of material," she added, rather indignantly)—drove him back to Europe, and eventual retirement in Lugano.

They needed a comedy director especially, and someone there had seen *A Scandal in Paris.* So they signed him—to do comedies at first, six of them in his first two years at the studio, none of them very funny or otherwise remarkable, but graceful and painless, with some apparent wit in their pacing and staging, and a surprising complexity (for such films) in the visuals (foregrounded images, multiple frames, deep-focus interiors, and so on). They were folksy, "family-type" comedies—as their titles promised and their studio more or less required: *Weekend with Father, No Room for the Groom, Has Anybody Seen My Gal?, Meet Me at the Fair.* They are also—for all the invitations they offer to whimsy and cutesiness—almost rigorously uncloying and unsentimental (even when they deal with cute orphans, as in *Meet Me at the Fair*). And there are patches at least of real unforced charm in some of them—especially *Has Anybody Seen My Gal?* (1951). It's a Charleston-dance, raccoon-coat, backfiring-jalopy comedy with period songs (in the public domain), and it's Sirk's first movie in color: you can see how he takes to it; it's *always* a nice film to look at. But the comic teamwork of Charles Coburn (happily, *he* wears the raccoon coat for us) and "little" Gigi Perreau, as the childless grampa and the elderly child, is often lovely and funny. (Rock Hudson and Piper Laurie are the romantic pair.) And the splendid Coburn's air of gruff benevolence reminded me forcefully—in spite of no *other* resemblance—of Sirk himself, when I saw the movie after his death.

It was toward the end of this apprenticeship (in 1952) that Sirk was assigned by the studio to work with a man who could have been—even *should* have been, given their temperamental and cultural oppositions—his producer from hell. But their creative alliance, continuing to the end of Sirk's career, worked out—on balance, at least—*very* differently from that.

Twenty-Four

ROSS HUNTER

Clifford Groves (Fred MacMurray) is a wealthy toy manufacturer in Los Angeles, and the movie he's a main character in, *There's Always Tomorrow* (1956), opens with an exterior shot of his factory-showroom. It's raining heavily, and the camera follows a young woman in a slicker crossing the street in front, going in the door, and appearing in the next shot at the receptionist's desk inside. There are toys on display all around. "What a dreamy place to work in!" says the girl, a messenger, to the receptionist (who doesn't reply). You know what she means, but you don't believe it. The place is grayly lit (it's a black-and-white film) and looks cheerless—as much because of all those toys as in spite of them. And the scenes that follow tend to show them—dolls, marionettes, clowns, stuffed animals, et al.—either startlingly foregrounded (as if to say what-the-hell-is-*this?*), staring blankly ahead at the side of the screen, or else ranged on backlit shelves in falling-away diagonals into the background, while the rain streams on the skylight windows above.

It's not too surprising, then, when you find out later on that Cliff's favorite new item (he designs his own toys) and prospective hot seller is a number called Rex, the Walkie-Talkie Robot Man. Talk about creepy: it looks like an industrial-age golem, shaped like a pyramid with the point sliced off, with cudgel-like legs and hands that swing when it walks, metal knobs studding the chest, and light-bulb eyes that wink and glow as it whirs and lurches across the demonstration table and toward the camera. Cliff is showing his new creation off to his old friend Norma (Barbara Stanwyck)—who expresses a quite improbable enthusiasm. "Oh I adore him!" she cries, picking "Rex" up. "And the children will be crazy about him!" It's the sort of moment (what children?) that briefly makes you wonder where you are—the answer being, of course, that you're at one of Douglas Sirk's Ross Hunter movies, where seemingly misguided enthusiasms ("What a dreamy place to work in!") get regularly announced.

The sense you get in that scene above of something intentionally not

Ross Hunter (left) and Douglas Sirk (right)
hold a casting conference.

quite right, of some troubling elusive under-meaning, though characteristic of Sirk, becomes especially strong in the movies he did with Hunter—a
result, at least in part, of their opposing temperaments. Their collabora-
tion resulted in some fine movies (*Imitation of Life, There's Always Tomorrow*)—and also in some routine and perfunctory ones (Sirk did up to three a
year at Universal): movies like *Battle Hymn, Interlude, Taza,* and *Son of
Cochise* that must have seemed hopeless from the start. Also, and more
interestingly, in movies—*far* from routine—that seem sort of monstrous,
even calculatedly so. Maniacally articulated kitsch like *Magnificent Obsession* (1954), their first monster hit. A soap opera with a famously preposterous plot, but infused as well with a smarmy New Age–like religiosity,
embodied in a mysterious and avuncular raisonneur (Otto Kruger), who
counsels the hero to align himself "with the forces that go up and on,"
comparing spirituality to an electric outlet (plug in and turn on). There is
also a blind heroine, whose courage inspires everyone around her, who
wears black-lensed spectacles with gay Harlequin frames (very popular in
the fifties), and who recovers her sight at the end (the hero studies medi-

Barbara Rush, Agnes Moorehead, Jane Wyman, and Gregg Palmer
in *Magnificent Obsession*

cine and operates), laid out like a corpse, in the shadows, wrapped like a
mummy, only her flat planeless face emerging from the bindings into the
light. And the last thing the Technicolor movie shows us (in this era of
location shooting) is a painted flat of a sunny landscape, accompanied by
the voice of the hero's guru with all its sonorous fakery sounding the
mantra of the movie's title (". . . and it'll be a mag-*ni*-ficent obsession!") as
the exit music (an angelic choir) rises. "There has to be some parody going
along with the sincerity," Sirk said about another scene in this movie—
where Kruger appears like a vision in the glass of the viewing room above
the operating theatre, inspiring the offscreen choir to vocalize and the hesitating hero to take up his scalpel and cut.

The problem here, of course, is not so much with the parody as with
the sincerity. The people who champion this film (I'm not one of them)
find various ways of reading it: sometimes as an allegory, like *The Faerie
Queene* ("a commentary," writes one, "on the role of artist in a world where
God has died"—"God" in this example being the heroine's late husband),
or as a triumph of form over content (the convoluted plot "tellingly coun-
terpointed by the clean compositions and straight lines" of the hospital
and clinic settings, and so on), but most commonly as a "text" endorsing
middle-class values combined with a subtext by Sirk that subverts them

("an attack on bourgeois conformity and rationality"). But then, later on, when Sirk—in a picture with the same producer and stars, Rock Hudson and Jane Wyman—has at last a *text* that attacks middle-class values, the antibourgeois message being quite explicit, he subverts that *too*. Or so it seems, with *All That Heaven Allows* (1956). Was it something about Ross Hunter? Or that Hudson-and-Wyman combination?

Carey (Wyman) is a respectable, well-to-do widow who falls in love with a younger man, Ron Kirby (Hudson), who also happens to be her gardener, scandalizing (and titillating) her friends at the country club and alienating her two stuffy, college-age children. Her dilemma is not only whether she has the courage to marry Ron in the face of all the disapproval, but whether or not she really can live his kind of life.

The kicker is that "his kind of life," when we see it, looks just like hers, only trendier. His closest friends, whose lifestyle, we are told, has been inspired by Thoreau (a shot of two lacquered Hollywood ladies, Wyman and Virginia Grey, frowning over a volume of *Walden* together is one of the movie's stranger high spots), live in a house that looks only a little less affluent than the heroine's. But they give parties and have loud and lovable ethnic guests. And Ron, it develops, is not really "a gardener" but an entrepreneur with a college degree in horticulture, planning to start a greenhouse business (it's like the love story of *Althea Bruce,* in *In a Lonely Place*—see p. 155). It's true that the place he calls his home is a big, dark, and unlivable barn. But in love, he renovates, and it becomes as lavishly overappointed and vulgarly opulent as all the other houses in the film—except his place seems more Beverly Hills than Mamaroneck. Carey's fateful big step, it seems, is unlikely to take her anywhere she hasn't already been.

And Sirk's sense of the upscale suburban home as a spectacularly overdecorated tomb ("a tomb of my own making," says Cliff in *There's Always Tomorrow*) never gets much livelier or nastier than it looks here. The movie takes a conventional Hollywood glossiness, with heavy infusions of *Better Homes and Gardens,* and pushes it to almost lunatic extremes of elaboration and rich deadness—in color. And like the best Sirk films, this one is full of disturbing imagery, not only inside those houses but outdoors too. Like the sight of the malevolent town gossip, with the splendid, Evelyn Waugh–like name of Mona Plash (Jacqueline DeWit), walking down a snowy Main Street in the thick sable coat that seems to be the townswoman's uniform, stopping by the butcher shop to exchange innuendos about "Carey and her nature boy" with the liver-lipped proprietor behind the counter—like two figures out of George Grosz. Even more

All That Heaven Allows: Virginia Grey (it worked for *her,* after all)
introduces Jane Wyman to Thoreau's *Walden.*

unsettling in a way is the sight of some strangely affectless children sitting together in a sleigh and singing Christmas carols to the unanswering houses, leading to a close-up of Carey's face, marked by a single tear, in perfect plangent isolation on her face behind the snow-frosted panes of her French windows—just as she is later framed in the dead-screen depths of her new television set.

Sirk told Halliday that "the picture is about the antithesis of Thoreau's qualified Rousseauism and established American society." But the Rousseauism represented by Hudson, in his impeccable plaids, is a little *over*qualified. And the movie's portrayal of "established American society" is both crude and unbelievable, the kind of "satire" that mostly reflects its own dumb and unearned complacency, aimed at targets who are setups and cartoons—like those slavering hypocrites at the country club, or Carey's daughter, Kay (Gloria Talbot), embodying one of Hollywood's ideas of a female intellectual: pedantic and foolish, she reads Freud and wears glasses and makes speeches about sex ("We call it an Oedipus complex") to her mother and to her bemused jock boyfriend, wearing tight, bulging sweaters and looking stern as she does so. But still, contemporary feminists praise the movie because it actually "validates" a mature heroine's sexuality—and in the fifties too. But it's a very fifties sort of validation: the on-screen relation between the two stars is so sexless it begins to seem almost sinister—especially with Hudson always towering over Wyman's Carey, with his look of private knowledge, and even the suggestion of a smirk. Given all this, it seems appropriate that this movie too should conclude with a view of a painted flat, representing a snowscape outside Ron and Carey's big new (that renovated barn) picture window—but even *more* appropriate that the freedom of natural feeling that Carey has finally gained with Ron should now be symbolized by the reappearance at their window of a wild fawn: the animal looking bewildered and trapped, as it clearly *is,* between them and the fake scenery.

That same year, director Robert Aldrich was at Columbia, where he was also filming a soap opera about an older woman who loves and marries a younger man, *Autumn Leaves* (1956) with Joan Crawford and Cliff Robertson—a movie *without* any of Sirk's complications of tone and attitude. Later, in an interview, Aldrich told how Crawford and he were initially at odds during the filming—until one day on the set she looked up from playing her scene and saw him wiping a tear away. (After that they got on fine, he said.) I think we can be sure, however, that Jane Wyman never had to look up and see a tear in Sirk's eye—which was almost certainly one of the coldest in Hollywood when he was on the job. "I have no talent for sentimentality," he said to me. And these two "tearjerkers" with Wyman and Hudson certainly bear that out. The big emotional moments, of heartbreak and transcendence, come regularly, at generically prescribed intervals, but the feeling is too oddly astringent: it's hard to imagine any audience, however affected or gratified, actually crying at these movies, with their air of ambiguity and unspoken ironies, their striking lack of "warmth." And their oddity stems at least in part, I would argue, from Sirk's deep and fundamental lack of sympathy for heroines like Carey, and for the American ideals of self-fulfillment that they enact. As well as from his differences with Ross Hunter.

I talked with Hunter in 1991, at his hilltop mansion in Beverly Hills— an eye-popping place, like a set from one of his Lana Turner movies. He was delighted to talk about Sirk, he said—a man he respected and loved, a perfect gentleman, a wonderful man, he could talk about him forever. And so we did for quite a while that day. And Hunter was more intent on emphasizing their differences than Sirk himself had ever been—but ebulliently. "Boy, he could have used some of my vitality!" he said. "I mean, he could have used a little more positive view of things!" Back in the fifties they had made ten films together at Universal—among the most successful of both their careers up to then. And when Sirk packed it in and returned to Europe in 1959, Hunter went on to become one of Hollywood's most important independent producers (for a brief while), graduating to mega-hits like *Airport* in 1970, and then to mega-bombs like the musical remake of *Lost Horizon* in 1973. ("Only Ross Hunter," observed the critic Judith Crist, "would remake a 1937 movie into a 1932 one.")

His partnership with Sirk began in 1952, with Hunter's first assignment to produce a feature film of his own. During the forties he'd been a minor actor (juvenile leads in a few B pictures), but that hadn't led anywhere. At Universal he rose from dialogue director to an associate producer. Now he was producing *Take Me to Town* (1953), a folksy Technicolor comedy about a backwoods preacher (Sterling Hayden) and a barroom hostess (Ann Sheridan)—and he asked for Sirk (who'd by then done seven routine studio films) to be his director. Sirk was fifty-two; Hunter was thirty-six—enthusiastic, boyish, irrepressible (much as he seemed at seventy-five when I met him), full of an ardent vulgarity and a soaring personal ambition. And just getting started: "Sirk couldn't *believe* my drive," he said. I *bet* he couldn't—even in 1977 Sirk had had the air of not quite believing it whenever he talked about Hunter. Ross, he said, "had a great manner with everyone. He was tremendously successful—very charming. 'Oh, but it's a crude charm,' someone said. Yes—but in Hollywood who will notice if you have a subtle charm? There is one word in the English language, and without this word you couldn't have an American—this word is 'wonderful.' Now this word was Ross's word. He used it to everyone, and everyone loved it. He could get anything he wanted."

"We didn't agree very often," said Hunter. "He was very pessimistic and I was very optimistic." But as he recalled those disagreements now, they were never bitter. *He* was in charge, after all. And the studio was in charge of both of them—sometimes assigning them projects that discouraged even Ross. Like June Allyson in *Interlude* (1957), filmed on location in Germany. "Sirk and I joked about it—we used to call it *Inner Tube.*" But by that time it had become just the sort of movie (their ninth together) they were most identified with: the so-called woman's picture, melodramas about nobly enduring heroines and their domestic-romantic travails. *Magnificent Obsession* and *Imitation of Life,* their two biggest hits, were just such movies. And both were also (as was *Interlude*) remakes of Universal originals that had been made in the 1930s by director John Stahl, the house director of the time and a specialist in the genre (*Back Street, Only Yesterday,* et al.)—just as Max Ophuls had been before coming to Hollywood, and Sirk as well, though to a lesser extent, in his early German career (the Zarah Leander films—nearly as cold-eyed as his American ones). And this was the particular genre that Hunter had set himself to rejuvenating in the

Ross Hunter, with Archie, his dog:
a private moment

fifties at Universal, setting out to reclaim the female audience—"because women were not coming to the movies anymore."

One thing Ross was adamant about: "the beauty of my stars. Douglas went along with me on that. And he was a close-up man—which I love." Their stars being generally the older ones that Universal would spring for, "I'd always guarantee them that whatever else went wrong, *they'd* look great. And I'd always tell everyone how good they were." "Ross was on the set continuously with Lana Turner," said Irene Heymann (about *Imitation of Life*). "He was kissing her hand and loving her all over the place." But she thought that Douglas had liked Ross, "though I think he *tolerated* him more or less." She agreed, however—as Sirk had insisted to me fourteen years earlier—that Hunter never interfered with Sirk's direction, leaving him free to do as he wanted on the set. The toleration went both ways, it seemed.

"He really was my father figure," Hunter said. "I was like his son. He was so thrilled at my success. He already had *his,* of course." Hunter

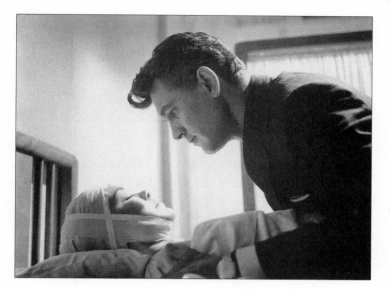

In a moment she's going to see again, thanks to him.
Rock Hudson and Jane Wyman in *Magnificent Obsession*

believed, starting out at the studio, that he could only "make it" there if he created "an image" for himself: "the image of someone who was stressing the beauty rather than the dark side of life." He believed strongly, he said, "that people on the screen should be beautiful." And from the beginning that's what he fought for. But against whom, I wondered. *Where* at Universal had been the champions of "the dark side," or of ugly people?

But of course they weren't there at all—they were merely everywhere else in Hollywood, as it must have seemed, at almost every big studio *except* Universal. Even Harry Cohn was making message movies and art films, with stars like Brando and Clift and producers like Stanley Kramer. The Method people and their allies, the controversialists, seemed to be taking over the whole town—in their cause of making the movies more "real," more like the new foreign films. But if, like Ross, you strongly wanted "beauty," you certainly didn't want to see something like Shirley Booth scratching her behind through a tattered housecoat (1952 Academy Award for Best Actress, *Come Back Little Sheba*), or a movie like *Marty,* where the people not only looked unbeautiful but talked about it (1955 Academy Award for Best Picture). Movies like these, of course, weren't burning up the box office, but they did seem to be changing Hollywood, and claiming its future.

But Hunter wanted to claim its past, more or less—to restore to movies the glamour of their still-recent golden age. Except that his notion of that glamour, unfortunately, was less one of romance and elegance than of sentimentality and tacky display—more like Liberace than Astaire and Rogers. And he managed to impose it on his very first production—and on Sirk, it appears. *Take Me to Town* has precisely that cloying, cutesy quality that the director had so strikingly managed to avoid up to then, in his earlier "family comedies" at the studio.

And worse was to come. Like the idea of remaking John Stahl's 1935 movie of *Magnificent Obsession* (from a Lloyd C. Douglas best-seller). The original, starring Irene Dunne, had made a star out of her leading man, Robert Taylor, and the studio was now hoping it would do the same for Rock Hudson (and so it did). But for Sirk (as he told Halliday) the prospect of doing "this goddam awful story," with its "combination of kitsch, and craziness, and trashiness," was mostly appalling, throwing him at first into days of "deep depression." Until he came to realize that the story's "craziness" might also save it for him, the way craziness often redeems trash. He was helped too by his propensity (carried into later interviews) for intellectualizing his assignments, especially the unlikeliest ones: after all, *Alcestis* has its believability problems too, as well as much the same theme, of "one person pacifying death by taking the place of another"; and so on. But he was helped most in the end by knowing, and reminding himself, that movies are not theatre: "If I had had to stage *Magnificent Obsession* as a play I wouldn't have survived"—that the language of a film is not in the words (thank God) but in (as he said to me) "the lighting and camerawork, in the *style* that the director is imposing on the cheap material." And in the editing afterwards—which he claimed neither Hunter nor the studio ever interfered with (Universal was too cheap to have previews).

The story is about a playboy who accidentally more or less causes the death of a famous and saintly doctor (a boating accident)—and then when he tries to make it up to the heroine, the doctor's widow, accidentally causes her to go blind (a car accident). It's love, of course—or at least its clumsy beginnings—driving the playboy to forsake the high life he's been leading and become a brain surgeon (and win a Nobel Prize in the original) so that he can operate on the heroine and restore her sight at the end. Where Stahl had tried to disguise the outrageousness of the material (and with some success, even), Sirk heightens and plays it up. Though not, of course, in any way that might tip off the "undiscriminating audience"—or the front office—so that the movie's intended irony, he later conceded, is "a bit buried." Nor is there any sign that its two stars were alive to it ("No, no. Actors you shouldn't tell about technical matters")—let alone the

The Tarnished Angels: Jack Carson, Robert Stack,
Dorothy Malone, and Rock Hudson

ebullient Ross. The director, Sirk said, is always "a very lonely man . . . the only one who knows what the film is aiming at." What about the writer? I asked. What does he know? The answer was an equivocal one: "The writer is *always* your comrade in a way; he is always your friend. Often he's the only intelligent guy in the whole crowd, the only one you can really talk to." In any case, at Universal you had very little chance to change any script when you were shooting—"and then only in such a hidden way that the studio won't object." He summed it up: "You are tied mostly to a piece of trash."

But pulp trash—for Sirk as for most of us—was better than the kitsch kind. That preference formed one of the bonds he had with his *other* important Universal producer, Albert Zugsmith—a pulp specialist (producer of *Touch of Evil* as well as *The Incredible Shrinking Man* and *Sex Kittens Go to College,* among others). And if Sirk sometimes "tolerated" Ross, he truly liked Zugsmith. "And Zugsmith adored him," Irene Heymann said. "Zug," as he liked to be called, was the kind of shlockmeister Sirk could warm to—i.e., not a phony, in his view. "There was no bullshit, no arty pretensions," he told Michael Stern in a 1976 interview:

> "Doug," he'd say when we were doing *Written on the Wind,* "give me some bosom." . . . I said, "Zug, I can't. They'll cut it out." "Let's try

it anyway," he said. "As much as you can get away with." . . . What a character. I never knew him without the baseball cap on his head. He has newspapers, TV stations, radio, and movies. The man dabbles in everything—except art and culture. "That's why I hire you and Orson," he told me. I really liked him very much . . . As a producer, he never interfered, except to ask me to show more bosom.

"Zugsmith never gave him an argument," said Heymann, "gave him anything he liked." Including—after the great success of *Written on the Wind*—a project Sirk had been cherishing the hope of for years (and unthinkable for Ross): a film version of *Pylon,* Faulkner's novel about barnstorming aviators in Depression America. *The Tarnished Angels* (1958) was the closest thing to an art movie he ever got to make at Universal. It's about the tensions in a kind of ménage à trois, between a daredevil pilot (Robert Stack), his parachutist wife (Dorothy Malone), and his faithful mechanic (Jack Carson). There's a little boy too, and a sympathetic, observing reporter who drinks too much (Rock Hudson). And the movie seems—in spite of the action, the plane races and crackup scenes— becalmed, its mood a kind of choked desolation (Stack remarked later that at least it did very well in Europe), its main action the aggrieved and damaged characters circling each other warily and talking, in shabby diners, half-lit apartments, empty airplane hangars, while a distinctly sinister Mardi Gras (the locale is New Orleans) goes on outside. They are all in different ways in love with the Stack character, with deep investments in his recklessness and his ambiguous heroism, and they are only freed—or cut loose—by his death, partly self-willed, in a crash at the end. The performances—especially Malone's and Carson's—are affecting. Stack's role seems to have been a bit botched in the writing (quite important *here*); you never feel you know the character well enough. And Hudson seems mostly out of his depth, especially his drunk scenes (one of them involving a very long and fancy speech). But he's nice with Malone, yearning after her so convincingly that the big kiss when it comes has real dramatic power.

It wasn't a moneymaker, of course—even with Hudson top-billed in the ads (his role was really secondary). And Sirk himself was disappointed with it, feeling he hadn't quite pulled it off. He partly blamed (wrongly, I think) Malone's performance—not nuanced enough, he thought—and the fact that he had to use black and white (studio economy again) instead of color. And his cameraman for a change was not Russell Metty, his favorite. In addition to that, it was in CinemaScope, a screen width that Sirk—in contrast to Nick Ray—was never comfortable with. And so forth. But with all its faults, it's a movie that gets under your skin, that you don't forget.

Both Sirk's Zugsmith films have a different look from the Ross Hunter ones: almost *under*decorated by comparison. "Simplified" and "stripped down" was how Sirk described the "optical style" of *Written on the Wind.* He had had the opportunity on that movie, he said, to furnish the rooms and interiors more "lavishly," and in fact

> . . . the studio expected it. But I determined to do the opposite. This material, I decided, is poster material—what you call *placatif.* And the whole picture is in a kind of poster style, with a flat, simple lighting that concentrates the effects. It's a kind of expression-ism . . . And I avoid what a painter might call the sentimental col-ors—pale or soft colors. Here I paint in primary colors—like Kirchner or Nolde for example. Or even like Miró. I have the flash-ing [sic] red of a car and I want that to be just as red as possible.

The Tarnished Angels is even more "stripped down"—it looks almost at times like an old Warner Bros. film, in their low-budget tabloid style, with no-nonsense, clean, and uncluttered compositions throughout.

That sort of austerity didn't seem to be an option with Ross. According to him, "Sirk was not particularly fond of the beauty of the sets"—"*my* sets," as he also called them. "He was always upset at me about them. He always thought they were too polished." Like the woodland residence of Otto Kruger's guru character in *Magnificent Obsession:* it was supposed to be "a shack," Hunter said. Not in *his* movie: "I made it something chic and stylish, the sort of place everyone in the audience would want to live in!" (It looks like some big CEO's getaway lodge.)

Such eat-your-heart-out displays were characteristic of a Ross Hunter production, even when it wasn't directed by Sirk—e.g., *Midnight Lace* (1960), *Portrait in Black* (1960), *Madame X* (1965): all made by other directors, on Hunter's "polished" sets and photographed by Russell Metty, but not one of them looking remotely like a Ross Hunter film directed by Sirk. Like *Magnificent Obsession,* for example, with all its settings of well-to-doness in color (country clubs, manorlike homes, resorts, private clinics, even a Swiss chalet-hotel), and the dominant look (and feel) of the movie is funeral-home chic, with shadows and cut flowers everywhere and charac-ters who seem (backlit and sidelit) carved out of a darkness that only seems to spread as the movie goes on—toward its happy end (that painted land-scape). Sirk has turned Ross's sunniness, as it were, into creepiness. It might be nice to be able to afford those interiors, but I don't think you'd want to live in them.

Or in Clifford Groves's house in the suburbs in the black-and-white *There's Always Tomorrow.* It's a posh two-story building, with high-ceilinged rooms on a ground floor that opens to a patio, upper rooms that open onto balconies. The furnishings are "early American" (as the style was called), pricey but homey, and the rooms are full of tchotchkes—but still the place looks empty, even forbidding, and never brightly lit; it's always overcast outside or else it's night. Sometimes the camera looks in from there, prowling along the trellised and ivy-covered outside walls, peering at the inhabitants through the open shutters and French doors and cross-hatched windows. Once it goes inside, you notice the shadows, the sharp angles and unyielding lines of the place—and the subtly unbalanced compositions that often put the people at the bottom of the frame so that the space above almost seems to weigh on them.

And especially on Cliff (Fred MacMurray), who is often seen alone there, or else standing apart from the others. He is alone the night when an unexpected visitor appears at the door—his old girlfriend Norma (Barbara Stanwyck). What a surprise—and she in turn reacts with delight at seeing where he lives. "The house is beautiful!" she exclaims. "So warm and cheerful!" Okay—but almost better if she hadn't said *anything*—just as you feel when she tells him a bit later, "You look so happy!," followed by a close-up of his collapsed face and uneasy eyes.

Cliff the family man is in the throes of a midlife crisis—in another Universal remake (of a 1934 programmer of the same title, with B players Frank Morgan and Binnie Barnes in the MacMurray and Stanwyck roles). It's another Ross Hunter "woman's picture" directed by Sirk and photographed (black and white) by Metty—except that this time it's not a woman but a beleaguered man who is at the center of things. Cliff suffers not only from the passing of youth but from the awful family he seems to have passed it with—his wife and three children, who have become oblivious not only to his suffering but even to his presence. The marriage is officially "happy," but his ditzy wife, Marion (Joan Bennett), has become so absorbed in her role of upper-class suburban matron, so preoccupied with "the kids and the house," that she has no attention to spare for her husband's anxieties—which are mainly about now never escaping their trap of routine and everydayness. "Don't you ever want to get out of this house?" he says to her, desperately, "to go places? to move around?" "But I'm *constantly* moving around," she replies laughingly. "That's how I keep my figure." Bennett's Marion is the one time in her starring career (nearly at its end by 1956—she got above-the-title billing, but it's a supporting role) that she had to play such an entirely (and improbably) clueless woman.

The Cliff we first see in his own home is like a petitioner, humble and used to rejection. He has two tickets to a hit show, but he can't get anyone to go with him. Marion has promised to go to their little girl's dance recital. The oldest kid has a date. His younger sister has "emotional problems" to discuss with her friends, and besides is "not in the mood for the theatre." Even the cook (he's asked her too) is busy that night. And so Dad is left alone at home. That, of course, is when Stanwyck's Norma turns up—he answers the doorbell (in an apron) and there she is, smiling at him. "His youth comes back," said Sirk, "—knocks right on the door."

There's Always Tomorrow: Fred MacMurray in the apron, Barbara Stanwyck in the doorway. "His youth . . . knocks right on the door" (Sirk).

At first he doesn't recognize her—it's been over twenty years. Her name is Vail now, not Miller, and she's become quite glamorous, along with her great success in New York as a women's clothes designer. He hasn't seen her since they were both young and planning his toys together for his fledgling company. She'd left town—he never knew why—around the time he got married. Now here she is—in Los Angeles to set up her own branch store there. Married briefly and divorced, she has carried a torch for Cliff ever since she left California. But he is no more aware of that now than he seems to have been when they were young together and starting out. So they resume their old friendship—innocently.

But they are soon being watched—without innocence—by his teenage kids. It's Vinny, the oldest one (William Campbell), who instigates the surveillance, pursuing it with Ken Starr–like zest, helped by his equally self-dramatizing younger sister Ellen (Gigi Perreau), and in spite of his more sensible girlfriend (Pat Crowley), who keeps telling him, without effect, how appalling he is. Then, at a family dinner, suggested by Marion, the two older kids behave with such pointed rudeness toward Norma, the putative guest of honor, that Cliff is infuriated. "That was a pleasant evening," the ineffable Marion says afterwards as she and Cliff get ready for bed. "It was a hideous evening!" he retorts, and complains about the kids—fruitlessly, as usual. But Marion—who seems to have been oblivious to everything else—has seen how unhappy Norma really is (you imagine she *would* see that): "I think she's lonely. Did you see the way she looked at the kids?" Nonsense, replies Cliff—she's a famous and successful woman. Comes the inevitable rejoinder: "She's missed what any woman really wants," says Marion (leaving Cliff and the rest of us to name it). "I feel sorry for her."

But Cliff soon realizes that Norma, in spite of her intention to conceal it, is in love with him still, and he with her. But when he urges her to run away with him, she resists. Though not quite finally, it seems—she agrees to another meeting at her hotel room. But Vinny and Ellen turn up there ahead of him, and accuse Norma of trying to take him away from his family. She accuses them in turn of ignoring and neglecting him. "Can you blame anyone but yourselves if he *is* thinking of leaving you?" Don't they know how much they mean to him? They do now—and so does she. When Cliff comes for their appointment, she sends him back to his family—it's too late, she says. He can't deny it.

So she takes a plane back to New York—alone. The now chastened Vinny returns home to tell his girl that at last he understands it's unselfish love that is the most important thing—she's glad to hear it. Inside the house, Cliff, standing at the window, watches Norma's plane fly off, as Marion comes up beside him. She's noticed (!) that something's been bothering him, she says, and she's worried about him. "I'm all right now," he says as they link arms—adding: "You know me better than I know myself." "I *should*!" she answers, dimpling up at him, "—after a lifetime with you." And they walk off together, as the now happy kids watch them from the next room, declaring before the fade-out that they make "a handsome couple."

You don't believe any of this, of course—and Sirk would say you weren't meant to, any more than you believe Norma when she tells Vinny and Ellen how worshipfully their father talks about them and "how his eyes shine" when he does. You haven't heard that, or seen it: what you've seen in his eyes instead is a kind of dismay whenever he looks at them—or even (at one point) at their framed photo on the table beside his chair (he angles his newspaper so as to block it out). As usual in Sirk's films it's the kids, not the grown-ups, who are the *true* phonies (Vinny compares their family problem to *An American Tragedy*). He seems to have disliked American teenagers almost as much as Nick Ray doted on them.

Sirk had planned another sort of ending, of course. As he described it: Cliff alone in his showroom as he watches Norma's departing plane through the skylight, with Rex the mechanical man (his symbolic surrogate) behind him, lurching and whirring across the demo table and falling over the edge to the floor. The fade-out would then show Rex upended on the floor, his wheels spinning in the air. But Ross and the studio (who were about as likely to permit such an ending as Harry Cohn might have been to make that blind-people-ceaselessly-tapping movie) vetoed it. "It wasn't that they didn't get it," Sirk assured me. "They got it—unfortunately." Of course—it wasn't too subtle, after all.

"Sirk had a viewpoint on life completely the opposite of mine," reiterated Ross in 1991. "He was definitely pessimistic about life and what it brought. He thought life never did supply happy endings." But Universal supplied them—so did Ross. And Sirk seems to have lost the arguments about them every time. But that mattered even less perhaps than *he* seems to have thought. It was Sirk, after all, who *filmed* the endings. For example: "You know me better than I know myself," says MacMurray—saying the line resignedly, as if it were more about indulging her than believing it himself. A discouraging point.

In any case, no imaginable final scene or set of scenes could prevent the movie from seeming a very bleak one right to the end. What makes it more than that, what makes it moving, is the *rigor* of its bleakness, and the way Sirk sustains that rigor with the help of his two stars, against the soap-opera world the movie also inhabits—Ross Hunter's world, so to speak. MacMurray, of course, was a past master by this time at suggesting the panic of contingency, the depths of unease that come with the passing away of things. It's the same deep-down discomposure (a lurking incompetence and cluelessness, a what-am-I-doing-here? air) that kept him from ever being in his long career a completely satisfying romantic lead—the discomfiture that he was covering with dumb bravado in *Double Indemnity,* that had settled into seedy sullenness, a sort of curdled discontent, by the the time of *Pushover.* Here it's anything but settled—it's stirring painfully, mostly in his eyes. As in the suddenly alarmed, half-intimidated way Cliff looks at that insufferable son—realizing that the kid is actually condescending to him, but then *why* shouldn't he? It's just an unwilling glance, but MacMurray conveys with it every nuance of the character's humiliation.

And Stanwyck's Norma shows—as this actress usually does—a complicated consciousness from the start, when Cliff first opens his front door on her. She is glowing, but nervously. She brings a radiance to the house and to the movie that they both need. But she gives the sense that "glowing" is also something Norma has to sort of work at here. She really wants to know that he is happy—she almost needs him to be, it seems—and she doesn't want to talk about *her* life, she wants to hear about his. There is an air of diffuse, only half-acknowledged sorrow about her, even at her most enthusiastic ("The house is beautiful!"). They go out, and she asks him to show her that haunted toy shop. Which he does.

It's one of the richest scenes in the movie, with its sense of their intersecting delight—her pleasure at what she's seeing, his pride in her pleasure, their mutual sense of the past, their sudden happiness together: they're both a little high on it, even a bit dazed by it. That it's highly provisional doesn't make it less real. Because of them, and in scenes like this (there are others to come), *There's Always Tomorrow* may be the closest to a truly romantic movie that Sirk ever did—in spite of "Rex" and the rest of it.

Norma is specially delighted, among the multitudinous toys, by a miniature barrel organ that grinds out "Blue Moon" when she turns the handle—it's their old song, as they both now remember. Nearly "everybody's" old song (even Bob Dylan has recorded it)—genus American love song, so of course it's about loneliness ("You saw me standing alone . . . /Without a love of my own"—the words unheard here). The lilting and familiar Rodgers melody, so playfully and wittily "blue," then gets taken up by the soundtrack orchestra, surging into a string-section epiphany, then subsiding—as Stanwyck, alone in a close shot, speaks. It's been a wonderful evening, she says—then adding, slowly and thoughtfully: "You know, tonight . . . for a little while . . . time stood still . . ." She says it—movingly—raptly, less to him than to herself, with a genuine wonderment. But even miracles in this movie are melancholy. They leave and turn out the lights, and the camera dollies in to an unsettling close-up of the toy barrel organ in the dark (a shape like a bier) as the "Blue Moon" melody declines into a music-box tinkle.

We already know what's bothering *him,* but the emptiness of her life— an obligatory point in the fifties (and we don't need Marion's help to take it in) about *any* "career woman," even the married ones—is sketched in by a brief scene showing Norma in her new store: in her brusque, irritable manner toward her saleswomen employees, and in an encounter with a presumably typical client—a stereotype rich-silly woman with a little dog in her arms who gushes at her about the upscale new establishment, calling it "a special place for special people," the sort of thing "Los Angeles has always needed." Norma accepts the tribute impassively.

But none of the options people have in this movie are meant to be happy ones. You're left feeling not so much that "family" is good or bad as that it's probably better to have one than not. Because what else *is* there? . . . Certainly not what Cliff finally proposes to Norma—let's run away together. Not at *their* ages—or in the middle of their particular lives. "You can't go back," she tells him in their final scene. "None of us can." And when he starts to protest against this, she explodes in a sudden anger, all her buried rage at this self-deluding man she still cares for finally surfacing: "Oh, *face* it, Cliff!" she says—then adds bitterly, crushingly: "*I've* had to face it . . ." And Stanwyck's expression and suddenly breaking voice make the moment so large and powerful that all the stale formula meanings it also conjures up (the embittered career woman, the too-late romance, etc.) are simply swept away. When she also tells Cliff in this scene that she's had "twenty years of being a career woman, with an eye to design and merchandising," just as he has had "twenty years of being a husband and father"—Stanwyck invests the neutral words "design and merchandising" with such a depth of bitter feeling that you're startled and moved, and you're taken far beyond the boring knee-jerk career-woman point into a more pervasive regret, into those feelings of irretrievable waste and loss ("a special place for special people") that fill the whole movie and that make it in the end so haunting.

This was in fact the second Ross Hunter production that Sirk and Stanwyck worked together on. The first, three years before, was *All I Desire* (1953)—a simpler and less problematic vehicle that never aspires to be disturbing. But it's made with Sirk's usual grace and fluency, and it's almost consistently involving. Stanwyck is Naomi Murdoch, a turn-of-the-century independent woman with a failing career in vaudeville: "Not quite at the bottom of the bill yet, and not quite at the end of my rope," she says in the narrative voice-over that opens the film. Because of a letter from her daughter Lily, Naomi resolves to return to the small Wisconsin town she'd left in disgrace years ago, when she was driven away by the scandal of her quickie affair with a local lover named "Dutch" (Lyle Bettger) and her betrayal of her schoolteacher husband (Richard Carlson). She hasn't seen him, or the town, or the three children she abandoned when she left, in years.

This was the particular film that prompted Sirk's recollections of Stanwyck in 1977. "A great star," he said—

. . . Unfortunately I couldn't give her any great parts in those days. I did see *All I Desire* again—after Halliday praised it to me. And you know there is nothing, *nothing* the least bit phony about her ever. Because she isn't capable of it. That insignificant little picture she did with me and she played it all right out of herself. And yet she is so discreet—she gets every point, every nuance without hitting on anything too heavily. And there is such an amazing tragic stillness about her at the same time. She never steps out of it and she never puts it on, but it is always there, this deep melancholy in her presence . . .

And the way she acted between takes was very different. Most people, as soon as the camera stops, you know, go straight to the mirror to check. But every time, she would go to a corner of the set, hardly talking to anyone—until we were ready to shoot again, and she was always ready and always perfect.

But that was a very rare thing. She impressed me all the time as someone—what can I say?—someone who had really been touched deeply by life in some way. Because she had depth as a person . . . I wish I could have done a really great picture with her . . .

"Depth as a person" is certainly what Stanwyck has on the screen. And if the two movies she did with Sirk are hardly "great," they are certainly pretty good ones—if only, in their different ways, as movies "about" her.

Sirk cited as an example the sequence, early in the film, where Naomi goes to see her daughter Lily (Lori March), an aspiring actress (who mistakenly believes her long-absent mother is a famous one), in the lead of the high-school play, *Baroness Barclay's Secret.* The daughter has been desperate for her mother to attend, and the townsfolk are all agog over the glamorous and scandalous prodigal. It's a fraught occasion, and Naomi, wearing a jeweled choker and a regal white gown, handles it with perfect aplomb, seated with Lily's father in a front row of the audience. As the lights go down and the curtain up, Sirk's camera sweeps forward into a close-up of Naomi, as she turns her face into the stage light, ready to be diverted: with that knowing semi-smile, reflecting an almost daunting self-composure and shrewdness, that Stanwyck often has in repose. And from here on, the film alternates views of the stage performance (looking up from the audience), with Lily always at its center, and close-ups of Naomi watching and reacting. Now that self-composed look has vanished: she appears struck by what she's seeing, almost alarmed, and as the kids' voices from the stage fade away, Stanwyck's voice on the soundtrack begins (an andante violin beneath it, the melody of Liszt's "Un Sospiro"), the camera tracking slowly, near-imperceptibly in on her face ("It was just an amateurish school play, but Lily was delightful . . ."). And her stricken

Naomi (Stanwyck) at the high-school play with her estranged husband,
a local teacher (Richard Carlson), in Sirk's *All I Desire*

expression—her head now inclining toward the side ("She knew how to
hold her head, use her hands"), her mouth falling slightly open ("When
she said she knew what she was doing up there, she was right")—gives
way very gradually to a radiant sort of smile, dazzled and tender and verging on tears: dazzled by her daughter . . . until the show is over and she is
on her feet leading the applause, then rushing backstage to congratulate
"everybody!"

It's a lovely scene. And it comes not just from Stanwyck, of course, but
from Sirk's response to her—the way he tracks and frames her, the way he
paces and times it, and so on. It's like a synchronicity of inspiration
between them. Movies in general—unlike plays, where the performer
never has to endure a close-up—are necessarily about the people who are in
them. Sirk's talent wasn't just his skill at directing actors, but knowing
better than most directors how to make a movie *out of* them, whether the
screenplay or production helps or not—out of what seem to be the actor's
deepest qualities, giving not just a personal vision of his stars but (in the
broadest sense) a moral one.

In many ways, he was the ultimate (to borrow Manny Farber's term
again) "termite artist." More, I think, than any other of the fifties filmmakers in this book. At Universal, he seems to have had less room to

The final scene of *The Tarnished Angels:* Nebraska-bound Dorothy
Malone says a last goodbye to the reporter (Hudson), who gives her
a book by Willa Cather.

maneuver and invent, less control over the choice and preplanning of his
projects than even Nicholas Ray going from studio to studio had had, or
Max Ophuls working for John Houseman or Walter Wanger. Sirk told me
that he "never ever planned any picture in advance." And I assume that
was at least partly because so much to do with the "advance" of his pictures
felt beyond his control. He presented it otherwise, though—as a strategic
and artistic preference:

> Because you can't plan ahead, you can't plan things. In my first
> picture experience I had a stage director's idea. I had worked out
> everything, and nothing worked out . . . No, no, you have to take it
> from the people. And from the set . . . An actor on a set is in a com-
> pletely different position from what you can imagine ahead of time.
> And in every picture you improvise. Even if you are making a
> completely trite picture, you have to take it from the last word, the
> last gesture . . . As a director, you are building instinctively, even
> musically . . .

And movies like *Written on the Wind* show how much he did "take it" from
his actors. So do, it seems to me, failures like *All That Heaven Allows.* You

could make a case, I think, that the oddities of that movie, and the entertaining excesses of *Magnificent Obsession,* are a kind of response to the fundamental imperturbabilities, the unyielding depthlessness, of their leading actors.

One of the anomalies of Sirk's Universal career was the extent to which it was bound up with Rock Hudson's. The project of turning the actor into a major star, begun in the early fifties, was studio-wide, much of it falling of course on Sirk and Ross Hunter, the house director and the house producer, respectively. Between 1952 and 1958, Sirk made eight films with Hudson (five of them produced by Ross), working tirelessly and patiently by all accounts (both Heymann's and Hunter's) on Hudson's acting and even his general education. And Sirk was still wondering in 1977 if he had really "succeeded" with the actor. And in the two Zugsmith films, the roles themselves seem to express Sirk's own reservations about his amiable star: the "coldish" (in Sirk's own words) and "not very interesting" hero of *Written on the Wind* and the reporter in *The Tarnished Angels,* who doesn't even get the girl at the end (Sirk told Halliday how he prepared Hudson at one point by reading him "The Love Song of J. Alfred Prufrock"), but who does get to give her, before she departs in a prop plane, a copy of *My Antonia*—one of the director's favorite books.

Twenty-Five

IMITATION OF LIFE

Imitation of Life is the movie that, still today, most evokes the fifties for me. It was a big hit in 1959—the biggest in Universal's history—and it was Sirk's last movie. "I couldn't go on making those Ross Hunter pictures," he said, about his departure from Hollywood that same year. But he made the best one last—the picture where all the discordancies of those earlier ones get triumphantly resolved. In part, it's a movie about its own genre, the tearjerker, about the genteel pop culture that it itself exemplifies—and about the genre as a way of looking at American life, seeing what Sirk saw: the "creative generosity" and optimism, the complacency and willed innocence, the denial of death and the emptying-out of life, the endemic racism. It's above all about different forms of "imitation" ("I would have made it for the title alone," Sirk said), about "phonies" of different sorts, and their opposites, about American blacks and whites and the connections between them. Fassbinder called it "a great crazy movie about life and about death. And about America." Is it ever. And not *only* about the America of forty years ago.

Sarah Jane (Susan Kohner) is white enough to "pass"—that is, if she can get far enough away from her unmistakably black single mother, Annie (Juanita Moore), who thinks "it's a sin to be ashamed of what you are, and it's even worse to pretend." Her mother thinks she's working at the library, but what she's doing instead is singing and dancing under an assumed name at a sleazy joint called Harry's Club, a small underground room, full of smoke and raunchy atmosphere and leering old men—where Sarah Jane, in a black corset, now performs a sexy song, leaning on the tables, posing near a phallic candle, showing lots of leg and cleavage to the appreciative clientele. She's not very good, but she *is* fairly blatant (by the standards of the time) and is having success with her audience.

But for the second time in this movie (which is entering its final half hour), Annie blows her daughter's cover. She's been there, behind a louvered screen, watching the whole spectacle. "Sarah Jane Johnson, get your

Imitation of Life: Annie (Juanita Moore) on the phone;
Susie (Terry Burnham) at left, Sarah Jane (Karen Dicker) below

clothes on and get out of here!" she says—just as Sarah Jane, after her act,
is flirting with one of the cute guys at the club. She tries to brazen her way
through the embarrassment: the woman's crazy, she says; "make her go
away." But Annie's not going anywhere without her daughter. And the
men, of course, are amazed—they would never have *guessed* . . . (It's almost
kind of titillating.) But anyway she's fired. (This was a time in America
when you *could* be fired for not being white.)

And when she packs her suitcases and leaves, guess who's out there
waiting for her—in a doorway? "Sarah Jane!" cries Annie, as the girl goes
by, furious and silent. "What do you expect me to do when I find you
dancing in a low-down dive like that?" What would they say at the teachers' college—"*Think,* honey," she implores. But Sarah Jane retorts that she
"wouldn't be found dead in a colored teachers' college." So come home,
have coffee, we'll talk, pleads Annie, as they stop and face each other:
"Nobody's all right about anything," says Annie urgently, "and nobody's
all wrong. Now if you don't want to be a teacher, all right, we'll talk about
what you *want* to be." But Sarah Jane isn't having any—she wants to be
white, and there's no talking about *that,* not with her black mother. She
turns away without replying and goes on, leaving Annie behind, calling

Annie has just gotten her daughter fired from her job at Harry's Club,
and now she wants to stop her from going away. Susan Kohner
is the grown-up Sarah Jane.

her and sitting on a nearby stoop. What Sarah Jane doesn't know, as we do,
is that Annie is ill—that the movie, in the conventionally tactful and
unspecific way of such movies, has already let us know that Annie "doesn't
have long."

So Sarah Jane disappears. And as Annie's time dwindles, she determines
to see her daughter one final time, and *not* to reproach or dissuade her:
"I've settled all that in my mind," she says. I should emphasize that Annie
by now—and in spite of what that Harry's Club scene might suggest
about her—is almost inarguably the most sympathetic character in the
movie. Sarah Jane is her only competition, as the white characters have
become less and less so. What starts out, as Fassbinder observed, as a movie
about Lana Turner has turned into a movie about Annie, her maid. Who
now goes to Hollywood: private detectives have informed her that her
daughter is working (an assumed name again) as a chorus girl at the
Moulin Rouge nightclub there. It's a real place, and the next sequence was
filmed there on location.

And suddenly there she is: this genteel "colored" matron, in the middle
of the crowded, glitzy lobby, as jazzy music blares on the soundtrack, and

she slips up the staircase past a tuxedoed host greeting people and into a room with a gridded purple ceiling and hot-pink walls and milling couples, all white. She looms above the camera, looking confused, making her uncertain way through the crowd, and looking just like what she is— Somebody's Maid—in her boxy bluish coat and round black hat. The film now cuts between her progress through the lobby and the show inside that we know she is headed toward. It's a confused-looking production number, as we first see it (before she does) in a long shot: a vast multileveled stage where showgirls in massive headdresses move vaguely about to the jittery music amid Dalíesque truncated pillars and stairways, while sprightly chorus girls in feathers dance onto and down a circular runway that takes them out among the audience's tables. Back to Annie in the lobby, looking around. Back to the show: a male dancer in striped coat and straw bowler is leaping and prancing around an insouciant chorus girl who is inciting him with her plume, as the girls on the runway pass by in front. Back to Annie, seeming to find her way now. Then a shot of her from behind, close and low-angled, and we see, as she moves away from the camera and down an aisle through tables, that she is inside the theatre, and then at the edge of the runway. Where she stands, looking up at the chorus girls as they whip by just above her.

Now something else is happening on the runway: in the far background you can see that the chorus girls are being followed by a slowly moving turntable track of showgirls seated in lounge chairs; as they emerge from the wings you can just see Sarah Jane among them. Chugging along, they perch coquettishly on the edges of their chairs, which have high backs— which they rock to the music. They are wearing gold-colored corsets, with long trains that fall between their legs, and they have ice buckets beside them and are pantomiming the pouring of champagne into goblets and drinking. There is some more synchronized-to-the-music business—arch and mischievous and disturbingly pointless. In close-up Sarah Jane shakes her shoulders and winks. On the floor below, a waiter approaches Annie and whispers at her; she follows him back up the aisle, stopping at the end to look back at the stage—where the routine goes on, Sarah Jane looking suddenly distressed. She and the girls rise and go behind their chairs, leaning on them provocatively. Annie goes out. The girls get back into their chairs and stretch out on them, lying prone and rocking as their turntable begins to move them off. The camera moves with it, fixing Sarah Jane in a disturbing overhead view—laid out on her chair, traveling past the politely applauding tables, arching her back, lifting her pelvis toward the camera, raising an arm to hold the goblet aloft, holding the pose until she

The show at the Moulin Rouge: Sarah Jane is among the sexy champagne drinkers (the fourth one from the left) in the bottom row.

is shunted into the wings and offstage. As the turntable moves slowly to a stop, she relaxes (also slowly), gets up off the chair, and peels off her long blue gloves—frowning. A carrot-haired friend from the next chair asks her if anything is wrong. No, nothing, she replies—"just a funny feeling." What she doesn't say, of course, is that she thinks she has seen her mother.

The sequence is very short—less than three minutes—but it focuses so much complication of feeling and meaning, in such gathering, stunning, and total control, that it feels a lot longer: the crosscutting between Annie outside and the show inside, both undercutting the glitzy spectacle and at the same time heightening its excitement; then Sarah Jane's performance with its disturbing undertones, and Annie's impassive witness (like some dream reversal of the primal scene: your parents watching *you*); the intersection between public and private meanings, between the show and Sarah Jane's place in it, and the meaning that *both* get from Annie's inapposite, improbable presence. It's not surprising, then, that before the sequence fades out, Annie makes a final apparitionlike reappearance, passing quickly through the backstage wings as Sarah Jane and her showgirl friend exchange reminders about their after-the-show dates ("Don't forget—the guys are picking us up at twelve-thirty").

But at least it's a step up from Harry's Club, isn't it? Classier, "cleaner," bring-the-whole-family as compared to Sarah Jane's brassy self-display at the "low-down dive." So why does it feel so much worse?

For one thing, Sirk shows that champagne routine (the actual show at this place) without any obvious satiric slant but in a way that makes it feel both nasty and dumb. Just as he highlights (through his cutting and angles) the nattering, dithering quality of the big stage show—you feel it's like something gibbering at you. The sleazy life of Harry's Club has emptied out into this chaotic spectacle, the cold mechanistic tease of those relax-a-bed lounge chairs and fake champagne bottles, into the familiar hectic vacancy of popular entertainment.

But that vacancy is finally and importantly what passing for white comes to mean in this movie—and what Sarah Jane is seen to be finally pursuing. And that building revelation is part of what makes the next scene—where Annie visits Sarah Jane in her motel room to say goodbye to her—as harrowing as it is.

It was principally because of the latter scene, and Annie's death and funeral at the end, that the 1959 reviews would say things like "the most shameless tearjerker in memory," *Time* magazine suggesting that theatre owners would "have to install aisle scuppers to drain off the tears." *That* prediction was nearly right: Sirk's film quickly became famous for its uniting effect on big audiences, the way *Psycho* would a year later, though with a very different kind of effect. But *Imitation of Life* made even more money, more than anything out of Universal before it, in fact. "The sobs," as Pauline Kael would later observe, are virtually "torn from your throat."

That's true enough—but on the other hand, as between having such a reaction "torn" from you or "jerked," you could conceivably prefer the former approach—the all-outness of it, the frankness of the aggression. Why not? It would never work that way, of course, if you didn't also believe the pain, didn't feel that the excess embodied a truth of some kind—in the actors, in the scene itself.

Sarah Jane is dressing for that double date when Annie surprises her in her motel room: "It *was* you," the girl says—and then: "Why can't you leave me alone?" "I tried, honey," says Annie. "You'll never know how hard I tried." The look of this scene is almost Dreyeresque: the bare, dimly lit room, with brown wood furnishings, straight right-angled lines, and blue-and-black-inflected colors, a mirror (of course) framed in brown wood, and

(at the beginning) the arc of a wooden chair arm in the low-angle foreground, bisecting the frame in an ominous dark curve. Sarah Jane is in a
black sheath cocktail dress, Annie in her dowdy coat and hat. Sarah Jane,
upset and angry, supposes she might as well pack her bags again, that her
mother's already seen the boss about her. No, says Annie, she hasn't, and
she means never to interfere with her daughter's life again. But she's
expecting someone, says the girl, only partly reassured. "I'll only stay a
minute," Annie says. "I just want to look at you. That's why I came." And
then: "Are you happy here, honey? Are you findin' what you really want?"

It's said with love, but it's still a terrible question—whether it's yes or
no, you feel, the answer has to be unhappy. As it turns out, it's yes. "I'm
somebody else!" Sarah Jane answers, distraught—turning around, the
camera tilting upward and turning with her until it shows her reflection in
the mahogany-framed mirror. "I'm white," she says into the mirror, with
her black mother in the bleak gray-wall background of the shot—then
repeats the word ("—white, *white!*") with rising hysteria. Then: "Does
that answer you?," turning back to her mother—who says that it does.

It's not Sarah Jane's agitation that controls these early moments as
much as it is Annie's sorrowful serenity. The scene itself, as you recognize
from its beginning, is an almost obligatory, conventional one, with a prescribed shape and development: the renunciation scene, where the heroine
(or hero, though rarely) gives up the beloved other—Marguerite sends
Armand away, Stella Dallas rejects her daughter, Lorrie, Annie relinquishes Sarah Jane—for what she feels is the other's good. This always
involves some painful masquerade—Marguerite doesn't love him, Stella
doesn't want her, Annie is just tired, not ill—which amplifies the heartbreak. And the heroine's belief that she is doing the Right Thing is
always at least open to question: causing both Armand and Lorrie to suffer cruelly—and relinquishing Sarah Jane to—well, *what*? A life of
"imitation" . . .

But someone will come soon: she wants her mother to go now, please—
and to promise if they should ever meet again, not to know her. Annie
agrees. But Sarah Jane must promise her that if she's ever in trouble or
needs help ("—and you shouldn't be able to—get in touch with me"), she
will let them know at home. And one more thing . . . Sarah Jane looks
frightened: What? she asks. And from this point, as Annie's emotion bears
down on her more and more, so does the camera, trapping both of them, as
it were, together and separately, almost unbearably it seems at times, in an
escalating series of tighter and tighter close shots. Annie says: "I'd like to
hold you in my arms once more—like you were still my baby." "All right,

Mama—all *right!*" says Sarah Jane, with a kind of irritable distractedness (a response, the way Kohner inflects it, that seems to summon up a whole bygone adolescence), turning her face away and bracing herself against the chair back. And when Annie then hugs her, Sarah Jane—in a close-up— looks half-dazed, almost unhinged, by the impact. "Oh, my baby!" says Annie, sobbing now, "my beautiful, beautiful baby . . . I love you so much. Nothin' you ever do can stop that." And next Sarah Jane is saying "Mama, Mama!" and hugging her still closer. She was right to be frightened . . . Annie's love is a powerful and terrible thing: it can't be a light matter to be its object.

An offscreen knock at the door and Sarah Jane's showgirl friend comes in, dressed up, wearing a fur stole. "Come on, Linda," she says (that's Sarah Jane's current name), "they're waiting." Then, seeing Annie: "Say, listen," she says, in a voice of reasonable grievance, crossing the room to Annie, "if you're the new maid, I want to report that my shower is full of ants." It's perfectly polite, even a little shy, not at all imperious; but the remark lands brutally—for *us,* too—as reminder of one of the larger meanings of what we've just been watching, and it's a surprise. So is Annie's reply: "Oh, I'm sorry, miss," she says, with her lovely smile, "that must be very uncomfortable"—generous, splendid, somehow more noblesse oblige than self-abasing. "But I just happened to be in town, and I dropped in to see Miss Linda. I used to take care of her . . ." And she approaches Sarah Jane, who is standing apart in a half-shadow, facing the camera—Annie beside her now in profile. She'll be running along now, she says, catching her plane, and so forth. "Goodbye, honey," she says to "Miss Linda"—who turns to her, silently saying the word "Mama," as Annie turns away and goes out. The friend, who has been watching all this, is impressed, and comes strolling forward: "Well, get *you,*" she says to Sarah Jane. "So, honey child, you had a mammy . . ." "Yes," says Sarah Jane, crying quite openly now, leaning with her back against the door that has just closed behind Annie. "All my life." Fade-out.

This coda with the showgirl friend is also conventional: multiplying the painful masquerades (Annie must pretend again, and Sarah Jane too this time) ups the emotional ante, giving you an extra pang or two. And you're aware of the manipulation—and, in this case at least, the cleverness (e.g., the several meanings of "mammy," and of "All my life," and the adroit use of them; the instinctive snobbery of the showgirl's reaction). But you're equally aware of how the truth of the performances and the scene itself (the wasting-and-destroying aspect, the final hopeless impasse, of parent-child love) trumps the self-declaring artifice, even redeems it—and that's part of what makes the scene moving altogether: the refraction through a conventional form.

Oddly enough, Sirk himself claimed, when I asked him, to have been surprised when he heard how emotionally audiences were reacting to his film. That was the American audience, he pointed out (the Germans, apparently, remained dry-eyed—the movie failed there). He was still puzzled, he said. "It may be. It may be—I have no talent for sentimentality. So perhaps I simply don't recognize it." I thought then that he was being disingenuous—how could he *not* know? (Later he wanted to omit this exchange from the published interview.) But today I'm not so sure. These scenes with Annie and Sarah Jane have the same formal absorption and intense artifice, the peculiar mixture of coldness and passion, both fracturing our attention and concentrating it powerfully, that mark his best work—in *Written on the Wind,* for example, as different as that movie otherwise is from this one.

And it has those two extraordinary performances from Kohner and Moore. Kohner's dark, vulpine prettiness and angry, intelligent eyes make a remarkable contrast to Moore's air of acquiescence. Sarah Jane is the severe one, with a nice-girl-going-on-tough-cookie quality that's both upsetting and moving—and that gives an entertaining ironic edge to those public performances of yielding sexuality she gives. Moore, with her broad brow, deep-set, large eyes, and high, wide cheekbones, has the kind of face that looks both beautiful and bountiful at once—with such a force of genuine good nature that the Lana Turner heroine's early capitulation to it seems foregone. But you notice, as the movie goes on, that Annie never, even at her most radiant, looks unwatchful. Nor, even at her most nurturing and "mammylike" does she ever seem less than the smart and authoritative woman she is—almost certainly the smartest person in the film. And to the degree that the character assumes a kind of monumentality— the film's representative of historical suffering and injustice ("How do you explain to your child, she was born to be hurt?")—Moore makes it seem (as it should) the opposite, as if the monumentality were assuming *her.* Both actors in their different ways have this kind of sincere, unfaked power. And the rapport between them makes their scenes together one of the wonders of the movie era.

They were both Sirk's casting choices: the studio wanted Pearl Bailey for Annie, and for Sarah Jane, Ross (it's true) wanted Margaret O'Brien (a *young* old star for a change). By comparison to those, Sirk's candidates were both unknown and untried. Moore (then thirty-six—two years younger than Turner, the star) was a former singer and chorus girl who'd been doing small roles (mostly maids, of course) in minor movies, occasionally in a major one like Raoul Walsh's *Band of Angels* in 1957, appearing briefly as a sexy wanton slave who taunts Yvonne De Carlo, the virginal heroine. "Sirk really stuck his neck out for me," she said in 1998. And his patience, she said, was inexhaustible: she recalled being so nervous at the start of shooting that he had to do twenty-two takes of an insignificant early scene with Lana Turner (who was also patient). "He'd say to me, 'You know, if you're no good, Juanita, the movie's no good.' " He was simply the kindest man she had *ever* worked for, she said, before or since. But that's not the way Susan Kohner remembers her experience with him: he was very tough on her (Moore and Heymann both corroborated this)—stern and remote and demanding and, to the twenty-two-year-old she was then, sort of frightening, certainly intimidating. But whatever he was up to in all this, she admits, he seems to have gotten what he wanted from her on the screen. The movie was the peak of both actresses' careers—unhappily, there were never such roles again for either of them (they were *both* nominated for the supporting-actress Academy Award that year; Shelley Winters won).

It was—once again—a remake of an earlier Universal movie by John Stahl. The original, starring Claudette Colbert, was released in 1934 and was a great success—though nothing to touch the remake's. Both movies, based on the Fannie Hurst novel, follow the fortunes of two mothers and their two daughters. Both of them begin when the white heroine, a struggling widow, takes in a homeless black woman to be her housekeeper, along with her light-skinned little girl. The two girls grow up together, and in each version meet the same sort of problem: resolving to "pass," in the one case, and in the white daughter's case, falling in love with her mother's boyfriend. In both pictures the white mother rises to riches and the black mother dies, with a spectacular funeral near the movie's end, and her repentant daughter sobbing over her coffin.

In the Stahl original—which closely follows the Fannie Hurst novel—Bea (Colbert) opens a pancake house on the Coney Island boardwalk, using the secret recipe that her new housemate and cook, Delilah (Louise Beavers), has shared with her. Soon they are selling it in boxes, with Delilah's grinning face on the outside ("Aunt Delilah's Pancake Flour"), and Bea is running a company. But when she offers Delilah her rightful share in the business, the woman refuses, preferring her station as Bea's housekeeper and live-in friend.

Annie, on the other hand, gets no such offer. Sirk's version makes essential changes in this material: instead of a businesswoman who becomes a

Louise Beavers, Ned Sparks, and Claudette Colbert in John Stahl's *Imitation of Life*. Here Delilah (Beavers) is being offered a share in her mistress's business.

magnate, the Lana Turner heroine is an actress who becomes a star. But in spite of this fundamental revision, the remake reproduces all the dramatic highlights of the Stahl film, and even many of their details (Sirk never watched the original, he claimed, but the many writers assigned to his film did), but always in an inflated, hyperbolized way. The climactic funeral, for example, is much longer and more operatically rendered in the Sirk version. As is the black mother's death scene: in the Stahl film, she goes rather quietly, slipping discreetly away to the accompaniment of distant "darkie" singing, while Colbert stifles her sobs in a trailing chiffon handkerchief at some nearby windows; whereas Annie has quite a lot to say before *she* goes, and when she finally does, the heroine collapses at her bedside, screaming her name.

In both movies the black mother catches her little girl "passing" at school by turning up unexpectedly at her classroom. The humiliated child in the first version then walks slowly, agonizingly, up the schoolroom aisle, past the whispers and stares of her classmates, to where her mother waits for her at the door; in the next scene, they are back home again. But in Sirk's film, the girl dashes past her mother, grabbing her coat in the cloakroom and rushing out into the falling snow, her mother following, while an offscreen choir shrills and ululates in alarm—in a deep-focus long shot that foregrounds a bright red fireplug. And the effect—like a visualized howl—is stark, beautiful, appalling.

And the original of the Harry's Club scene—the one where you first see the grown-up daughter "passing"—could hardly be more opposite. In the Stahl film, Delilah finds Peola—as the Sarah Jane figure is called in both the novel and the 1934 movie, where she is played by a "real" (i.e., technically) black woman, Fredi Washington—working as the cashier in a tearoom. When Stahl's camera first picks her up there, she is sitting at her register by the door, facing the customers in the dining room, leaning forward on her elbows, looking heartbreakingly happy, and smiling into space—in a private rapture of achieved gentility. That is, until her mother comes in, and asks her what she's doing there—with the predictable results.

The fact is, as this tearoom epiphany suggests, that Peola's situation registers as almost unrelievedly dreary. Where Sarah Jane—angry, rebellious, sexually provocative—is movie-size "tragic," Peola seems mostly depressed (an *angry* black woman would have too disturbing a figure in 1934 to be offered as sympathetic). When *she* faces a mirror in order to deny her own blackness (another moment echoed in the later film)—"Am I not white!" she says in her velvety alto voice and painfully "correct" English—she sounds plaintive and heartsore, more defeated than defiant.

And Stahl evokes the trap of her life with marvelous economy again and again. The first time we see her as a grown-up, it's the occasion of one of Bea's lavish house parties, with Peola and Delilah in their quarters belowstairs—listening to the party music as it drifts down to them from above. Delilah is dressed up, wearing a corsage—still, there seems to be no question of her or her daughter actually *going* to the party upstairs (they're still ahead of Annie—who cooks and serves for the parties at her place). Peola is stretched out on the couch reading. But her mother, sensing her moroseness, says with blundering benignity: "Come on, honey—*I'll* dance with you." I'm reading, retorts Peola—can't you leave me alone? But the moment evokes at one touch all the pitiableness of the daughter's life and prospects.

The Delilah, Louise Beavers, is certainly the "mammy" type, as it was conceived in those days (Delilah calls her mistress "honey chile," for example, and even offers to share her rabbit's foot with her)—like her contemporary and colleague Hattie McDaniel, she was relegated through her long career mostly to carrying trays and playing comic maids. But where McDaniel could be acerbic and formidable, and even tantalizing (as with Paul Robeson in *Show Boat*), Beavers is wistful and childlike and lost-looking—Mammy without sting or threat, a lovable primitive. Her

"Passing" in two different movies—and failing in both because of Mother.
ABOVE: Annie brings Sarah Jane's galoshes to school. BELOW: Delilah turns up
(with her mistress, Colbert) at the tearoom where Peola (Fredi Washington,
behind the counter) works as a cashier (Paul Porcasi, right foreground, is her boss).

Delilah is lumbering and overweight and slow-witted ("Just two hundred pounds of mother, fighting to keep her baby," as the Colbert heroine embarrassingly describes her; Delilah corrects her: "Two hundred and forty, ma'am"), as good-hearted as she is long-suffering: just the kind of mother who would have been an embarrassment to a daughter like Peola even if she'd been white. It's just that sort of mundane, shaming point—not an outrage but a nasty little truth—that Stahl's quiet realism excels at making.

"Realism" is always relative, of course. And while it's true that Stahl's heroine, in the course of her rags-to-riches-to-heartache story, eventually becomes quite movie-star-glamorous (wearing swank soigné gowns and striking languid poses), she at least doesn't become the toast of Broadway, as Lana Turner does. It's the restraint and comparative true-to-lifeness of the Stahl version that make many people (Pauline Kael among them) at least prefer it to Sirk's and Ross Hunter's—with its unrelenting flamboyance and obvious falsities and Hollywood gloss. The tearoom turns into a low-down dive. Delilah turns into Juanita Moore's Annie, a figure of unshakable dignity (and thin, too). Peola has become "white"—that is, played by an actress the audience knew to be white. And the heroine has the kind of romantic and professional career that's closer to Danielle Steel than to Fannie Hurst.

But there is an irony directed at this heroine that has no counterpart in either the book or the earlier film. You've seen it before, of course, in Sirk's earlier Ross Hunter movies, directed at the Jane Wyman heroine, but less controlled, less focused and coherent than it is here. Lora's rise to stardom, for instance, is almost offhandedly preposterous, treated in a way that highlights its daydream unreality. She is a struggling, unemployed actress when she first meets Annie and brings her and Sarah Jane to live with her and Susie, then only eight, in their coldwater flat. When she finally lands a part in a play, she almost loses it at rehearsal. The playwright, David Edwards (Dan O'Herlihy), objects to the way she's acting her scene; she tells him that the scene is unactable: "You're far too good a writer to have such a scene in your play." He is, of course, impressed by this ("You've got spunk," Lou Grant once said to Mary Richards. "I *hate* spunk!"). "Tell me—what would you do with that scene?" he asks her. "I'd cut it," she replies briskly, "drop it entirely."

EDWARDS: That's not a bad idea. Let me think. Yes—but the scene has a couple of lines that are important . . .
LORA: Give them to Amy.

ABOVE: Delilah comforts the child Peola (Dorothy Black). BELOW: Annie consoles her "child"—Lora (Lana Turner) is just back from a day of making rounds.

EDWARDS: Yes—it *would* work! Huh! Think *you* could play Amy?
LORA [*thrilled*]: *Amy?*
EDWARDS: Of course we'll have to work very hard together, Miss
Meredith . . .

It's the role that makes her a star. And the movie charts her rise to even
greater heights in a montage: showing her taking successive curtain calls,
against improbable backgrounds in equally improbable costumes (in a
bonnet and hoop skirt, in an apache dancer's tight black skirt and blouse,
in a leopard-skin coat against painted palm trees, and so on), her name and
face appearing above show titles like *Summer Madness* and *Sweet Surrender*
and (nicest of all) *Born to Laugh.* "A sophisticated actress in this part would
not have been any good," Sirk told Michael Stern, about the casting of
Lana Turner. "This character is supposed to be a lousy actress. She got to
where she is by luck, or bullshit, or, what-do-I-know, by dumb audiences."

On her way up, Lora has a brief, sophisticated affair with Edwards, the
playwright. The other men in her life are Allen Loomis (Robert Alda), her
cynical, lecherous agent, whose advances she spurns ("You're trying to
cheapen me—but you won't!"), and photographer Steve Archer (John
Gavin), her true love (or at least the one in the genre position to be), the
one who wants to marry her and whom she rejects to pursue her career. In
any case, she is seen to be neglecting her daughter, Susie (Sandra Dee)—
prompting the girl to fall back on her mom's friend Steve, and then to fall
in love with him: a potentially disruptive development once Lora decides
at last to marry him, but one that only Annie seems to know about at first.

A typical Lora-and-Annie scene: It's after one of Lora's big parties, when
she is rich and famous and reclining on a sofa in her boudoir, wearing a
rose-colored, fur-trimmed lounging robe, her feet up and resting in
Annie's lap, at the other end of the sofa. Lora reminisces: "You and I have
been through a lot together, haven't we?"—as Annie massages her feet for
her. Both daughters are growing up, and the years, as Annie says, are flying by. But Annie herself looks unwell—there are dark circles under her
eyes, and Lora asks if she needs any money. Annie says no; thanks to Lora
she is "well fixed," she says, with enough money for both Sarah Jane's college education and her own funeral. "Oh, Annie, that *funeral* again!" says
Lora. "It's the one thing I've always wanted to splurge on," says Annie—
and she's made a list of all the friends who will come to it. Lora takes notice
of this: "It never occurred to me that you had many friends—you never
have any visit you." But Annie says she knows all kinds, hundreds even,
through her church and all the lodges she belongs to. They are both stand-

After the foot massage. "You and I have been through a lot together . . ."

ing now, in a medium two-shot, with Lora reflected in a mirrored door behind them. "I didn't know," she says quietly. "Miss Lora (as she always calls her, even on her own deathbed), Annie replies gently, "you never asked."

That's a recurring theme about Lora. "What do *you* know about controversy?" Edwards challenges her, apropos of a script with a "colored angle." "Nothing!" she replies. "And I don't *want* to know. I only know that it's a good script and they're not easy to find." Lora is as much characterized by general unawareness, by blindness to matters both near and far from herself, as Colbert's heroine was by her clearsightedness, by her unsleeping perceptiveness and good sense. Where it's the black woman who is childish in the Stahl film, here it's the white one.

Lora is unaware not only of Annie's rich life outside their home, but of the one she leads inside it as well. Beginning with their coldwater flat, where Annie not only sustains the "family" morally and emotionally but even materially. When Lora is out of work and making rounds, not only does the unsalaried Annie take care of the two little girls and generally be the "housewife," cleaning and cooking and taking phone calls ("Miss Meredith's residence"), she also earns money for them as well—addressing envelopes, taking in washing, schmoozing the tradesmen they owe money to, and so on—enabling Lora to pursue her "dream," without noticing.

Nor does Lora ever notice—though *we* are certainly invited to—how much, however discreetly, Annie runs *her.* But constant visitor Steve is aware of it—as we see early on. He and Annie are sitting together one night at the kitchen table in the coldwater flat (he's watching her address envelopes), waiting for Lora to get home from one of her discouraging work-hunting days. It didn't go well today, either, and Lora breaks down,

Annie tells the Christmas story, and Lora intervenes.
(Note the mirror reflection.)

going directly to Annie, to be soothed and comforted in her arms, while Steve looks on. But then Annie rises, returning to the kitchen—the camera following her as she passes Steve, to show her signaling him with a movement of her head and eyes to go to Lora. Which he promptly does. And in a few minutes, she also lets him know—through the open kitchen door, and with the same eye movement—when it's time for him to go home. Which he promptly does. She doesn't have to tell *him* twice . . .

Annie, for Lora, will always remain partly invisible—will always be much like the legion of unseen but indispensable menials who underpin *any* comfortable life. *Except* that the two women are friends—that part of Annie is not invisible to Lora (as it was to Lucia Harper about Sybil in *The Reckless Moment*). But friend or not, Annie is still Lora's cook and maid. And later on, when Lora is a big star, she becomes her dresser too. Around their splendid new suburban house, she wears a uniform. Neither woman, of course, would be likely to question such arrangements (Annie even refuses Lora's offer of another servant to help her). Annie, unlike her daughter an implacable conservative, "knows her place"—more honestly, at least, than Lora is willing to know it. They may indeed have been, as Lora says, "through a lot together." But it's not (nor could you even imagine it) Annie who is getting the foot massage.

What Lora brings to her perception of the outside world is not insight, or even a desire for it ("And I don't *want* to know") but a rather indomitable will. "Maybe I should see things as they really are, and not as I want them to be," she says, in a rare early moment of faltering. But faithful Steve comes to her rescue again: "If I know *you*," he says, grinning and leaning over her, "they'll have to be the way you want them." "Thanks, Steve," she replies—the danger past—"you're so good for what ails me."

One night during the Christmas season, just before the little girls' bedtime, in the tiny living room of their flat, Annie is holding Susie and Sarah Jane on her lap and telling them the story of Christ's birth. Lora is occupied learning lines, walking back and forth with a script in her hand. Sarah Jane interrupts her mother's narrative with a question: Was Jesus white or black? *This* gets Lora's attention—something to be corrected, and quickly. "Well, it doesn't matter," she says, gently but firmly, addressing both children. "He's the way you imagine him." Of course. But the little girl's disturbing specificity persists: it seems that Annie has told them that Jesus was a real person, not a "pretend" one, as Susie puts it. And now Susie too wants to know what color Jesus was. An impasse—which even Annie seems unwilling to break. Until the camera moves in on Sarah Jane's face, looking spookily rapt (low, ominous music). "He was like me," she says softly, with centerless absorption, "—*white . . .*"

Little Sarah Jane (Karen Dicker, the child who plays her, is remarkable) is clearly a "troubled" child: self-willed, obsessional, even verging on delusional. But as this scene invites you to notice, her He's-white-like-me obsession is not so far from Lora's whatever-you-want-Him-to-be complacency—different ways of bending reality to your will. Sarah Jane—and as she grows up and becomes Susan Kohner, it becomes even clearer— is Lora's true counterpart, her real "imitator." And she even goes into showbiz.

But the movie sometimes shows a kind of animus toward Lora that it never shows toward Sarah Jane—and shows it even crudely at times. In the scene above, for example, when Annie, telling the Christmas story, gets to the birth itself and says (offscreen), " 'Heavenly hosts sing Hallelujah!,' " Sirk shows Lora coming upon herself in a nearby mirror—and regarding the image with satisfaction. Later on, when Sarah Jane, after that motel-room scene with Annie, leans back crying on the door that has just closed behind her mother, an image (in a simple black dress) of tragic devastation, the scene fades in and out on Lora, coming through a door in her home, wearing Day-Glo orange, a sleeveless blouse and toreador pants and girlish headband (one of the most outlandish of the star's advertised thirty-four costumes), her hand held to her ever-more-plasticene-looking hair.

This last juxtaposition might even seem like a meanspirited joke, even if an unintended one (a reflex of a general aversion), if it weren't that just such ironic juxtapositions—mostly much subtler ones—are at the heart of the way the whole movie works, from early on. As when Annie and Sarah Jane the child come home from the grammar school, after the girl's imposture has been humiliatingly exposed. Lora is already home with Susie, who is out of school too, and in bed. The situation is just as it all was in the Stahl version—with a crucial difference: in the Sirk movie it is clear, in the midst of Annie's and Sarah Jane's upset, that the white mother and daughter are merely playing at calamity, both of them knowing that Susie's sickness is a sort of game. "Why, you're *practically* normal!" says Lora, looking at the thermometer, and the two of them falling into collusive giggles as a result—while the distraught Sarah Jane and Annie go by in the background.

And this is an early foreshadowing (one of many) of a notion that becomes more insistent in the film as the characters age: the idea that Annie and Sarah Jane have what even Lora herself will later call some "very real problems"—in contrast to Lora and Susie, who have the problems of narcissism, of the spoiled and self-absorbed, of Lora's vanity and ambition, of Susie's sentimentalism. In contrast, in Stahl's film that whole mother-and-daughter-in-love-with-the-same-man is taken straight and treated very seriously, as in soap-opera tradition. And the Colbert heroine, in the movie's final sequence, resolves to give the guy up (at least temporarily), reconciling with the daughter and reaffirming her first commitment, to being a mother. (In the novel, the mother gives him up to the daughter.) The parallel moment in Sirk's movie is *very* different. "I'll give him up!" says Lora, dramatically. "Oh, Mother, stop acting!" says Susie (Sandra Dee's one moment of triumph in the movie). And that, it seems, takes care of *that*—we never hear about it again anyway. Susie goes away to school to recover (and out of the movie), only returning for Annie's funeral at the end.

No black movie actors have been *more* misused than Paul Robeson and Ethel Waters were, James Baldwin wrote in 1975 (in *The Devil Finds Work*). And partly, he argues, that was *because* of their talent and power on the screen—they brought too much "reality" with them, posed too much of a threat to the prevailing Hollywood falsity, having "enough force, if unleashed, to shatter the tale to fragments." Major black artists were segregated in their movies as they were in society, put in "special" sequences apart, in their own musical numbers (the Nicholas Brothers, Lena Horne, et al.), for example, or, as in a multistory film like Julien Duvivier's *Tales of*

Manhattan (1942), in their separate episode, as Waters and Robeson were in that film, in a story about a Negro shantytown, at the end of the movie (where they could be more easily excised by southern exhibitors)—and kept at some distance from the white stars in the same film, like Edward G. Robinson and Henry Fonda and Ginger Rogers.

It's Rogers that Baldwin zeroes in on, comparing her face on the screen to an ice-cream confection: "something to be placed in a dish, and eaten with a spoon—possibly a long one. If the face of Ethel Waters were placed in the same frame, the face of Little Eva would simply melt." The important thing becomes, then, to keep "the black performer" away from her, "sealed off into a vacuum."

Well, that seal is certainly broken in Sirk's film—as it was and had been in many other movies of the fifties, but hardly in any of them to quite such effect as here. For one thing, Turner's face at times seems vacuous enough to make Rogers look like Falconetti. And Moore, though younger than Waters was in 1942, less roguish and more conventionally beautiful than her predecessor, is every bit as authoritative and resonant, it seems to me. Turner's face, of course, never "melts"—even metaphorically: it looks too impermeable for that. It's Moore's face that succumbs to age and dying, while Lora's only looks younger. But the contrast, of course, is not to the white woman's advantage (as it is, as much as it exists there, in the Stahl movie). It enacts for us a familiar and central experience: the sense some people give you—whether they are good or bad—of a certain moral and personal authority and size. There are, after all, superficial "characters" in life as well as in fiction. And Juanita Moore on screen has that sort of authority, of course. So in her tortured adolescent way does Susan Kohner. Lana Turner and Sandra Dee, in different ways, lack it. It's the discrimination between shallowness and depth, between what we can take seriously and what we can't, in ourselves and others. And it's often the difference between the movie stars we like or are interested by and those we can't or aren't. And it's that sort of discrimination—the continuing contrast, for example, between Lora's fussy, driven emptiness and Annie's unfailing dignity and inwardness—that Sirk's movie is finally organized around: the juxtaposition of Lora and Annie and of (though to a lesser extent) Susie and Sarah Jane.

Because it is, as Sirk said it was, a movie *about* imitation, about living superficially. And Lora has gained the kind of life that our American plenitude often seems to promise us, to hold out as an ideal: an achieved shallowness. It's not that Lora, like everyone, doesn't have serious crises in her life—it's more that she doesn't believe in them, tending to act rather than live them, what a feminist critic approvingly calls "her refusal to suffer." It's a negative condition that the black characters in the movie implicitly criticize—both by being in a world quite apart from it, as Annie is, and by "imitating" it disastrously, as Sarah Jane does. And Annie especially, for all her considerable misguidedness, embodies the kind of tragic recognition that almost everyone else in the movie resists and opposes: the sort of meaning, according to Baldwin again—in *The Fire Next Time*—that the Negro in America carries with his skin and history, and suffers for, because he reminds "the white American" of precisely what the latter does not *want* to be reminded of at all. Namely, "reality—the fact that life is tragic . . .": ". . . simply because the earth turns and the sun rises and sets, and one day, for each of us, the sun will go down for the last, last time . . . It seems to me that one ought to rejoice in the *fact* of death— ought to decide, indeed, to *earn* one's death by confronting with passion the conundrum of life . . . But white Americans do not believe in death . . ." ("Oh, Annie, that *funeral* again!")

But to respond only to the irony about Lora—as audiences now tend to do, almost exactly reversing the way the audience in 1959 took her—is really to misunderstand the movie, I think. She's a phony, perhaps—and she may be ineducable in certain areas. But who isn't? Still, Lora is no monster (as, in a way, Annie *is*). On the contrary, she's a genuinely nice person, open and generous, a warm and unfailing friend to both Annie and Sarah Jane, and by her lights, dim as they may be, a good and loving mother. And she cares about Sarah Jane, it's clear, almost as much as she does about Susie. And Turner makes all this very believable.

So that when Sarah Jane tells Lora—on the night that Lora is having some important people over—that she's sorry but she can't help her mother serve because she has a date tonight, Lora seems more pleased than not: "A *date?*" she repeats, brightening instantly (she and Annie have been concerned about the apparent absence of boyfriends). She is standing below the white-railinged stairway of her spacious new house, looking up at Sarah Jane, who is standing on the level above, looking down. (Turner looks terrific here—and regal, in a shoulderless white gown with a wide blue strap across the chest.) "Is it the Hawkins boy?" she asks the girl eagerly. It's the wrong question: Sarah Jane frowns in response—what Hawkins boy? The son of the chauffeur down the road, says Lora—he's been asking her about Sarah Jane. "No," says Sarah Jane, rather sullenly, "it's with someone else." (It turns out to be with the very white Troy Donahue, who doesn't know she is "colored," and beats her up when he finds out.) "Oh," says Lora, turning away, a little disappointed her guess wasn't right, reflecting now on the inconvenience: "Well, all right . . . you run along. I'll try to manage here." As the doorbell rings.

Sarah Jane goes back to the kitchen, where Annie, in her uniform, is busy preparing the food, laying out plates—and looking exhausted. And the girl gets the same sort of line from her mother: "Look, honey, why don't you go over to the party at the church? . . . You're young, you shouldn't be sittin' around. Miss Lora feels the same way—she'll lend you her car." "Oh, she will? How nice of her!" Annie persists: "I'd be happy knowin' you're meetin' nice young folks." But Sarah Jane knows about those nice young folks at the church: "Busboys, cooks, chauffeurs!" she retorts angrily. "Like Hawkins!" "I don't want to fight with you, honey," says Annie. "Not tonight—I don't feel too good." And she asks her to take a tray of hors d'oeuvres in to "Miss Lora and her friends." "Why, certainly," says Sarah Jane, very sarcastic, "anything at all for Miss Lora and her friends." And by the time she gets to the living room, where the small group is gathered, she is balancing the tray on her head and doing a darkie imitation—to the dismay and embarrassment of Lora and her guests. She's just showing them something she learned from her "mammy," Sarah Jane says—"who l'arned it from Old Massa, befo' she belonged to *you*!" And she goes out again.

But Lora is furious. She follows Sarah Jane back to the kitchen, where Annie says wearily that she heard the whole thing. So what was that all about? Lora asks the girl. "You and my mother," says Sarah Jane, "are so anxious for me to be colored, I was going to show you I could be." What she was *being* was "childish," Lora says—and she doesn't understand how she could want to hurt her mother so, "or me." "I told her she has to be patient," Annie says, "—things'll work out." "*How?*" says Sarah Jane— who is by this time more ashamed than defiant. She turns and appeals to Lora: "Miss Lora, you don't know what it means to be—different." Lora's reply to this is quick and indignant: "Have *I* ever treated you as if you were different?" she demands. "Has Susie? Has anyone here?" This question— addressed as it is to someone who has just called her "*Miss* Lora" (as Annie and Sarah Jane always do)—seems just another example, though flagrant, of Lora's habit of incomprehension. It's Sarah Jane's reply that is startling. "No," she says, slowly and uncomfortably, "you've been wonderful . . . but . . ." But *what?* But Sarah Jane doesn't finish the sentence—she doesn't know *what*. Some ideologically minded critics have found this moment wanting: Sarah Jane, writes one, "should attack Lora for treating Annie as her servant." Sure she should—except for the fact that Annie *is* her servant. And for the same reasons, known to us all, that Hawkins is

The kitchen scene: Annie and Sarah Jane

inevitably a chauffeur, and that the party at the Negro church will inevitably be attended by busboys and cooks (and that Juanita Moore's career will go downhill after this role, in spite of her Academy Award nomination). To be sure, Lora's kind of unconsciousness helps to sustain these arrangements—but within their constraints, and on the "personal" level, Lora has been unimpeachable, and more, in her relations with Annie and Sarah Jane—even "wonderful," as Sarah Jane has just put it. What *else* could Sarah Jane say or think? It satisfies Lora. "Then don't *ever* do this to us again," she says, "—or to yourself." Then adds, tearfully, tenderly: "It won't *solve* anything, Sarah Jane . . ." And she goes out again, back to her guests.

This is a bigger Lora moment than it sounds like—implying more imagination than we've come to expect from her. And Turner is surprisingly touching here: the sudden inflection of pained tenderness toward Sarah Jane is powerful. It's Lora's most sympathetic and appealing moment so far—the first time we've been invited to see Lora too as someone trapped in a racist mythology and culture. Not as fatally as Sarah Jane and Annie, but just as surely.

Annie sits down wearily—at left-screen foreground—saying nothing. Sarah Jane approaches, bends down to her, crouching and looking up into her face, which now looks collapsed, impassive, drained. "Mama?" says Sarah Jane. Annie's eyes are cast down, her mouth slightly moving. "Try to understand," the girl pleads. Annie turns her head and looks at her. "I didn't mean to hurt you," says Sarah Jane, and throws her arms around her neck: "I love you!"—burying her face on her shoulder, Annie still in the foreground, hugging her back. "Oh, I know, baby," she says, patting the girl's shoulder, looking more wastedly beautiful than ever. And then she offers Sarah Jane her typically shattering sort of comfort, with its mixture of love and total insufficiency: "Oh, I know, baby. You're just like a puppy that's been cooped up too much. That's why I wanted you to go to the party . . ." And it's a terrible moment—we register that right along with Sarah Jane. "Oh, Mama," she says, drawing back and looking at her hopelessly, ". . . don't you *see* that won't help?"

Of course, Annie doesn't *see*. Not-seeing, in one form or another—from Lora's "Is it the Hawkins boy?" to Sarah Jane's "You've been wonderful . . . but . . ."—has been the connecting thread through this whole sequence. And this is where you get your strongest sense yet that the incomprehension doesn't belong only to Lora: they are *all* trapped in it. And with that perception, the movie's tone has shifted from a detached, ironic sort of observing to something more involved, more like sympathy. And now, you can no longer depend on Lora being excluded from it.

But that doesn't prevent Annie—as the movie goes on—from beginning to look at her (Lora, when she speaks, is usually looking off) with a certain (and growing) subtle, final lack of interest. Not that she flags in her concern or ministrations for both Lora and Susie, or defaults on her role of nurturer, advisor, supporter, listening to their problems and offering her judgments (she approves of Steve, and disapproves of Edwards, the playwright). But you can see that she's wearing out, and that they are wearing her down more or less. Even when she's in her sickbed confined to her room, Susie is there too, nattering away about her crush on Steve, sitting in the foreground of the shot, and (like her mother) looking off as she talks and eats dinner from a tray—while Annie, in the background, is propped up against the headboard of her bed, looking ravaged and ill and even a little irritable for a change. It's not that she isn't listening to Susie; it's that she'd rather go to sleep, and soon does. Soon Lora is visiting her too, to talk about Susie (you begin to feel they're chatting her to death!).

But at her last moments, it's Annie (at last) who commands the room and the audience (which includes doctor and minister, Steve and Lora)—even the camera (the shots of the others are from her point of view). And she does it with an almost frightening power. With Lora crouching and sobbing at her bedside, Annie has a kind of dry-eyed fierceness that makes you think of a prophetess at a shrine ("You're dying, not crying," Sirk had told Moore, when she played the scene too moistly at first) as she gives them all her last instructions. Steve must find Sarah Jane again (he will, he assures her); Lora must tell her that Annie knows now that she was selfish, and that "if I loved her too much, I'm sorry." She leaves her fur stole to the preacher's wife, and her pearl necklace to Susie, for her wedding: "Our weddin' day, and the day we die, are the great events of life." And fifty dollars for Mr. McKinney. Who?—Lora is baffled. It's the milkman who gave them a break on their bills when they lived in their coldwater flat. "You've been so good!" Lora says on a sob. Annie hopes so: she wants to "be standin' with the lambs and not with the goats on Judgment Day." And finally, she's left detailed written instructions about that big funeral she wants, and tells Steve to get the envelope from her drawer.

STEVE: . . . I've got it, Annie.
ANNIE: I wanta go—the way I planned—especially the four white horses, and a band playin'—no mourning—but proud and high-steppin'—like I was goin' to glory!
LORA [*sobbing*]: *No!* I won't listen! There isn't going to be any funeral! Not for a long, long time! You can't leave! I won't *let* you!
ANNIE: . . . I'm just tired, Miss Lora. Awfully tired . . .

And that's all. She seems to drift off. But the passing is an event we see only as it registers on Lora's face, in close-up, as she watches—and then screams, calling Annie's name, her face turning into a kind of rictus mask of horror and grief, sobbing and burying her head in the bed next to Annie—as the camera pans from her face in death to Sarah Jane's framed photograph on the table next to her. Dissolve to a church interior and the funeral in progress—on the unmistakable (as it was in 1959) and thrilling sound of Mahalia Jackson's singing voice.

So it was finally Lora's turn to be a little frightening. That scream at Annie's bedside is startling—and yet in a way feels overdue. The face is not, after all, so impermeable. And you're brought to the recognition that Lora's friendship with Annie was probably the deepest thing in her life, beyond even Susie's place there—at least from what we've seen. (And forget Steve.)

And yet—also from what we've seen—it's in some ways even less than a friendship. Annie's place (however Lora may have denied it) was so fixed that her relation to her "Miss Lora," even at their fondest and closest, had

Annie's death

something quite impersonal about it. As the movie makes clear: at best Lora only half-apprehends Annie, showing neither curiosity about nor interest in her other life—the black one. And that indifference hardly seems to change even after it's been pointed out to her ("Miss Lora, you never asked"). But then it hasn't been as necessary for Lora to *know* about that life as much as to have it in the background of her own quite different one. Like a beloved pet, Annie is both remote and intimate to her at once: a ground of Lora's reality, as it were. So that her death is a loss of *meaning* as well as of a friend—just the sort of meaning that gets defined by the funeral that follows.

It's the most famous set piece in the movie (it's what people always remembered from the earlier one, too)—extending the heart-wringing effect even above and beyond Annie's death scene. Not only into the funeral service—with Jackson in a pulpit singing against stained-glass windows, the coffin amid banks of flowers below, the familiar faces (even the milk-man's) in the crowded pews—but past that into the funeral cortege itself, and the dramatic and unexpected return of Sarah Jane, throwing herself on her mother's coffin in an agony of regret and remorse, declaring "I killed my mother!," until Lora gathers her into the funeral car, with herself and Steve and Susie. Then the funeral parade, spectacular by any standard—

even Annie's, you would suppose—with the majestic and ornate glass-windowed hearse, the marching band from the colored lodge, and, best of all, those four high-stepping black-plumed white horses. No mourning—going to glory. And the streets along the way crowded with mourners, almost all of them black, many shown in close-up, weeping and doffing their hats, paying tribute to Annie.

It's another example, an extended one, of pulling out all the stops (the Stahl movie confined itself to the church facade and a glimpse of the horses). But Sirk denied to me that that was anything like the intention. "The funeral itself is an irony," he said. "All that pomp." It's certainly true that it comes as slightly jarring when the otherwise levelheaded, no-nonsense Annie first tells us and Lora that her funeral is "the one thing I want to splurge on. I really want it elegant." It's too close to one of those Negro clichés—like Delilah's rabbit's foot or Rochester's dice—that now makes us squirm, that even did in 1959: a white person's patronizing idea of black culture and folklore, and sort of cute as well, good for a condescending chuckle at least. But in this film any whiff of condescension, any suggestion of a picturesque ignorance in action, is disposed of at the first notes of Mahalia Jackson's surging and billowing voice lifted into the words of the spiritual—

> *Soon I will be done—*
> *Trouble of the world, Lord,*
> *Trouble of the world . . .*
> *I'm going home to live with God.*
> *No more weepin' and wailin' . . .*
> *No more weepin' and wailin' . . .*
> *I'm going home to live with my Lord . . .*

In the end, it seems, Annie is as unknown to us as she was to Lora—and that feels right too. Annie, you realize, stands for something you don't quite understand or apprehend—for something dimly perceived perhaps, but clearly opposite to the emptiness and sterility of the white characters' lives. Even *they* know that—and Lora in particular, whether she remembers it or not (probably not). In any case, Annie's funeral has become so resplendent, visually and aurally, that it comes to seem almost the equivalent of Dietrich's "What does it matter what you say about people?"—seeming in the end to have as little to do with the character of Annie as with that of Mahalia Jackson. But of course quite unthinkable *without* either of them . . .

The funeral procession; the four white horses are at far right.

There is at least one extraordinary, half-hidden (of course) and very Sirkian touch during the funeral procession—which is shown in a montage of different points of view, one of them (very brief) through the display window of a store from the inside. Just visible are the outlines of some mannequins arrayed in things like knights' and ladies' outfits, and on the window itself the store's logo reads COSTUME RENTALS—only for us, printed in reverse—and beyond that the uniformed band, the plumed horses, the hearse and coffin. "All that pomp" is right. Annie has become in the end not only that generic hope of hers, a Judgment Day "lamb," but an impresario, even an artist ("I really want it elegant"), giving us, and orchestrating to its details, this final but strange and beautiful show.

Apparently, there was to be one more and final sequence after this one. Susan Kohner showed it to me in the final shooting script she used in the original production and has saved. It's a scene between Lora and Steve (and parallels a similarly placed and concluding scene in the Stahl film between Colbert and Warren William). Lora announces her intention to adopt Sarah Jane and her wish now to postpone their wedding, so that she can take both Susie and Sarah Jane "away from here . . . This place, the people,

New York—the memories are still too strong for the way we all feel now. I don't have the answers yet—I only know they both need love and understanding—and a mother. That's what I intend to be, Steve." Maybe she'll go back to her hometown in Iowa. She'll go in for country living again—cooking and washing and ironing. And Steve laughs—calling her "ham clear through to the bone." At first affronted by this, she laughs too. They both laugh, then kiss, and then kiss again—for the final fade-out.

No one to my knowledge has ever seen this scene, and Kohner is pretty sure that they never even filmed it. How could they—even at Universal—after Mahalia Jackson?

Twenty-Six

CONCLUSION

The films and filmmakers I've talked about the most in this book—beginning with Tourneur's *Out of the Past* and ending with Sirk—have in common, as different from one another as they otherwise are, some qualities that I'd like to call moral: a certain impersonalism and refusal of self-pity, a respect for a kind of final mystery in their characters and in their materials, a commitment to what Stark Young (see p. 146) calls "that distance in art that style requires." Because, against the odds of their time and place, these moviemakers were stylists—however subtly or covertly.

The fifties were a time, you might say, when the movies, mainly due to the impact and vitality of the new Method performers and directors, discovered the self—eroding the aesthetic distance between us and the movie screen as much as they could, the separation that the old stars and the old genres had more or less maintained, and that the mannerist filmmaking of the fifties engaged in preserving, though in more self-conscious forms, through directors like Welles and Hitchcock and Sirk et al.—even Nicholas Ray.

But by now, of course, the "self" has been discovered so much and often that it's turned a bit rancid: it's become the thing inside us that we are urged to empower or actualize or realize, most of all to celebrate (it's even had a mass magazine named after it). If the curse of the fifties was complacency (as we're so often told), the bane of our own, surely, is narcissism—what art critic Mark Stevens calls "the endless whine of me-me-me in modern culture." When someone like Brando or one of his heirs says (as Brando did to Kazan) that he feels like a faker when he acts, you think: yes, of course, but not because he isn't leveling with us when he acts, but exactly because he *is*—and then some. And we discover that it's tiresome. Or at least has become so.

"He could open you up and psych you out," Geraldine Page said (admiringly) about Kazan the director. The sort of thing they *all* said about him, and yet exactly *not* the sort of thing you could've imagined any-

One of the fifties' great "stylists." Frank Sinatra in *Young at Heart*

one saying about Welles—or Sirk or Ophuls, for that matter—let alone about Hitchcock. What they were after from and through their actors were higher reaches of imagining than the psychological insight. Only rarely, if at all, was it the kind of exposure and personal probing associated with Kazan and other Method directors. Sometimes it would seem almost the opposite to that—a pulling back rather than a zeroing in. When Lucia Harper weeps for the mortally injured Donnelly, she does it facedown in shadow, stifling her sobs on top of her bed. When George Minafer finally feels the "comeuppance" he's been asking for, bitterly repenting his arrogance at last, he is kneeling turned away in darkness, while Welles's voice-over tells us what's going on. How does one render the "inside" of a character or experience? Godard asked rhetorically in a 1962 interview. And answered: "Precisely by staying prudently outside."

Just as writers often do. As in, for example, Flannery O'Connor's great comic novel, *Wise Blood,* where we are not always told, even at climactic moments, what her characters are thinking or feeling, but we are nearly always told—with photographic immediacy and objectivity—exactly what they are looking at. As, for instance, when the haunted, God-obsessed young hero, Hazel Motes, having stalled his "new" car, a junkyard special, on a Georgia roadside, makes his way on foot to an isolated gas station—a shack with a single pump outside—and Sabbath Hawks, his indefatigable would-be girlfriend, comes trailing up behind him. It's because of her that he sees it:

> . . . [She] went over to a cage about six feet high that was at the side of the shack. Haze had not noticed it until she came up. He saw that there was something alive in it, and went near enough to read a sign that said, TWO DEADLY ENEMIES. HAVE A LOOK FREE.
>
> There was a black bear about four feet long and very thin, resting on the floor of the cage; his back was spotted with bird lime that had been shot down on him by a small chicken hawk that was sitting on a perch in the upper part of the same apartment. Most of the hawk's tail was gone. The bear had only one eye.

And that's it really, nothing else: the garage man gives them a lift to their car and the story goes on. But it's just the sort of recurrent detail, both appalling and comic at once, where you find, over time and repetition, a central meaning of the novel: the yawning gap between promise and reality in the world around Hazel and Sabbath, with its pathetic-grotesque aspirations to glamour ("TWO DEADLY ENEMIES . . ."). It's implicitly how the novel asks us to see *our* world, with all its commercial-material-airhead brightness. And yet it's exactly the pathos of that brightness—its utter final inadequacy amounting almost to a kind of candor—that partly saves it for O'Connor. Just as it almost saves the experience of late-forties Manhattan for Salinger's Holden. And for both these authors that discrepancy has a religious implication—just as the transforming objectivity of the movie camera has for André Bazin. Even a simple photograph, he writes, can enable us "to admire in reproduction [what] our eyes alone could not have taught us to love."

Much as Nabokov's Humbert admires Lolita's tennis game—though not in reproduction but at first hand—in spite of what he knows as her impending treachery, and cursing himself that he has no camera to record it, but "filming" it nonetheless, for himself and us, in words:

> My Lolita had a way of raising her bent left knee at the ample and springy start of the service cycle when there would develop and hang in the sun for a second a vital web of balance between toed foot, pristine armpit, burnished arm and far back-flung racket, as she smiled up with gleaming teeth at the small globe suspended so high in the

zenith of the powerful and graceful cosmos she had created for the express purpose of falling upon it with a clean resounding whack of her golden whip.

It had, that serve of hers, beauty, directness, youth, a classical beauty of trajectory . . . That I could have had all her strokes, all her enchantments, immortalized in segments of celluloid, makes me moan today with frustration . . . Now . . . on that particular day, in the pure air . . . on that admirable court leading up to Champion Hotel where we had spent the night, I felt I could rest from the nightmare of unknown betrayals within the innocence of her style, of her soul, of her essential grace.

This is the language of love, of course ("My Lolita . . ."), but it's also the language of art and of the movies. This act of heightened seeing, it seems to me, is finally what movies are about.

The quasi-religious character of the movie experience has been remarked on almost since the movies themselves began—the congregation in the hushed dark before the enormous light-filled screen, and so on. Movies at their best—even the comedies—inspire awe. And that experience is surely connected to the sort of vision Humbert describes for us here. It's no accident that he sees Lolita—in spite of lacking a camera—as if in a movie: in montage, close-up, high- and low-angle shots, even a touch of slow motion, and so on. A movie that transcends ordinary seeing—that sees instead a kind of essential Lolita, even a truer and more real Lolita: a "soul" rendered through "style," and "an essential grace."

In one way or another, this sort of exalted seeing is what movies at their best both ask from us and give us. It's what makes some of them seem even better with time.

SELECTED BIBLIOGRAPHY

Alpi, Deborah Lazaroff, *Robert Siodmak* (Jefferson, N.C., and London: McFarland and Company, 1998)

Bacher, Lutz, *Max Ophuls in the Hollywood Studios* (New Brunswick, N.J.: Rutgers University Press, 1996)

Baldwin, James, *The Devil Finds Work* (New York: Dell, 1976)

————, *The Fire Next Time* (New York: Dell, 1963)

Bazin, André, *Orson Welles: A Critical View* (New York: Harper and Row, 1978)

————, *What Is Cinema?* (Berkeley and Los Angeles: University of California Press, 1976)

Bernstein, Matthew, *Walter Wanger, Hollywood Independent* (Berkeley, Los Angeles, London: University of California Press, 1994)

Bosworth, Patricia, *Montgomery Clift* (New York: Harcourt Brace Jovanovich, 1978)

Brady, Frank, *Citizen Welles* (New York: Scribners, 1989)

Brando, Marlon, with Robert Lindsey, *Songs My Mother Taught Me* (New York: Random House, 1994)

Bresson, Robert, *Notes on Cinematography* (New York: Urizen Books, 1977)

Brown, Peter Harry, *Kim Novak: Reluctant Goddess* (New York: St. Martin's Press, 1986)

Cagney, James, *Cagney by Cagney* (New York: Doubleday, 1976)

Cahiers du Cinéma—The 1950's: Neo-Realism, Hollywood, New Wave, ed. Jim Hillier (Cambridge, Mass.: Harvard University Press, 1985)

Carringer, Robert L., *"The Magnificent Ambersons": A Reconstruction* (Berkeley, Los Angeles, Oxford: University of California Press, 1993)

————, *The Making of Citizen Kane* (Berkeley: University of California Press, 1985)

Ciment, Michel, *Kazan on Kazan* (New York: Viking, 1974)

The Collected Works of Harold Clurman, ed. Margaret Loggia and Glenn Young (New York: Applause Books, 1994)

Considine, Shaun, *Mad as Hell: The Life and Work of Paddy Chayefsky* (New York: Random House, 1994)

Dalton, David, *James Dean: The Mutant King* (New York: St. Martin's Press, 1974)

Dunne, Philip, *Take Two: A Life in Movies and Politics* (New York: McGraw Hill, 1980)

Eisenschitz, Bernard, *Nicholas Ray: An American Journey* (London: Faber and Faber, 1993)

Ephron, Henry, *We Thought We Could Do Anything: The Life of Screenwriters Phoebe and Harry Ephron* (New York: Norton, 1977)

Farber, Manny, *Negative Space: Manny Farber on the Movies* (New York: Praeger, 1971)

The Film Criticism of Otis Ferguson, ed. Robert Wilson (Philadelphia: Temple University Press, 1971)

Godard, Jean-Luc, *Godard on Godard: Critical Writings,* ed. Jean Narboni and Tom Milne (New York: Viking, 1972)

Green, Martin, *Re-Appraisals: Some Commonsense Readings in American Literature* (New York: Norton, 1965)

Greene, Graham, *The Pleasure Dome: The Collected Film Criticism 1935–40,* ed. John Russell Taylor (London: Secker and Warburg, 1972)

Grobel, Lawrence, *Conversations with Brando* (New York: Hyperion, 1991)

Halliday, Jon, *Sirk on Sirk* (New York: Viking, 1972)

Higham, Charles, *The Films of Orson Welles* (Berkeley: University of California Press, 1970)

Hitchcock on Hitchcock: Selected Writings and Interviews, ed. Sidney Gottlieb (Berkeley: University of California Press, 1995)

Holding, Elisabeth Sanxay, *The Blank Wall* (New York: Ace Books, 1947)

Hotchner, A. E., *Doris Day, Her Own Story* (New York: William Morrow, 1976)

Houseman, John, *Front and Center* (New York: Simon and Schuster, 1979)

———, *Run-Through* (New York: Simon and Schuster, 1972)

Hurst, Fannie, *Imitation of Life* (New York: Harper & Row, 1933)

Huston, John, *An Open Book* (New York: Alfred A. Knopf, 1980)

Johnson, Nora, *Flashback: Nora Johnson on Nunnally Johnson* (New York: Doubleday, 1979)

The Letters of Nunnally Johnson, ed. Dorris Johnson and Ellen Leventhal (New York: Alfred A. Knopf, 1981)

Kael, Pauline, *The Citizen Kane Book: Raising Kane* (Boston: Little, Brown & Co., 1971)

———, *For Keeps: Thirty Years at the Movies* (New York: Dutton, 1994)

———, *I Lost It at the Movies* (Boston: Little, Brown & Co., 1965)

———, *Kiss Kiss Bang Bang* (Boston: Little, Brown & Co., 1968)

Kazan, Elia, *A Life* (New York: Alfred A. Knopf, 1988)

Kotsilibas-Davis, James, and Myrna Loy, *Myrna Loy: Being and Becoming* (New York: Alfred A. Knopf, 1987)

Lambert, Gavin, *Mainly About Lindsay Anderson* (New York: Alfred A. Knopf, 2000)

Leaming, Barbara, *Orson Welles* (New York: Viking, 1985)

Leigh, Janet, *There Really Was a Hollywood* (New York: Doubleday, 1985)

Lewis, Robert, *Slings and Arrows: Theater in My Life* (New York: Stein and Day, 1984)

McCarthy, Mary, *Sights and Spectacles, 1937–1956* (New York: Farrar, Straus & Cudahy, 1956)

MacDonald, Dwight, *On Movies* (Englewood Cliffs, N.J.: Prentice-Hall, 1969)

McGilligan, Pat, *Backstory 2: Interviews with Screenwriters of the 1940s and 1950s* (Berkeley: University of California Press, 1991)

Mailer, Norman, *Marilyn: A Biography* (New York: Grosset and Dunlap, 1973)

Manso, Peter, *Brando: The Biography* (New York: Hyperion, 1994)

Maugham, W. Somerset, *Christmas Holiday* (London: Heinemann Ltd., 1939)

Nabokov, Vladimir, *Lolita* (New York: Putnam, 1958)

O'Connor, Flannery, *Wise Blood* (New York: Farrar, Straus & Giroux, 1949)

Oppenheimer, Joel, and Jack Vitek, *Idol: Rock Hudson* (New York: Villard, 1986)

Ray, Nicholas, *I Was Interrupted: Nicholas Ray on Making Movies,* ed. Susan Ray (Berkeley: University of California Press, 1993)

Renoir, Jean, *Letters,* ed. Lorraine LoBianco and David Thompson (London: Faber and Faber, 1994)

———, *My Life and My Films* (New York: Atheneum, 1974)

Rollyson, Carl, *Marilyn Monroe: A Life of the Actress* (New York: Da Capo Press, 1986)

Ross, Lillian, *Picture: John Huston, M.G.M., and the Making of "The Red Badge of Courage"* (New York: Proscenium, 1952)

Sabin, Margery, *The Dialect of the Tribe: Speech and Community in Modern Fiction* (New York: Oxford University Press, 1987)

Salinger, J. D., *The Catcher in the Rye* (New York: Little, Brown & Co., 1951)

Sarris, Andrew, *The American Cinema: Directors and Directions, 1929–1968* (New York: E. P. Dutton, 1968)

Sayre, Nora, *Previous Convictions: A Journey Through the 1950s* (New Brunswick, N.J.: Rutgers University Press, 1995)

———, *Running Time: Films of the Cold War* (New York: Dial Press, 1982)

Schary, Dore, *Heyday: An Autobiography* (Boston: Little, Brown & Co., 1979)

Sirk, Douglas, director, *Imitation of Life,* ed. Lucy Fischer (New Brunswick, N.J.: Rutgers University Press, 1991)

Southern, Terry, *The Magic Christian* (New York: Random House, 1960)

Stern, Michael, *Douglas Sirk* (Boston: Twayne Publishers, 1979)

Strasberg, Susan, *Marilyn and Me: Sisters, Rivals, Friends* (New York: Warner Books, 1992)

Tarkington, Booth, *The Magnificent Ambersons* (Bloomington and Indianapolis: Indiana University Press, 1989)

Truffaut, François, *The Films in My Life* (New York: Simon and Schuster, 1978)

————, *Hitchcock* (New York: Simon and Schuster, 1967)

Tomkies, Mike, *The Robert Mitchum Story* (New York: Ballantine, 1973)

Vidal, Gore, *Palimpsest: A Memoir* (New York: Random House, 1995)

Weatherby, W. J., *Conversations with Marilyn* (New York: Mason/Charter, 1976)

Welles, Orson, and Peter Bogdanovich, *This Is Orson Welles,* ed. Jonathan Rosenbaum (New York: Da Capo Press, 1998)

Welles, Orson, director, *Touch of Evil,* ed. Terry Comito (New Brunswick, N.J.: Rutgers University Press, 1985)

INDEX

Page numbers in *italics* refer to illustrations.

ILLUSTRATION CREDITS

Museum of Modern Art/Film Stills Archive: page 145

Red Barn: pages 330, 396

The Kobal Collection: pages 34, 253, 297, 317 (bottom)

Photofest: pages 6 (bottom), 9, 13, 18, 49, 53, 57, 63, 80, 110 (bottom), 118, 124, 133, 136, 141, 156, 159, 165, 167, 169, 180, 185, 191, 198, 207, 212, 234, 241, 257, 260, 262, 263, 265, 273, 281, 289, 291, 301, 334, 336, 345, 355, 363, 368, 372, 373, 375, 378, 379, 381, 385, 391, 406 (bottom), 425

James Harvey: pages xii, 4, 6 (top), 8, 15, 19, 20, 26, 30, 36 (both), 40, 48, 50, 62, 69, 73, 78, 82, 84, 87, 90, 95, 97, 103, 109, 110 (top), 111, 114, 115, 123, 125, 126, 128, 130, 131, 134, 137, 142, 146, 149, 152, 172, 175, 176 (both), 181, 184, 187, 188, 189, 194, 203, 225, 230, 238, 247, 255, 270, 274, 286, 297, 306, 308, 312, 315, 317 (top), 323, 324 (both), 325, 327, 351, 357, 358, 365, 392, 395, 398, 404, 406 (top), 408 (both), 410, 411, 417, 420, 422

A NOTE ON THE TYPE

The text of this book was set in Garamond No. 3. It is not a true copy of any
of the designs of Claude Garamond (ca. 1480–1561), but an adaptation of
his types, which set the European standard for two centuries. It probably
owes as much to the designs of Jean Jannon, a Protestant printer working in
Sedan in the early seventeenth century, who had worked with Garamond's
romans earlier, in Paris, but who was denied their use because of Catholic
censorship. Jannon's matrices came into the possession of the Imprimerie
nationale, where they were thought to be by Garamond himself, and were so
described when the Imprimerie revived the type in 1900. This particular
version is based on an adaptation by Morris Fuller Benton.

Composed by North Market Street Graphics, Lancaster, Pennsylvania
Printed and bound by Quebecor Printing, Fairfield, Pennsylvania
Designed by Iris Weinstein